The
L/L Research
Channeling Archives

Transcripts of
the Meditation Sessions

Volume 1
March, 1972 to February 15, 1976

Don
Elkins

Jim
McCarty

Carla L.
Rueckert

Copyright © 2009 L/L Research

All rights reserved. No part of this book may be reproduced or used in any form or by any means—graphic, electronic or mechanical, including photocopying or information storage and retrieval systems—without written permission from the copyright holder.

ISBN: 978-0-945007-75-3

Published by L/L Research
Box 5195
Louisville, Kentucky 40255-0195

E-mail: contact@llresearch.org
www.llresearch.org

About the cover photo: *This photograph of Jim McCarty and Carla L. Rueckert was taken during an L/L Research channeling session on August 4, 2009, in the living room of their Louisville, Kentucky home. Jim always holds hands with Carla when she channels, following the Ra group's advice on how she can avoid any possibility of astral travel.*

Dedication

These archive volumes are dedicated to Hal and Jo Price, who faithfully and lovingly hosted this group's weekly meditation meetings from 1962 to 1975,

to Walt Rogers, whose work with the research group Man, Consciousness and Understanding of Detroit offered the information needed to begin this ongoing channeling experiment,

and to the Confederation of Angels and Planets in the Service of the Infinite Creator, for sharing their love and wisdom with us so generously through the years.

Table of Contents

Introduction 8
Year 1972 10
    March, 1972 11
Year 1973 14
    August, 1973 15
    December 18, 1973 17
Year 1974 20
    January 4, 1974 21
    January 6, 1974 23
    January 7, 1974 26
    January 8, 1974 28
    January 10, 1974 30
    January 12, 1974 33
    January 13, 1974 37
    January 14, 1974 38
    January 15, 1974 40
    January 16, 1974 43
    January 17, 1974 44
    January 21, 1974 47
    January 21, 1974 49
    January 23, 1974 51
    January 25, 1974 53
    January 26, 1974 54
    January 27, 1974 58
    February 1, 1974 59
    February 2, 1974 61
    February 3, 1974 63
    February 4, 1974 65
    February 9, 1974 66
    February 10, 1974 70
    February 11, 1974 71
    February 11, 1974 74
    February 13, 1974 76
    February 15, 1974 79
    February 17, 1974 80
    February 18, 1974 82
    February 18, 1974 87
    February 20, 1974 88
    February 21, 1974 89

February 22, 1974	91
February 23, 1974	92
February 23, 1974	99
February 25, 1974	102
February 25, 1974	104
February 25, 1974	107
February 27, 1974	109
February 27, 1974	114
March 2, 1974	117
March 4, 1974	119
March 5, 1974	120
March 6, 1974	122
March 8, 1974	124
March 9, 1974	127
March 10, 1974	130
March 11, 1974	133
March 17, 1974	137
March 18, 1974	139
March 19, 1974	142
March 19, 1974	144
March 23, 1974	146
March 24, 1974	148
March 28, 1974	151
April 2, 1974	154
April 3, 1974	156
April 8, 1974	158
April 10, 1974	160
April 12, 1974	162
April 13, 1974	165
April 14, 1974	168
April 14, 1974	171
April 15, 1974	173
April 16, 1974	175
April 17, 1974	177
April 19, 1974	179
April 20, 1974	181
April 21, 1974	183
April 22, 1974	184
April 23, 1974	186
April 24, 1974	188
April 25, 1974	191
April 26, 1974	193

April 27, 1974	197
April 29, 1974	200
April 30, 1974	203
May 1, 1974	205
May 2, 1974	208
May 5, 1974	210
May 8, 1974	212
May 11, 1974	214
May 12, 1974	216
May 13, 1974	218
May 14, 1974	220
May 15, 1974	223
May 16, 1974	225
May 17, 1974	228
May 18, 1974	230
May 19, 1974	232
May 23, 1974	235
May 24, 1974	237
May 25, 1974	240
May 26, 1974	243
May 27, 1974	246
May 28, 1974	248
May 31, 1974	251
June 1, 1974	254
June 2, 1974	256
June 2, 1974	258
June 5, 1974	260
June 5, 1974	263
June 6, 1974	265
June 6, 1974	267
June 7, 1974	269
June 8, 1974	271
June 9, 1974	274
June 11, 1974	277
June 12, 1974	279
June 13, 1974	282
June 21, 1974	287
June 22, 1974	289
June 23, 1974	291
June 29, 1974	294
July 2, 1974	297
July 3, 1974	299

July 14, 1974..302

July 23 1974 305

July 28, 1974..309

July 30, 1974..311

August 6, 1974...315

August 6, 1974...318

September 21,1974...320

September 22, 1974..323

October 4, 1974...327

October 13, 1974...329

October 31, 1974...331

November 1, 1974...336

November 10, 1974...339

November 12, 1974...342

November 15, 1974...344

Year 1975..347

January 31, 1975...348

November 2, 1975... 351

November 23, 1975...352

November 30, 1975...354

December 7, 1975..356

December 21, 1975..359

December 21, 1975..362

December 28, 1975..364

Year 1976..368

January 4, 1976..369

January 11, 1976..373

January 11, 1976..375

January 18, 1976..378

January 25, 1976..382

February 1, 1976..386

February 1, 1976..391

February 15, 1976..397

Introduction

Welcome to this volume of the *L/L Research Channeling Archives*. This series of publications represents the collection of channeling sessions recorded by L/L Research during the period from the early seventies to the present day. The sessions are also available on the L/L Research website, www.llresearch.org.

Starting in the mid-1950s, Don Elkins, a professor of physics and engineering at Speed Scientific School, had begun researching the paranormal in general and UFOs in particular. Elkins was a pilot as well as a professor and he flew his small plane to meet with many of the UFO contactees of the period.

Hal Price had been a part of a UFO-contactee channeling circle in Detroit called "The Detroit Group." When Price was transferred from Detroit's Ford plant to its Louisville truck plant, mutual friends discovered that Price also was a UFO researcher and put the two men together. Hal introduced Elkins to material called *The Brown Notebook* which contained instructions on how to create a group and receive UFO contactee information. In January of 1962 they decided to put the instructions to use and began holding silent meditation meetings on Sunday nights just across the Ohio River in the southern Indiana home of Hal and his wife, Jo. This was the beginning of what was called the "Louisville Group."

I was an original member of that group, along with a dozen of Elkins' physics students. However, I did not learn to channel until 1974. Before that date, almost none of our weekly channeling sessions were recorded or transcribed. After I began improving as a channel, Elkins decided for the first time to record all the sessions and transcribe them.

During the first eighteen months or so of my studying channeling and producing material, we tended to reuse the tapes as soon as the transcriptions were finished. Since those were typewriter days, we had no record of the work that could be reopened and used again, as we do now with computers. And I used up the original and the carbon copy of my transcriptions putting together a manuscript, *Voices of the Gods*, which has not yet been published. It remains as almost the only record of Don Elkins' and my channeling of that period.

We learned from this experience to retain the original tapes of all of our sessions, and during the remainder of the seventies and through the eighties, our "Louisville Group" was prolific. The "Louisville Group" became "L/L Research" after Elkins and I published a book in 1976, *Secrets of the UFO*, using that publishing name. At first we met almost every night. In later years, we met gradually less often, and the number of sessions recorded by our group in a year accordingly went down. Eventually, the group began taking three months off from channeling during the summer. And after 2000, we began having channeling meditations only twice a month. The volume of sessions dropped to its present output of eighteen or so each year.

These sessions feature channeling from sources which call themselves members of the Confederation of Planets in the Service of the Infinite Creator. At first we enjoyed hearing from many different voices: Hatonn, Laitos, Oxal, L/Leema and Yadda being just a few of them. As I improved my tuning techniques, and became the sole senior channel in L/L Research, the number of contacts dwindled. When I began asking for "the highest and best contact which I can receive of Jesus the Christ's vibration of unconditional love in a conscious and stable manner," the entity offering its thoughts through our group was almost always Q'uo. This remains true as our group continues to channel on an ongoing basis.

The channelings are always about love and unity, enunciating "The Law of One" in one aspect or another. Seekers who are working with spiritual principles often find the material a good resource. We hope that you will as well. As time has gone on the questions have shifted somewhat, but in general the content of the channeling is metaphysical and focused on helping seekers find the love in the moment and the Creator in the love.

At first, I transcribed our channeling sessions. I got busier, as our little group became more widely known, and got hopelessly behind on transcribing. Two early transcribers who took that job off my hands were Kim

Howard and Judy Dunn, both of whom masterfully transcribed literally hundreds of sessions through the eighties and early nineties.

Then Ian Jaffray volunteered to create a web site for these transcriptions, and single-handedly unified the many different formats that the transcripts were in at that time and made them available online. This additional exposure prompted more volunteers to join the ranks of our transcribers, and now there are a dozen or so who help with this. Our thanks go out to all of these kind volunteers, early and late, who have made it possible for our webguy to make these archives available.

Around the turn of the millennium, I decided to commit to editing each session after it had been transcribed. So the later transcripts have fewer errata than the earlier ones, which are quite imperfect in places. One day, perhaps, those earlier sessions will be revisited and corrections will be made to the transcripts. It would be a large task, since there are well over 1500 channeling sessions as of this date, and counting. We apologize for the imperfections in those transcripts, and trust that you can ascertain the sense of them regardless of a mistake here and there.

Blessings, dear reader! Enjoy these "humble thoughts" from the Confederation of Planets. May they prove good companions to your spiritual seeking. ♣

For all of us at L/L Research,

Carla L. Rueckert

Louisville, Kentucky

July 16, 2009

Year 1972

March, 1972

L/L Research

L/L Research is a subsidiary of Rock Creek Research & Development Laboratories, Inc.

P.O. Box 5195
Louisville, KY 40255-0195

www.llresearch.org

Rock Creek is a non-profit corporation dedicated to discovering and sharing information which may aid in the spiritual evolution of humankind.

ABOUT THE CONTENTS OF THIS TRANSCRIPT: This telepathic channeling has been taken from transcriptions of the weekly study and meditation meetings of the Rock Creek Research & Development Laboratories and L/L Research. It is offered in the hope that it may be useful to you. As the Confederation entities always make a point of saying, please use your discrimination and judgment in assessing this material. If something rings true to you, fine. If something does not resonate, please leave it behind, for neither we nor those of the Confederation would wish to be a stumbling block for any.

CAVEAT: This transcript is being published by L/L Research in a not yet final form. It has, however, been edited and any obvious errors have been corrected. When it is in a final form, this caveat will be removed.

© 2009 L/L Research

Maturity Meditation
March, 1972

(The day of this channeling is unknown.)[1]

(Don channeling)

I am Hatonn. I greet you, my friends, in the love and the light of our infinite Creator. It is a great privilege to be with you once more. I am always privileged to be with you. These are the thoughts of the one known as Hatonn.

I am speaking through this instrument. I will speak to you on the subject of maturity, for this you have requested. As you have already indicated, this concept may be somewhat different from that which is generally appreciated by your peoples.

---

[1] Carla: I was writing a paper on Maturity for an educational and developmental psychology class I was taking at Spalding College while pursuing an advanced degree. It was a direction I did not pursue, but it was in order to take a job with the school system of the whole county of Louisville and surrounding areas as the AV Librarian, and I needed three courses, which I got, for my emergency certification.

This channeling took place after I had done extensive research on what the people in the field said about maturity. It all had to do, for the normal psychologists, with behavior, how you behaved. I felt that was unacceptably shallow, as maturity has so many levels, not all of them behavioral. But nothing in the literature covered this. So I turned to Hatonn.

This channeling was perfect in that it agreed with my feelings, and I used it to write my paper. The poor professor! She gave me an A, but said please don't share the paper with anyone, as she could get into trouble for allowing a discarnate source. I put this channeling in as an appendix to my paper.

Maturity, my friends, is in truth a maturity of the spirit, for in truth there is nothing but the spirit. Physical illusion which you appreciate in your daily lives is of no consequence other than for its result in action upon the spiritual self.

Maturity, my friends, is first the realization of this fact. Secondly, maturity is the ability to control one's own consciousness in such a way so as to propagate the continuance of this maturing process.

Maturity, my friends, then is realized in the ability to control one's consciousness. Unfortunately, upon the planet which you now enjoy, there is but very little true control of the basic consciousness. And, therefore, there is very, very little maturity. It is necessary first to realize the value of each thought you have, and then to reject those of little or no value. Most of the thoughts that we are able to discern occurring in the daily lives of those who dwell upon this planet lack maturity. For this reason, you might consider the planet upon which you live a planet of children. Their daily thoughts, communicated to one another, hold them in this state. It is a self-propagating thing, communicated from one to the other.

It is necessary to reject thoughts that continually infringe upon your mind from your present environment and to carefully select each thought that you generate in order to reach a state of true mental maturity.

You might ask how it is possible to select thoughts of value from thoughts that are meaningless, or of little value. It is very simple, my friends. All that is necessary is for you to analyze the thought with respect to the real objectives of your person. If the thought has true consequence, if the thought is of a true developmental nature—that is to say, if it develops either your consciousness or the consciousness of someone else with whom you are communicating—then it is a worthwhile thought. If it does not develop the consciousness, then it is probably of very little value.

Now, how will a thought or concept develop into consciousness? There are several ways. One technique of development is simply evolving the ability of analyzing the merits of your thoughts. After this has been done, the thoughts themselves will act as generators of the maturing process.

Each thought you have is important. It is important either in a negative or a positive sense. If it is a thought that is of no consequence, it is important to recognize this thought as being of no value. If it is a thought of consequence, then it is necessary that you amplify it and utilize it and communicate it, or it too will be of very little value.

Maturity, my friends, is first the ability to think in this manner. It is second to act in the manner in which you think.

There are millions and millions of thoughts generated by the people of your planet each day. A very, very small percentage of these thoughts have to do with maturity. That is, a very, very small percentage of them have to do with creating a better environment for the growth of the spiritual self. By this I mean actively causing spiritual development.

What is spiritual development? It is the process of maturing; the process of maturing, the process of analyzing everything that you are aware of in a true and unbiased sense. In order to do this, one must be able to recognize truth. It is only possible for one to recognize truth by the process of allowing truth to communicate the absolute base for truth which is ever present throughout the universe. This communication is accomplished primarily through the technique of meditation.

There is a separation of maturity into primarily two aspects: intellectual and spiritual maturity. They go hand in hand, and one generates the other. However, it is not necessary to acquire intellectual maturity in order to acquire spiritual maturity. It is, however, necessary to acquire spiritual maturity in order to acquire intellectual maturity, for the intellect cannot accurately evaluate concepts without a true spiritual basis.

There are three more things which I would like to speak about concerning maturity: the concept of infantile maturity; the concept of general or induced maturity; the concept of absolute or total maturity.

The concept of infantile maturity is highly misunderstood upon this planet. An infant, upon incarnating into your environment, has a certain amount of maturity that he normally brings with him. It is not necessary to induce this quality of maturity through any system of education to the infant. It is only necessary that he be alerted to the possibility of generating a continuance, through his own intellectual processes, of his own spiritual evolution and, consequently, spiritual maturity. Unfortunately, your religious systems do not provide, for the most part, this stimulus.

It is recommended that, in order for infantile maturity to progress at an acceptable rate, the infant be made aware at the earliest age possible of his responsibility in creating an intellectual communication with his total self. This is usually done through techniques of ritual and appreciation of the natural forces of the universe. The ritual that is employed by most of your religious systems upon your planet is highly ineffective, since it is generated primarily by force, and is not freely offered, to be accepted or rejected.

Those, even in an extreme infantile state, who are appreciative, due to their previous growth of the proper ritualistic communications, will accept them, and continue, at their own pace, and should not be forced to attend weekly meetings at specific hours for these purposes, since they reach a peak of spiritual attunement that is a function of their own cyclical activities, and therefore should be able to seek out, at any time, spiritual communications and should be provided with a place for seeking. And this should be the limit of that which is expected of them. Your present system drives most of your people from spiritual seeking at a very early age due to the aspect of force which should be totally removed. This is what we have experienced, and what we have found to be most beneficial.

The second aspect of which I speak is that of induced maturity, occurring in most unusual aspect among the peoples of your present society. This maturity, which is a false maturity, is induced by the social systems which are presently in effect upon your planet. Each system intellectually communicates an aspect of assumed maturity, which has nothing to do with real or absolute maturity. Therefore, much strife and confusion is realized by those who attempt to orient their thinking so as to reach the accepted state or level of the assumed concept of the mature mind. This concept is usually heavily intellectual, for your society at present is primarily an intellectual society, with very, very little awareness of the existence or function of what you would call a spiritual society.

Therefore, to mature within the boundaries of your present society and be accepted as a mature person, it is necessary to be able to communicate with it in its accepted intellectual jargon, which includes primarily a ridiculously long list of totally meaningless concepts. These should be, if one is to attain true maturity, rejected as meaningless, for they are extreme transients and have nothing to do with spiritual maturity.

The last aspect of maturity upon which I wish to speak is that of real maturity. My friends, there is only one way to reach real maturity: that is through meditation. We have said this many times. You cannot get there by intellectual mechanisms. You cannot get there by analyzing each of your thoughts, and labeling it either worthwhile or worthless. All of these things are aids, but with the foundation of daily meditation you cannot use this analysis, for the result of this analysis is insulated from the total self by a boundary. This boundary is permeable, but this boundary is only permeable when the mind is conditioned through meditation. Lack of meditation reduces this boundary to an impermeable state, all intellectual functions occurring on the surface, and having little effect upon the growth of the true self.

So you see, my friends, there is a dual process occurring. However, the meditation is always of the primary and greater importance. Once, however the art of meditation has been fully mastered, the intellectual mind becomes a useful tool in the development of spirit. It is of little consequence until this state of communication between the two is mastered. Therefore, my friends, all is of no avail until receptivity is made possible through daily meditation. This not only breaks down the barrier between the intellect and the spirit, it also breaks down all other barriers between the spirit and the one great All.

I hope that I have been of some service to you in this discussion. I realize that it is difficult to speak to you on this subject because it is a difficult subject if one is to use the parameters of your present society. We consider it very, very simple. Therefore, any true discussion of the subject should require no more than a few sentences.

It has been a privilege to speak with you. Adonai, my friends. I am Hatonn.

(At the end of this transcript is the following announcement.)

LOUISVILLE SPACE MEDITATION GROUP MEETING

Sunday—Introductory meeting

8:30 p.m.—Talks questions, films, et cetera on meditation and the space story.

9:30 p.m.—Meditation *(Name, address and phone number)*.

If you have any questions about the time or location of this meeting, please call the number given above.

(Tape ends.)

Year 1973
August, 1973 to December 18, 1973

Sunday Meditation
August, 1973

(The day of this channeling is unknown.)

(Don channeling)

I am Hatonn. I am with this instrument. I greet you in the love and in the light of our infinite Creator.

I am aware of your problem. It is an understanding of time. I will attempt to instruct you as to the nature of time. It is not very simple to you, I am sure, but it is very simple to us. simply because we are aware of time in a different way than you are aware of time.

Time, my friends, is in your mind. There is only now, and there is only here. The reason that there appears to be a reciprocal nature between space and time in your world is because your world is, shall we say, designed to produce this illusion. It is an illusion necessary for certain catalytic actions that you enjoy in your present state for the purpose of your continued spiritual growth and evolution.

Time, however, is totally independent of space, and space is totally independent of time, for in truth they have no relationship—for in truth neither has meaning. There is one place, and there is one time. Therefore, there is no interdependent relationship between the two.

I am going to at this time, if you will excuse the pun, call on another to speak to you, for it may be of some help to hear his words, as they will be somewhat less simple and therefore more time-consuming. I am sorry to be, shall we say, in a joking mood this evening, but I am afraid I find the subject somewhat of a humorous one.

I will leave you at this time. Adonai.

(Pause)

I am Oxal. I am with this instrument. I have been called for the purpose of speaking to you on the nature and reality of time. Time is a field, like unto your electric field, your magnetic field. But what is a field, my friends? A field is an effect. A field is in your minds. A field has different effects at different distances. So does time. As you have recently stated, time and space are dependent, one upon another. It has also been stated that they are totally independent, and have no relationship.

Both of these statements are true. It simply depends on your point of view. The people of your planet at present do not appreciate the number of dimensions that are available for one to experience the creation. All of these dimensions are made up of a single place and a single time, and, for that matter, a single dimension, which has no dimension. But it is necessary to go from where you are to where you will be. Therefore, we shall speak of time as you know it and try to lead you to that place where you will know it.

Time is a field. It is space-dependent. Space is a field and is time-dependent. For this reason you recognize a reciprocal nature. The relationship between the two is the third power [of] displacement in either. This may be recognized by a simple equation or formula. T^3 divided by 3 is equal to S^3. S^3 divided by 3 is equal to T.

There are three dimensions: therefore, the numeral "3" is used, both as a power and as a constant. Permeability of the field is dependent upon the speed of the reciprocal field. Your present constant, that which you call the velocity of light, is the basic speed of the field. The permeability of that which you know as matter is dependent upon this constant. In other words, my friends, the densities of which your world is composed, and the densities of the other planes of existence as you know them, are time-dependent. Their permeability is a function of apparent speed.

Condensation in dense form results from oscillations between reciprocally related space/time entities and permeability, or the basic density of this material, is a function of the apparent velocity of what you call light. There are six spaces and six times in each density. In your present form and state of awareness you recognize three. The other three you travel in in the state of sleep. In doing this. you become, quite often, mismatched with your awareness you possess in your waking state. For this reason you are able to perceive events that will occur in what is to you in the waking state the future. However, the future is an illusion, as is the past, for there is only the present. It is possible to slide, shall we say, along with respect to your awareness of time in the waking state simply by removing through the process of normal sleep the confines of the physical illusion. Space and time are then, as before, reciprocally related.

It in a difficult subject upon which to speak, and will require considerable intellectual thought for you to apply or communicate to others within the present illusion. How can one reduce to a mathematics fabricated within a system of illusion a truth that is totally outside the boundaries of that system? It may be possible, however, to make certain statements regarding the relationships between space and time in any system that will help to guide an individual attempting to work within a limited system to understand the truth of the actions and the limits of that system of phenomena of time. It would, however, be much better to eliminate from the individual's consciousness preconceived notions of the nature of both time and space, for they are not what they seem to be, as depicted by their phenomena within the boundaries of your present limitations.

Space may be thought of as linear, if time is thought of as volumetric. Or you may reverse the process, as you do within your limitation, and consider space volumetric and time linear. Either is true. And either may be perceived to be true, depending upon the limitations of your thought. It is possible to move linearly in space and volumetrically in time, all with the same movement. You can be aware of what you call the past, the present, and the future, simultaneously.

Time is not so much time as it is space, and space is not so much space as it is time. They are one and the same thing, and yet they are reciprocally related. For is not 1/1=1? For there is only one thing and we are all parts of it.

There are six dimensions, but you must speak of three. And time is a field, and radiates from each nucleus of matter in all directions and may be evaluated as $T = S^3/3$, where T is time and S is space.

I will be happy to speak with you in the future regarding this subject. However, it is thought that it will be necessary to consider that which has been given to you before further instruction will be of great benefit. It is a very difficult bridge to travel, between a world of semantics and a place of being. But we will serve you in any way that we can.

I am Oxal. I will leave you at this time. Adonai vasu borragus. It has been a great privilege. Peace be with you. ☥

Tuesday Meditation
December 18, 1973

(Unknown channeling)

I am Hatonn. I am very pleased to be with you this evening. It is always a great pleasure to be with you. I greet you, my friends, in the love and the light of our infinite Creator. I and my brother Laitos are here. We will condition you as I speak to you. It is very important, my friends. to spend time in meditation. Very important.

We of the Confederation of Planets in the Service of the Infinite Father are with you, my friends, and you are with us, in a single effort. Our effort, as I have said before, is to awaken the people of this planet to truth. This has been tried many, many times. They are sleeping very, very soundly. Yes, my friends, they are asleep, dreaming a dream that is fantastic. It is beyond the belief of those who know truth that such a dream could be a dream, but this is the case. Many of your people have dormant within them the memory of truth. Many others have a less accurate memory. And a few have no memory at all. The truth, however, is within them, for it is within all men, in all places.

For those of the first category, it is relatively easy to awaken them from their slumber. The second category is much, much more difficult, and the third, for the present, will be impossible for you to awaken. Do not concern yourself if an individual rejects an attempt you might make to awaken him. This simply means he is not yet ready for this truth to be given unto him. Concern yourselves with those who would seek the truth, and make it available to them in any way that you can.

There are many people upon your planet at this time who are attempting to cloud the memory of this truth. They are not aware of what they are doing. This is not their fault, but it is unfortunately the condition. It is not a simple task that we have outlined, and I am afraid it will require a great deal of effort. We have not been as successful as we had hoped to be when we initiated this project some years ago. The people of your planet do not actually wish to be awakened for the most part. Those who are sleeping very, very lightly are all too few. However, you will know them as you find them, and you will recognize their lightness of slumber by their activities, for they will not be as enmeshed in the insanity, if we can call it that, that is so prevalent on your world today.

These people are already seeking. In this case, it will be but a simple matter for you to convey to them that which they need. It is, however, very important that you be able to give them what they need. For this reason, we suggest that you continue to meditate, for only in this way can you be prepared to serve them. I speak not only of the preparation to act as does this instrument, as a vocal channel, but also a preparation of your own thinking, so that you will know the truth with no doubt or hesitation in speaking it. It is within you, my friends, and we will reawaken it within you, for your slumber is but very, very light. It is only necessary that you avail yourself to us through meditation.

There are many wondrous things that we would freely give you, if you would simply avail yourself to us. Those gifts are freely given. It is not only our pleasure and our privilege to do this but our duty, as it is your duty to pass them on to others, for this is the plan of the creation. The creation is a single entity. Each part of it is designed to aid and help all the other parts. This is the original plan. It Is a very simple thing for you to understand if you will relax and look at the original true creation and forget that which was created by your fellow man upon the surface of your planet that you now enjoy, and think of the plan and the working of the Father's original creation. It is quite obvious that each part was designed to aid and benefit each other part.

Unfortunately, due to the action [of] the free will that He gave to its parts, there have been some errors, shall I say, made by some of the parts, and they have strayed from the original plan, confusing themselves and confounding the workings of this plan. It is only necessary to realize the truth of this plan to know its workings. It is only necessary that you meditate to have all of these things given to you, or reawakened within you, for all of this knowledge was originally given to all of the parts of this creation. It dwells within every living thing—and every thing in this creation lives.

We of the Confederation of Planets in the Service of the infinite Creator are living as closely to the plan as we possibly can. We do this because we know it to be the only logical and rational way of living; to divorce yourself from the plan is only to confound the true workings of nature. Your people at present are totally unaware of such a plan. Your scientists ignore it. They are extremely interested in plans of their own. Unfortunately, their plans do not follow the plan of the Creator. Therefore, they waste much of their time and energy, and build devices that have no real valuable purpose. They are transient, I can assure you.

Your scientists should realize that there is a purpose to the creation that far surpasses what they suspect. They should avail themselves to the purpose in meditation. Then they would find that they would begin to understand the plan, and thereby they would be able to use their knowledge to build within the plan, not as they do now with no heed at all to the truth, and with plans of their own which have no relationship to truth.

Your governments make the same error. They do not work within the plan. They are not aware of the plan. They attempt to make law, but their laws do not work. They appear to have some value, but very shortly much strife is generated, and the result is war. They do not understand that the reason for this strife is that they have ignored the natural plan of creation, the natural order of things, and the law of the Creator that devised this. Your leaders should avail yourself in meditation to truth, as we do.

We are aware that at this particular time it is impossible for your scientists and your leaders to do such a thing, for they are in the a vast depths of slumber, and cannot at this time be awakened, for the most part. There are only a few, many—many too few, who are very lightly slumbering. It will be necessary, therefore, to concern yourself with those whom you contact in any and all walks of life, the ones who are lightly slumbering, the ones who will seek on their own, after they have been made aware of the possibility of seeking.

It is our plan to alert as many of these people as possible, so that when it becomes obvious, to your leaders and to your scientists, that we are real, and we are what they suspect that we might be, there will be a sufficient number of awakened entities on your planet for some form of communication to take place between those who are already awake, and those who are lightly slumbering in the future. For, as time passes, those who are in the depths of slumber now will begin to awake. Those who you cannot contact at all now will begin to awake. It will be a self-generating process, so that large numbers of your people will be given the truth. It is a very, very big task.

It will be up to you, and those like you, to help us in carrying this out. We have said before that we would very much like to land upon your surface and contact your peoples directly but we have explained that this is not at all feasible.

I am aware of many planets such as this one that have gone through a cycle of awakening. Many planets made this transition with considerable ease, because they were following the plan. Unfortunately, this planet has lagged in the natural scheme of things. This is what you might refer to as a borderline case. There will be those of your people who make the graduation, and those who don't. This is not always the case with all planets. In some instances, all individuals are ready for the graduation that you now approach. In some unfortunate instances none are ready. In your particular place, it is a combination of both instances.

Therefore, do not be dismayed if your ideas are totally rejected by some, for this is to be expected. And this is the major reason that we cannot come among you, for it would be a direct violation of one of the laws of which I earlier spoke. Due to their conditions, it is necessary for those of you who would help us, who are on the surface of your planet, to help us. We request that you meditate. This is all that is necessary. This is all the help that we need. Because, if you meditate, then you will know what to do. And this is all the help that we need, or all the help that we would desire, for this is also part of the plan.

It has been a privilege to be with you this evening. I am Hatonn. I will leave you in His love and in His light. Adonai. Adonai vasu.

Year 1974
January 4, 1974 to November 15, 1974

Saturday Meditation
January 4, 1974

(Don channeling)

I greet you, my friends, in the love and in the light of the infinite Creator. I am here with you in the room. I will condition the ones known as Carla and S. They will both feel my presence. It is a great privilege to be with you, and to aid you in your ability to receive our thoughts. I am Laitos. Adonai.

(Pause)

I am Oxal. I am with this instrument, and I am using control, because he is not used to channeling me. I am sorry that it is necessary to use this type of control for a little while, but he must be able to speak, using my thoughts.

I am a member of the Confederation of Planets in the Service of Our Infinite Creator. I am here, as are my brothers, to serve your people. This has been told you this evening. But there are some other things that should be told unto you at this time. We of the Confederation of Planets in the Service of Our Infinite Creator are here for another purpose. This purpose is to serve ourselves. For, my friends, in serving you, we serve ourselves. This is the way that the creation is built. It is made so that if you serve anyone or anything in this creation you are serving yourself. This is a truth that cannot be varied. The creation, my friends, is one thing, and it is impossible in this creation to act without affecting yourself. This is not realized by most of the people of your planet, and for this reason they have affected themselves in a miserable way. We are very sorry for this, because in doing this they have not only affected themselves, they have affected us. They have made us very sad.

We are sad because we are very sorry to see people as miserable as are yours. It is not necessary, my friends, to be miserable. It is necessary only to be extremely ecstatic at all times, for this is the way that our Creator intended it. When it is understood that all things are one and it is impossible to serve anything without serving yourself, then the state of ecstasy that I spoke of becomes reality.

I am sorry that I am required to control the instrument, but I wanted to give these thoughts to you with no possibility of misinterpretation. I am Oxal. I shall leave you now, in His love and light. Adonai vasu borragus.

(Pause)

I am Philip of the Brotherhood of the Seven Rays. I greet you, my friends, in the love and in the light of the infinite One, Creator of us all. Creator of all things in all places at all times. In His light, my friends. We have said this many times: "… in His light." Consider, my friends, what we mean when we say, "His light."

Yes, my friends, the Confederation of Planets in His Service is here to serve you. They orbit your planet in their craft. They come in swarms, by millions and millions they come from all of creation. They come to you at this time to serve you. Will you not let them serve you? For they are here, now. If you will look, you will see them, for they will show themselves to those of you who would wish to know them. They would greet you openly but they cannot, for most of the people of your planet have so willed it. It is already known the exact reactions that would occur if a direct meeting were to take place at this time. For this reason it is very necessary that you continue in more active service. It is very necessary that more and more of your peoples learn the truth. Only this will bring about a condition which will enable direct contact to take place.

Many your peoples at this time would wish to know exactly what has happened, but they are not provided with the correct intonation. The information they are given should be correct. And it can be given them only by those who understand what is correct, or those which are channels and can speak directly, using our thoughts. Many people are crying out for this knowledge, but they are confused. They are confused by so many, many erroneous thoughts and erroneous sayings and erroneous deeds.

In the past, our space brothers contacted some of your people and attempted to pass on through them certain information. In each case, this resulted in failure. These contactees were not understood or believed. It led to their ridicule, and a considerable waste of effort on the part of the Confederation, and a considerable waste for those who were contacted. For in some cases, it did them harm. It seems that each time your people are contacted, it does them harm, to some degree.

So it will take strength to serve at this time. It will take strength to be a link between our brothers in space and our brothers upon the surface of your planet. But this is very necessary. More necessary, my friends, than anything else that you could do at this time. It will not be an easy task, but it is not an impossible task to alert those of your people who would wish to know what is actually occurring. It will be necessary that enough of your people believe in what we say for the Confederation to land upon your surface. It is not necessary for the people of this planet to believe in the Confederation; it is necessary that they believe in the Creator, and that they believe what the Confederation says.

There are many people here that already believe this, that already know this, for it is truth. However, this knowledge is lying dormant, below their level of consciousness. It is necessary that this knowledge be brought to their surface. A reawakening, a reexamination of their inmost thoughts is necessary for them to release themselves from the hypnosis created by their present social conditions.

It is therefore necessary that channels such as yourselves act at this time, to give to the people of this planet a reminder. A reminder of truth. Those that are ready will awaken. Those who are not ready will ignore.

Act wisely, and remember the mistakes of those who have gone before you. Do not become a stumbling block in the way of those who would be awakened, because of the peculiarity of your action. But do act, for this is now necessary.

I will leave this instrument at this time. I leave you in His love and in His light, and extend to you all of the love from all of the peoples in the Creation. For it is yours, and yours is theirs. My peace be with you. I am Philip. Farewell, and love.

Sunday Meditation
January 6, 1974

(Don channeling)

I am Oxal. I greet you, my friends, in the love and the light of our infinite Creator. It is a great privilege to be with you this evening, as it is a privilege to be with you every evening. For, my friends, we cannot be separated. For we are one person, you see, and it is impossible to be separated.

I am using control for this instrument's vocal mechanism.

We of the Confederation of Planets in the Service of the Infinite Father are here. We are here now. You can see us if you look for us. We are here now even more so than we were previously. We are here now because it is time for us to be here. Things are progressing now that we have spoken of previously. You will see many changes in the coming year. These changes will be both of a natural type and a man-made type. There are certain things that will take place. But do not be alarmed, for you will be with the Creator.

I am with you at all times. Do not forget this. It will be important in the days to come. I am with you at all times. All that is necessary is that you ask and you shall receive, as it is written in your *Bible*. I will provide for you what is necessary. It is a simple matter.

I am at present in a craft far above this house. I am a physical being such as yourself. I am enjoying much more freedom than yourselves. But you too may soon enjoy this freedom. It is only necessary that you understand how to enjoy it.

(Pause)

I shall continue. I have allowed the instrument to rest, for this method is very tiring for the instrument, but it allows a more accurate transcription.

We of the Confederation are here, as I have said, in great numbers. We are allowing your people to see us; at present we are allowing more of your peoples to see us. You can see us, as this instrument has. I will appear to you in the very near future. I will be seen in your skies. It is only necessary that you continue in your seeking. You see, my friends, it is truly written that in order to find, you must seek. That is the scheme of things at this time. All of our efforts have been directed toward fulfilling this simple phrase: "Seek and ye shall find." Why do you think we have been so elusive? This was wisdom, my friends, that it is necessary to seek in order to find.

You will understand this wisdom if you think about it. It is a very old and tried system of producing an increase in the awareness of an individual, for only he himself can produce this increase in awareness. We cannot impress it upon him. But he can very easily increase his awareness many, manyfold. But the seeking is necessary. It is not quite so important as to his method of seeking as it is that he simply seek. Seek knowledge of the Creation. Many of your scientists seek, and they find. But many get confused about what they are seeking. When we speak of seeking, we speak of seeking a truth that is within all things.

I will leave you now, but with one final thought. This thought is that all of us are one. If we are one, then we share all of the knowledge that there is. Avail yourself to this knowledge. It is yours to begin with. Do this through meditation. You will understand all there is to understand. It is a simple process. I am Oxal. Adonai vasu borragus.

(Pause)

I am Yom. I greet you in the love and light of our infinite Creator. It is a privilege to be with you. I am aware of certain things that you wish to know. I am Yom. I will tell you what I know of these things.

We are here now, where we are. And we are going to be someplace else, at a later time. But both places are one place. Each is possible. Each is true. It depends on your awareness.

I would suggest that you would observe a bubble at the bottom of a glass of water. It is originally smaller than when it rises to the top. If you take this bubble to an extreme depth, it will flatten to a form that is lenticular. This is because of the extreme differential of pressure. The gradient at that depth is sufficient to cause this formation. This same gradient exists in space. It is responsible for the galactic shape. This pressure is external pressure to the galactic system, causing a lenticular shape. Within the system, there are planetary systems. These systems are within a flattened orbit. This is because that they naturally, due to this pressure, find themselves in one plane of rotation. All galactic systems are lenticular in shape, except for those that are extremely close to other systems. The creation has the property of creating this shape. If there is sufficient freedom of materials in the galactic system, this freedom exists; in the bubble at the extreme depth, this situation exists.

Now let us consider the cause for the pressure creating the shape. If the gravitational theories that your scientists support were correct, galaxies would be spherical. Sufficient freedom being allowed, they would coalesce into a simple ball. There is a scheme to the Creation that provides for separation of systems. There is no inertial expansion of the Creation, as many of your scientists believe. There are forces holding all bodies in their position. and forces causing the rotation of those bodies. These forces are external to the bodies. They are not generated within the bodies. They are a property of the great creation in general, and not an interactive force between bodies. Observe the placement of galactic systems with respect to other systems. They are separated by several major diameters or less. At this relatively close proximity, if the gravitational theories were correct, there would be an influence of one system upon the other, creating in a relatively short period a combining of the two systems. It is therefore suggested that your present theories of gravitation are incorrect.

Each system of stars exists in a field that has a gradient in the direction of the minor axis. The entire thing becomes a large wheel. Within this wheel we find many small wheels. These are the planetary systems. They also experience this gradient and therefore are flat, or within the same plane. Although your science is unable to discern the numerous planetary systems within the galaxy, if it could it would find them all to be oriented so that the planes of their rotations are parallel. And this plane of their rotation is parallel to the major plane of the galactic system, which includes its major diameters. Each planetary system rotates around its central axis. This axis is parallel to the central axis of the galactic system. The entire system rotates around its central axis. All of this was planned. All of it has meaning. All of it has purpose.

You are on a system which is relatively close to the outer edge of the galactic system. The angular velocity results in a relatively high linear velocity of your system with respect to the central axis. This linear velocity of your planetary system thereby passes you through much more space thanthose who dwell near the center of the galactic system. You are moving now from one zone into another, due to the rotation of the galaxy. The space transversed by your planet and its system is close to the maximum per unit time that can be appreciated within a system of planets within this galaxy. There is a reason for this. The reason is that your system is in an early stage of evolution, and therefore there must be a long, angular path resulting in … I should say a long arc of experience for your system. If you were dwelling much closer to the center of the galaxy, or at the center of rotation, there would be no progression through space with respect to the central axis of the galaxy. As you experience night and day, and seasons of the year due to rotation, you also experience seasons of spirituality due to rotation. These exist within the rotation of the galactic system.

I will return to this instrument another time, for he is becoming fatigued. It is difficult to use control for a long period. It is difficult to translate all that I have to say to an understandable framework for you, because of limitations of concepts. But we will continue, and we will attempt to bridge this gap. I am Yom. I leave you in His love and in His light.

Monday Meditation
January 7, 1974

(Unknown channeling)

I am Hatonn. I greet you, my friends, in the love and the light of the infinite Creator. It is a very great privilege to be with you this evening. I and my brothers are here. We have been here for many years, and we have given freely to your people that which we had to give, our knowledge of truth. Unfortunately, there has been too little dissemination. Most of your people are unaware of contacts, and if they are aware of them, they have been misled. They do not understand what we have for them.

Your people are somewhat unique. We have visited other planets, and made contacts such as this one, and we are listened to, for they recognize truth when they hear it. The people of your planet do not seem to recognize truth as easily as the other peoples of which I just spoke. The peoples of your planet are quite hypnotized by a false illusion created by themselves. At an earlier period in your history, many more of your people would have paid attention to our words, for they were, as you might say, more superstitious at that time. It is only necessary that our words be made available to your people. Those who will recognize them as truth will do so. Those who cannot recognize them as truth will not. It is as simple as that. There is no need to impress this information any further upon your people than simply exposing them to it. This, however, has not been carried on in sufficient quantity. It is for this reason that we are now attempting to impress upon channels such as this one the need for greater dissemination of that information that we have to present to your people.

We of the Confederation of Planets are here, and have a job to do. We have been working diligently at this job for many of your years. We are aware of the problems that you face in attempting to make more of the people of your planet aware of our communications, but we will assure you that we will aid you in doing this. As time progresses, more and more aid can be given. You will have noticed that in the past twenty years attitudes have changed considerably. Things that were very difficult to talk about with the general population are now relatively easy to talk about. Their acceptance of our presence is much greater than it was in the past. Your own expeditions into space, however slight, have aided greatly in the acceptance of your general public's attitudes toward possibilities of extraterrestrial contact.

We of the Confederation of Planets in the Service of Our Infinite Creator are here to contact you now. We must emphasize this: we are here to do this. This is our purpose. We must, however, make this contact very, very carefully, in a predetermined way. That is what is happening in this room at this instant. There can be no variation from this technique at this time. We have had many experiences in contacting peoples. It has always been found that it must be done with extreme caution. There are grave consequences when an alien society is impressed directly upon another society, especially when technological separation is as vast as is ours.

Your people would not understand at all. They would not accept us for what we are. We could not walk among them and be accepted, and this is what we wish to do: be accepted. For, my friends, we are all exactly the same. We could not speak directly to your people and have them gain benefit from our teachings, for they would feel that they must accept, without question, what we say. This is of no benefit, my friends. You are here, at this time, as we are where we are, primarily to seek. To seek in our own way that which is the path back toward the Creator of us all. An interruption that is too great in this personal seeking is not a very good thing. For this reason, we are unable to directly contact your people. We must provide them, however, with that which they need. And this we are doing to the best of our ability.

However, it is of extreme importance that those of you who are available to help us do so. You will find that, at first, you may have considerable difficulty in doing this because, as this instrument has stated, it is a tricky business. You must always remember that the individual must seek. If you provide information, then do it so that it is understandable, simple, and in no way forced upon the recipient. We of the Confederation of Planets in the Service of the Infinite Creator are always with you. We are constantly serving you. It is only necessary that you avail yourself to us, and we will be there. In the future, in the very, very near future, you may expect much, much more support from us, in a physical way, for time now grows very, very short. Reach out to your brothers in space, as we do to you.

I will leave you now. I am Hatonn. I leave you in the love and in the light of our infinite Creator. Adonai vasu.

(Pause)

I am Oxal. I greet you, my friends, in the love and the light of our infinite Creator. It is a great privilege to be with you. I and my brothers are here. This you have heard, and it is true. We are here, and we will remain here, until the entire program on your Earth is complete.

We are here for a special purpose. We are here to serve. Think of this. We are here to serve. This is important. As you now near the end of a master cycle, there will be changes in your physical world. These changes should not be feared. They should be welcomed. For they are signals to you that a new age is dawning. If you understand it, and walk among your people unafraid, then you too will serve. For they will see in you an inner knowledge, which we will provide you. We will also serve you through the absolute limits of our ability. There are cycles in time, and cycles in space, and all things operate in cycles. Your planet now approaches the end of a great, great cycle of time. This has been a learning time, an evolving time, a time of growing. And many of the people of your planet are now ready for a transition to a much more glorious existence.

But they will not understand this transition unless they are told. There have been many contacts speaking of this transition, but too few of your people are presently aware of what is shortly to take place. It will be necessary to provide them with the reasons for what they experience. It is only necessary that you avail yourself in meditation to be able to understand and therefore serve. This is your call. This is why you are here, where you are.

We of the Confederation of Planets are aware of all of the problems which confront you, for we are in contact with you at all times. It is not an easy place to exist, your world. But pay it no attention, for it is not a lasting world. Everything that is happening and will happen is not really of any importance. It will shortly be gone. We speak of a lasting creation. An unchanging, but infinite, creation.

We will at all times serve you. This is our duty. If you will meditate, and avail yourself to the truth, you will understand your true position, and you will know your duty. I am Oxal. I will leave you now. I leave you in the love and the light of our infinite Creator. Adonai vasu borragus.

Tuesday Meditation
January 8, 1974

(Unknown channeling)

I am Laitos. I am with this instrument. I greet you, my friends, in the love and the light of the infinite Creator. As you know, it is my privilege to condition those who are to become channels. I am here this evening to condition each of you. I will condition the one known as Carla; also the one known as S; also the one known as T. Each of you will feel my presence and the effect of my conditioning. All that is necessary is that you avail yourself to me. If you desire my contact, you will receive it. This is my duty and my privilege. I am Laitos. Adonai vasu borragus.

(Pause)

I am Oxal. I am with this instrument. I am using control. I greet you, my friends, in the love and in the light of our infinite Creator. It is a great privilege to be with you this evening. Yes, my friends, I am here with you. I am Oxal.

We of the Confederation of Planets in the Service of the Infinite Creator are here now. Now is an important time. It is time, my friends, for your people to be awakened. It is time for them to understand what is happening. They have slept for a long enough time. We are going to accomplish this, with help. We will be seen much more often in your skies in the coming months. Many questions will be asked. Many of your people will become much more inquisitive. It is important for you to prepare yourselves now, so that you do not confuse them. If it is necessary, then we will work directly with them, but you must be very careful in your attempt to serve, for the service that you perform must be correct or it will only confuse them.

This is the reason that you are here now. This is the reason for your choice. Service, my friends, is very natural. It is the way of the Creator. It is the plan of the creation. Everything in the creation is performing a service. The vegetation that is abundant on your planet performs a service. But your people ignore this. The animals upon your planet perform a service, but this is largely also ignored. The flowers, the very air, the water, perform a service, but this is ignored. If it were taken fully into consideration, it would become obvious that everything in the creation is there to perform a service.

This includes all the Creator's children. Each of you is here to perform a service. This is the plan of this infinite creation. This is how it works. It is only necessary to understand this, and then all things are possible. Unfortunately, upon the planet that you now enjoy, this principle is not understood. Very, very few of those who inhabit the surface of this planet understand the simplicity and totality of this plan. It is the way the Creation functions. It is only necessary that you understand this, and then perform, with the best of your ability

Perform these services to your fellow man, and then you too will be functioning the way that the Creator of us all planned.

We of the Confederation of Planets in the Service of the Infinite Creator are here to serve you. It is a great privilege, yet we must remain aloof. This is our understanding of proper service, for in serving your fellow man, it in necessary that you serve his exact wants and needs. You cannot determine for him what these are. Therefore, if his wants and needs lie outside the limits of your ability or your desire to serve, it is best that you remain aloof, as we.

There are, however, many, many of your people who desire exactly our service. We are hindered by those who do not desire our service. For this reason it is impossible at this time to come among you. For this reason it is necessary at this time to act through instruments such as this one. Your fellow man cries out in many ways, for many things. He is looking, but for the most part he does not know what he seeks. Shortly, he will seek your service. Prepare yourself now, for there is very little time remaining.

We of the Confederation of Planets in the Service of the Infinite Creator will be seen in your skies. It is only necessary that you look for us. We will be there.

It has been a privilege to be with you this evening. I am Oxal. Adonai vasu borragus.

(Pause)

I am Hatonn. I greet you, my friends, in the love and in the light of our infinite Creator. It is a great privilege to be with you this evening. I am aware of certain questions. I will attempt to answer these questions at this time.

There are many, many things that will happen in your future. There are many things that have happened in your past. Each of these things has a meaning. Each of these meanings can be known. It is only necessary to avail yourself in meditation, and you can know what these things are. Many of the interpretations are not possible in the language of the people of your present planet, where they have no concept to include these meanings.

The meanings can be known to you in full. There are many wondrous things in this creation, so many more than the people of your planet imagine, that I could not begin to give you an idea of what exists. There are seven ways to choose that which you would seek. There are right ways, and there are wrong ways, but the paths are not labeled. There is a path through woods; a path by a stream; a path by a highway; a path through a door; a path that is lighted; and a path that is not lighted; and a path that goes nowhere, but returns upon itself.

But who made these paths, my friends, and why are they there?

Six principles are linked to these paths: the principle of Light; principle of Sound; principle of Motion; principle of Vibration; principle of Time; and the principle of Energy. Five types of people embark: the Light; the Dark; the Yellow; the Red; and the last, which has no color. And they go four places: they go North, South, East or West. And experience three things: Love, Hate and Tranquility. Which leads to two poles: Good or Evil. But each of these things leads to one, my friends, and that one is the Creator.

(Transcript ends.) ❧

Thursday Meditation
January 10, 1974

(Unknown channeling)

I am Hatonn. I greet you, my friends, in the love and in the light of our infinite Creator. It is a great privilege to be with you this evening, as it is every evening. I am in a craft, high above you. I am aware of your thoughts, even though I am quite some distance above. I am, at this time, in a craft which is capable of interplanetary flight. This craft has been seen by some of your people. It will shortly be seen by more of them. It may shortly be seen by yourselves, if you look for it. The time is closely approaching now when we must be seen much, much more by the people of this planet. The time is now closely approaching when we must create a high degree of inquisitiveness among your people. They are quite inquisitive at the present, but they are not yet seeking. This is what we intend to do: we intend to provide a stimulus for them, to increase their seeking. The larger percentage of your people, although interested in our craft, are not sufficiently interested to seek an answer to what they see. This we intend to alleviate by stimulating a more intense interest.

There is, unfortunately, considerable false information as to our purpose, our reality, our motives, and our being. It will be a great help to our effort to have additional vocal channels such as this one. These channels will be able to talk directly to the people who initiate seeking as a result of seeing our craft. If we are able to do this in sufficient quantity, then we will be able to circumvent discrepancies and wrong information with respect to our presence. We of the Confederation of Planets in the Service of the Infinite Creator are engaged in a definite program of action. This action, for the past twenty or so years, has been limited. It has recently become less limited. Certain aspects of your civilization and its intellectual growth have made possibilities for greater stimulation, through a greater showing of ourselves, a distinct possibility. In other words, many, many more of the people of this planet are open to suggestions of a nature that would have seemed all too radical just a few years in your past.

Many of your people are now ready to open their minds to things that were beyond belief for them just a few years ago. There has been a great increase in the dissemination to the general public of information with respect to both travel in space and what you call metaphysical phenomena. This attitude makes it possible for us to initiate what I will call a second phase in our program in awakening the people of this planet to the truth that they so badly desire.

We of the Confederation of the Planets in the Service of the Infinite Creator are about to embark upon a most interesting phase of our mission. It will be interesting for us, and it will also be interesting for you. If you are to be of service in the program we are now instituting, it will be necessary that you—very, very carefully—control what you say to those who seek from you, and it will also be necessary that you are very careful about the way that you act. In this way, you can be of maximum service. It has been said in your language, "Physician, heal thyself." If you do not demonstrate in your daily living an understanding of the teachings of those of the Confederation who profess the understanding of the way of the Creator, then you will not be of as much service in your attempts to help enlighten your people as you would be if you would so demonstrate this knowledge.

We of the Confederation of Planets in the Service of the Infinite Creator are most eager to join with you who dwell upon the surface of this planet in bringing this light and this love to the people who so much desire it. There are, of course, those upon your surface at this time who do not desire this light or this love. At this particular time, we cannot do anything for those who do not desire this, for they will not believe what is given to them. There will be no way, in this case, to help them, for it is a necessary fact of the mechanism of this creation that the individual must evolve within himself an understanding of its working.

For this reason, we have been very, very careful about contacts, and for this reason, we have been very, very careful about arousing too much attention with respect to our craft in your atmosphere. There are, however, at this time, enough seeking what should be given unto them for us to take what I will call a more drastic action. You must, I am afraid, be a little patient, for this will not take place overnight. But I will assure you that in a very short period of time, there will be considerable activity with respect to our presence, and considerable awareness of this form of contact. At this time, those of you who can serve us will have a great duty to perform, for you will, like us at that time, be actively and directly in the service of our infinite Creator.

Join with us, members of the Confederation of Planets in His service, to act as a steppingstone from the darkness that now abounds upon your planet to the light that is so ever present in this infinite creation.

I am very privileged to have spoken with you this evening. I am Hatonn. I will leave you in the love and the light of our infinite Father. Adonai, my friends. Adonai borragus.

(Pause)

I am Oxal. I am with this instrument. I have for you a little story. I greet you, my friends, in the love and in the light of our infinite Creator.

I am at this time in the room here with you. If you look, you can see me, but I am afraid that you have not totally learned to look. Be patient, and you will see me. I am Oxal. It is really a very great privilege to be with you here. And it is, I must assure you, an extremely interesting and glorious thing to do, to be able to be in this place at this time. We of the Confederation are constantly moving about with your people, moving into their homes and industries, offices, wherever they my be. We do not intend to snoop, my friends, but it is necessary to know what is happening upon your surface, and what is going on, you might say, in the minds of your people. For this reason, those of us who are so able to do this are constantly moving about on the surface of your planet. We are called to instruments such as this one by a so-called direct telepathic thought. This is the way that you explain it in your language. We do not think of it this way. We do not think of it [as] a possibility of separation. Since the creation, my friends, is one thing, it is very difficult for us to suppose that you could separate mind.

We share a mind, my friends. The people of your planet have simply, for quite some period in the past, denied this possibility of sharing. This is the natural way for things to be, my friends. It is very natural that we should share a single mind, as we share everything.

As I was saying, I am here with you in this room now, and since I am sharing with you your minds, I am sharing with you your thoughts. It is apparent to me that each of you is somewhat confused about certain things that we intend. Do not let this trouble you, my friends, because certain things are very difficult to understand from your perspective at this particular time. I can tell you, however, that we intend to do everything that you have been told tonight. We definitely intend to awaken the people of your planet. We have gained enough knowledge in the way that I have spoken of about the actions and thinking of the people of your planet to know them almost as well as we know ourselves. We have spent considerable time studying the people of this planet, and we have found that there are a reasonably large number of them that can join us in the peace and the love of our Creator's infinite creation.

For this reason, we are here now. If there were none of your people ready for this, we would have no task. We would be incapable of arousing people that do not wish to join us in this love and light to do so. It is not possible for us to do this, my friends. It is only possible that the individual do this. Each of you must arouse himself to a state of seeking that which we hold out to you as the only worthwhile objective in the creation: that is, the love and the light of the creation itself. We of the Confederation are very, very privileged to be here and to do this at this time. It is something that we have desired for a long time. We have waited impatiently to be here and to help you, for this is a service that gives us much, much pleasure.

We are aware that it is very difficult for you, who have been, shall I say, stuck on the surface of your planet for quite some time, to fully encompass in your minds the grandeur and the magnitude of this project, but it is possible for you to do this, my friends. The only thing that is necessary is for you to avail yourself to this knowledge through meditation. We are speaking of something that is so much beyond anything that you have previously experienced that you would find no comparison. There will be certain problems for you, but if you will keep foremost in your mind that the objective which we share is to bring truth to a people who are for the most part totally unaware of this truth, then, my friends, we will be triumphant, and we will, working together, accomplish a satisfactory culmination in the great scheme of our Father's creation.

I am at this time going to attempt to contact each of you more directly. Please be patient, relax and await my contact. I will leave this instrument now and move around the room to each of you. Adonai vasu. I will be with you. Adonai vasu.

Saturday Meditation
January 12, 1974

(Unknown channeling)

I am Hatonn. I greet you, my friends, in the love and in the light of our infinite Creator. I am with this instrument. It is a great privilege to be with you this evening. I am at this time in a craft high above your house. You could not see me if you looked, for I am much too high. I am aware of your eagerness to meet with us. We will attempt to arrange this at some time in the future, but for now you must be patient, for we cannot at this time greet you openly.

We are sorry that this is the situation, but it is at this time impossible. But in the relatively near future, we will be glad to greet you directly. We, the Confederation of Planets in the Service of the Infinite Creator, are waiting to meet as many of the people of your planet as would wish to meet us. The reaction of the people of your planet is quite varied [as] to their realization of our presence. Some of them seem convinced that we are here now. Some of them do not believe in us at all. That is exactly the condition for which we have strived. It is a condition which will produce a maximum effort on the part of the individual to seek: to seek the truth of our existence, or of our nonexistence. This seeking will lead him upon other ideas. These ideas have been presented in many forms in your literature in the past many hundreds of years.

In his seeking he will, if things are correctly progressing, discover certain truths that have been available throughout all time. He will also, if he is fortunate, come in contact with some of the material that we make available through channels such as this one to the peoples of your planet.

This condition of questioning, seeking and thinking about things is precisely the condition that we have attempted to generate by our rather nebulous contact. It is always much more satisfactory if the individual finds something out by his own efforts than it is if he is taught a principle. The mental activity required for the individual to seek out and find the basic truths of the creation allows him time to reflect and examine with his own point of view each one of the propositions offered to him. This results in an understanding of the propositions that surpasses any understanding that he could achieve if these propositions were made to him in a relatively short period of time.

This, of course, would have been necessary if we had landed upon your surface and directly communicated with the people of your planet. The ways of the Confederation in establishing contact with a planet that has no knowledge of their presence or the galactic Confederation or any of our peoples is now quite standardized. For this reason, we have chosen to limit our contacts severely. There is, however, only a certain amount of time available to make and establish a contact which will disseminate to as many of your people as possible the truth of this infinite creation, and the true workings of man in it.

We will, therefore, be much more in evidence in your skies in the very near future. As I have stated earlier, many, many more of your people are ready for the truth that we bring than were ready a few years ago. We therefore increase our activity, in hopes that it will increase the seeking of individuals in an attempt to understand us. We must emphasize that this understanding can come only through an effort put forth by the individual to do so. Without this, there will be very little progress in his development of understanding.

I hope that I have been of some service in helping each of you to understand our purpose and motives with respect to our relatively unusual form of contacting the people of your planet. It has been a great privilege to give you these thoughts, and we are in hopes that it will aid you in understanding the importance of your own seeking, for this, my friends, is a great truth: that it is necessary to seek in order to find. It is necessary to seek, my friends, in order to grow. Do not be neglectful of your personal seeking. It is the most important thing that you do.

I hope that I have been of service. I will leave you now, and will allow this instrument to be used for contact by one of my brothers. I am Hatonn. Adonai vasu.

(Pause)

I am Latui. I am with this instrument. I greet you, my friends, in the love and the light of our infinite Creator. It is a very great privilege to be with you, my friends, for I have not been with you before. I have been with this instrument before but not with you, in a sense that I have not spoken with you. We, of course, cannot be separated in our totality.

I am Latui. We of the Confederation of Planets in the Service of the Infinite Creator are always privileged to speak with the people of your planet. We are sorry that we have to use this method, but the reason for this method has been adequately explained by my brother. I will, therefore, continue using this instrument to give you certain thoughts, which I truly hope will help you in your seeking.

This planet, my friends, is a ball in space. It is a ball of light. But it does not appear to you as what it really is. The reason, my friends, that it is a ball of light is that all things in the entire creation are comprised of nothing but light. This is the basic building block of all of the material creation. When we greet you in His love and His light, we greet you in the only existing ingredients of the creation: love, the formative force, and light, the building block.

I am aware that it is difficult for you to conceive of light as matter, but this, my friends, is the actual situation. Light is one of the two things that we always mention at the beginning of a contact. There is a good reason for this. There is a good reason for us to greet you in His love and His light. The reason is that this encompasses everything. And that is what we wish to do: include within this greeting everything and everyone in the creation. For, as we have told you, it is true that all of these parts are one single thing. Imagine, if you can, an infinitely large sphere of pure light. Impressed upon this is absolute love. Out of this, then, condenses the unimaginably vast number of created parts, each of those parts connected by this original force, the love of our infinite Creator. Each of us, my friends, and everything else, is made up of this single fabric—light.

It is only necessary to learn the truth of what I say in its totality to be able to return to that place and stature that was designed for you by the Creator. Light, my friends, is the substance of which you are made. Light is the substance of which I am made. Light is the substance of which everything is. Love is the substance which forms light into the forms that you know as living beings, as planets, as trees, as stars, as air. It is all one substance. This substance, my friends, can be affected only by love.

Love, my friends, is not what you think it is. The word in your language has a meaning that has various interpretations. But it is none of these things. We use the word when we speak to you, because it is as close as we can come to the concept, using your language. Love, my friends, is that force which does all of the things that are done in the entire creation. All of the things, my friends, even those that you would interpret as being without love. If it were not for that love, my friends, then the freedom of choice to do these things could not exist. It is only necessary that the individual realize the truth of what I am saying in order to be able to do those things that he was originally intended to be able to do by the Creator of us all.

The things that he was intended to be able to do are quite surprising. They extend so far beyond your present limitations that I could not possibly convey to you the scope and magnitude of these abilities. However, it is possible, let me assure you, through proper methods of advancing your understanding with respect to its present limitations, to regain what is rightfully yours, the knowledge that you have buried within you, the knowledge of the use of our Creator's light through love.

It is very, very important, my friends, that you seek an understanding of love. Do not be satisfied with your first interpretation of this concept, for it is much, much broader in scope than you might imagine. It covers everything that there is.

I am going to instruct the people of your planet on the use of love. This will be done in an unusual way, but please bear with me. We have found that it is necessary to do things in unusual ways, as far as you are concerned. It is necessary to teach to you a way of thinking that is not common to the people of your planet, if you are to rapidly gain understanding of the concepts that are of utmost importance in your present progression. There are three ways to achieve a knowledge of love.

The first way is to relax, and let your mind become at rest. This is the method of meditation. If this is done, on a daily basis, then it is not possible to shut out the love that is ever present. You will become aware of the true creation and its meaning.

The second way is to go forth among the people of your planet and serve them. They will return to you love, and you will absorb this love and store it within your being. I must at this time caution that this service to your people must be done in such a way that it is service that they wish. Do not make a mistake, as so many of your people have done, in trying to impress an unwanted or unsolicited service upon your neighbor. To go forth and to serve your fellow man at this time upon your planet requires much care and planning, for it is at this time rather difficult to accomplish, for interpretations of service vary greatly, and it is necessary that you understand what service is, in order for yours to be effective. This can only be done by following the first step, or plan, which is meditation.

The third technique is to give all that you have to your fellow man. If this is done, then you will not be encumbered by material possessions. You will no longer give part of your love to material possessions. Giving love to material possessions is an extreme waste of your abilities. This is a mistake that is made by most of the people of this planet. It is necessary, if one is to attempt this method of gaining love, to divorce oneself from the desire for material things.

Each one of these three avenues may be used. Each one will produce results. At present, it is very difficult to work and live within a society such as yours and to allow each of these programs for knowing love. It is therefore suggested by those of us of the Confederation of Planets in His Service that you employ the first method. Meditation. my friends, will allow you to decide to what extent you may employ the other two methods, for it is sometimes impractical to attempt to literally follow these two suggestions, in that those whom you attempt to serve will not understand. It is, however, recommended that you keep each of these methods in mind, for they are all important.

Much of the strife that has occurred upon your planet in its history is due to the attachment of the people of this planet for material possessions. They have a false concept, which is the concept of ownership of possessions. Everything is made of light. All of these possessions, everything that exists, is the property of our Creator. He provided ample materials for all people in all space. It is not necessary to covet any of these materials, for all of them are part of you. At present, there is much strife upon your planet. There is much coveting of properties, but this is of no avail to those who covet these properties, for even though they may acquire, as they think, these properties, their apparent possession is very, very short-lived.

I am Latui. I hope that I have been of service. Adonai vasu.

(Pause)

I am Oxal. I am with this instrument. I greet you, my friends, in the love and in the light of our infinite Creator. It is a privilege to speak with you, my friends. I am at present in a craft which is very high in your sky. It is several hundred of your miles high. I am, as you say, one of those who dwells within a flying saucer. I am trying to impress upon you this fact for a definite reason, so please bear with me.

I, Oxal, of the Confederation of Planets in the Service of the Infinite Creator, have for many of your years lived in a craft that orbits your planet. This has been my service and my duty. I am attempting to give to the people of your planet something that they need more than any other thing. I am attempting to give them love.

This is not an easy thing to do on your planet. What do you think would be the reaction if I met, on the street, a group of your people and told them this? I am afraid that it would be not at all effective. To give your people love is quite a problem. All of us in the Confederation are attempting to do this. Your people just do not seem to want our love. Oh, yes, some people are accepting us, but the vast majority are not interested in accepting our love. They are interested in us, but not in our love. What can we do to remedy this situation? What can we do to arouse within the people of your planet a desire to receive our love? Why is it necessary to bring to your people this love?

My friends, it has just been explained to you: this is what you need. This is the only thing that you need. The Creator has amply provided everything for you. We are just simply trying to redistribute the love that He originally planned for you, and that many of your people have rejected.

It is a long and difficult task, but we will be successful, for we will not tolerate a lack of diligence for ourselves. We will continue to bring to you the Creator's love. When you are fully able to accept this, then and only then can we land and contact the people of this planet in general. It is a very simple thing, and could have been accomplished in a few minutes' time, if your people would simply accept this love. However, as you know, this is extremely improbable.

We must accelerate our program of bringing this to the people of this planet. There will be a greater attempt in the future to arouse those who would wish to know of our purpose. So please bear with us, as we continue in our efforts to bring to you the only gift that is possible, for there is nothing else of value to give.

I am Oxal. I am going to leave you at this time. I leave you in the love and in the light of our infinite Creator. Adonai vasu.

Sunday Meditation
January 13, 1974

(Unknown channeling)

I am Hatonn. I greet you, my friends, in the love and in the light of our infinite Creator. It is again a great privilege to be with you. I am speaking to you from a craft known to you as an "otevana." It is a very, very large craft compared to your standards. It is several miles in length. We have been aboard this craft here above your planet for some numbers of years. It is like a world in itself, and is used for intergalactic travel. Aboard this craft we have all of the facilities that you have in your world, plus many others.

At this time, I and my brothers aboard this craft are pleased to be in contact with this instrument. You have some question about how we are always so available to your contact. We are aware of your thinking because it is also our thinking. When you have, shall I say, tuned your mind so that it will operate at the same vibration as ours, then, if you think something, it is a mutual thought between your mind and ours. This is the way that it should be. It is not as it was intended for minds to be individualized as they are upon your planet. This results in much confusion and difficulty in communication. Individualization of mind is something that we do not desire. Many of the people of your planet desire to separate themselves and their thinking from all others. This is their choice. It is a choice given to them by their Creator.

However, those of our planet are not so individualized. We are always able to contact those who avail themselves because we are always availing ourselves, for that is our mission and purpose at this time. There are always a great number of our people ready and willing to send to you that which you desire.

I am aware of certain questions about our contacts. We of the Confederation in the past have contacted directly many people on your planet. The early contactees, as they are known, were not too successful. They were unable to approach through channels of communications on your planet the people of your planet with our messages as much as we would have liked for them to. The reason for this was that the people of your planet could not understand such a form of contact, and they were not prepared to accept messages of the nature that we were able to give there. However, we are now in the position to give them much more. For this reason, we are going to support channels in a very direct way.

But there is a slight difficulty at this time. We in the service of the infinite Creator are here in great numbers. What we ask of you is very simple. We ask that you meditate. This is important, for if we are to contact you, this will be the way.

(Transcript ends.)

Monday Meditation
January 14, 1974

(Unknown channeling)

I am Hatonn. I am with this instrument. I am using control. We have had some difficulty in using this instrument. Please be patient.

I am Hatonn. I greet you, my friends, in the love and the light of our infinite Creator. We of the Confederation of Planets in the Service of the Infinite Creator are always with you. We have said this many times. It is true. We are always with you. As we have said, there is no possibility of separation, for we are one being. Therefore, we are always with you.

It has been the practice of the people of this planet to separate their thinking from the thinking of others. This is not a common situation. It is not a necessary situation. It is a false illusion. It is very simple, my friends, to rid yourselves of the illusion that your mind is a separate and unique entity. It is very easy to establish contact with us in the same way that this instrument has. It is only necessary that you first become aware of the creation in its true essence. This causes a variation in the attunement of your mind.

To develop this awareness, it is of course necessary that you meditate. I am going to speak tonight on meditation, and how to go about it in order to establish this contact.

Meditation, my friends, is a very, very effective tool if you are to accomplish anything. But first you must understand what we mean by meditation. We have stated that it is necessary that you clear your mind of thoughts. This is not always too easy to do, but it can be accomplished. There are many techniques that may aid you in doing this. Various sounds are sometimes used, and things to concentrate on are sometimes used, so that a single thought is allowed to remain. And then, from this single thought, no thoughts occur.

It is necessary that, if you are to be totally relaxed in meditation, you totally relax. It is, however, necessary that you do not go from this relaxed state to a state of sleep, for this defeats the purpose. It is therefore recommended that you remain in an erect sitting position. This, for the most part, eliminates a great deal of tendency to sleep.

I and my brothers are aware of your thinking. We are aware of your thinking because it is also our thinking, for our minds are as one. However, we are not aware of everything in your mind, because at times your thoughts are disrupted or cut off from us by the individualization that I earlier spoke of, that is so common with your peoples.

It is necessary, in addition to practicing this form of meditation, for you to become aware of the original creation, and not creation of man. Pay attention to that which is natural. Become aware of it. People of your planet are not aware of the original creation. They have created a very false illusion. Therefore, they are not in awareness of reality. If you think that you are totally aware of the original creation at this time, then you are mistaken. For, if you were, you would see us, for we are part of the original creation.

There is a technique for increasing your awareness. The technique will be given to you a little at a time, so that you may employ each step. The first step will be to seek to understand each thing that you see that is a portion of the original creation. Take those things one at a time, and consider them in detail, and try to establish in your mind a totally detached understanding of them.

If this part of the creation happens to be a leaf, then study it with care. Become aware of it. Do not rely on old impressions. Develop an awareness of each thing. This will be the first step.

We leave you at this time. I am Hatonn. I leave you in His love and light. Adonai vasu.

(Pause)

I am Oxal. I greet you, my friends, in the love and the light of our infinite Creator. It is a privilege to be with you. I am a member of the Confederation of Planets in the Service of the Infinite Creator.

What does this mean? Why should we so call ourselves the Confederation in the Service of Our infinite Creator? There is a good reason for this. It is necessary. It is necessary, my friends, to serve if you understand, for this is the only route open to us. I am aware that you have certain questions as to how one is to serve. There are certain problems in performing this service. We are very limited in our ability to contact your people, because we must be careful, because we know what these limitations are and why they should be as they are. It is necessary that each individual serve in his own way. If you can understand how to serve, then your service will be effective. It is necessary to avail yourself to meditation to know these things. Many of the people of your planet attempt to serve, in many, many ways, but they are not effective. They have not availed themselves to the Creator through meditation. Service, my friends, must be performed with care. However, it must always be performed.

We of the Confederation of Planets in His Service do not have the difficulty in serving our fellow man elsewhere in this creation that we are having at this time. There are so many limitations upon your planet at this present time that service is extremely difficult. However, it is possible for ones such as yourselves to serve the people of the planet in a much more direct way.

It is, however, necessary that you be qualified, if you are to serve. These qualifications include many, many things, each of which may be obtained through meditation. When the individual is fully ready to serve, then it is time to go forth and perform the service. It is not wise, however, to act beyond your limitations. You will know your ability to serve by availing yourself to this knowledge through meditation. Many of your leaders attempt to serve the people of your planet, but they are unaware of the necessity for meditation. If this is not done, then it is very difficult to serve with intelligence. It is necessary for all who are in His service to spend time in meditation. We cannot overemphasize this necessity. It eliminates the possibility of making errors that will result in nullifying the effect of the service.

I hope that I have been of assistance in your seeking. I am Oxal. Adonai vasu.

Tuesday Meditation
January 15, 1974

(Unknown channeling)

I am Hatonn. I am with this instrument. I greet you, my friends, in the love and the light of our infinite Creator. It is again a great privilege to be with you. I and my brothers are here. I have said this to you before. This is truth. We are here.

We are here to serve you. We will be here to serve you. We have been here to serve you. We are here to serve all of the people who wish our service. We cannot presume that our service is of value to all people in all places. Therefore, we can only offer what we have. You must accept or reject. Sometimes, you wonder why we give you what you might consider to be relatively elementary material, or material that is repeated. We do this because this is what it needed. In actuality, this is all that is needed. It is only necessary to learn to think in the original way planned by the Creator of us all to totally benefit from all of His gifts.

This is why we would prefer to continue speaking in what you might consider to be relatively elementary or simple terms. My friends, truth is very, very simple. The Creator's plan is very, very simple. It is not necessary that we weave a complex web of circumstance to lead you to the Creator. He is within you, and you are Him. It is only necessary that you realize this in its fullest sense for you to be aware of all the Creator's wisdom. The people of this planet have blocked their minds from this knowledge. We are attempting to teach the people of this planet how to remove this blockage.

It is a very simple process. Unfortunately, the people of this planet are more accustomed to complexity, and would therefore desire intellectual juggling of various propositions and theories. This, my friends, is not necessary. To get from where you are to where you should be requires an understanding that has nothing to do with the intellect. It requires, simply, a knowing of truth.

This truth is extremely simple. What I am trying to say is that when you become totally aware of this simple truth, then you will not use intellectual processes to understand anything that you wish to know. This knowledge will be yours, for all knowledge is linked in the Creator's universe. There is no separation. This separation occurs only when man desires it, through use of the freedom of choice that has been given him by his Creator. Return, therefore, to the Creator. Return to the knowledge and the wisdom and the power that is yours. Do this by giving forth only His light and His love. This is what was intended. Acting otherwise, and knowing otherwise, results only in the isolation and blockage that I referred to.

Consider very carefully these simple teachings that I offer to you, for these simple teachings are all that is required. There is nothing of a complex nature that is needed. We will continue in a program designed to bring the thinking of the people of this planet back to that which they desire. Those that avail themselves of these teachings will benefit greatly, I assure you.

I hope that I have been able to clarify certain things. It has been a great privilege to speak with you. Adonai vasu.

Questioner: *(A question concerning personal business decisions is asked.)*

I am Hatonn. I am with this instrument and I am using control. It is a great privilege to have a question asked. It is a privilege to have a question asked. I shall answer it in the love and the light of our infinite Creator. It is a very great privilege, and we welcome all questions. I am afraid, however, that it is impossible for us to interfere in the plans of the people of your planet. This is our policy. We would request that questions involving your understanding of the nature of truth be asked, for it is impossible for us to do anything to change what will occur upon your surface at this time. Each time we do anything—each time we are seen, each time something is written about us in your periodicals, anything that we do to cause your people to change their attitudes—is an infringement. We are attempting to balance our service so that the infringement that does occur will be at least balanced by the good that is created. This is why we can only accelerate our help for our teachings for the awareness of your people for us as they desire it.

I hope that I have answered to your satisfaction. I will gladly give to this instrument all that I can with respect to answers to questions that you might bring to me. But questions involving changes of your activities, especially of a physical nature, are completely beyond that that we desire to do. Please allow me to apologize for my lack of ability to act in this area, but this has been agreed upon by those of us in the service of the Confederation of Planets in the Service of the Infinite Creator. I am Hatonn.

(Pause)

I am Latui. I greet you, my friends, in the love and the light of our infinite Creator. It is a great privilege to be with you this evening. I am Latui. I have not been with you except for one previous time. It is a great privilege to speak with you. This instrument is not as familiar with my contact as he is with some others. Therefore, please bear with us.

My friends, I am what you call a space man. But so are you. For where do you dwell but in space? From our point of view, you are as much in space as are we. The only difference is that you are limited in your ability to travel to different points in space; you are at one place in space at this particular time.

Therefore, you are also a space man. You see, my friends, there is very little difference between yourselves and us. Our system of transportation is simply a little more refined. We enjoy certain other abilities which are much more useful than simple conveyances. They are available to all men in all places. All men are in space, they are all space men. For what you call space is infinite, and surrounds all of the creation.

We are no different. We are just slightly separated. Not by distances, my friends. By thinking. You have learned to think in a way that isolates you. It is not necessary that you remain in isolation. To do this, it is only necessary that you think in a slightly different manner.

It is not a difficult thing to do. It is a simple thing to do. Do not use the intellectual processes that you have used in the past. Learn to totally rebuke arriving at conclusions in what you consider a logical manner, for these conclusions will be based on suppositions that are made with very weak fabric, the fabric of the creation of man of Earth. If you wish an answer to any question, it is only necessary to base your knowledge on truth. This you can do through meditation. It is always available. It is not necessary to make a complex analysis.

There is a correct solution for every problem. Analyses based on the false fabric of your material world are short-lived, and the intellectual process that is so prevalent among the peoples of your planet is invariably based upon this falsity. It has been stated, "Know the truth, and the truth shall make you free." Free from what? Free from many things, my friends. Free from many, many things. For cutting yourselves off from truth begins to put more and more limitations upon you. It is a difficult thing to relay to you, because you have been accustomed to another way of thinking. You have been accustomed to the proposition of cause and effect.

The cause, my friends, is the Creator. The effect is love. This is all that there is. This is the simplicity of the truth. Hear my words and understand them. Man was created with this truth within him. It is available to all men throughout all time. It is available through meditation.

It is not necessary to try to understand, in an intellectual way. It is only necessary to know. It is stated that you should know the truth to be free. The word that is used is "know." Know what the truth is, my friends. Know it. Meditation will provide this knowledge.

I will leave you now. I am Latui. Adonai vasu borragus.

Wednesday Meditation
January 16, 1974

(Unknown channeling)

I am Hatonn. I greet you, my friends, in the love and in the light of our infinite Creator. It is once more a great privilege to be with you.

This instrument receives my thoughts, and relays them to you. These thoughts are not my exclusive property. They are the thoughts of an entire creation of our infinite Creator. It is not necessary for the instrument to be used for you to know these thoughts. They are available to all people in all places at all times, for they are the thoughts of the Creator. And these thoughts were meant for all of mankind, in all places. These thoughts are the thoughts with which the Creator created us.

These thoughts are very simple. They are a simplicity that is unique, for they are the very foundation of the creation. This is what we are attempting to give man on Earth, this original Thought. This is what he needs at this time. This Thought can only be approached using pure language. It is not a common concept among the people of your planet. This is the reason for their difficulties. The Creator never imagined difficulties in His creation. They are the product of man's erroneous thinking. We have said to you many times that meditation is necessary. Through this process of meditation, it is possible to know this Thought; we have called it love, but this can only be understood through meditation.

In an environment such as yours, meditation is of even greater importance than in an environment such as ours, for we have very, very little to overcome in our understanding of our fellow man. It is suggested, therefore, that through the process of daily meditation, you will develop an understanding of this Thought that created all of us.

I hope that I have been of service this evening. Adonai vasu borragus. ✧

Thursday Meditation
January 17, 1974

(Unknown channeling)

I am Hatonn. I greet you in the love and the light of our infinite Creator. It is a great privilege to be with you this evening, as it is every evening.

I and my brothers are with you. We are with you because you desire our presence. Yet this statement is ambiguous, for we cannot be separated. Nothing in this creation can be separated from anything else. For everything is one thing.

Therefore, when I say to you that I am with you, it has more than one meaning. I am with this instrument in a direct sense with respect to his ability to understand an intellectual communication. I am with each of you in an equivalent way. It is not necessary for you to be able to receive my thoughts in an intellectual way. This is only convenient if they are to be passed in a verbal fashion to others, as I am doing now. However, the same thoughts are also yours, for they are everyone's. It is only a matter of whether or not you desire the thoughts.

Those of the people of your planet who do not desire the thoughts of those of us who now surround your planet are not obliged to receive them. This would be a great error on our part. Those of the people of your planet who desire these thoughts receive them. Whether they may be translated into a verbal form or not is of no particular consequence.

We of the Confederation of Planets in the Service of the Infinite Creator are preparing to launch a new attack upon your planet, an attack of love. If one is to attack with love, it is necessary that it be done with utmost care. The only possibility, if one is to attack with love, is that the ones attacked desire that they be attacked. More and more of the people of your planet have become aware of this attack. More and more of them are now welcoming this attack. For this reason, it is possible to accelerate our program.

Many of those that are at this time aware of some form of attack are not welcoming it. This results in our limitations. It is necessary that we do not in any way infringe upon those of your planet who do not desire the attack. Therefore, we must remain a mystery; a mystery that can be rejected by those who wish to reject our presence. We must, however, bring to more and more of those of your people who wish to accept us the truth and understanding that they deserve, that is theirs, that is all man's. For this was given to him by his Creator. We are merely agents, acting in a way to bring that which is desired to those who desire it.

I am aware that many of the people of your planet consider that we have wasted too much time in our attempts to awaken the slumbering population of your planet. We would greatly prefer to act much, much more rapidly, but the speed and the degree of our activities must be regulated, not by us, but by you. The acceptance of us by the total population of this planet is the only governing principle that controls our activities.

We will, very shortly, increase these activities. More and more of our craft will be seen by the people of your planet. This can be done because they are beginning to accept us. We will do this in order that their curiosity will be stimulated. This curiosity will then lead them to seeking the truth of our presence. This truth is what they desire, even though they do not consciously realize it.

There will be a certain percentage of your population who will not desire, nor will they seek, knowledge of us. This we expect. This will limit us, but we will be able to act much more directly in the very near future. There has been, within the past few years, an increasing awareness of something outside the limitations of the material world which has held the people of your society for a very long time in a trance-like state. We are about our Father's business. We are about to give to many, many of the people of your planet the only thing that they need to progress. We are aware that many of you believe that we repeat ourselves too much. But we have actually only one thing to present to your people. This is truth, and it is very simple. If they would simply learn to accept this truth and utilize it, they would be free of their limitations. We have stated many times in our communications this truth, in many different ways. It is all that is needed. There is nothing more that is required, for once you are able to assimilate this knowledge, you are then in a position to know all things, for you are then in common with all of the creation. This is the way that you were created. Only through, shall I say, errors in experimentation with free will has man limited his thinking, and cut himself off from total knowledge.

The mind of man is not created so that it is isolated. It is created to be in contact with all consciousness at all times. It is possible through understanding, which is not intellectual in form, to realize the single truth that allows man of Earth to remove this limitation or separation from the infinite mind. It is only necessary that the individual avail himself to this infinite mind through the practice of daily meditation. It has been found by some of the people dwelling upon your planet. However, it was necessary for them to seek this mind through meditation.

At this time I would like to continue for a very short time on another subject. It is the subject of the principle of telepathic communications.

There are many ways of achieving a contact such as this one. There are several ways we can impress an intellectual thought upon an instrument. The form of contact that we are using most of the time with this instrument is a form that presents to him a concept, or a portion of a concept. He is able to use his own fabrications of language to describe the concept. At other times we use muscular control, to aid the instrument in forming words to fit the concepts impressed upon him. If the concept is of a totally new or different nature from his thinking or his realization in meditation, we use a great deal of muscular. control. If the concept is familiar to him, we allow him great leeway in his intellectual analysis of the concept, and therefore his verbalization of it.

You can experiment by saying a word to yourself without speaking. You will hear it in your mind. One part of your mind has said the word, and another part has heard it, although you have made no sound. It is possible for two, or more, or all minds to work in this manner. It is necessary that they don't, for this could result in an unimaginable confusion and constant noise in the mind. However, it is possible, by willing it to, just as you hear the unspoken word that you have thought in your mind, to direct the same word to another mind. It is also possible to direct a muscular action, a response, to another mind. It is also possible to impress an intellectual concept upon another mind. It is also possible to impress a non-intellectual concept upon another mind.

These are just a few of the simple principles of communication, mind-to-mind. We have some difficulty at times, and there is confusion. This instrument is aware of the possibility of generating thoughts and repeating them as if they were from a source external to him. My friends, I have stated earlier that there in only one source. It is the Creator.

There are seven planets in your solar system that are now inhabited by our craft and our people. Many of these would not be seen if you were to go to these planets. However, some would. There are a great number of us who are very interested in this solar system at this time. We are very interested in your planet at this time. We will be in your skies on the first day of the coming month. You will be aware of our presence at that time. I have attempted to give this instrument certain thoughts this evening that are difficult to relay. I am going to leave him now, for he is fatigued. I am Hatonn. Adonai vasu. 🌀

Monday Meditation
January 21, 1974

(Carla channeling)

[I am Hatonn.] … begins with an understanding of the Father.

My friends, of what substance is the universe made? We have told you that this substance is light. You may also call this substance energy, vibration [or] consciousness. And yet, my friends, by itself, this substance, this fundamental unitary substance would remain in an uncorporate state. The shaping force, my friends, is love.

And so we greet you in love and light. For there is nothing but these two substances which are, in fact, two aspects of the single building block of the physical and the spiritual universe. You, my friends, in your spiritual reality are articulated light shaped by love in such a way that you possess freedom and desire. Your light is shaped by the love of freedom and the love of desire.

Before we even consider that which you have called reincarnation, we simply say to you again, you are not in multiple, or a put together device. You are one being, part and parcel of the great universe which is the Creation. And your basic desire is shaped towards reunion with your Creator.

You are love and light—and yet, you have freedom. This is your spiritual reality: that you are a being articulated in light and fashioned in love, by your very nature destined to progress back towards your point of origin which is the Creator. But also, by your very nature having the freedom to choose just when you will decide to make that journey.

My friends, universes, such as the one you are now experiencing, are environments for beings, such as yourselves, to experience and enjoy. In order that each being may freely exercise each choice which is his, reincarnation, therefore, is not inevitable but will occur within beings, such as yourselves, if further experience within the physical is desired or if a being desires to be of service within the physical manifestation.

The mechanism by which this is done has been explained in many ways. And, although the instrument which I am using is not familiar, at all, with the material which she was shown, we accept the material as being what you may call a fairly good stab at analyzing that which seems like a process, but which is actually much simpler than a process. There are other explanations. The most familiar explanation to this instrument is the division of the deity into the Father, the Son, and the Holy Spirit. In this case, that which is known as the Holy Spirit would serve as aid within the physical and spiritual meeting place so that soul and body could join. Let us simply say that whatever those who analyze desire to call the various forms of energy which are used during the mechanism of reincarnation, each is a manifestation of love, shaping light in such a way that the soul may have the experiences which it desires.

We would like to comment, also, about the use of the term morality. We will simply say this, and you may take for what it is worth. It is difficult to understand intellectually. My friends, there is no morality. There is only love. If you will radiate love for all, you will never need to know what is right and what is wrong. The entire difficulty with morality is due to a desire to follow rules rather than a desire to follow the Father. Meditation, correctly pursued, quickly shows the basic simplicity of the way of the Father. That which you term moral decision is within each and available to all. No matter what the conscious frame of mind, and no matter how many chances have been missed, that which is redeeming lies always within, and not one bit has been taken away from anyone.

This, only, we would adjust within the scheme which you presented for our appraisal. Each of us is perfect. Manifestations often do not indicate our knowledge of our perfection. But this, my friends, may be corrected from within.

I am aware that there do remain questions, but I think, at this time, I will simply ask for further questions.

Questioner: *(Inaudible).*

I was aware that you might wish that this be accomplished. I am very pleased to have had this chance to aid you. I would like to encourage you. I can say no more. But let it be known that we are with you at all times.

I will leave this instrument if there are no further questions.

(Pause)

I am Hatonn. My brothers and I greet you and say farewell. ☙

Monday Meditation
January 21, 1974

(Unknown channeling)

I am Hatonn. I greet you, my friends, in the love and in the light of our infinite Creator. It is a great privilege to be with you again this evening. It is always a very great privilege to speak.

We of the Confederation of Planets in the Service of the Infinite Creator are here for the purpose of speaking with you and giving you directly our thoughts as you meditate. These thoughts are yours to accept or reject. They are constantly available to you. It is only necessary that you desire them, if you wish them. This is our service to people of the planet Earth at this time. This is not our only service, but it is our most important service.

Why are your people at this time not very interested in these thoughts? We have said, time and time again, that thoughts of this nature are what the people of this planet need. And yet they show very little interest. This puzzled us at first, until we became more familiar with the reasons for the thinking of the population in general of this planet. We are now aware of some of the problems involved in bringing truth and understanding to a people so very long in the darkness that has been generated by those that have gone before them in the history of this planet.

It is a very difficult thing to change thousands of years of erroneous thinking in a very short time. It is something that we will not be totally successful in doing. However, we will be, and we have been, partially successful in bringing certain [information] to those who would desire it. This is the key, my friends: desire. If the individual does not desire what we have to bring to him, then he will not receive it. This is exactly how the creation is designed: so that each entity, no matter where he is or who he is or what he is, will got exactly what he desires.

Unfortunately, in some places certain actions of one entity with respect to another cause an infringement that was never designed by our Creator. This results in a discrepancy in the plan of the creation, and creates unfortunate situations, as it has upon your planet. It is necessary for man on planet Earth to realize this, and to individually correct his understanding of himself, in order to bring himself back into alignment with the plan and design of our Creator.

Each individual must make up his mind, and he must do it now. He must decide whether he is going to attempt to understand and to serve in the light of the infinite, or whether he is going to seek for himself, and follow a pathway that has been laid down for him by man on Earth, rather than that provided by the Creator of us all.

It is very necessary that the people of this planet at this time be made aware of the plan and the design of their Creator. Without this awareness, they may continue in their erroneous and unintelligent ways of acting. Each individual will interpret information given to him in a slightly different way, if it is of an intellectual nature. Some individuals will not be able to interpret information of this type at all. This is why it is so necessary that man of Earth at this time meditate and go within. For that which he obtains in this fashion will be information which is not of an intellectual nature. It will be the truth, the understanding of the original creation. Within every individual in the universe is this knowledge. It is only necessary to seek it out through meditation. If this is done, there will be no question in the mind of the individual. There will be no need for interpretation of information, for this is not of an intellectual nature.

Man on Earth considers that he has many problems. But these problems are not reality. They are an illusion, developed by his thinking. Nothing in this universe follows the laws man on Earth considers the laws of the generation of events. I have stated before that the only cause is the Creator. Man on Earth interprets cause and effect in a very illusory manner. This is not the way that the creation is designed; it is not the way the Creation works. It is only necessary that an individual give forth love and light. If this is done, this is what will be returned to him. It is not necessary to consider complex propositions and plans in order to reach an objective that is assumed to be of great benefit. It is only necessary that you generate the love that is amply provided by the Creator of us all.

This is how we were meant to live. Man on Earth has forgotten this very simple principle. He believed that he can generate, through plans and activities, great pleasure that will come to him as a result of these plans and activities. And then he goes forth and does these things in great complexity. And very seldom does he glory in their product, but he does not learn, for he does not meditate. For within him is the truth, the truth of the pathway to the ecstasy that awaits him. It is not a complex pathway. It is not a product of his intellect, or of his ability to act in the physical, producing great changes in the many things that he desired for his pleasure.

The pathway, my friends, is simply love, a total and universal love, expressed for all things and all peoples, and demonstrated daily in his activities and thoughts. And then, my friends, everything is returned. And this love that he generates is reflected on him a thousand-fold. For this is the plan, this is the design. This is the gift of the Father. It is so very simple, for the Father is very simple. He did not mean for His children to find it necessary to generate complexities in order to achieve the state of ecstasy that He designed for them.

It is only man on this planet that has become confused, and drifted away from this knowledge. This knowledge is deep within you. It is part of you. It is part of everything that exists. Seek this knowledge within yourself. And then, go forth in your daily activities demonstrating to your fellow man this knowledge, and it will be reflected one thousandfold.

It has been a very great privilege to be with you this evening, and I hope that I have been able to give to you some understanding of that which man on planet Earth so badly desires and needs, an understanding of the principle of love. I am Hatonn. Adonai vasu. ☥

Wednesday Meditation
January 23, 1974

(Unknown channeling)

I am Hatonn. I greet you, my friends, in the love and in the light of our infinite Creator. It is once more a great privilege to be with you. It is unfortunate that I was unable to use either of the instruments the previous evening. However, anyone who wishes to continue availing himself to my contact will be successful.

We of the Confederation of Planets in the Service of the Infinite Creator have used this method of contact in many, many places, with many, many people. Upon your planet at present there are people in almost all areas that are receiving our communications. There are many of these people who do not understand what is happening to them. They do not understand who we are, as do you. They simply receive communications. The reason they have no idea who we are is that they have no concept of people coming to them from the stars.

This is unimportant. The only thing that is important is that they understand the message that we give to them: the message of love and brotherhood. There are many other people who receive our messages who do understand our identification. In this case, it is also only important that they understand the message that we bring to them. This is what we are here for: to bring this simple, single message. This is what is necessary for the people of your planet to learn at this time.

We of the Confederation have lived an example of this knowledge for many, many of your years. We are totally aware of the results of living the type of life that results from the understanding of the principle of love. We are not unwise in our attempt to give these principles to you, for we have experienced the effect of using these for quite some time.

I am aware that these principles are not understood by the people of your planet, not even the people who have been given them directly, through channels such as this one. There seems to be a barrier to this understanding that has been generated through thousands of years of an ignorance of these truths. This barrier is so solid at this time that it is very difficult, even for those who desire this knowledge, to accept it and put it to use. They are able to hear the words and understand them, and even though they agree totally with the concepts that we present, they are still unable to assimilate them into their own thinking. We have suggested many times that in order to assimilate this knowledge into your thinking it is necessary that you meditate. But this is something that is also misunderstood.

It is extremely difficult for the people of this planet to remove their thinking from the hypnotic state that has been created. Everything that they experience is created by their own thinking. You cannot experience something that you cannot think, because this is all that there is: there is nothing but thought. It is found in many forms and expressions, but thought is the source of all that there is: the thought of the Creator.

And this is what you are. And you are able, like the Creator, to generate thought. The thought that you generate is your responsibility. The people of this planet each generates thought, and communicates these thoughts to others. If the thoughts that are generated are of a low quality, then they will in turn generate low-quality thoughts in others. This is a self-perpetuating action. And this is the reason for the strife and confusion that is so abundant with the people of this planet. It is erroneous to say that you cannot do anything about the situation as complex as this one which has been created by millions and millions of minds through thousands and thousands of years. It is only necessary that the individual remove himself in thought from this sea of confusion, and express himself in the true love and light of the infinite Creator.

This may be done at any time. It is up to the individual. If he desires to do this, then it is only necessary that he do it. This has been demonstrated to the people of this planet many times in the past by the teachers who were here to demonstrate to the people of Earth life and the expressions of the Creator as they were intended. It is a very simple lesson, but man on Earth desires to ignore this. Very few accept these teachings and stand in the light and express only the love and understanding of the Creator of us all.

This is unfortunate. It is a situation that we who are in the service of our infinite Creator are attempting to remedy, by giving instructions which are not only verbal, and which have difficulty in penetrating the barrier which the mind has erected, but instructions of a nature that will bypass this intellectual barrier and reach the spiritual self directly. This is done, of course, during the process of meditation. This is why we have stated for so many years that meditation is extremely important. It is only necessary that you avail yourself to these concepts for those concepts to begin to cause the individual to realize once more his proper stature and position in the Creator's scheme of things. It was stated by your last great teacher, "Know ye not that ye are Gods?" This man understood the true created purpose of all of mankind.

Why is it necessary for people, especially people who have been made aware of truth through their seeking, to stop short of achieving the knowledge of their true created purpose and being? We have been puzzled at times by the inability of the people in general of this planet to be awakened to this simple truth. We suggest that it is necessary to maintain a continual awareness of your objective. We suggest that that objective is to realize your true position in the creation, and then to act in a manner intended by the Creator. In order to do this, it will be necessary that a considerable effort be put forth. We find that the state of hypnosis brought about by the evolution of thought of the people of this planet is so great that if an individual is to free himself from it, it is necessary for him to maintain a constant awareness of his spiritual nature and purpose, and to augment this awareness with meditation. The effort put forth to do this will be much more rewarding than any other activity that the individual can engage in.

This step must be successfully made by each individual of this planet at some time or other. Wouldn't it be reasonable to do it at the earliest possible time, for it is an extremely beneficial step. We would suggest that if progress is seemingly slow, then additional meditation may be necessary, for only in this way can the people of planet Earth free themselves from the erroneous thoughts that have been impressed upon them for so very long.

I hope that I have been of service this evening. At this time, I would accept most gladly a question.

(Pause)

If there are no questions, I leave you at this time. I leave you in the love and the light of our infinite Creator. It is all around you. It is you, as it is I. Open your minds and your hearts, and let it fill you with its love. Adonai vasu.

Friday Meditation
January 25, 1974

(Unknown channeling)

I am Hatonn. I greet you at this time in the light and the love of the infinite Creator. I would speak to you at this time concerning spiritual development.

Daily meditation is a necessity. As we near the climax … of this chapter in your planet's development, the vibratory rate will steadily increase until your planet …

(Transcript ends.)

Saturday Meditation
January 26, 1974

(Unknown channeling)

I am Laitos. I greet you in the love and in the light of our infinite Creator. I will condition each of you. I will speak through the instrument known as R.

(R channeling)

I am Laitos. I would speak to you at this time regarding your personal daily meditations. This is becoming increasingly necessary as we near the coming events upon your planet. I will be with you upon request, for this is our purpose, to serve. There is some difficulty in this channel receiving my thoughts.

(Pause)

(Unknown channeling)

I am again with this instrument. I am sorry for the difficulty, but it will be remedied. Please bear with me.

(Pause)

(R channeling)

I am again with this channel. Your daily meditation is necessary in order that the veil might be lifted, and all things which you have been promised will be shown. This higher vibration will enable you to perform such things as healing with little difficulty. Again there is some difficulty with this channel.

(Unknown channeling)

I am Hatonn. I am with this instrument. I am Hatonn. I greet you, my friends, in the love and the light of the infinite Creator. It is a great privilege to be with you this evening. We are very happy to see that one more channel is being developed. My brother Laitos will continue to work with the one called R until he receives our thoughts as clearly as this channel. It is actually a very simple process, and requires only that you continue in your meditation, availing yourself to our contact.

We of the Confederation of Planets in the Service of the Infinite Creator are experienced with this form of communication, and we can say at this time that each of you in this room will be able to receive our thoughts with little difficulty in the near future.

I would like to speak with you today about a subject that concerns your very near future. I would first like to speak to you about the definition of this term, "future." You see the future as something that will come to you. We see the future as an event that is presently here. This is a difficult thing to translate into your language, but I will attempt to give you an understanding of what you know as time.

Time, my friends, is an illusion. The creation is, in fact, timeless. You are at a particular point in the evolution of the creation. There seems to be a progression of time. But there is actually a continuing stream of consciousness. It is only necessary to displace yourself along this stream of consciousness to be at any point along the stream that you call time.

In other words, it is possible to move through time as you understand movement through space. Each of these concepts is as real as the other. We have stated to you previously that there is one place and there is one time. This place and this time are the creation. We are able to move through space. We are also able to move through time, for in actuality these things are the same thing: they are the creation.

The illusion that is now impressed upon you because of your limitations in a physical condition, as you call it, are limitations that are not at all ordinary. They are limitations that are impressed upon those who desire them for certain experiences. Each individual in this creation is able to select precisely what he desires. This is exactly the plan of the Creator. He not only gave man free will, but he also gave man the ability to select exactly what he desired. There are many, many paths to take through this creation—in actuality, an infinite number—and the choice is always left up to the individual.

Some of those who have explored have explored in a direction that led them away from the all-knowing One, the all-loving One, the Creator. In wandering away, there were conditions encountered that were at that time desired by the individual who was wandering. But as he wandered farther and farther, he became more and more immersed in an illusion that he created. This illusion is at present so very strong that many of the children of the Creator find themselves confused and unable to easily find the pathway back to the infinite light.

It is necessary that they realize for themselves how to do this, for the principle given to them by their Creator is still totally in effect. It allows them to do precisely what they desire. It is therefore necessary that they realize for themselves what they desire, and then it is necessary that they seek this realization. In order to do this, it is necessary that they become aware of the techniques of bringing about this understanding. This is our purpose, at the present time: to help those who are presently seeking the pathway that will return them to the love and the light that they now desire. It is necessary for us to help those who desire this, in order to act within the plan of the creation. It is necessary also that we do not overly disturb those who do not overly desire at this time such activity.

For this reason, we are somewhat limited in our abilities to reach out to the people of this planet at this time. It is possible for you to eliminate certain conditions that you are now experiencing, and it is possible for us to help you do this. We are acquainted with certain aspects of what you would call the future because of an ability to move not only in space, but in time. However, due to the action of the freedom of desire that was given to each of the Creator's children, it is possible for them to cause alterations in the stream of consciousness, and therefore, as events change due to these desires in what you know as the present, so do they change in what you know as the future.

It is therefore not possible to travel through time in exactly the same sense that you travel in space, for it has properties that are dependent on the action of free will, just as special properties are dependent upon this action. Time and space are in many way very similar in their properties, and we are aware of the nature of action, not only in space but also in time. We would attempt to give you aid in understanding how to free yourself from the illusion of being trapped in a continuous and unchanging stream of time, for this is an illusion, an illusion that has been sought by a large number of individuals.

It is difficult to relay to you these concepts, for they are not at all familiar within the illusion that you now enjoy. I have spoken of this at this time to give you some clue to the problem of living as you do. The illusion is so strong that you become accustomed to understanding events in a way that is not at all real. You become accustomed to a relationship between the illusion of past, present and future that is not actually real.

In the past, many of your people have traveled in the dimension of time. Many are experiencing this dimension now in what you know as dreams. We who are aware of the possibility of traveling in both space and time find that an additional understanding allows for an instantaneous or immediate transportation [of one portion] of the creation to any other. This how you were created, with total freedom.

I am going to leave you at this time, and allow another of my brothers to speak using either instrument. I hope that I have been of some service in attempting to bring to you some understanding of a subject that is quite difficult for you at this time to realize.

I am Hatonn. I leave you in the love and light of our infinite Creator.

(Pause)

(Unknown channeling)

I am Hatonn. I am with this instrument. I greet you once more, my friends, in the love and the light of our infinite Creator. It is a privilege to speak with you once more. My brother Laitos was attempting to use the instrument known as R. However, there were certain difficulties.

I am going to speak with you at this time on another subject. I am at this time in a craft that is high above your planet. You may ask why we utilize craft, if we are able to travel through space and time. My friends, there are many things to be experienced in this creation. There are many things of different natures, and we, as you, enjoy experiences of different natures. We are able to move in space, as you do, using craft. We are able to move in time, as I have just spoken to you, using nothing but our understanding. Both of these concepts or realms were meant to be utilized by the children of the Father. This is why there are so many of our craft near your planet at this time. It is possible to get here from elsewhere by moving through that dimension you know as time. This is why we state that there is only one place, and that is the creation, for you may move from one place in the creation to any other place using the dimension you know as time. In actuality, you are in the same place. Also in actuality you are in two different places. It depends upon your awareness.

There is much about this creation that the people of your planet are not aware. I have stated that the principles are extremely simple. Everything is provided for the individual. All knowledge is yours. It is only necessary that you seek it out within you. Everything that we do is within the abilities of everyone else. All of the people of your planet are also able to do all of these things. It is only necessary that they return to an awareness of these abilities. This awareness is an awareness of the love and understanding that they were originally created with.

This is the only thing that blocks them from their abilities and their knowledge. It is recommended, therefore, that through meditation it is possible to regain this knowledge and these abilities. For this reason, we continually impress upon you the need for meditation, and the need for understanding your fellow men. For only through this process can you return to your rightful position.

The people of your planet are not aware of the simplicity of this process. If they could learn how very simple it is, and not forget this, then they would not any longer have the difficulties that they experience. I must be very emphatic about this, that the entire process is of an extremely simple nature. It is only necessary that the individual realize that he is a part of the creation, and that the creation is one single thing, and that in so being, he and all of his brothers and sisters throughout all space are one being. This realization will result in an ability to demonstrate only one reaction to anything: that reaction will be love.

It is extremely simple. First it is necessary to realize your relationship with everything that exists. It is then impossible to realize anything but love. This is the realization of the Creator. This is the principle upon which everything was created. It is that orientation of mind that is necessary to know all knowledge and to demonstrate all of the things that were intended for you to demonstrate through the expression of the Creator's love.

Do these simple things. Do not sway from this understanding and this love. Do this, and only this, and you will reach a state of ecstasy that is enjoyed by all of those of the Creator's children that are living in His light.

I cannot overemphasize this simple truth. It is easy for an individual to forget this truth in his daily activities, especially in an environment such as the one you experience at this time. However, it is possible to overcome the illusions that are impressed upon you by your present environment, and when this is done, you will know and feel the intense love of the Creator, and then you will know that you have found the pathway that leads to Him.

This has been stated to you many, many times. This has been given to the people of this planet by many, many teachers. It has been stated in many, many ways. And yet it is so easily forgotten. Do not forgot this. It is what you desire. We are in a position to know what you desire. If you did not desire this, we could not tell you this. We could not say to you that you should do these things, for this would be against the will of the Creator.

Remember these simple teachings. Remember them throughout each instant of your daily activities and express the principle of love. This is all that is necessary. This can be done if you remain constantly aware of the need for doing it. In order to remain aware of this need, it is necessary to meditate. Do this, and join us in the kingdom of heaven, for this was what was meant for you. This is what is your destiny. It is what you desire. There is a strong illusion, which is in a way a test of your abilities, and this test was designed by you, for you are always the recipient of that which you desire.

Do not falter and do not reject that which you desire. Remain aware of your true desire. And express it through love.

I hope that I have been of some assistance in reminding you of that which each of you is seeking. I will leave this instrument at this time. I am Hatonn. Adonai vasu.

L/L Research

Sunday Meditation
January 27, 1974

(Unknown channeling)

I am Hatonn. I greet you, my friends, in the love and the light of our infinite Creator. I and my brothers in space, as you call it, are here with you. Yes, we are here in space, and we are also here. This is a concept that is not too familiar with your peoples, that it is possible to be in more than one place at one time. However, we have told you that there is only one place. There is an ambiguity of concept when viewed from your limited state of awareness which you presently enjoy. However, it is possible to be, from your point of view, in two places or many places at one time. To us, they are all the same place.

This concept is not entirely new to the people of your planet, although it is not understood but by a very few of them. It is necessary that an individual reach an understanding of the reality of the unity of the creation in order to understand the reality of this concept.

There are many ways to state in an intellectual way this idea, but it is more revealing to experience it. This experience is available to all of the Creator's children. It was how they were originally created. Only through your own desires have you cut yourself off from the ability to experience the reality that is all about you. It is not necessary to be limited as you are. It was not intended that you be so limited. It is only your desire that you be so. It is a simple process to free yourself from the thinking that limits the people of this planet to their present locations. These locations are simply a consequence of their thinking, since in actuality, all places are one place.

This does not seem possible to most of the people of your planet. However, this condition is the true condition. The dimensions of the creation that you experience in your present form and understanding seem to be of such a magnitude that it would be impossible for you to travel through any great distance. We do not have these limitations. The reason for our lack of these limitation is simply our understanding of the truth of the concept of total oneness. This oneness is the original Thought that was provided all of the children of the Creator. Return to this Thought. Have no other thought but this Thought: a Thought of total and complete love. This will enable you to know all of the fruits of our infinite Creator.

I hope that I have been of help this evening. I am Hatonn. Adonai vasu borragus.

Friday Meditation
February 1, 1974

(Unknown channeling)

I am Hatonn. I greet you in the love and in the light of our infinite Creator. It is a great privilege to be with you. We of the Confederation of Planets in the Service of the Infinite Creator are at all times at your service, for to serve you is to serve ourselves. We have stated this to you, but at this time I wish to state it once more: to serve you is to serve ourselves. This truth is not only what you might call a philosophical truth, it is also a truth that is of a direct physical nature. Its origins, although [they] may lie within the realms of the philosophical nature of the creation, do in fact take their action within what you know as the physical or material expressions of the creation.

This is how the creation functions. It was initially conceived by our Creator to be of a property so as to reflect the impressions given to it by man. It was so designed as to express his desires in any way that he chose. There are various levels or densities in this creation; levels and densities that are not yet suspected by your physical scientists. Each of these levels is expressing the desires of those of the Creator's children who are acting within it. Each level or density is moldable or may be acted upon by the thoughts of the individuals within it to a greater or in some cases a lesser extent than that appreciated by those who dwell upon the surface of your planet at this time. It is only necessary to desire an effect to create it. This is what the Creator of us all provided for us. This is not understood at present by the population of the surface of your planet. However, it is in actuality the truth of the Creation that they are experiencing at this time. The conditions that you experience in your daily activities are a result of your thinking and the thinking of those about you and others on your surface.

There are also effects manifesting upon Earth's surface that are caused by the thinking of those who occupy other levels of existence within the physical boundaries of your planet's mental system. It in much more obvious to us that this statement with respect to the physical manipulation created by mind is a true and active portion of reality than it is to the people on the surface of this planet at this time.

Everything that you experience has been created by mind. It is in some instances obvious that this is true. In others, it is less obvious. If you consider the creations of man, whatever they may be—his cities, his homes or factories, or vehicles for conveyance—all of these things are expressions of his thought. They have been brought into existence through a physical manipulation of his physical body. However, they are no less a direct manifestation of thought.

We have stated that the entire creation is an expression of thought, the original Thought of the

Creator. It is possible for you to appreciate this statement by considering what is in evidence about you. About you, you find the expressions and manifestations of the creations of man. This preoccupies most of the people of this planet. In addition to those creations, you find the expressions and creations of the Creator. However, upon considering this, it should be noted that man is an expression and a creation of the Creator. Therefore, his creations are simply an extension of the original Thought and the original creation of the Creator. It is therefore evident that all creations throughout this infinite creation are the works, in either a direct or indirect sense, of the Creator of us all.

It is unfortunate that the people of this planet are unaware of the principles that are provided for the extension of the principle of creation. Our Creator provided each of His children with abilities quite similar to His own. Each of you has within you these abilities. They are not possible to be removed. They are within all of the children of the Creator, and will always remain with them. It was so designed by our Creator. He wished for all of His children to have and to use the abilities to govern and mold their environments at will. Unfortunately, the people of this planet have forgotten the principle that was within each of them. It is only necessary that this principle be remembered for each of the children of our Creator to fully manifest them. The teacher that was known to you as Jesus was able to use many more of the abilities than the people of this planet. He was no different from any of you. He simply was able to remember certain principles. These principles are not at all complex. They are very simple.

And an understanding of these principles is what we of the Confederation of Planets in the Service of Our Infinite Creator are attempting to give to the people of this planet who would desire them at this time.

Those principles are not necessarily of an intellectual nature. They are of extreme simplicity, and may be realized by anyone at any time. It is only necessary that you avail yourself to our contact through meditation in order to begin to re-realize that which is rightfully yours: the truth of the creation and the truth of your position in it.

Unfortunately, on this planet there is what we might term as interference. This interference occurs because of erroneous thoughts that are manifested in most of the areas of your planet. These erroneous thoughts are of a nature so as to cause a problem in the realization of truth. These erroneous thoughts must be totally obliterated from the thinking of an individual if he is to be successful in returning to the original thinking with which he was created.

We have attempted many times to suggest to you that this original thinking is one of total love and brotherhood. This is not enough. It is very difficult for the people of this planet to understand these concepts in an intellectual way. They have for a very long period of time been mentally conditioned by erroneous thinking, so that they cannot easily become intellectually aware of the principles that are simplicity and truth themselves.

It is therefore suggested that the intellectual mind be circumnavigated, and the principles be directly communicated to the soul or spiritual mind through the mechanism of telepathic impression in a non-intellectual or a conceptual sense. This we have found to be highly effective with respect to any attempt to get from an intellectual thought to a deeper understanding and awareness of the truth of the principles of our infinite Creator. It is for this reason that we have asked that the individuals who wish to understand these truths avail themselves in daily meditation, so that these impressions may be analyzed by them at a deeper level, and therefore a true and complete understanding be arrived at.

If this process of daily meditation will be continued, then each of those who avail themselves to this will find that they begin to become aware of things about them in a new sense, and that they find that they begin to appreciate the true creation in a greater and more beautiful way.

I hope that I have been of service in attempting to communicate to you the importance of daily meditation, and what the benefits and goals are, for this is the road to the future. This is where you are going to be. It is only necessary that you go. This is where all of mankind will eventually be. We extend our hands so that we may assist our brothers, wherever we find them, to find their way back to the light that was created for them.

I will at this time leave the instrument. I hope that this communication has been helpful. I am Hatonn. I leave you in the love and in the light of our infinite Creator. Adonai vasu. ☥

Saturday Meditation
February 2, 1974

(Unknown channeling)

I am Hatonn. I greet you, my friends, in the love and in the light of our infinite Creator. It is once more a great privilege to speak with you. We of the Confederation of Planets in the Service of the Infinite Creator are always most privileged to speak with any of those of your planet who would hear us.

This privilege, my friends, is one that is given to us, and it is a privilege that we accept with great gladness, for this opportunity to serve our fellow man is a rare one. It is not often that it is possible for us to directly aid our fellow beings in such an important way. The people of your planet view service in many ways. However, my friends, we of the Confederation of Planets in the Service of Our Infinite Creator view service somewhat differently than most of those who dwell upon your surface.

Service, my friends, is an extremely difficult task to perform effectively. It is necessary first to define the objectives of true service in order to understand how one may serve. There are two classifications under which all services may be divided. The first classification includes those services that are of a transient or unlasting nature. These are the services that you perform in your daily activities for your fellow man, and they are truly services.

But there is a test that may be administered in order to determine whether the service performed is of a transient or unlasting nature, or whether it should fall into the second classification, which includes all services of a permanent and not transient nature. The test is to determine whether or not the service is of such a nature to cause spiritual growth for the one served. This, my friends—whether it is known to the individual or whether he has forgotten—is in truth his only real objective.

The people of your planet are, for the most part, in a state of ignorance with respect to their real objective, which is the evolvement of their spiritual awareness. This, then, is what must be served if the second classification for service is to be met.

Each of these two classifications are desirable, and we would like to perform for the people of your planet acts which would be classified under both classifications. However, since we are aware that the second classification is by far the more important of the types of services that may be performed, it is necessary at this time to postpone performances of services of a direct way, to aid in a physical or more transient nature. We are quite fortunate that we are able to act as we are doing now, to provide the people of this planet with information that they may use in order to augment their seeking in a spiritual sense.

It is necessary that [if] an individual is to make progress in a spiritual sense, that it be a result of an inner-directed seeking of his own, rather than an outer-directed commandment given to him by an organization of a religious or other nature. For this reason, it is necessary that we do not make ourselves too generally known and accepted by the people of your planet. If we were to do this, then the inner direction of their seeking would be for the most part lost.

This is the basic reason for the conditions that you experience in your present physical environment. These conditions have been selected by yourselves, and by others, and they are a natural consequence of the creation, so as to act upon the consciousness of the individuals and create an atmosphere which will produce the inner-directed seeking for truth of which I spoke.

Unfortunately, many of the people of this planet at this time are so involved in activities that are of an extremely transient and unimportant nature that they do not have opportunities for experiencing the growth of an awareness that is necessary in order to accomplish the seeking that they actually desire.

We of the Confederation of Planets in the Service of the Infinite Creator have attempted to balance between too much exposure of our craft to the people of this planet and too little exposure. If we were to become too much a common phenomenon, so that our presence was beyond question, then we would eliminate, at least in part, a large interest in seeking for spiritual truth. This may seem to be a strange or unusual point of view, but we have observed this in the past, and since the basic reason for the physical isolation of a people such as yourselves is to cause an inner-directed seeking, then it is evident to us that we should follow, as closely as possible, this plan.

Our craft, and our people, have visited this planet many, many times in the past. This was done only after the civilization that we visited was ready to accept us. This was done only after the civilization had reached a satisfactory level of inner-directed seeking of the truth of the creation, and therefore it was displaying the principles of love and brotherhood that is the product of this seeking.

We are at this time forced by conditions over which we have no control to visit the civilizations of your world, even though they have not reached a state of spiritual awareness satisfactorily high enough for our contact. We are aware that some of the people of this planet are, however, already sufficiently aware of their spiritual nature and are sufficient}y demonstrating the love and brotherhood that is necessary for our contact. This presents a problem. The problem is that we must approach a part of the peoples of his planet without distressing the rest.

We are attempting to do this. It is necessary that the evidence of our visits and our communications be of such a nature that it can be rejected or accepted by anyone who is exposed to it. There will be, unfortunately, a degree of infringement upon those [of] the people of this planet who do not wish to accept our contact. This is an unfortunate condition, but it is one with which we must deal, since at this time it is necessary that those of the people of this planet who are seeking truth be given truth.

It will not be necessary to prove to these people that what we are giving them is truth, for if an individual has reached an understanding of truth through the inner-directed seeking of which I spoke, then he will recognize this truth when it is given to him. It is therefore only necessary that we, by some means that will not disturb those not seeking our contact, give to the rest of the people of your planet that which they seek in a form that is suitable.

This, then, is our service: to lend a helping hand up the ladder of spiritual evolution to that part of the people of this planet at this particular time, a time that is unique in the history of this planet; a time that must be dealt with in a more direct and forceful way than previous times and experiences in the history of this planet. We are extremely privileged in being able to offer this service to those who seek it, and our service is largely given to them through the process of their daily meditation. If they are to avail themselves to this service, it is necessary that they do so through meditation.

At this time I will leave this instrument. But I am always with each of you, and I am always at your service in your seeking of the love and the light that is the true creation. I am Hatonn. Adonai vasu. ☥

Sunday Meditation
February 3, 1974

(Unknown channeling)

I am Hatonn. I greet you, my friends, in the love and the light of our infinite Creator. It is once more a great privilege to be with you.

I am aware of the subject of which you have requested that I speak tonight. We of the Confederation of Planets in the Service of the Infinite Creator are always available to you for information and guidance on subjects of this and other natures. It is of great privilege to be of service in attempting to give you our viewpoints. We hope that these viewpoints will be of benefit in your understanding of the truth that is in you.

This is where we obtain the answer to questions such as the one you have asked. It is possible for you, like us, to directly find these answers, for they are within you as they are within everyone. However, we realize that conditions on your planet sometimes make it difficult to readily accomplish this understanding of truth that is abundant for all of us.

For this reason we endeavor to use instruments such as this one to help in guiding you so that you may, using the information that we present, find similar truths within your own consciousness, for these truths are the ones that are of great value. We only hope to remind you that you have these within you. We only hope to help guide you to a remembrance of what you seek.

There is no necessity to establish within one's thinking an appreciation of self. For this presupposes that it is possible to separate self from the entire creation. If one appreciates any part of the creation, then one appreciates self, for they are one and the same thing. The elimination of the concept of self is an important one in your spiritual seeking. It is necessary only to appreciate the Creator and His product, the creation. In appreciating any part of the Creation, one must appreciate all parts, for they are inseparable.

It is therefore important to act in unison with the creation rather than out of harmony due to a lack of confidence in a state of oneness. It is possible to achieve this understanding of oneness with all by availing yourself to this knowledge and understanding through the process of daily meditation.

We of the Confederation of Planets in the Service of the Infinite Creator extend our hand to the people of this planet. It is not necessary that we appreciate ourselves in our attempts to serve. It is only necessary that we serve. This will be appreciated by the Creator, for, my friends, the Creator is all that there is. It is as impossible to separate the Creator from the creation as it is impossible to separate yourself from the creation.

Appreciate, then, this unity. Appreciate your oneness with the Creator and the creation. If this is done, then other objectives will be of very little value. For this is what the Creator meant for all of the parts of the creation to do: to act in such a way as to serve. He did not specify this service, and He did not demand it. He simply provided the opportunity.

It is not necessary that you seek out opportunities to serve. It is only necessary that you serve as best you can as the opportunities present themselves. It is impossible to serve if one is not knowledgeable as to how to serve, and it is not possible in your particular state of awareness to know how to serve, unless this knowledge is sought through daily meditation.

The process, therefore, is quite simple. It is only necessary that an individual become aware of how to serve through meditation. It is then only necessary that he serve as the opportunities for service present themselves. If these simple tasks are performed, he is fulfilling all of the requirements that were specified by our Creator.

I hope that I have been of service tonight. I hope that I have been able to act as the opportunity presented itself. I am Hatonn. I leave you in the love and in the light of our infinite Creator. Adonai vasu.

(Pause)

(Unknown channeling)

I am Hatonn. I am again with this instrument. I greet you once more in the love and the light of our infinite Creator. It is always a very great privilege to be with you. Do not hesitate to call on me and my brothers for service, for this is why we are here. We are here to serve you. This is our only purpose.

In the fields of your planet grow many things that are edible. These things are given you by your Creator. They are given to you to sustain life in your present physical form. There is much wisdom in this arrangement. It is necessary for you, if you are to exist in a physical way as you know it, to sustain the body with food. However, the food that you select is up to you. There are some things in your environment that are impossible to eat. There is a very large variety of things that can be eaten. However, what is eaten is up to the individual. Selections may be made dependent upon his desire. The Creator provided for the fulfillment of desire, and it was His plan that each individual should have exactly what he would desire. We have said to you that it is necessary to meditate in order to understand. This understanding includes the understanding of desire.

I hope that I have been of service. It is only possible for me to say that with an understanding achieved through daily meditation, it is possible to fully understand desire. I will leave this instrument at this time. I am Hatonn. Adonai vasu. ☥

Monday Meditation
February 4, 1974

Group question: Why do animals have to kill each other? Why do earthquakes have to kill people?

(Unknown channeling)

There is no death. There is experience. Each entity experiences what he desires. The concept of dominion is unclear. However, the concept of awareness is clear. Speaking with respect to the planet which you know enjoy, the higher degree of awareness is experienced by the people or individuals upon the planet. In this respect, they enjoy a dominion over the other forms of life. However, all the forms of life are one form: the Creator. They all express His love.

The concert of dominion, in the sense that there should be a separation by rank or privilege, was never a portion of the original Thought of our Creator. There are many experiences allowed the children of the Creator. There are many experiments which they may perform. However, there is only one truth, and it is the truth of unity and love.

You speak of the concept of vibration, and in your mind you think of various grades. We do not think in this manner. There are simply different experiences for an entity to choose. Different experiences, but the same creation. An infinite creation, experiencing an infinite number of experiences, separate but the same, graded but ungraded. Separated by vast distances, but all in the same place. Expressing many thoughts and desires, but being only one: the Thought and desire of the Creator.

(Tape ends.)

Saturday Meditation
February 9, 1974

(Unknown channeling)

I greet you, my friends, in the love and in the light of our infinite Creator. It is a very great privilege to speak with this group this evening. It is always a very great privilege to speak with the people of this planet.

We of the Confederation of Planets in the Service of the Infinite Creator are here for one purpose. That purpose is to communicate with the people of your planet. This communication takes many forms. However, the most important of these forms is that communication which you receive in your daily meditation.

We are able to use channels such as this one to communicate concepts for your intellectual evaluation. However, these concepts are always of a limited nature. We find, however, that it is helpful for many of those of your people who have not yet learned the necessity for daily meditation.

We will continue making contacts such as this one, and developing new channels for communication, and we will hope to reach more and more of the people of your planet as time progresses.

I am attempting at this time to use the channel known as R, for it is important for channels to become accustomed to this type of contact. And I will use this channel if there is a difficulty with communications through the instrument known as R. If he will avail himself to my contact at this time.

(R channeling)

My friends, as I was saying, the most important contacts are made during periods of meditation, and are more of a spiritual nature than of an intellectual one. It is our purpose to aid your peoples in their spiritual development through stimulating your peoples intellectually to seek truth. As we have said many times before, daily meditation, constant self-analysis, and love are the keys which open the doors to truth.

It has been said, "Seek and find. Seek and ye shall find." And this is so. I will now attempt to use the instrument known as M.

(Pause)

(Don channeling)

I am with this instrument. I am sorry, but the instrument known as M is expecting too much control. He will not receive the amount of control that some other of the instruments receive. He will be able to speak, however, using my thoughts. If he makes en error, I will use this instrument to correct it. He should have no fear of these problems. I will return to the one known as M, and continue to use him.

(M channeling)

I am now with this instrument. I am Hatonn. I greet you, my friends, in the love and light of our infinite Creator. As I speak through this instrument, I ask your patience and indulgence, as we are attempting to develop new channels for your group. This process takes time and patience, my friends. I am Hatonn.

(R channeling)

I am again with this instrument. This difficulty with the other new instrument will soon be alleviated. As I was saying, seek truth, and you must surely find it. Ask, and it will surely be given. These truths are in your sacred books. This is a law of the universe, for your desire sparks cause and effect.

(Don channeling)

I am with this instrument. I am Hatonn. Your desire, my friends, is the key to your existence. Your desire is extremely important, for the Creator planned that all of His children throughout all of the universe would get exactly what they desire. That is how the universe works. That is how the Creator planned it.

The people of your planet at this time do not understand this, though it is evident to us that this is the cause of all of the conditions that you enjoy on your planet. These conditions range from those that you would call enjoyable to those that you despise. However, my friends, all of these conditions are a result of desire. Man on Earth does not realize that he creates everything that he experiences through the mechanism of desire.

This, my friends, it why meditation is so very important at this time. It is because man on Earth does not understand his desires, and, since he does not understand his desires, he does not understand the gifts of the Creator. He interprets them quite erroneously. And, my friends, the Creator never planned for His children to be the recipients of that which they did not desire.

However, man on Earth is desiring things that he does not want. But he does not realize this. He can realize this, very simply, through the process of meditation. He may know himself and his true objective. That objective, my friends, is the same for all people throughout all of the creation, even though, as on your planet, they do not realize the objective. The objective, my friends, is the Creator. A return to Him. A return to the true creation.

Many of His children have wandered far from truth. They have forgotten that condition in which they were originally created. They have wandered from this condition due to a desire to experience other things. And these experiences have led them to other desires which have led them even farther from the original Truth.

Man on Earth at this time is in a state of ignorance with respect to the principle of desire. This principle has been stated many times. You know of it as, "Ask, and you shall receive." We say, "Knock, and the door shall be opened."

Open to what, my friends? Open to truth, a truth that will make you aware of what you actually desire. "Seek and ye shall find," it has been said. Seek this truth, and know your desire.

But first, my friends, it is necessary that you desire to seek. All of you here tonight desire to seek, and you are seeking. But many of your fellow beings upon the surface of this planet are not even aware of the possibility of seeking, or of the fruits of seeking. They continue living in a state of desire that is erroneous to that which their true being would achieve.

It is necessary that we make available to as many of the people of this planet as would receive our thoughts the principles upon which the creation actually functions. It is necessary for the people of this planet to understand the principle of desire. We were, for quite some time, confused about the conditions that are manifested upon your surface, and the reason for the turmoil. It took us some time to understand the state of total ignorance that is in evidence among your peoples. This is not a condition that is often found in this creation, for the Father has given to each of His children an understanding that is within them.

This understanding is within all of the peoples throughout all of space, and it is within the people of this planet. However, since they have not sought this understanding that is theirs, that is a part of them, they have continued in directions brought about by desires that have nothing to do with truth. Desires created by intellectual games played in their waking state. They come in contact with truth only during their sleeping state.

And if they did not come in contact with their innermost thoughts at this time, they would long since have ceased to exist, for a being cannot long exist in a condition of total lack of the Creator's truth. For this reason you find it necessary to sleep. Sleep, my friends, is not a normal condition. It is something that the people of your planet do out of necessity.

Unfortunately, this condition of sleep does not totally satisfy the requirements that are necessary if the truth of the creation is to be revealed in its totality. It is therefore necessary, if they are to return to this truth, to avail themselves to it in daily meditation.

This, my friends, is why we cannot come directly to you, and land upon your surface and speak with you, for it would do no good. We must provide a spark, a clue, something for a start. A start of seeking, seeking that results in finding the truth that is within you.

This, my friends, is the only way to help the people of your planet. For they must help themselves. They must find the truth that is within them. They must initiate the seeking. All that we can do is to provide a stimulus for their own initiation of seeking.

Unfortunately, only a small percentage of those contacted initiate this seeking, and only a percentage of those continue the seeking for any satisfactory period of time. We are always available to aid in guiding your seeking. But, my friends, we cannot do this if you do not seek.

This message is not meant so much for this group as it is for those who will read it at a later time, for this group is seeking.

Seek, my friends. Seek. This is the word that opens the door to everything that exists throughout all of space and all of time. Seek. Seek.

And what will you find? You will find love, for that is all that there is to find. For that is all that there is.

I am Hatonn. It has been a privilege to be with you this evening. It has been a privilege to be with you at this time. Adonai vasu borragus.

Questioner: I have a question. *(The questioner asked Hatonn the question in silence.)*

(Unknown channeling)

I am Hatonn. I am once more with this instrument. It is a great privilege to be of service, for that is our purpose. That is our desire: to serve. This, my friends, is also a principle of the creation, for in serving you, we serve ourselves. For it is not possible to serve anything within the creation without serving yourself. The creation, my friends, is one thing. You are simply a part of that one thing. It is impossible to separate yourself from it, because you are it.

The people of your planet are living an illusion. This illusion includes the concept of the possibility of separation; the concept of the individual.

There is difficult in using your language, for it was evolved with concepts that are erroneous. It is necessary in using it to use terms such as "the individual." However, this term should be simply, "the Creator."

As you look at your fellow man, see him for what he is: the Creator. For there is no part of this creation that is any more or less than any other part. Each part is a portion of the Creation. Each holds equal rank.

I am aware that there are many upon your planet who would not understand this concept. They feel pain, if it is within their individual being, but they do not feel the pain of others.

This is not so with the Confederation of Planets in the Service of the Infinite Creator. We feel your pain, and this brings us to you at this time: to serve you. For in doing so, we serve ourselves, since you and we are one. Your pain is felt throughout all of the creation, and for this reason there are many, many here to serve you at this time. We serve you in the very best way that we can: to eliminate this pain. We give to you the information that you need in order to eliminate this pain. It is something that may be done in the twinkling of an eye. It is the way that the Creator planned. He did not, however, anticipate that His children would create from their own desires the pain that we now feel emanating from your planet.

This is a result of the desire of the people of this planet. Unfortunately, these desires affect not only the ones generating the desire, but also others who live on the surface. It is what you call a contagion. It requires an extreme degree of understanding to live upon your surface and not experience this contagion.

It can be done, my friends. It is only necessary that you know and demonstrate the Creator's truth in every thought and deed. And then you will be free from the effect of the desires of your brothers who live about you on the surface of your planet.

I hope that I have been of assistance. I am Hatonn. Adonai vasu.

Sunday Meditation
February 10, 1974

(Unknown channeling)

I am Hatonn. I am with this instrument. I greet you, my friends, in the love and light of our infinite Creator. It is a great privilege to be with you this evening. It is always a great privilege, for this is our purpose, to serve those of the people of this planet who seek.

We of the Confederation of Planets in the Service of the Infinite Creator are here for this express purpose: to serve those who seek. Our service is, unfortunately, very limited, but these limitations are limitations impressed upon us by those who are dwelling upon your planet. We are limited to use of a channel such as this one in order to serve those of the people of this planet who are seeking our service: who are seeking truth.

We are apologetic for the conditions that make it difficult for us to serve you to the extent that would be desired this evening[2]. However, we find that at this time it is not desirable that we perform this service as it will be performed in the very near future quite adequately.

We request that you avail yourselves to our service and to this instrument in the near future, when conditions are more suitable, and we will extend our service to you, to our fullest extent, for this is our purpose; this is the reason we are here.

I hope that I have been able to serve you in some slight way this evening. It is a very, very great privilege for us of the Confederation of Planets in the Service of the Infinite Creator to do this, for in serving you, we also serve ourselves. For it is impossible to serve any part of this creation without also serving yourself.

I will leave you now in the love and in the light of our infinite Creator. Adonai vasu.

---

[2] At this session there were the parents of a very restive baby who was in another room.

Monday Meditation
February 11, 1974

(Unknown channeling)

I am Hatonn. I am with this instrument. I greet you, my friends, in the love and the light of our infinite Creator. It is again a great privilege to be with you.

This evening I would like to speak to you on the subject of light. We have spoken recently to you many times on the concept of love, and what this word really means. Tonight, however, I would like to speak to you on the subject of light.

We greet you each evening, as we speak through this instrument, in the love and in the light of our infinite Creator. These are the ingredients that comprise all of the creation. All of the creation, my friends, is composed of love and light.

We use these two words because they are the words that are closest in definition in your language to the concepts that we wish to communicate. However, they are, unfortunately, extremely lacking in depth of definition. I will attempt, this evening, to clarify, to some extent, the meanings of both of these words.

Love and light. As I have stated recently, love is the force that creates. Light is what it creates. My friends, the Creator is love. You are love. You are a part of the Creator. Therefore you are love, but your love is expressed through the manifestation of light.

Light is the substance out of which the creation is formed. The Creator's love causes vibrations. This is what is meant when the term "vibration" is used. It is a condition of love. These vibrations are the building energies that compose all of the creation, in its entire infinite and boundless sense.

These vibrations produce a manifestation that you have come to know as the visible creation—the visible creation, and many, many invisible creations; invisible to you at this time, however, not inaccessible.

These vibrations produce the basic particle that you understand as a particle of light. This particle is associated with these vibrations. And therefore it manifests as a function of the rate of these vibrations, and produces the creation, the creation in which you and all of your fellow beings experience that which you desire.

Since both you and the Creator are one, both you and I and all of the creation is a product of love. This love is a concept creating a real force, which is interpreted as a vibration. This vibration is measurable, and occurs in different intensities. The intensities are a function of the intensities of love that generate the vibration. It is possible for the parts of the Creator who act through the free will of their own to generate these vibrations using their love, and so producing the particles known to you as light.

These particles are arranged by this expression of love to produce all of what you consider your physical world and its inhabitants, and all other worlds and their inhabitants, be they what you consider physical or non-physical, for this is how all of the creation is manifested.

From this explanation it should follow that it would be possible for an individual, understanding the principles of creation, to express this love to create for himself that which he desired. This is done all of the time. We consider this activity normal, and the Creator considered this activity normal, for it was this original concept. Each of you, then, as do each of the Creator's children, have the ability to create through love anything that you desire. It in only necessary that you express the love that is yourself.

This was demonstrated recently to the people of this planet. Many teachers who understood this principle have demonstrated it in the history of this planet. The one that I refer to at this time is the one best known to yourselves, the one known as Jesus. He was able to, by the simple expression of the love that was himself and all of the creation, create this vibration and then, through desire, there was formed of this vibration the light as was originally conceived by the Creator.

This light, then, was formed to the wishes and desires of this man. This is considered a normal activity for each of the Creator's children, for this was their birthright, and was planned by the Creator.

If desire is to be intelligently employed, it is necessary to employ it through the principle of love, for this is the generative force which produces the vibration condensing, you might say, out of space the particle known to you as light. All of your material is composed of this single basic particle. If any desire is to be fulfilled, then one should act to do this using the creative force: love. It is possible to return things considered to be lacking in perfection to their original perfection through this principle. This is how the healing that was evidenced by the man known as Jesus was accomplished. This is how all healing of a spiritual nature is accomplished. This is, in fact, how all healing is accomplished, although your science is not at this time aware of this.

We find that it is more logical to arrive directly at the result desired, rather than to achieve this state through intermediate actions such as are performed upon your planet. These intermediate actions are performed due to a lack of understanding of the use of the creative force. This creative force may be understood by anyone at any time.

The understanding of this force is within all people throughout all of the creation. It is only necessary to realize it. Unfortunately, upon your planet at this time there is much difficulty in realizing this principle.

The conditions that have manifested through long periods of time have focused the attention of the preponderance of your people on other concepts. The concept of which we speak is not of an intellectual nature. Therefore, it is necessary to become aware of it in a sense that is not intellectual. For this reason, we have suggested that meditation is the best avenue for acquiring the non-intellectual understanding of the use of the creative force.

This is possible for anyone at any time. It is only necessary that they avail themselves of the knowledge that they already possess. It is a difficult thing to do sometimes, when surrounded by vibrations created by desire that is of a nature never intended by the Creator. We understand the difficulty arising in realizing this simple truth when impressed with the thoughts of those who would desire other than this truth.

However, it is quite possible to insulate one's consciousness from these infringements of thought and realize the truth of one's origin. The one known to you as Jesus was able to do this. Do not believe that this man was unique in his ability. He was demonstrating to you that this was possible. He was demonstrating that each of the Father's children could do the same thing that He did. It is only necessary that you meditate to realize this, and then it is only necessary that you demonstrate your knowledge of it through your thoughts and your actions.

You, then, as did he, will be able to use that force that is yours to use: love. This is the word, my friends: love. But it is not understood. Love: it means all that you think it means. But it means much more. Learn what it means, and you shall truly be free.

I leave you now in my love, and in His love, and in all of the love of all of the Father's children throughout all of the Father's creation. I am Hatonn. Adonai vasu. ☥

Monday Meditation
February 11, 1974

(R channeling)

I am Hatonn. I greet you in the love and the light of our infinite Creator. I would speak with you at this time on …

(Unknown channeling)

I am Hatonn. I greet you, my friends, once more in the love and the light of our infinite Creator. It is a great privilege to be with you. I am sorry that we were unable to use the instrument known as R. However, this is of no consequence.

I am aware of your thoughts. I will attempt at this time to speak to you on a subject that would concern you. This is the subject of landing one of our craft to meet you. This instrument is at this time questioning this communication. He has always questioned communications of this nature. But I can assure him that this is a communication from the one known as Hatonn.

At this time I occupy a craft that you know as a flying saucer. It is a small craft, approximately thirty feet in diameter, and is capable of landing at any point upon your surface. I am aware of this instrument's feeling of skepticism towards messages such as this one. I am going to suggest that he totally relax, and clear his mind of thoughts. In this way, I will be able to use him as an instrument in relaying this message.

I and my brothers in the Confederation of Planets in the Service of the Infinite Creator are in your atmosphere, and we are also around your planet outside your atmosphere. We are constantly keeping your planet under surveillance. We are constantly ready to serve in any way that we can. We are aware that you are extremely anxious to meet us, and we, my friends, are extremely anxious to meet you. Nothing would give us greater pleasure than to walk upon your surface and meet you directly.

This instrument is still skeptical in regards to this communication. He has always been skeptical of communications of this nature. I can assure him that I am Hatonn, and am communicating through him from a craft, and that the thoughts that I have given him and the words which he has spoken are correct. And if he will kindly maintain a clear and open mind, I will use him as an instrument. He should not think of anything. He should not try to analyze these communications. He should not be skeptical of what he is saying. He should simply relax and allow me to use him as an instrument. I am sorry that we are having some difficulty.

Questioner: Is it possible for us to meet now?

I am Hatonn. I will attempt to answer your question. You must relax. He must relax because he is at all times skeptical of this type of communication, but I can assure you that I am

Hatonn and I am in a craft. At this time I am over the building that you are in. In fact, I can at this time reveal myself to both of you. I would suggest that you put on your coats and go into the back yard. I will reveal myself to both of you.

(Both went to the back yard. One saw nothing. One saw a white star-like object which moved very rapidly across the sky, with no trail, and then disappeared.)

(Unknown channeling)

I am Hatonn. I am again with this instrument. I greet you, my friends, in the love and the light of our infinite Creator. It is always a great privilege to be able to speak with you. I am aware of your thoughts.

(R channeling)

I am Hatonn. I am aware of your thoughts. You are wondering why you could not see our craft. Because you were not looking as we told you to look. I am aware of your thoughts. You are questioning the source of this information. I am Hatonn.

(Transcript ends.)

L/L Research

L/L Research is a subsidiary of Rock Creek Research & Development Laboratories, Inc.

P.O. Box 5195
Louisville, KY 40255-0195

www.llresearch.org

Rock Creek is a non-profit corporation dedicated to discovering and sharing information which may aid in the spiritual evolution of humankind.

ABOUT THE CONTENTS OF THIS TRANSCRIPT: This telepathic channeling has been taken from transcriptions of the weekly study and meditation meetings of the Rock Creek Research & Development Laboratories and L/L Research. It is offered in the hope that it may be useful to you. As the Confederation entities always make a point of saying, please use your discrimination and judgment in assessing this material. If something rings true to you, fine. If something does not resonate, please leave it behind, for neither we nor those of the Confederation would wish to be a stumbling block for any.

CAVEAT: This transcript is being published by L/L Research in a not yet final form. It has, however, been edited and any obvious errors have been corrected. When it is in a final form, this caveat will be removed.

© 2009 L/L Research

Wednesday Meditation
February 13, 1974

(Unknown channeling)

I am Hatonn. I greet you, my friends, in the love and in the light of our infinite Creator. It is once more a great privilege to be with you. We of the Confederation of Planets in the Service of the Creator are always extremely privileged to speak directly to those who dwell upon the surface of this planet.

We would prefer to speak with all of the people of this planet. However, there are many who would not wish to hear us. They would not wish to know us. And they would not understand anything that we said, even though, my friends, we are able at this time to use, fluently, any of your languages. It takes a considerable amount of time, as you know it, to establish a base for communication when the concept from which we generate ideas is as largely displaced from yours as is ours. When I say "yours," I am speaking of the general basis for concepts of the majority of the people of your planet.

The bases for our concept are what we consider universal truths, truths that are unchanging, and that are the reason for the creation that is all about us and is us and is you. Unfortunately, the people of the planet upon which you presently dwell are not aware of the truth behind the functioning of the creation in which they find themselves. This is not an abnormal situation, but it is not normal, either.

There are many other peoples throughout the creation who are not aware of these truths. However, there are a very, very large number who are.

There are a certain percentage of the people within your population who are ready to be instructed, for they have reached a state of understanding so that they may easily assimilate the little more knowledge that they need in order to understand the truth of the functioning of this creation.

This is what we are attempting to do at this time, and this evening we will endeavor to do this so that each of you will be able to make one more stop in your journey towards a complete understanding of truth. Most of the problems that you encounter in understanding this truth have to do with false impressions given to you by the society in which you now find yourselves. If you had been living in a society that had always been aware of truth and of the true nature of the creation, you would have no difficulty in applying the truths, since they would be a part of your life. It is difficult to do this when living in a society that continues to focus its attention on things that are very far from the Creator's plan.

The society as you know it as present has focused its attention at present on many things. Very, very few of these things that it is interested in have anything at all to do with the basic truth of the functioning of the creation in all of its ways and all of its parts.

Your people on this planet seek many things. However, they seek these things in what we would consider to be a very strange way. They seek the result of their desires almost exclusively within what they know as the physical illusion that they now enjoy. Since they are unable to experience in their waking state anything but this physical illusion, they then think that this is all that exists, and they attempt to find expression of their desires strictly within this illusion.

This results in the fulfillment of false desires. The people who fulfill these false desires wonder why, having filled them, they do not find happiness. This has been demonstrated upon your planet many times, but little heed has been taken of it. The desires still remain very strong, and the people about you strive with much energy to fulfill them.

Having fulfilled them they then, as I have said, wonder. They wonder why they still have desires, for as soon as they have fulfilled one, they have generated another.

We are going to attempt to give you instruction at this time on the proper use of desires so that you may work within the truth of the creation and become once more knowledgeable about its function. There are certain desires that every individual has within him. These desires are a natural state, and they should be fulfilled. The reason the individual has these natural desires is that he is a part of the creation, and the Creator had an original desire, which continues throughout all of time and all of space.

This desire of the Creator was to provide an experience for all of His parts that would fulfill in totality the desire of all of His parts. But since all of His parts have this same desire, then it should be evident that this desire is to serve the other parts. This is how we have interpreted the functioning of creation. This is why within each individual throughout all of the creation there dwells a desire to serve the creation in any way that he can.

This dwells within each of the people, all of the entities of this planet, for all of them are a portion of the Creator.

It is possible to fulfill this desire. As we have said, the Creator has attempted to provide only good for all of His children. But since all of His children are a part of the Creator, and since all of us and everything is in actuality one thing, then we have this necessity occurring within each individual in all of the parts of the creation, an attempt to serve. This is natural. The planet upon which you now stand serves you. The growth that comes from the planet serves you. Its atmosphere serves you. Its water serves you. The entire creation serves you. You feel the energy from your sun. It serves you.

This principle is simply the original concept of the Creator being expressed through all of its parts, for this concept remains undiminished. For this reason, you will find that you will achieve what you actually desire only if you are to serve the rest of the creation. This is a law that is natural. This law is the creation.

The people of the Confederation of the Planets in the Service of the Infinite Creator are just that: we are in His service. But we are in our service, and we are in your service, and we are in the creation's service, for we have recognized that, in being a part of the Creator, and having within us the expression that was originally generated, it is only possible to fulfill desire through service. For this reason we are here now, to give to you our service. This fulfills our desire. This fulfills the Creator's desire. The entire process is simplicity itself.

And, my friends, this is the creation: simplicity. It is only necessary that you understand this, and then act in such a way as to carry out your desire in its true sense for you to once more unite in totality with the original and true creation.

We have stated many times that meditation is very necessary. If you are to understand what and how to serve at this time, it is necessary that you find this through meditation, for this is the only process that will allow you to understand in its totality this information. So, it is necessary that you spend time each day in meditation, and become aware of the technique of fulfilling your desire to serve.

When you have done this, you will find that you are experiencing something that is phenomenal. It will be an event that is beyond your wildest dreams. It will be of a nature that you might consider impossible at this time, but it will take place. Many of the people of this planet are serving at this time. They serve in many different ways. However, only a small percentage of them are actually fulfilling their desire to serve, for what I will call "blind" service is not as effective as service that is performed as a result of the knowledge gained in meditation.

It is important, then, to learn how to serve, and whom should be served. As I have said, it would seem that we would perform a service by coming among your people and helping. Our meditation reveals to us that this is erroneous. For this reason, we contact you in this way. We request that you do as we do, if you are to know how to serve, and whom should be served at this time. Meditate, for this knowledge is within all people throughout the creation, for they are the creation, and this is His desire: to serve, to serve all of His parts, so that each experience the ecstasy that He originally created and that exists all about you.

I hope that I have been of service this evening, for this is my objective. I will leave this instrument now for a short period. If there are any questions, I shall return shortly. I leave in the love and the light of our infinite Creator. Adonai vasu.

Questioner: *(Question asked silently to Hatonn.)*

(Unknown channeling)

I am Hatonn. I greet you again in the love and the light of our infinite Creator. I would attempt to speak on a subject of interest. The subject is love.

This is a subject that is necessary to understand if you are to be effective in fulfilling your desire of service. In serving your fellow man upon Earth, it is necessary to give him love. This is sometimes difficult to do in your present society, for these expressions are often misunderstood.

Love is very misunderstood among your people. We express total love for all of your people. We cannot help doing this, for we express total love for all of the creation. It is impossible to do otherwise, when you are aware of the love expressed by the creation. In order to achieve this awareness it is only necessary to meditate, and then to serve, for with each service effectively performed, love will be reflected. This will generate within you more love, and the process will be repeated, or recycled.

This process will be self-generating and will continue to build. This is what occurred with the teacher you are most familiar with, the one known as Jesus. Why was this man much more effective in generating this love than others who have attempted this recently? The reason, my friends, is that he was able to fulfill his desire for service intelligently. He was able to do this in an intelligent manner because he sought answers to the questions of how to fulfill his desire for service through meditation.

Many of those upon your planet who seek to serve their fellow man at present, seek to serve him in ways that they have learned intellectually, from others, or from readings. And they find, in many cases, difficulties in performing the service that they so much desire to give. And the love that they desire and expect as a return for their service is not reflected, for the service that they have attempted is not desired, and is therefore not a service.

A service is only a service if it is desired. Man has free will. He is free to choose anything that he desires. It is necessary, if you are to serve, that you understand the desire of those served, not in an intellectual sense, but in a sense that you gain through meditation. A knowledge that transcends the intellect. A knowledge that results in effective service.

I hope that I have been of assistance in explaining this particular point. I will leave this instrument. I am Hatonn. Adonai vasu.

Questioner: Was that an answer to your question?

Questioner: Yes, that was a specific answer to my question. ☥

Friday Meditation
February 15, 1974

(R channeling)

I am Hatonn. I greet you, my friends, in the love and in the light of our infinite Creator. It is again my privilege to be with you.

There is some difficulty in using this instrument, for he is relatively new and not yet adept at receiving our thoughts.

We are using more control at this time because he so wishes it. I would speak to you at this time concerning your spiritual development. As we have said many times, it is good that you gather in groups such as this one, for this enables us to aid you.

Perhaps it is hard for you to realize how your spiritual development is progressing. This is because this development cannot be measured, as you would say, on a day-to-day basis. It is possible to realize the progression of your spiritual development more readily over a period of months.

We realize the frustration encountered at times by those of your peoples who would seek higher spiritual life. But remember, it has been said that one makes his spirit—one makes his greatest spiritual strides during these times. Look upon your frustrations and doubt as spiritual tests. Look upon these as things to be overcome. It is a most interesting paradox that these great hardships can bring such great reward.

I will attempt to use this instrument.

It is hard for peoples to realize how great a gift these frustrations and doubts are, as it is difficult for many of the people of your planet to realize how great a gift it is to be able to experience the vibrational change upon your planet. How great a gift it is to be able to serve your fellow man!

It has been my privilege to be with you at this time. I leave you in the light of the infinite love of our infinite Creator. For, as you know, that is the only way that I could possibly leave you. I am Hatonn. Adonai vasu borragus. ✣

Sunday Meditation, H's Meeting
February 17, 1974

(Don channeling)

I am Hatonn. I greet you in the love and in the light of our infinite Creator. It is a very great privilege to be with you this evening. It is a very great privilege to be with you at all times. We of the Confederation of Planets in the Service of the Infinite Creator are here to serve you. This is sometimes difficult. We have attempted to contact the people of this planet through many different ways. We have not always been successful. There have been, in some instances, misunderstandings about our contacts. There have been, in some cases, misrepresentations, through no fault of the contactee, of what we would bring to the people of this planet.

We are attempting to bring to you one thing. We have attempted to do this in many ways, but still we have but one thing to bring to you at this time. We are bringing to you love. This is all that is necessary, for when you are able to receive this love, with it will come the understanding that many of you now seek.

We of the Confederation of Planets in the Service of the Infinite Creator are attempting, therefore, at this time to bring to you love. If the people of this planet can accept this, then understanding will occur with no other effort. For, my friends, there is only one thing to understand, and that is the actual interpretation of the word "love."

This word is misunderstood among your peoples. It does not mean exactly what most of your peoples believe it to mean. The concept has been demonstrated many times in the history of your planet. The demonstration that you are most familiar with is the demonstration of the man known to you as Jesus. This man performed what you would call miracles. However, these were not miracles, in the true sense of understanding of this concept. These were simply expressions of this man's love, for in expressing this love in its true and total sense he was able to use the single force of the creation given to each of the Creator's children as their birthright.

Yes, my friends, each of you here tonight has the same birthright, for each of you is equal in all respects to all of the Creator's children. The man known to you as Jesus understood the concept of love. We are here to bring to you the understanding of this concept. Nothing else is of any real importance, for once this is understood, all is understood. And this concept, my friends, is simplicity itself. It is only necessary that you realize the truth of this concept that is within each of you. This is why we of the Confederation of Planets in the Service of the Infinite Creator are here. This is the only real service that we can perform for any peoples at any time.

There has been considerable confusion about our real purpose, and this we understand. There are many pathways to the single truth that lies within each individual. And each individual finds his own route back to the knowledge that was his birthright. It is only necessary, however, that you become aware of this birthright through meditation, for this knowledge is within you. For you, like ourselves and like every being within this infinite creation, is a part of this creation. We are all one thing. We are the creation of the Father, and in so being we have within us His love, for this is what created us—a great force. A force that permeates everything that exists. The word that expresses it in your language is love, but this force goes far beyond the concept of this word. Each of you can know this force, for it is part of you, and you cannot separate it from you. Spend time each day in meditation, and you will become aware—aware of the force that is the creation. This, my friends, is the first step, and it is also the last step, in knowing all that there is to know.

For with this awareness, comes all awareness. This is what we bring to the people of this planet at this time: an education. For many of them have lost direction and have become involved in a complex illusion.

At this time, I will attempt to transfer this contact to the instrument known as R.

(Pause)

(R channeling)

I am with this instrument now. I am Hatonn. As I was saying, many upon your planet have been deeply immersed in a hypnotic state. It is desirable to awaken from this state. We have presented a method of awaking from this state through daily meditation, constant self-analysis, and love. You will come to a deeper understanding and will begin to lay your claim upon your birthright.

I will now attempt to speak through the instrument known as H.

(H channeling)

I am with this instrument now, my friends. I only wish to present a few brief remarks before leaving you. Be aware, my friends, that a great opportunity is presented to all of your peoples at this time. Those among your peoples who can raise their consciousness rapidly enough can take part in what you might call a great graduation. Your planet moves to a higher vibratory area and is even now at the entrance to this higher vibratory area. Only those individuals whose vibration can be raised along with that of the planet will continue into the Golden Age which will soon dawn upon your surface, a spiritual age of beauty, grandeur and true love, of which I speak.

As an individual, each of you have everything to gain by following our simple suggestions which will raise you in consciousness, and which will raise your individual frequency of vibration. You have nothing to lose but a small particle of what you call your time.

Ask yourselves, my friends, in all honesty, do you not find the time for those things which are important to you? It may simply be a matter of readjusting in your own thinking that which is important to you.

I will leave you now, my friends, with that thought uppermost in your minds. May you put forth the necessary effort. May each of you grow rapidly in love, which will bring about understanding and a new awareness to you.

It has been my very great privilege and pleasure to be with you at this time. I am Hatonn. Adonai vasu borragus.

Monday Meditation, First Meeting
February 18, 1974

(Unknown channeling)

I am Hatonn. I greet you, my friends, in the love and the light of our infinite Creator. It is a great privilege to be with you. It is always a very great privilege to be with those of the population of this planet who are seeking—seeking a truth that is singular, a truth that is the only objective of those who have become aware.

We of the Confederation of Planets in the Service of the Infinite Creator are here at this time to aid you in your seeking. This is a great opportunity, for us and for you. For it is not too often that the condition that you are soon to experience in its total sense occurs. This experience is the reason for our visitations, and it is the reason for your present meeting. Each of you will become channels of communication between we of the Confederation of Planets in the Service of the Infinite Creator, and the multitudes of the population who dwell upon the surface of the planet you now enjoy.

This service which you perform will be very great. We are aware that, at this time, there are difficulties in performing this service, for at this time very few of the people upon this planet are seeking anything outside of the physical illusion that so constantly busies their minds with trivialities.

We of the Confederation of Planets are aware of the trivial nature of the things that involve most of the people of your planet. Their things seem of great importance to them. However, the importance of their activities is a function of their inability to still their active minds, and return to the awareness of reality that is possible through meditation.

The activities that seem so important to the people of this planet at this time are so very transient as to be in reality negligible, as are all activities within the physical, except for that activity of service to one's fellow man. For through service, one builds one's awareness of truth. This is the reason for life, as you know it, in the physical.

The reason is to experience service. For this is very effective in creating a deep and complete understanding of the Creator's plan for the creation. In this plan was the concept of service. Through His love, He instilled in each of the parts of this creation the desire to serve. This desire to serve is within everything that exists. It is within the planet that you walk upon. It is within the vegetation, the atmosphere itself. Everything about you exists to serve, and unless an entity becomes involved too deeply in thoughts generated as an action of his freedom of choice, he will maintain this awareness of his desire to serve, as does the vegetation upon your planet; as does the atmosphere that you breathe; as do we of the Confederation of Planets In the Service of the Infinite Creator.

This, then, this experience, is what is needed for many of the peoples of this planet at this time: an opportunity to act and to demonstrate this desire to serve. Many people who now live upon the surface of this planet act in such a manner so as to serve their fellow man. Some of these desires for service are unfortunately misdirected. This is not a bad thing for the individual for all that is necessary is that this desire be realized. However, it is sometimes unfortunate that the service is misunderstood and misdirected, for it is not as effective in this case as it would have been with more intelligent direction.

For this reason we have suggested that everyone who will attempt to serve first avail themselves to a knowledge of how to serve. This they can do through daily meditation, and only in this way can they serve intelligently.

We of the Confederation of Planets in the Service of the Infinite Creator avail ourselves to this knowledge through meditation. For this reason, we do not come among your people, giving them our services directly, for we are aware of detrimental effects upon them in doing this. Our service is aimed at what they actually desire. What they actually desire is an ability to realize truth. In order to give to them this ability, it is necessary that we bring about a condition to cause within them a personal seeking of service and a personal seeking of knowledge of the truth of the creation. Only through this process can they understand the truth that is within them. It is something that cannot be too effectively given to them in an intellectual manner.

We therefore suggest that, in order to create an atmosphere desirable for service, that each of you avail yourself to the knowledge of how to go about this, that is within you. Do this through meditation, and then your service will be effective.

There are many ways to serve; however, a knowledge of the real objective of service is of great importance. There are many illusions of service that result in little or no service. Before attempting your service, spend time in meditation. You will realize what is necessary if you are to serve in an effective manner. We are serving you at this time by conditioning you, if you desire it, so that you can receive our thoughts. We find this service to be effective, for these thoughts generate in you your own thoughts, and augment, to some extent, that which you are able to seek within yourself. It will also be important in the future that we have instantly available channels of communication, and this technique is highly effective, especially when the channel is as trained as this channel.

It is a simple process, and if you desire this form of communication and this form of service, it will be given unto you. We can only do as much in this area as you desire. For this is the limitation of all of our service: to do only as much as is desired.

We are at this time going to attempt to use each of the instruments in this room. It is suggested that each of you avail yourself to our contact, for this is our service at this time. It is only necessary that you desire this service.

(R channeling)

As I was saying, it is only necessary that you avail yourself to this service to receive it. Gradually it will become easier for you to receive our thoughts. We realize the difficulty in discerning our thoughts from your own. This is why our thoughts will be of a spiritual nature. It would not be of service to add confusion to your illusion. As we have said, once you have become proficient in receiving our thoughts, it is possible to do this with each other. However, any thoughts which are not of a spiritual nature would again only add to your illusion. It is for this reason that we suggest that you maintain as high a spiritual consciousness as possible at all times. This is a difficult thing to achieve. However, as you grow spiritually from your meditation, it will begin to manifest.

I will now attempt to speak through the instrument known as M.

(M channeling)

I am now with this instrument. I am happy to be with you, my friends. As I was saying, all of you are capable of helping to raise the spiritual vibration of your planet. All you have to do is open your consciousness through daily meditation. Avail yourself to the creative intelligence of our infinite Creator.

Our purpose, as I have said before, is to aid your peoples as your planet moves through the major cycle change. All that is required, my friends, is that you open your consciousness. Open your consciousness, my friends, through meditation.

I am Hatonn, my friends. This instrument is in the process of learning to channel. As we have explained before, it takes time and patience.

I will attempt to continue through another channel.

(Side one of tape ends.)

(Don channeling)

I am Hatonn. I am now with this instrument. I greet you, my friends, in the love and in the light of our infinite Creator. It is a great privilege to work with you in conditioning new channels. It requires some experience in receiving our thoughts to communicate as easily and accurately as does this instrument. However, even this instrument at times questions as to whether the thoughts are from those of us who identify ourselves as the Confederation of Planets In the Service of the Infinite Creator, or thoughts generated within his own thinking. We can assure this instrument and those who are present here this afternoon, that if there are errors made by him due to misinterpretation of what we relay to him, that we will correct this, by using control. He has experienced total control several times during communications in past weeks, and is quite familiar with this technique. We use more control with new instruments than with instruments who are as experienced in receiving our thoughts as this instrument is.

Each of you can arrive at this ability very easily. It only requires that you spend some time in availing yourself to our contact to receive as clearly and as rapidly as does this instrument. He too went through a long period of training and conditioning, but through the years of his practice in availing himself to us, he has developed the ability to receive our communications at his convenience.

It is only necessary that he think that he wishes our contact, and he has it. For this, as we have said, is our service to you. We are available to you at all times, and we only require that you desire our contact for the contact to be made.

It is helpful to be able to channel our thoughts as does this instrument, for there will be many of the peoples of this planet seeking truth who have not become aware of it through meditation, simply because they have not been aware of the necessity for or the technique of meditation. This will be the service of the channels such as yourselves: to initiate the concepts of meditation and the concepts which we of the Confederation of Planets in the Service of the Infinite Creator have become aware of.

There will be many of the peoples of your planet who do not desire this information, and who do not desire that it be proved to them, as they express it, that such information is correct. This we do not wish—that this, our concept of truth and the concept that we know to be true, be forced upon individuals who do not accept these concepts and would rather bury within them the realization of this truth. This is the Creator's plan, my friends: that each of the Creator's children have what they desire, regardless of the consequences.

This, then, is the reason for the state of confusion on this planet at this time. It is the gift of the Creator that each of His children should live as they desire. Unfortunately, there are certain natural laws. I say unfortunately—this is not correct, but it is unfortunate for those who choose to ignore them. These natural laws are as simple as the laws that your physical science experiences. The creation was generated by the pure love of the Creator. In generating this creation, He conceived of a creation in which all of the parts would serve all of the other parts. In order to create this creation, it was necessary to build it upon certain principles of love. These principles permeate all creation, and if properly understood, as is the right of all of the Creator's children, it is possible to live in total harmony.

If these laws have been forgotten, as is the case with many of those who dwell upon the planet you now enjoy, then the consequences are somewhat unusual. These consequences are now being experienced by many of the peoples of this planet. These consequences, which they do not desire, are a result of their desire, a result of a desire that is not based upon understanding of the truth of the creation. There are, unfortunately, conflicting actions that result in creations and experiences that were never intended by the Creator. However, certain principles govern, and cannot be misinterpreted or misused.

This is our understanding of the manifestation and reality of the creation.

(Pause)

Questioner:

(A question is asked silently.)

I am aware of your question. You have spoken of the concept of antichrist. My friends, this is a source of confusion. The source of confusion, my friends, is the concept of Christ. Once this concept is understood, then the concept of antichrist is understood. Therefore, I shall speak upon the meaning of the one known to you as Christ.

This man known to you as Jesus was born into the physical upon your planet. He was able to realize the truth of the creation, and then he was able to demonstrate this truth to those about him. This man came into the physical on your planet as have many teachers in the past. Each of these teachers came into the physical for the purpose of serving the people of this planet. However, it was up to them to carry out this service. Each of them did it in his own way. This is within the limits of our understanding of the intent of the Creator.

These teachers were limited: limited by the same conditions that each of you and that each of all the people on the planet experience. The people of this planet have misinterpreted the meaning of these men. The people of this planet are at this time misinterpreting the meaning of the man known to you as Jesus. His purpose in his life was to demonstrate that it is possible through an awareness of the Creator's truth to experience what the Creator planned for each of us. This man worked what was called miracles. These were truly miracles to those who thought of them as miracles, but this was given to each of the Creator's children. He was simply demonstrating the result of thinking in the original way as planned by our Creator. He was also demonstrating that it is possible for anyone, at any time, to demonstrate this type of thinking, and therefore, the abilities that accompany it.

Unfortunately, the people have very much misinterpreted this man's life and teachings. He was attempting to provide an example of understanding so that each of the children of the Creator could seek the same understanding.

This is the task of any teacher upon this planet or any other place in the creation. This is our task at this time. You have spoken of the term, antichrist. What then is the meaning of the term? It is simply the ignorance of the knowledge of this truth. This ignorance is widespread upon this planet. This is what is known as the antichrist: it is the ignorance of truth. We speak to you, through instruments such as this one. We do this because it would be a mistake to speak to the people of this planet in a more direct manner. It is necessary that the ignorance of truth be eliminated from within, for this is the only possibility available to the individual, if he is to achieve a true awareness of truth. The concept of antichrist is with you but it is a false concept. If there exists an individual who would be called the antichrist, then there exists an extremely ignorant individual. Should this be a threat to any of the Creator's children? I think not!

Questioner: Well, are there people working against you, directly, as has been stated by researchers?

There is no possibility of working against us. We are in the service of the creation. We are attempting to serve those who desire our service. We extend our service to all of the creation. We extend our love to all of the creation. This is in no way limited. There is no possibility existing for a portion of this creation to work, as you say, against us, for it is part of us.

Questioner: Let me state it another way. On one of the tapes, you said that a group of people beyond the constellations of Orion called the Satanians were responsible for the destruction of Atlantis and Lemuria. I believe the message was from Hatonn.

I will relinquish my contact with this instrument and make available another source. The instrument will be conditioned for a short period. We will attempt to serve you in any way possible.

(Unknown channeling)

I am with this instrument. I am using control. There is no concept in the one which spoke for what I tell you. I am aware of your question. There are thoughts in this universe. You think of one thing. Hatonn thinks of one thing. Sometimes there is misunderstanding.

There are people in this universe. They are infinite. They do many things. They speak to you. You listen. They come to you. Into your consciousness come thoughts. What comes into your consciousness is what you desire. You are limited because of your desire to be limited. Everything that you think is possible, if you desire it. Many things have occurred.

I am attempting to tell you that there are things that have occurred in your past, as you call it. There are many of the Creator's children who experienced what they desired. These desires are varied. There are activities which you would like to call evil. Is this possible? A creation that was formed of love supports what you consider evil? Is this in the creation, or is this in your consciousness, or are these two things one thing?

Questioner: It's as much a part of creation as any other duality?

There are many activities that occur upon the surface of the planet at this time that are considered to be evil. There are groups who express themselves in ways that were never considered by the original Thought. The original Thought, however, provided for no limits on expression. It is possible, therefore, for any of the Creator's children to express themselves in any manner that they desire. For this reason, throughout the creation, there are individuals and groups expressing themselves in infinite numbers of ways. You, at your present state of understanding, consider some of the expressions to be evil. We consider them to be expressions. We find, for our purpose, certain expressions to be of a more beneficial nature to our own enjoyment than others. There are, however, expressions of an infinite quality and an infinite quantity occurring throughout the creation. We attempt to serve those within the creation who desire our service. They desire our service because they are interested in our concept of truth. We believe that our concept of truth is correct. In our understanding, we know that our concept is correct. There are many who would disagree with what we understand. This is their privilege. There are such groups as the one to which you have referred. They express themselves in a way that we do not desire.

They do not desire our service. We would freely serve them in any way that we could. However, they do not desire this. Therefore, we do not serve. There are groups known as the type which you have mentioned. The concept of Satan, of which you have spoken, is to some extent correct. This concept is as follows.

The one known as Satan was interested in experiencing the result of a desire, a desire of individualization. A desire for isolation. There are many of the Creator's children who are at present desiring isolation. In our understanding, this is not possible. The creation is full of the expressions of the Creator. Isolation is only possible through the creation of illusion. In creating the illusion of isolation and intense individuality, the one known as Satan has experienced his desire. He has attempted to serve others in giving to them the experience of isolation. And many have sought this experience. For this reason, there are many groups who actively seek to experience isolation. This, then, is occurring, and has occurred, within the creation. This is a part of the original Thought of the creation, that each of the parts might fulfill their desires.

I hope that I have been able to act through this instrument to bring to you our understanding of this concept.

(Transcript ends.)

Monday Meditation, Second Meeting
February 18, 1974

(Unknown channeling)

I am with this instrument. I am Hatonn. I am with you once more in the love and the light of our infinite Creator. I am going to speak, as requested, on the subject of meditation.

We of the Confederation of Planets in the Service of the Infinite Creator suggest that there are certain things that are important if you are to effectively meditate. The first and most important is that you allow the conscious mind to relax. It is necessary to relieve it of thoughts that are of a transient nature and we find that thoughts concerning most of the daily activities are of a transient nature.

In order to allow the mind to become receptive to things of other than a transient nature, it is suggested that you sit in a quiet place with the spine erect. This is the most important of the techniques of meditation. A silent place is very beneficial; however, not necessary. It is more beneficial to an individual who is starting to meditate than it is to an experienced individual.

In order to remove the concepts of an intellectual nature that involve the mind in transitory thoughts, it is suggested that something to fascinate the intellect can be at times of use, such as music, or what you have called a mantra. This, however, is not necessary.

What is necessary is that thoughts that are of an intellectual nature be allowed to leave the consciousness.

Are there any other questions on this subject?

(Pause)

Questioner: What technique do you use for clearing your mind? Mantra? Do you just be quiet? And make sure that your mind slows down, stops?

(The instrument stated that he would speak himself, rather than channeling.)

(Tape ends.)

Wednesday Meditation
February 20, 1974

(R channeling)

I am Hatonn. I greet you at this time in the love and the light of our infinite Creator. I am privileged to be with you at this time.

I would address those of you at this time who are receiving conditioning. We are attempting to form the word "I." We will attempt to form the words with your mouth that we are attempting to communicate to your mind.

This helps you to realize the thought that we are sending. In time, we are sure you will be able to act as an instrument to channel our thoughts to others. It would be of assistance if you could constantly remember why we are doing this.

I will leave this instrument at this time. Adonai, my friends. I am Hatonn.

Thursday Meditation, Second Meeting
February 21, 1974

(R channeling)

I greet you, my friends, in the love and the light of our infinite Creator. It is once again my privilege to be with you.

I would like to speak with you at this time on the subject of desire. This instrument is not receiving my thoughts very well at this time. I will continue through another instrument.

(Don channeling)

I am with this instrument. I am Hatonn. I greet you, my friends, in the love and the light of the infinite Creator. It is a privilege to be with you. I am sorry that [we] could not use the instrument known as R. All that is required is that he continue to avail himself to my contact in order for him to receive my thoughts as does this instrument.

There is a need for him to totally clear his mind of thoughts and to attempt not to analyze what he is saying, but simply to say it, as does this instrument.

There is a common difficulty when using new instruments. That difficulty arises due to their inability to accept that they are receiving thoughts and then speaking the thoughts that they receive. In many cases they believe that these thoughts originate within themselves, and for this reason do not wish to speak those things. It is a simple task to act as does this instrument, as simply a receptacle with no thoughts of his own.

This is something that each of you can learn to practice. It requires meditation and practice in speaking without thinking. This instrument is doing that now—in fact, he has but little knowledge of what is to follow each of the words that he speaks and by long practice is able to clear his mind of the transient thoughts that disrupt a communication such as this one.

I suggest therefore that each of you who is new to this method of communication simply relax and allow the mind to think of nothing. It is better that you make errors in communication—which we later correct—than it is for you to fight, as it were, the concepts which we impress upon you.

I shall continue speaking through this instrument on the subject of desire, for this was a subject of interest, and there are a few points which should be investigated for further use in molding your daily activities.

Desire is a thing that dwells within each of the Creator's children. The desire of each of them, however, is different. What this desire is, is dependent upon the vibratory level of the individual. The lower the vibration, the more basic the desire. The higher the vibration, the higher the desire. You will find, as you increase your vibration through meditation and seeking and service, that your desire will change. The things that are desired by those that are tightly locked within the physical illusion are not those desired by those on the verge of freedom. And the reason for this verge of freedom is the desire, which goes hand in hand with the increased awareness or higher vibration.

How, then, is it possible to achieve what you actually desire, and that is to remove from your thinking desires of any nature except those of unity with the creation and those of service for your fellow man? The technique for doing this, my friends, is a simple one. We have stated it many times. It is to avail yourself to the reality and truth of the creation through meditation, and then act upon the desires generated by the availing. These desires will be somewhat different from the ones you experienced before you spent time in meditation and seeking. The desire to seek will be generated from seeking. It is a self-perpetuating phenomenon. We have belabored this point many times, and we will continue to do this.

Why do we do this, my friends? Why do we continue to tell you to meditate? To understand your desires. To understand yourself, and to become aware of seeking and what it is you actually do. Why do we spend so much time on these subjects that so many on your planet would consider to be trivial? The reason for this, my friends, is that these are the only subjects that are not trivial. It is of no value at all to seek within the illusion that you now know as your physical world. What you seek there, and what you find, is not lasting. It is stated in your world that you cannot take [it] with you. This is fact. What you take with you past the boundaries of the physical illusion is one thing. That is your mind. This mind that you take with you is, in reality, all that there is. You dwell, now, in an illusion that is designed for the schooling of this mind. However, the teachers provided for this schooling are seldom heard. The schooling, however, takes place …

(Tape ends.)

Friday Meditation
February 22, 1974

(R channeling)

[I am Hatonn.] … clear his mind, and not to analyze what is being said. I will continue, on the subject of desire. As I was saying, we cannot overemphasize the need to realize the truth that one only experiences what one desires. We realize this is a completely different way of thinking, on your planet, but it is necessary that you realize this.

When you are meditating, when you are in a receptive state, your mind is being programmed. The things that you program your mind [with] are things that will manifest, for you program your mind with the things that you desire. In other words, whatever you sow in the fertile fields of the mind, you also reap in the physical manifestation. The people of your planet are constantly programming themselves into undesirable experiences. This is completely unnecessary. It is ignorance.

It is difficult to fully comprehend the power that a man has at his use through his desire.

I will leave this instrument at this time. I am Hatonn. Adonai.

Saturday Meditation, First Meeting
February 23, 1974

(Unknown channeling)

I am Hatonn. I greet you, my friends, in the love and the light of our infinite Creator. It is a great privilege to be with you once more this evening. I and my brothers are with you at all times, but it is also a very great privilege to speak with you using an instrument.

I am aware of certain conditions that are occurring upon the planet that you now inhabit. The reason for this awareness is simple. We of the Confederation of Planets in the Service of the Infinite Creator are aware of conditions because of our awareness of truth. We have observed, for many, many of your years, conditions manifesting upon your planet. We are aware of what you would consider to be natural law—the law of the Creation. We are also aware of much of the working of this law. We are at this time attempting to give to this channel some information that he is not familiar with. If you will be patent, we will give him this information.

(Pause)

I am Hatonn. I am with this instrument. I am using control. This instrument will relay my thoughts using some control. This will be necessary for he is not aware of any of the information that he is giving to you.

It is possible to give to this instrument concept which he then channels directly without control. However, the concepts which we have for him at this time are outside what he is aware of. Therefore, it will be necessary to use control. Please be patient.

I am Hatonn, and am using control …

(There is a period of nonsense channeling while control is developed.)

We will rest for a short time between each attempt at communication to allow the instrument to rest. This type of communication is quite tiring.

(Pause)

I am with the instrument. I am Hatonn. There will be conditions manifesting shortly upon your planet, conditions that will be obvious to many of the people of your planet. They will be conditions of physical change. These conditions will bring about much seeking among the peoples upon your surface for one reason or another. It will be that in this time there be many channels such as yourselves there to speak, using our thoughts, for we have an understanding of these conditions and of their consequence.

This instrument at this time is being controlled, for many reasons. One of the reasons is that he is reluctant to speak of these things. However, at this time it is necessary for we must speak to you, the ones in this room.

There are problems that will confront the people of this planet very shortly. We have said this before, but the time now grows very short. We have ways of telling this. There will be a need for channels of communication, whether they be of the type of this instrument, who can directly channel our thoughts, or whether they simply be of the type able to relay this information from groups such as this one to groups who seek it and direct them to a group. We have far too few groups of this type to accomplish that which we seek to accomplish: to bring to the people who desire our aid the aid that they desire.

Please be patient. I will condition this instrument.

R: Hatonn, what kind of time span? Two years? Two months? Not that it makes much difference, but …

If the one who asked the question will avail himself to my contact, I will attempt to use him.

(R channeling)

I am with this instrument. I am Hatonn. I cannot answer your question as specifically as you would wish. I can state, however, that the time will be much less than the span of time that you would call two years. It is because of this that we find that there is some amount of urgency in reaching the people of your planet.

I will now leave this instrument and continue through another.

(Don channeling)

I am again with this instrument. I am Hatonn. I am with you, my friends. I will attempt to use this instrument now. I was saying that there is a shortness of time in alerting a sufficient number of the people of this planet to the possibility of communicating with us who are of the Confederation in the Service of the Infinite Creator. I am sorry that I have had to use control, but this instrument requires such control when he is channeling information of a specific nature. He requires this and desires it, for he has had experience with communications of this type and finds control to be beneficial in communicating the concepts that are of a specific nature.

I will now continue. Shortly upon your planet there will be conditions which will alert all of the people to something. Many will not understand what has happened, but they will know that something has happened. It is a situation where the people of the planet will have their attention focused upon something that they will all be able to speak of in common. It will be a natural phenomenon of a great magnitude, from your point of view. This will be something that many of the people who dwell upon your surface will fear. However, groups such as this one will be able to aid them by not fearing this phenomenon. There is no fear necessary.

I will continue now, since this instrument is able to receive my thoughts without using control. My friends, many of the people of this planet will know, for the first time in their present life, that there is a creation, because, my friends, the illusion that man has created upon this surface will suddenly became totally insignificant. They will be awakened from their slumber and look about them in amazement, and see about them the creation of the Father for this first time in its reality.

Unfortunately, this awakening for most of them will include the reaction of fear. And this was never intended by the Creator. And this reaction, my friends, will be because of their ignorance. These of you who wish to serve with us of the Confederation of Planets in the Service of the Creator will have the task of educating those of the people of this planet who would seek an education. And, my friends, many, many will do this. For, as I say, many will have been awakened,

It will not be an easy task, and there will be many at your door. And there will be much misunderstanding. My friends, there is one thing that is always understood, and that is love. Your demonstration of this principle will be the greatest benefit that you can offer to those that seek to learn.

It will be necessary that you prepare yourselves so that you demonstrate your knowledge of truth and the creation of the Creator. It is written in your holy works, "Yea, though I walk through the valley of the shadow of death, I will fear no evil, for Thou art with me." These words are not false words, my friends. Those words are meant for you. You have heard it spoken through a channel that, "He does not leave their shepherds without their staffs." These are not false words, my friends. All that is necessary is that you desire to seek, and then desire to serve, and then you shall do both of these things.

You shall seek understanding, and you shall gain understanding. And you shall serve, and give to those who seek it, understanding, for this is the Creator's way. There will be many, many of the peoples of this planet who cannot be served, for they will not seek. They will not seek the understanding that you offer. They will not be able to comprehend these concepts for the illusion which they have created will be much too strong.

This is unfortunate. And these are the ones that you will not be able to serve. And this will sadden you. But there will be a great, great number who will seek. And these are the ones whom you will be able to serve. And this will give you great joy. For this, my friends, is the source of true joy: to serve. To serve in a way that provides that which is actually desired.

Within each of us—within each individual in the entire creation—there is this desire to seek. But many, many have buried this so very deeply within them that it will take even more than you shall shortly experience to uncover it. Concern yourselves, therefore, with these who seek.

R: What is the event that is going to be happening?

(Don channeling)

I am again with this instrument. I will use control. There are several events that will occur. There will be events of a physical nature. These events will be, from the point of view of those who are living within the illusion, of a very destructive nature. However, there is no such thing as destruction. There is only change. This you must understand. If you understand this, then you will understand the truth of what is to occur.

There will be change, a physical change. This change will be very beneficial. However, the people of this planet who view those changes from their present state of ignorance will consider them to be quite destructive.

This is unfortunate. However, the people of this planet have had a sufficient length of time to become educated. They have, however, sought to educate themselves in the ways of their illusion rather than the ways of the Creator. This illusion is so strong in their understanding that most of them have no awareness, in a waking sense, of reality. These people will be very difficult to communicate with. They will view the changes in their immediate creation as destructive and irreversible.

R: Well, is it going to be an earthquake, like, or a depression, or what?

The changes will be of a physical nature. The depression of which you speak is of no consequence. It would be viewed as nothing compared to the physical changes that will occur. It will be necessary for members of groups such as this one who wish to serve to understand fully the reality of these changes, and to understand fully the accuracy of the statement made in your holy book which states that, "Although you walk through the valley of the shadow of death you will fear no evil." This must be kept uppermost in your consciousness, for you will walk through this valley and you will demonstrate to those who seek your knowledge of truth, and only your ability to demonstrate this knowledge will alert those who seek the knowledge that you are a true and knowing channel, for many false channels will at this time be lost, for they will not be able to demonstrate their knowledge of truth, for they will cling to the illusion that has surrounded them and will display the fear that this illusion brings upon them.

This change is looked upon by those of us who understand it as an extremely beneficial change. It is also looked upon, by those members of groups such as this one who have realized the truth of this information, as extremely beneficial to all the peoples of this planet. It will be difficult for some of the members of groups such as this one to demonstrate an understanding of these truths, since they have been strongly affected by the illusion that has been created by the people of this planet. However, this understanding is a necessity to be demonstrated.

R: What is going to be happening, exactly?

Physical change, of all types.

R: And it's going to be within the next two years?

Don: This is me, and I don't get a thing on that.

(A period of conversation follows in which Dave and Ralph wonder aloud just what will be happening.)

(Don channeling)

I am Hatonn. I am again with this instrument. I am sorry that I have not made myself precisely clear. I am with you, my friends, in the love and the light of our infinite Creator.

There will be massive destruction wrought upon your surface. It will be of such a nature as to totally change the surface of your planet. This destruction is within your planet at this time. It has been put there by thought. It has been put there by the thought of the population of this planet through thousands of years of thinking this thought. This thought is of a vibratory nature. You are at this time passing through the last portion of what you know as the third-density vibration. Shortly, your planet will be sufficiently within what you know as the fourth-density vibration. At this time, there will be a disharmony between the thought that creates the vibration that is your planet, and the thought that dwells within the density that is the fourth.

Much energy will be released of a physical nature. This energy will create physical changes within your planet. There will be changes within your land masses, changes in your atmosphere.

R: Changes in the atmosphere?

Changes in all of the physical manifestations of your planet. This will be of a nature that will be considered to be cataclysmic. This is a very good thing. However, it will not be considered good by those that are within the illusion.

Labeling this change good or bad is something that is dependent upon the individual observing the change and his orientation. My friends, the reason for this change being of a cataclysmic nature is that the thought that has been generated upon and in your planet for the past several thousands of years is a thought that is out of harmony with the new vibration that your planet now goes into. The Creator never conceived of the condition that is shortly to manifest upon your planet. This condition is manifested as a result of the desire of all the individuals that dwell on this planet. They are not aware of this desire, but their desire has created this.

They have created a condition by their desire that is shortly to be severely out of harmony with where they will physically be. Due to this, there will be a large energy release, which will manifest itself upon your planet in the form of earthquakes, storms, volcanic eruptions and in fact a shift of the poles of your planet with respect to their orientation in space.

This change that will shortly manifest itself upon your planet is, as I have said, a result of the mismatching of vibrations of your planet and its new position in space. This change will alert many of the people of your planet who are very lightly slumbering, and many of the ones who are slumbering relatively deep. Many of those people will at this time be what is known in many of your religions as "saved." It will save them, because they will get the violent awakening that is necessary to cause them to raise their vibrations that last amount that is necessary to get them off the fence, so to speak.

There will be those who are more deeply slumbering, so to speak, who will not make the transition. It is up to you to provide those, who will be awakened with the information that they desire. We have stated that this transition is both good and bad. Ultimately, in its most broad sense, it is a good transition; however, it is an unnecessary transition. In a normal transition there would be no energy released, since in a normal transition the vibration of the planet would match closely enough and be in harmony with the new and higher vibration. This would result in no energy release, and the planet would continue in a relatively normal sense from a lower vibration to the higher. Your planet is an aberration in the evolution of the spirit of the people of the planet and the planet. The change that will take place will be a beneficial change. However, the mechanics of the change will seem anything but beneficial.

Those of the people who dwell upon this surface at this time who are totally aware of the results of this change, and the reason for it, will not in any way be affected by this change. These who are not aware of this, but who are aware of this in a spiritual sense, will be affected only emotionally, because they will not understand. These are the people we wish to communicate with.

You might ask, why is [it] that we cannot do this using your networks of communication at the present? It would seem simpler to many of you that we just present this information to the governments of the world at this time and have it given to the people of the world at this time.

We are unable to do this. We are unable to do this because many of the people upon this planet do not desire this information. And this is the only reason that we are prevented from giving it to them in a direct and unquestionable sense. Since they do not desire it, it is necessary that we present it in such a manner that it can be rejected totally by them. This may be a difficult concept for some of the people who dwell upon this planet to understand. But it is our understanding of the intention of the Creator in providing for the desires of all of his children to be met at all times.

In the future, when the conditions have manifested of which we speak, and many of the people upon this planet have initiated seeking, there will be groups of people who, having initiated seeking and having been educated by channels such as this one and channels of other groups, will then be in a state of understanding sufficiently enlightened so that they may meet with us directly. We will at that time provide direct and physical aid to these people. There are many, many more of us than you could imagine waiting to act in this fashion, in the service of the Creator, for that is how we label ourselves. And this service at this time will include a direct service to those groups of people who are desiring our service. It will be necessary, however, that these groups be somewhat isolated from groups of individuals who do not desire our service. This will be done in many ways, and these will be made apparent to you at a later time, for you do not at this time have an understanding of the many, many ways in which we can serve you.

We have said many times in the past that it is necessary for you to meditate. We have said this as an instruction to allow you to erase the illusion that has grasped so many of the people of this planet within its clutches. This meditation that you perform brings you to an understanding of reality. Reality is all about you. But it is not the illusion that continually occupies the thinking of the larger number of your planet.

We have said this to you many times. It is up to you to understand what we are saying. And there is only one way to understand it. This way is to understand it in meditation.

I am at this time going to ask if there are any other questions?

R: Can you give us some confirmation on the time?

I am going to try to use an instrument that is new to channeling. If you will avail yourself.

(Carla channeling)

I am Hatonn. I am with this instrument. I am having much difficulty with this instrument.

(An unrecorded question was asked: "Can you land and meet us on the land we bought in Mario County?")

(Don channeling)

I will speak through this instrument. It is impossible to own a piece of the creation. I do not wish to sound as if I do not appreciate the problems which you find within your illusion, for the illusion is very strong, and this is the reason that we have recommended that you avail yourself to truth, in meditation, for all of these things are within you. You have simply been given the thoughts of those that built the illusion that is so strong on your planet.

There will be aid given to groups. These groups will number in the tens of thousands. It will not be necessary to convince the illusion that the groups have rights and privileges. These rights and privileges are the gifts of the Creator. The illusion will very rapidly cease to exist, as the change of which I have spoken manifests itself.

R: Is physical contact with you possible?

This is possible. However, as this instrument is aware, it is necessary that this be desired by each member of the group.

R: So, if four or five people were on the property and everyone there stated during a period of meditation that we wanted you to land, that you would?

This is not true. I have stated that it is necessary that each individual desire this contact.

R: To want something and to desire it, then, is not the same?

I have stated that each individual in the Creation receives exactly what he desires. This statement is true. Many of the people of this planet receive things that they believe that they do not desire. However, in truth, they desire precisely what they are receiving. In order for us to meet with a group of your group, it will be necessary that this desire is a true desire. This can only be achieved by meditation. This can only be achieved if the individual desires it.

The interpretation of this concept, "desire," is different in your language and in our understanding. Desire is the word that is used to most or best conform to the concept. However, to understand your desire it will be necessary that you avail yourself to this understanding in meditation.

We have met with individuals of this planet many times. We have met with those who desired this meeting.

R: How about if everybody here really desired to meet you? Could you do that?

I have stated that if this desire manifested itself, then the meeting could take place.

R: So, what you're saying is the people in this group right here don't really desire to meet you?

(Inaudible)

D: I feel like I desire stronger control. Is that a confusion on my own part, or is that just a means of easing me into channeling?

Through meditation you can know your desire. I will give an example. I use this example because it is best known to the members of this group. There was a teacher once, known to you as Jesus. This man had desire. His desire was to serve his fellow man by demonstrating a knowledge of the Creator's love. Through this desire he accomplished things that you know as miracles. This man had true desire. It is only possible to achieve true desire by initiating this yourself. If you are able to initiate a desire that is a true desire, then you will achieve what you desire, just as the man known to you as Jesus achieved what he desired. He achieved what he desired because he desired to serve his fellow man in a way that was in harmony with the desires of the Creator, for he realized his unity with the Creator.

We desire to serve our fellow man, as he desired to serve. We desire to serve you. We must serve you to the best of our ability. This will include meeting with you when this will result in what you desire. What you desire is that you grow in a spiritual sense, so that you may better serve your fellow man, fulfilling your desire, his desire, and the desire of the Creator. When our meeting with you will increase your spiritual growth and therefore meet your desire, we will desire to meet with you. I hope that I have made this point more clear.

You are desiring at this time what you are aware of that is desirable. The reason that you are not aware of what you actually desire is that you are conditioned to understand that which has been given to you as the illusion. If you will avail yourself to truth through meditation, then you will understand what you desire. What you desire is that you grow in a spiritual sense in order to serve your fellow man and in order to fulfill your desire, his desire, and the desire of the Creator.

R: So, to spend energy to meet you would not— would be a rather selfish use of energy?

This would not be your true desire.

D: Am I to understand then that the most important thing is to think within ourselves?

The most important thing is for you to meditate, for these things will be made clear to you by this simple process. This instrument has spent several of these past years in meditation. For this reason, he is aware of the things that he just channeled. For this reason, it is only necessary for me to give him these concepts in order for him to channel without control, for he already is quite sure of the veracity of what is relayed through him.

It is necessary to use control at times when we are attempting to give information of a very specific kind. It is possible to achieve a knowledge of all of these things simply be availing yourself in meditation, for they are within all of the individuals of this planet. This instrument, however, was not aware of the exact relationship of desire with respect to the evolution of the spiritual self that was just communicated through him. He was aware of those concepts in a conceptual sense rather then a specific sense. For this reason it is more effective to channel through the instrument, rather than to use him as a teacher, for we have found that it is very difficult for an individual to express the concepts which he achieves through meditation with words, which were never designed with those concepts in mind. We are simply at this time confirming what this instrument had considered conceptual truths. These were given to him in meditation many years ago.

There are several ways of becoming aware of your desires but there is only one that we recommend: this is meditation. Each of you has all of the information that this instrument has given you before he gave it to you. You have all of the information that he is going to give to you. We of the Confederation of Planets in the Service of the Infinite Creator are unable to give you any new information, for you are already in possession of all the information that exists. Each individual in the creation possesses all of the information in the creation, for each individual is a portion of the creation. The only reason for a lack of availability of this information is that this individual has desired to limit himself for the sake of his own experience.

For this reason, we have stated many times that it is necessary to meditate. Through this process you regain the communication with yourself that is necessary to be aware of all the information of the creation. There is one, single, simple Thought behind all of it. This Thought is the original Thought of the creation. In your language, this thought is expressed as love. This word most closely approaches the concept, although it is totally inadequate for an expression of the love that is the creation.

The process of giving information to you through a vocal channel such as this one is at times quite varied, and is only a small aid in creating a condition by which you can avail yourself of the total knowledge of the creation. We do find, however, that in using channels such as this one, that there is a service performed in helping those who desire it to seek the knowledge that is within them.

There are some misunderstandings about the uses of instruments. For this reason, a new instrument sometimes has difficulty in channeling our thoughts, for he confuses his thoughts with our thoughts. But in all of these processes, we are simply awakening in you the part of you that is us, and the part of us that is you. It is what you might consider a reduction of your isolation, so that instead of being isolated, you are in unity with the creation. For this reason, it is sometimes difficult for those of you who are so much conditioned by the illusion that is created on this planet to understand within the boundaries of the language that we are forced to use when speaking through an instrument the concepts which we are attempting to give you. It is necessary that an instrument such as this one spend much time in meditation, so that these concepts may be developed within him. A new instrument is able to communicate relatively simple concepts or messages of a completely controlled nature. If he is to develop into an instrument such as this one, or such as other instruments who are able to communicate concepts of a more involved …

(Tape ends.) ❧

Saturday Meditation, Second Meeting
February 23, 1974

(Don channeling)

I am Hatonn. I greet you, my friends, in the love and in the light of our infinite Creator. It is a very great privilege to once more be able to speak with you. We, of the Confederation of Planets in the Service of the Infinite Creator, are always very privileged to be able to speak to those, the people of Earth, who wish …

I was saying, we of the Confederation of Planets in the Service of the Infinite Creator are always very privileged to speak with those, the people of Earth, who desire our services.

This evening I would like to tell you a story. This, I believe, is an interesting story, for it has several aspects. There once was a man who dwelled upon this planet who had such wealth he had what he thought to be great security, for with his wealth he was able to do or have done whatever he wished.

I will continue. I am having some difficulty. I will condition the instrument.

(Pause)

As I was saying, there was a man who lived upon this planet who had such wealth, in this wealth he saw great security, but this wealth that he had was not a wealth you would interpret today to be wealth, for the wealth that this man had was a wealth or knowledge, and in this wealth of knowledge, he saw great security, for the knowledge that he had was the knowledge of truth. And in this truth, there was knowledge of security. For, my friends, in the knowledge of truth, there is the only security.

Today, upon your planet, security is sought by your peoples. They seek wealth as security and yet they do not have it for they do not know what wealth is. Wealth is thought of today in its material sense by most of the people of your planet. Only a very few understand true wealth. We are attempting to give you true wealth and true security. The wealth that we are attempting to give you cannot be taken from you. Even though you may leave your physical body in death, it is a wealth that can be carried with you. It is a security that encompasses all of the Creation, for in this knowledge and in this wealth you are once more in total harmony with all that exists. And, therefore, you are in possession of all that exists, and this is the ultimate wealth.

It has been said that you should think not of what is to come tomorrow, but you should exist for a service in the present and take no thought of that which will come to you in the future. This is truth, my friends, for everything has been provided for you. It is not understood, at present, by your peoples, but it is impossible to create a security by acting in such a way as to accumulate material wealth. This security does not exist. It exists only within the illusion that you now enjoy.

It is very difficult for a peoples such as yours, who have been conditioned to think strictly within the boundaries of their present illusion, to break from these thoughts and to exist in the true creation. If this is done, there is no need for the accumulation of wealth in any sense, for there is nothing to accumulate. You are then in possession of everything that exists, for you are part of it and it is part of you.

It is very difficult for an individual living in your society to realize this, for all of the thoughts impressed upon him or those about him indicate that what I am telling you is erroneous and that he must, in order to survive and in order to hold his rightful place within the society, accumulate wealth. He must plan for each day in the future, in order that he will continue in surroundings that he designs for himself.

My friends, surroundings in which you exist are not designed by any of us. They were designed by the Creator. The food that you eat was designed by the Creator. The sun that brings you the light and the warmth that sustain you was designed by the Creator. Everything was provided for you. Man on Earth has strayed into darkness and he has built an illusion that causes him to think that it is necessary to struggle against problems that he considers to be a natural part of the Creation. Problems against which he struggles are not a natural part of the creation. These problems that he creates in his struggling, as one entangled in a mesh of brambles, becomes more entangled in struggling. So does man on Earth become entangled in his own manifestations. In his lack of understanding of the true source of supply of that which supports his life, not only in the physical as he appreciates it at present but through all other stratum of existence, he is supported and continued in all instances by one source, the Creator.

And yet, man on Earth continues to struggle, continues to enmesh himself more deeply and deeply into the web of his illusion, confusing his thoughts and believing sincerely that the Creator will not provide for him what he needs. And this belief is generated to such an extent that the illusion suggest to him that the provisions are not available. And he does not find them and he therefore suffers. But who is created to suffer? He has created it himself in his lack of understanding, and this is not necessary, my friends.

We of the Confederation of Planets in the Service of the Infinite Creator want for nothing; we do not struggle against that which was given to us freely. We accept it, for it is a part of the creation and it is ours, for all of the Creation is ours, for we are a part of that all.

It is impossible to sustain the physical life upon this planet without assimilating foods that are provided for you. This is what is believed by the people of your planet. My friends, there is no lack in this creation for anything. There is ample supply at all times and at all places. It is only necessary that this be realized. I am aware that it is difficult to realize the truth of what I am attempting to tell you at this time, for within your illusion the concept of supply is quite extraordinarily changed from that as we understand. Consider the birds and animals that exist in what you consider a wild state. The Creator has provided for them that which they need. Unfortunately, upon this planet there are certain lacks in awareness that extend even to the animal life, which is brought by the general state of ignorance that permeates the thinking of a major portion of the population.

I do not wish to seem judgmental in stating that a condition of ignorance prevails. However, it is the most accurate way of expressing the understanding of those who dwell upon this planet. They are not aware of their true position and their true being in this universe. An awareness of this is all that is necessary for an individual to function as he was intended. All of the supply for the sustenance—what you understand as physical life on your planet—is provided by one source. That source is the Creator. If this was not supplied by the Creator, then you would not exist in a physical form. It is not possible to exist in the physical form as you now appreciate it, unless all of these things are provided for you. If all of these things are provided for you, how is it possible to doubt the objective of the Provider?

The men of science of your planet, bound in the state of ignorance of which I spoke, have interpreted the source or provisions that sustain you as occurring as a function of chance. We think this to be unusually ignorant. We suggest that you spend time considering how your physical beings are supported by those foods and other necessities that are given to you. Man on Earth has created an illusion which is very complex with respect to his concept of sustenance of his physical body. He has created an illusion that is very complex with respect to his interpretation of his concept of security. None of these illusions are even remotely correct. The truth of his sustenance is, as are all truths, related to a single source. For this reason, it has been stated that it is not necessary to give thought of the future. To live in the present and serve the Creator in any way that you find opportune; this is your reason for existence—to serve. For this is the Creator's reason for existence—to serve.

My friends, each of you is part of the Creator. Understand this principle and you will no longer be burdened with the illusion that has been passed on to you by your fellow man, who has dwelled for very long in a state of ignorance. Why should you learn lessons from those who know nothing, who know less than nothing, for they have built a complex illusion that is not even remotely related to truth? This creates many problems and difficulties for those that accept it. We suggest that you reject it in all of its forms and return to the understanding of your true being which you have within you. Become aware of your position in this universe. Become aware of your at-oneness with the creation, and then go forth and serve your fellow man, for in this way, you create that condition which the Creator desired and in this way, you are able to function in exact harmony with the original Thought.

When this occurs, all of the illusion is meaningless. For you then are your own creator, and all that you desire is yours. For, my friends, the desires you have at that state of understanding are far different from the desires that exist within the illusion. So give them up, if you wish, for they are desires which have been given to you by those who are quite ignorant. And, my friends, their ignorance is no more their fault than it is your fault. It is simply an ignorance due to a lack of education.

We of the Confederation of Planets in the Service of the Infinite Creator are here to remedy this lack of education. We will continue to attempt to speak to you on many subjects until we have accomplished a service. This service must be desired by those to whom we give it. If it is not desired, then we cannot serve them, for this is our understanding of truth.

I will leave this instrument at this time. It is my sincere wish that I have been of service in speaking to you this evening on our understanding of truth. I will leave this instrument at this time. It is my sincere wish that I have been of service in speaking to you this evening on our understanding of the concept of supply and the concept of the state of being of the individual with respect to the rest of the creation. I am Hatonn. Adonai vasu.

Monday Meditation, First Meeting
February 25, 1974

(Don channeling)

I am Hatonn. I am with the instrument. I greet you, my friends, in the love and in the light of our infinite Creator. It is once more a great privilege to be with you. It is always a very great privilege to be of service, for there are far too many of your people to serve. We are here with you this evening. We will condition you. We will speak through this instrument.

Be patient, for all things come to those who seek. Seeking, my friends, is the most important thing that you do. All of us in this creation seek. What we seek is the important thing. Many of your people seek, but they do not seek things that are of value. Every day you are given suggestions of things that you should seek, but if you will examine them you will find that most of them are of very little value. When you seek that truth that is permanent, and everlasting, then you seek that which is of significance.

We of the Confederation of Planets in the Service of the Infinite Creator are here to help your people with their seeking. As I have said before, there are all too few of them who are even aware that such seeking is important. Actually, they have chosen their physical incarnation, at this time, for the purpose of seeking the truth of which I speak. They are, however, for the most part unaware of this. This is unfortunate. We are attempting to remedy it in many ways and we are enlisting as much aid as we possibly can, for your people, at this time, are in very great need of knowledge of how and what to seek. They have been seeking for so long within the material realms that most of them are totally unaware that seeking is possible within the spiritual realms.

The religions of your world have, for the most part, eliminated the responsibility for individual seeking. This, however, is an extremely erroneous point of view. It is very necessary for the individual to seek truth, knowledge and the ultimate and supreme level of the Creator if he is to grow in strength and spirit and understanding and take at some future time his rightful position in the Father's creation. This, my friends, is why seeking is so important. It is the only way for your people to get from where they are to where they should be. All of the people of this planet should not be where they are at this time. Unfortunately, they are in a state of trance. I have spoken of this before and at this time will reiterate that they are truly in a state of trance. They have been hypnotized by suggestions of social systems which have been built up by erroneous thinking through many centuries. The only way to break the chain of foolishness that reigns upon your planet is to awaken your people with proper information.

Unfortunately, as I have said, most of them at this time are not really seeking this type of information for they see no need of it. Your societies have grown to such a state of confusion that the importance of that which is real has been subjugated to nothingness; where the importance of that which is man has been elevated to the only state of importance. Unfortunately, this condition is not being remedied at the rate that we would hope for at this time. We are striving and doing our utmost to help your people and to make them aware of the situation they are in, but they are not paying attention. We can only do so much. The more attention your people pay, the more that we can do. It is a simple matter of direct free will. If the population of a planet asks for our services then we may give them freely; if only a portion of that population asks, then we must limit our services. If none of the population asks for our services, we are unable to give any of our services. For this reason, you find us in a state of hiding, you might say, at this time. For far too few of the people of this planet have asked for our services. Consequently, we must act through instruments such as this one to speak to you and tell you of the problems that now exist for us and for you and for the rest of the population of your planet.

We suggest that you, as individuals, attempt to evolve as best you can on an individual basis and at the same time attempt to, in your own way, act as examples of this evolution. By doing this, you will draw attention by maintaining a knowledge of truth. Through meditation you will be examples. You can be nothing else. Those of your people who are in great need of truth and of understanding will notice that you are different. They will notice that you will have an inner peace and tranquility. They will notice many things about you, then they will seek you out for information. At this time, you will be able to serve them as we are able to serve you.

It is a difficult thing, my friends, to serve all of the people of your planet that wish service. Many of them do not know that service is available and they do not know how to recognize the service once it is offered. Each one of them is a different problem and there is not too much time left, my friends. Shortly, many of your people will be seeking much information. More and more of them, at this time, are seeking information. But they are difficult to communicate with because of their mixing with those who do not wish to be served. We must, therefore, increase the number of channels such as this one and we must increase the amount of information that is given to your people by other means.

I am sorry that I have taken a little more time than I expected to on this particular aspect. But at this time, we consider the dissemination of our information to the people of your planet of utmost importance. It must be remembered through, that caution must be used. And, as a general rule, the information should be presented so that it may be rejected. It is necessary to create within the individual an intense seeking that is his own, rather than to force upon him information that he does not request. Therefore, act as you are directed through your daily meditations. And we will, with you, succeed in bringing the truth that your people require at this time to them.

I will leave this instrument now. I am Hatonn. I shall speak with you at a later time. I have been very pleased to be with you this evening. Adonai vasu borragus.

Monday Meditation, Second Meeting
February 25, 1974

(Don channeling)

I greet you, my friends, in the love and in the light of our infinite Creator. It is a great pleasure to be with you this evening. As always, it is a very great privilege to be with you.

I have been listening to your conversation. This instrument is correct in what he says about his reception about what we give him. He is an advanced instrument. He has been practicing a long time. He is able, now, to make his mind a blank and this is necessary for ease of transmission. It is only when you clog your mind with your own thoughts that it is very difficult for us to get through to you. This is why we request that you spend time in meditation. This is the only way that you will become practiced enough to transmit our thoughts as easily as this instrument does.

He has been practicing, now, for many years. It was difficult for him at first because the people of your planet are not used to this form of communication. And, therefore, are not aware of the simplicity with which it may be accomplished. It is not at all complex, my friends, and thinking about nothing is not at all complex. It is, as has been stated by this instrument, something like learning to ride a bicycle. Once you learn it, you do not forget it, but you must practice it to maintain a high degree of efficiency. Sometimes, this instrument has difficulties and at those times it is necessary for us to condition him further.

This conditioning, my friends, is simply a means of causing the individual to be helped to think of nothing. We hope that each of you, here in this room, will learn to do the same because then you will be able to receive and speak our thoughts as readily as this instrument. He sometimes begins to wander in his thoughts as we transmit to him. When he begins to think of something or begins to think of the transmission, rather than simply relaying it to you, it sometimes becomes garbled, shall I say, or somewhat difficult. For this reason it is necessary at times to stop and condition him once more and then resume the communication. Errors are possible due to this same phenomena, but we correct these if these are out of limits of what we wish to give you.

The limits of what we wish to give you are always limited by those receiving. We can only transmit that which is acceptable to those who are receiving it. We cannot, shall I say, go over the heads of the receivers. For this reason, we are hopeful that the grades of people who receive our communication are not too mixed. We would request that groups of relative advancement be made. Putting a new person, who is unfamiliar with what we have to give to you, with a group that is somewhat advanced in its study of philosophy limits us to a communication that would be acceptable to a new person. It is, therefore, requested that you keep this in mind when forming groups of people who listen to our communication.

My brother Laitos is in the room with you this evening. And he will condition you as this instrument is speaking. I have concluded this portion of my communication and I will allow this instrument to rest for a short period. And then I will continue with another communication. I thank you very much for your patience in listening to me. And I hope that what I have given to you will be of service to you in your evolvement as channels.

(Pause)

I am Laitos. I greet you, my friends, in the love and in the light of our infinite Creator. I am with you this evening in the room. It is my duty to condition each of the new instruments. You will feel my conditioning. It is only necessary that you think of nothing and you will be most receptive to my conditioning. Please allow your body to follow any of my suggestions. You will feel the effects of my conditioning. Do not be alarmed, for this is very natural. It has been done for thousands of your people.

It is somewhat different from what you normally experience. But we, of the Confederation in the Service of the Infinite Creator, are very familiar with these types of contacts. They are a way for us to work across the boundary that seems to separate you from us. Actually, there is no separation. It is an illusion, but it is very strong for you at this time. So, please be patient and help me to work through this barrier and communicate with you. It is a great privilege to have this duty and I am skilled in doing this. Please bear with me for it takes a little bit of experimentation for each new vocal channel, for each person is, shall I say, tuned in a slightly different manner. Therefore, try to relax and think of nothing.

I will leave this instrument now. I am Laitos. Adonai.

(Pause)

I am Hatonn. I greet you, my friends, once more, in the love and in the light of our infinite Creator. We have been conditioning this instrument. It is helpful even in the case of an advanced instrument to condition him at times.

We will now meditate. Concentrate, my friends, on that which is all. Let your thoughts become one. For all is one. Become aware of the one great All. Become aware that you are one and that one is all. Do not separate yourselves from anything. My friends, you are not separate from anything. There is only one thing. That one thing is truth. Truth is. It is all about you. It speaks to you. Listen to it and you will know it. Truth is in your sky. It is in your trees, in your fields and in everything that is the Creator's. Do not be concerned with anything but this truth.

Questioner:

(A question was asked about changes in physical bodies due to physical vibration.)

I am Hatonn. I am with this instrument. I am requested by him to identify myself. I am Hatonn. I am with you in the love and in the light of our infinite Creator. These changes will have an effect upon physical bodies. They will destroy physical bodies. This has been occurring upon your planet for long in its history. There has been a physical destruction of what you know as the physical body.

I shall now speak through this instrument using no control.

I have said that there will be the destruction of physical bodies upon your planet. This is a necessary consequence of the physical change. We, of the Confederation of Planets in the Service of the Infinite Creator, are aware that within your illusion much attachment is in evidence with respect to the physical. The body that you know as your physical body is as much a part of the illusion that you now experience as the illusion created by the people upon this planet. It is only necessary to avail yourself to the knowledge of reality to understand the reason for what you consider the physical body.

It has been stated earlier this evening that it is necessary to understand the words written in one of the holy books that have been given to your people. These stated that even though you should walk through the valley of the shadow of death that you would fear no evil. These words have reference to that which you consider as the destruction of the physical body.

R: So what you're saying is that regardless of whether or not people raise their vibration, their physical body is going to be destroyed.

Your physical body will be destroyed. You are aware of this. There is not a single physical body upon the surface of this planet that will not be destroyed. At some time in what you consider to be the future. You have an awareness of this and expect it as do all of the people of your planet. This is what you know as death. It is a natural cycle for the physical body to be destroyed. It is alarming to most of the people who inhabit this planet to assume that their physical body will be destroyed before they expect it to be destroyed. However, it is possible at your present level of awareness in the physical to expect this destruction at any particular time.

R: Will all the bodies of all the people of this planet be destroyed during the changes that you have stated or will some people be taken with their bodies in your craft off the planet?

There will be a change of density of vibration. The physical body as you now know will not be in evidence in the fourth density of vibration. You would have no need for this dense a body. If you were to retain it, you would not pass into the fourth density. Do you wish to retain this and remain in the third density of vibration? I think not. Do you know what you desire? What is death? What is the physical body?

R: What's the process of translation that you have spoken of? Is it what we call death, or is it something else?

There is no death. The reason that you presently have the concept of death is that you are unable to communicate in your present state of awareness with those whom you consider dead. There will be no inability to communicate between levels of awareness when the planet has moved into what is considered fourth density. Therefore, there will be no awareness of the concept of death. All physical bodies that now exist upon this planet will in the future not exist. This would occur even if there was no change of density, for it has occurred in a cyclical manner throughout all of the history of this planet. Why would this process be of any importance?

R: Should we practice death during our meditation, so to speak? To make the transition easier? Practice the process of leaving our bodies?

There is only one thing to practice. That is meditation.

R: How long is it going to be before the big bang?

Don: So that he can get some more credit cards and cancel some more appointments.

(Don channeling)

I am Hatonn. I am Hatonn. I am with this instrument. I am with you, my friends, in the love and in the light of our infinite Creator. This instrument, due to his awareness of the nature of this question, is reluctant to attempt to channel this specific answer. However, I have given to him the concept, the technique for arriving at an answer to this question. The system of numbering to be used will involved years in your language. The number derived will be the number of years predicted by us to the best of our ability.

We are sorry that it is necessary to use this technique. However, this instrument is reluctant to attempt to channel information of this specific a nature for several reasons. One of these reasons is that it is information that is not desired. However, my friends, it is necessary, at this time, that we act within specific boundaries and limitations. Therefore, we are suggesting once more to this instrument that he give to you the ideas that we have presented to him.

I will leave this instrument at this time. I am Hatonn. Adonai vasu borragus. ☙

Monday Meditation, Third Meeting
February 25, 1974

(Unknown channeling)

I am Philip. I am Philip of The Brotherhood of the Seven Rays. I am using control over this instrument. I will speak with you this evening in love and light. I shall address you shortly as I condition the instrument. Please be patient. We are now with the instrument. I am Philip of The Brotherhood of the Seven Rays. Yes, my friends, I am here with you this evening and I am aware of your seeking. It is very difficult loving in the society that you now enjoy. So spend much time in seeking, for you are constantly confused and drawn into unimportant problems. Your daily lives are beset by many difficulties. And this makes it difficult for you to seek the Father through meditation. My friends, the Father is infinite and in everything you do and in everything you see and in everything you touch there is nothing but the Father. For He is and you are. He and you are one and I and you are one and we are all one, beloved ones. There is nothing else but the Father and I. When you go through your daily lives, know this truth. And demonstrate it in everything that you do. For this, my friends, is that which is truth. This is the truth that you seek. This the truth that we all seek. For when we know this, my friends, there is nothing else to know.

Throughout your planet, my friends, there are many, many peoples of many, many races and each of them think many, many things. But you must see them and you must know them as one. For each of them is a part of the Father as a part of you. And all that is necessary for you to realize this is to open your eyes and see. For man on Earth has these eyes, but what he sees is, for the most part, something that he designed for himself to see. The Father, my friends, made the creation. We are the creation. We are the Father. We are all one. It is impossible to be anything else. No matter where you are, what you think or what you do, this fact remains: that you and all of your brothers and sisters throughout all of this infinite creation are one single, great, living Being. Not only brothers and sisters, but all of life; and all of the trees and flowers and rocks and all of the foliage and all of the planets and stars are part of that one great Being.

And yet, man on Earth attempts to separate and divide and subdivide. And this is not truth. And yet he does not realize for he is yet in a state of ignorance brought on by his own misdirected thinking. And yet truth is simplicity itself and yet he has complicated this truth to such an extent as to kill his fellow creatures in great profusion. And he has generated such hatred for his fellow creatures and in doing so has generated this hatred for himself. For to hate your fellow men, my friends, is to hate yourself. And in doing so, he has brought upon himself terrible, terrible grief. For what could be worse than inflicting pain and destruction upon oneself?

And this is what he does. There are millions and millions and millions of planets throughout the creation. And these are inhabited by millions and millions of people. People like yourself. And yet, they do not hate. They do not fear. They do not envy. They do not show greed. They do not judge. For how is it possible to do any of these things if there is only one being? For in doing any of these things it is nothing but a self-inflicted wound. I and my Father are one. These are true, these spoken words. I and my Father are one. And each of you, as all people throughout all of the creation, one. One. Know this and this alone and you will know enough. But know it, my friends. Do not think it. Do not speak it. Do not accept it. Know it. For when you know it, you will then know love.

It has been a great privilege to be with you this evening. I am profoundly grateful for the opportunity. I leave you in love. For there is nothing else. My peace be with you.

Wednesday Meditation
February 27, 1974

(Don channeling)

I am Hatonn. I greet you, my friends, in the love and the light of our infinite Creator. It is a very great privilege to once more be with you. It is always a very great privilege to be able to speak to those of this planet who would hear us of the Confederation of Planets in the Service of the Infinite Creator.

I would speak to you this evening on a subject that I am sure each of you is interested. It is the subject of our contact with you. This contact at the present is what you know as a telepathic contact. This instrument is able to receive our thoughts. Each of you will be able to receive our thoughts as well as does this instrument in the near future. All that is necessary for you to do this is for you to avail yourself to our thoughts in meditation. There is a process of mental tuning, as you might call it, that is necessary. And this occurs while you are in meditation. It is much easier for us to contact you while you are in meditation since at that time you have rid your mind of many of the thoughts that constantly keep you from receiving what we would give to you.

Each of you here tonight desire our contacts. For this reason, you will receive our contacts. If you did not desire these contacts, you would not receive them.

There are several ways of contact. This instrument is demonstrating one of the ways at present. He is receiving my thoughts and repeating them verbally to you. At this time, I am not using control over this instrument. He has cleared his mind of other thoughts and is allowing me to speak through him rapidly using his mind simply as a relay station, so to speak. This requires some practice, and is quite difficult for a new instrument. For this reason, we use more control and operate at a slower speed with a new instrument. When this instrument was initially conditioned, it was necessary to operate at a much slower speed. However, each of you will be able to receive and relay our thoughts at this speed.

Some instruments do not receive conditioning, as you are aware of. They do not receive the muscular conditioning that some of you are aware of. They are conditioned in what you would consider a purely mental form, so that they receive our thoughts with no muscular control. There are certain reasons for this type of contact, and this will be the type of contact for some of your group.

This instrument is aware of my contact in more ways than one. However, it is sufficient to use him as a relay of our thoughts. In the future, we will contact you in a more direct way. This we would like to do at this time, but it is not possible at this time to contact you in a more direct way. However, in the future this will be possible. You will be responsible for this contact, not we. We cannot be responsible for this contact, for this would be a violation of what we understand as the Creator's design.

If you are to be responsible for our more direct contact with you, it will be up to you to generate a condition in which we can more directly contact you. This condition will be met by availing yourself to the knowledge of this condition through meditation. This condition is a condition of mind. It is a condition of the mind of your group.

In order to practice so that there will be a wider range of reception of these communications, I will at this time transfer this contact to one of the other instruments of this group.

(R channeling)

I am Hatonn. I greet you again in the love and the light of our infinite Creator. As I was saying, the condition that is required for a more direct contact with us is a higher spiritual consciousness. The development of your groups' mind will be necessary and will be achieved if it is desired by you. As we have said, a meeting of a more direct type will be entirely up to you. This is another reason why group meditations of this sort are advisable.

I will now attempt to use another of the newer instruments that we are attempting to develop.

(Don channeling)

I am with this instrument. I am Hatonn. I am having difficulty with the instrument known as D. It is only necessary that you relax and allow the thought to be stated by yourself. This instrument will be used to correct any errors that are made by the new instrument. Please avail yourself to my thoughts. I will return to the new instrument.

(Don channeling)

I am Hatonn. I am once more with this instrument. I shall speak for a short period of time on the process of channeling our thoughts. We are able to fully control your muscular actions. We implant a thought and then at the same time create a muscular response. If the thought is our thought you will get the response which is muscular. This will create an attempt to say what you are thinking. We are not able to form each word exactly in most cases. However, this may be done with some instruments. This, however, takes an exceedingly long time to develop. It is suggested that the new instruments use the muscular response he feels as a guide as to whether the thought he has is one to be stated or whether it is not to be stated. If he will simply state what he is thinking when the muscular response attempts to originate it, we shall be successful in giving our thoughts to this group through the new instrument.

At this time I will again try to channel a communication through the instrument known as D.

(D channeling)

I am Hatonn. I am Hatonn. I am Hatonn. I am … I … I am Hatonn. I am having a hard … (I guess he's trying to say he's having a hard time!) I am having … I am Hatonn … how hard I have tried. How hard I have tried and have been resisted. I am hopeful that I will achieve a smoother contact. I am having trouble because your mind is not focused. I have been trying about … I am sorry. I am Hatonn. I am having trouble. Avail yourself. All that is necessary is to avail yourself. All the way. I … I will leave. Adonai.

(Don channeling)

I am with you, my friends, in the love and the light of our infinite Creator. It is a great privilege to speak with you once again this evening. I am pleased with my ability to use the instrument known as D. He was resisting me previously. It is difficult for a new instrument at times to separate his thoughts from mine. This is not too important, for corrections can be made. And when we have achieved a good contact we can continue them without the necessity for repeating the phrases that is necessary for a new instrument.

It is only necessary that the instrument avail himself by clearing his mind of thoughts and then instead of trying to analyze each thought that comes into his mind, to keep his mind clear. And as this instrument does, simply speak what he thinks. We do not at this time use any control at all with this instrument, for he has relaxed and he is speaking exactly the thoughts that are in his mind. He is not thinking up these thoughts. He is just speaking them.

This is the technique that must be learned if one is to become a rapid and fluent channel. It is not necessary to analyze the source of the thought, it is only necessary to speak it. If this instrument speaks a thought that we do not wish him to speak as being one of our thoughts to be given to you, he simply will receive no thoughts after that and he will stop speaking. At this time we will be able to go back and rectify the erroneous communication that has been made.

This instrument at this time is speaking in a way that is slightly different from the way that the rest of you are accustomed to speaking. He is receiving what we are giving him in a conceptual form just a slight amount of time prior to his verbalizing. He is able to use his own words in speaking what we are giving to him to a certain extent. If what he says is sometimes slightly disjointed, it is because that he is relaxing and is not using his intellect to put the words exactly as they should be put together if it was to be appraised by one of your appraisers of your language.

We, however, do give him concepts which he attempts to relate to you by using the words which first come to his mind. For this reason, you find these messages somewhat less than a work of English manuscript. However, they are the thoughts, the concepts that we are trying to give to you that are of consequence and not the way that they are stated. If the instrument does not think about these things, and simply talks, then it will be much more rapid a communication and he will be able to give to you much more information in any period of time.

We sometimes use an instrument as we are using this one, talking in a state of, what you may say, some randomness in order to cause him to relax and get into a condition where he is stating our thoughts without at all analyzing them. In some instances, this instrument does analyze the concepts that we give to him and attempts to arrange the sentences in such a manner so as they are more suitable for your hearing or reading. However, this slows down a communication. It is possible to edit these communications after they are given to you through an instrument such as this one so as to make them more acceptable. This is of questionable value, since we are primarily trying to give concepts.

You will note that this instrument is speaking very rapidly. The only reason that this instrument is able to speak this rapidly is that he is not attempting to analyze what he is saying, he is simply saying it. And these thoughts that he is giving are thoughts that I am giving him. Exactly what I am giving him. I am not using words, as your language is composed of words. I am using concepts. These concepts are impressed upon the mind of the instrument which immediately transfers them into your language.

It is a process that is very simple. If he were to quit talking, he could get these concepts directly and understand them, but they would be of no value to him at this time for he already knows these concepts. This is another reason why it is so easy to communicate through him at this time for he has relayed similar messages to other new channels. It is sometimes difficult to relay messages that the instrument is not totally familiar with. And this takes [more] time and certain words that an instrument is not familiar with must be formed using muscular control. You will find, however, that as you gain confidence and ability in your communicating our thoughts you will be able to speak words that you are not familiar with, such as proper names and places, using muscular control. The muscular control that we are developing is also something that will be developed to a higher degree in the future.

You will find, as I am trying to indicate in this demonstration, that the main objective for an instrument if he is to become a good and rapid vocal channel is for him to totally relax, and to say what is in his mind. This instrument has been speaking exactly what has occurred in his mind for the past few minutes. If you think you can speak this rapidly using your own thoughts on any subject, I suggest that you attempt it. This instrument finds that he cannot speak this rapidly using his own thoughts on any subject for several reasons, for we are attempting to show to you at this time how you can best develop your ability to channel our thoughts simply by relaxing and speaking what is put into your mind. At a later time, we will use more control, for as you develop this ability to relay our thoughts you will also develop the ability to react muscularly to our control and therefore form exact words that we are attempting to give you. Please be patient and relax and allow yourself to speak what comes into your mind.

I will now demonstrate this form, if the instrument known as R will avail himself by relaxing and allowing me to attempt to speak more rapidly through him. I will now transfer this contact to the one known as R.

(R channeling)

I am with this instrument now. I am Hatonn. As I was saying, in the future it will be possible for you to speak at a more rapid pace if you will relax and allow the thoughts to flow freely through you. It is necessary, as we said, to relax and not to become tense. This instrument has a tendency to become tense when he is channeling our thoughts. In time, it will be possible for him to relax as more advanced instruments do. This instrument will note that every time he becomes tense it becomes more difficult for him to receive our thoughts.

We realize that this is difficult at this time because you have been conditioned to believe that you must put effort into using your mind. However, it is only necessary to let the thoughts flow through you. As we were saying, in time it will be possible to adjust muscular reactions in order to channel proper names and places and other concepts which are now foreign to you or difficult for you to receive. This instrument must remember not to become tense. As you become more proficient in channeling our thoughts you will be able to receive a channeled information of a more diverse nature. There is much we wish to give you that will require this greater ability to channel more specific information, information of a higher spiritual nature. These concepts which we would like to give to you are quite foreign to your planet's normal pools of ideas.

I will now transfer to another instrument.

(Don channeling)

I am with this instrument. I am Hatonn. I am with you, my friends, in the love and the light of our infinite Creator. I am Hatonn. I am greatly pleased with the progress we have made this evening in developing channels of communication. For we of the Confederation of Planets in the Service of the Infinite Creator are in need of many channels of communications of our thoughts to the people of this planet. We are in need of these channels because in the very near future there will be many of the peoples of this planet desiring to listen to what we have to say using channels such as yourself. At the present, people of this planet are not aware of reality. For this reason, they are not in great numbers seeking to hear what we have to tell them about reality. They are sleeping; however, they will very shortly begin to awake. It will be necessary at this time that there be many channels such as yourselves who can relay to them the information that they desire. This will be your major service; relaying to those of this planet what they desire. And, my friends, the key to giving to your peoples this information will be desire. For this is the way that it is planned.

It is planned to give to those who desire it that which they desire. It is planned to give them this in such a way that they may appraise its value on its own content of truth. Truth is always the same. However, different individuals interpret the truth differently at different times. For this reason we are allowing the people of this planet to interpret truth as they desire it. For this reason it is necessary that this truth be given to them through channels such as yourselves. We do not wish our understanding of truth [forced] upon your peoples. And this would be something that we would do if we contacted them directly. We could not help it, for our very utterance of truth would be accepted by many of your peoples as [inviolate]. We do not wish to be thought of as the ultimate representatives of the Creator's truth.

We wish to give this to your peoples in such a way so that they may accept or reject this at their own will. This, as we understand it, is a necessary provision in the spiritual evolvement of all mankind: that he be at some state of this evolution in a position to accept or reject what is necessary for his evolution. In this way and only in this way, can he know the truth—the truth of the Creator—that single truth that is the creation, the truth of the love of the creation.

It must be realized from within. It cannot be impressed from without. We are attempting to stimulate those of your peoples who would be stimulated to seeking this truth that is within them. It will be necessary for them to consider very carefully the messages that channels such as yourselves give unto them. They will have to weigh the value of what has been given to them and judge for themselves as to its validity. When they have become aware of its validity, then and only then can we meet.

This would seem to be a strange way of approaching the peoples of this planet to many of them. Perhaps it is strange. It is strange when you consider it from the point of view of those who have evolved in the structure of thinking that is prevalent on your planet. It is not strange from the point of view from those of us of the Confederation of Planets in the Service of the Infinite Creator. We have studied the creation of our infinite Father in much detail. And we find that it is always provided for that the individual seeking have all stages of evolution. We are seeking too. We are attempting to help those of the planet Earth who desire to seek truth to seek it also. Our seeking is somewhat different from the seeking of those of the planet Earth. We are seeking truth by coming to you at this time. This is a method that we have found in seeking truth, for in coming to your peoples at this time and offering to them that which we understand as truth and offering it to them in this way through channels such as yourselves, we find that we grow in our understanding of truth.

Spend time in meditation. Learn to understand our thoughts, whether it be while you speak them through channeling as does this instrument at this time or whether it be as you understand them in your meditations. Give us the only thing that we ask of your peoples—give us understanding. You can do this, my friends, through meditation. This is our understanding of how to achieve understanding.

It has been a great privilege to be with you this evening. I am Hatonn. I am Hatonn. Before I leave you I would like to express a greeting to the one known as Carla. I am sorry that it was not possible to meet with her this evening. I, however, will be with her at all times. I am Hatonn. I will leave this instrument at this time. I leave in the love and the light of our infinite Creator. Adonai vasu. ☙

Wednesday Meditation
February 27, 1974

(Don channeling)

I am Hatonn. I greet you, my friends, in the love and the light of our infinite Creator. It is a great privilege to speak to you once more this evening. It is also a very great privilege to speak to the ones who have joined this group.

I am at this time in a craft that is above you. I am going to speak of this, but through several other channels, if they will avail themselves.

(R channeling)

I am Hatonn. As I said, I would like to speak with you about our craft. I am attempting to give this instrument thoughts which he is not familiar with. I am in a craft above the house which you now occupy. Our craft would be visible to this group upon request.

We have said this many times. Desire is the necessary element in any communication with us, be it thought, visual or any physical medium.

I will now attempt to speak through another instrument.

(H channeling)

I am with this instrument. An aspect you may not have considered, one question which is asked many times, is, "Why don't those brothers from space meet us face to face? Why don't they bring a craft down where we can got a close look?"

My friends, one of the problems which we have encountered in contacting your peoples is what I should call an overreaction, either based upon fear or a semblance of what you might even call worship. Neither one of those attitudes is necessary or even desirable, my friends. Realize that when you have reached a maturity in your development that will allow you to meet us casually, as an equal—I should say, as a friend—when all of you can greet us in this way, then our meeting of face-to-face contact will be more possible, I shall say.

What I am referring to is not as much a problem with individuals such as yourselves as it would be with those among your peoples who do not have the background and the awareness which most of your group have.

I will attempt now to continue by using another of our newer instruments.

(Don channeling)

I am again with this instrument. I am Hatonn. I am with you in the love and the light of our infinite Creator. I am attempting to condition each of you. I am attempting to speak through one of the newer instruments.

(M channeling)

I am happy to be with you, my friends, once more. As new instruments are conditioned, communications are sometimes difficult. It is best that you meditate together in small groups, for as you do this you can feel more relaxed.

All of you in this room are capable of thought transfer. All that is required is that you desire it.

Our messages can be …

(Inaudible)

(Don channeling)

I am with this instrument. I am again attempting to condition each of you. I am also attempting to contact another of the newer instruments, if he will avail [himself] to our contact.

(Don channeling)

I am once again with this instrument. I am Hatonn. I am sorry that we are having difficulty. I will attempt to use another of the new instruments. I will speak by giving thoughts to you. Do not be afraid of making an error. I will use this instrument to correct any error that might be made. I am Hatonn. Please avail yourself to my contact.

(D channeling)

I … I … I am Hatonn.

(Don channeling)

It is a very simple process. However, it does require some practice. This instrument has learned to go ahead and speak with the thoughts that we give him. He has also learned to clear his mind to almost a 100 percent extent. This varies, somehow. This instrument has made an error. This varies somewhat, depending on the conditions that are surrounding him. At this time the conditions are quite good and he is receiving my words almost in a word-for-word fashion since I am familiar with your language and am also able to transmit the words that I wish the instrument to speak.

This type of communication is good for communicating information of a specific nature. It does, however, require a greater degree of control of the environment. In other words, the conditions for reception of my thoughts are at this time quite good, and this instrument is able to repeat word-for-word what I am giving to him. Each of you may learn to do this with practice. It is necessary to clear the mind of thoughts. You practice this through daily meditations and also through use of the channeling technique. You will not arrive at the fluidity of speaking which this instrument has without practice in doing so.

For this reason, we recommend that you simply relax and allow us of the Confederation of Planets in the Service of the Infinite Creator to impress upon your thinking our thoughts. And then, as these thoughts enter your mind, instead of analyzing them, simply repeat them. The analysis that you make of what you are doing is detrimental to the type of communication that we are making.

This instrument is doing very little analysis of what we are giving him at this time. He too at the beginning of his channeling had some difficulty because he analyzed, at that time, what he was saying. For this reason, it took a great deal of time to transmit a thought through him, and there was very little success in using this form of communication.

I am going at this time to tell a little story to you in order to allow you to focus your thinking on that which is necessary for you to focus your thinking upon in order to very simply receive our thoughts. This story has to do with a small child.

This small child listened to its parents, and its parents spoke to it. The child, before listening to its parents, could not speak, but after listening to its parents, it could speak quite fluently. However, the child was totally unaware of the process by which it learned to speak. It simply was there and it simply learned to speak. This is the process that we are using. Not to say that you are a little child. That is the problem! If you were as a little child, we could speak through you with no difficulty.

The problem is that you are not as a little child. We recommend that you think of yourself as you would of a little child and relax and know nothing. In this way you will very rapidly learn. This is what is necessary if you are to very rapidly learn to channel our thoughts. The child, you see, has no knowledge of what it is supposed to do. It simply speaks. This is how it is possible for you to learn to do this rapidly.

We have found that some people of your planet learn much more easily than others. We find people in a technological society such as yours sometimes requires great effort, because they have learned to question quite carefully everything that is presented them. If you do not question what we are attempting to do, but simply relax and let it happen, it will happen.

I hope that I have been of assistance in attempting to strengthen our contact. I will at this time attempt to communicate through one of the newer instruments.

(M channeling)

I am once more with this instrument, as he has relaxed sufficiently for communication to continue. We are aware continually of the activities of your group, as we are aware of the activities of all such groups on your planet. We are here to be of service to you. We bring you our love …

(Tape ends.)

L/L Research

Saturday Meditation
March 2, 1974

(Don channeling)

I greet you, my friends, in the love and in the light of our infinite Creator. It is a great privilege to be with you this evening. I am Hatonn. I am Hatonn of the Confederation of Planets in the Service of the Infinite Creator.

Yes, my friends, in the service of the infinite Creator. There are two possibilities. One is to be in the service of the infinite Creator. One is to be otherwise. The definition of "in the service of the infinite Creator" is very simple. It is applied to those who go forth, in this infinite universe, with a purpose that they understand to be a purpose desired by their Creator. This purpose they have determined through an understanding of the principles which govern this creation.

There are many ways to be in the service of the infinite Creator. We are demonstrating only one of these ways. It is possible for an individual to demonstrate a knowledge of this service at any time. In order to do this, you must understand what you are doing. In order to understand what you are doing, it is necessary for you to meditate, to avail yourself to the knowledge provided by the Creator of us all.

Upon your planet at this time, there are many, many individuals, performing many, many services. Very few of these services, however, are services of a nature that we would consider to be in the service of our infinite Creator. We find that upon this planet, man is primarily concerned with serving himself.

There are many ways to serve, and there are many attempts at service. However, much of the service performed upon this planet, which is an attempt to serve, as we do, our Creator, is not service of this nature.

The reason for this is always the same. It is because of a lack of meditation. We have said to you many, many times that it is necessary to meditate. This is the most important truth that we bring to you, for if one practices meditation, then one has no questions about service.

Each of you here this evening desires to serve, and each of you are serving and will serve to an even greater extent in the near future. However, in order to be of the most efficient service, it is necessary to prepare for that service with daily meditation.

Upon a planet such as yours, which is not at all used to service, there is considerable difficulty in serving your fellow man. And he is in dire need of that service. There is considerable difficulty for us of the Confederation of Planets in serving man on Earth. Man on this planet is extremely confused. For the most part, he has lost sight, almost entirely, of reality. He has built a myriad of illusions, and these illusions are so very strong that he is locked within them and cannot be served.

For this reason, it will be necessary for him to experience the strong catalytic action of his physical environment, in order for him to break his self-made illusion. Many of those who are locked within an illusion of their own are, nonetheless, of a nature willing to, and eager for, service in the light of our Creator. These will be the ones who must be contacted. These will be the ones who must be educated. And this will be quite a large problem.

Groups such as this one will have information given to them by we of the Confederation of Planets. This information should be of a form that is available to the many who will seek and understand this information when their illusion is destroyed.

Unfortunately, there has been much misinformation about us, and much misunderstanding, even of the ones who are aware of us, of our real message. We have attempted to maintain a simple message, for man on Earth has confused himself for many generations with complexities. We have attempted to maintain a simplicity in our teachings, in order to remove man on Earth from the web of his entangled complexities. What we here present to the peoples of this planet who would desire it is the simplicity of truth itself: the truth of this creation, and the truth of man's part in it.

It is, my friends, very, very simple. It is not necessary to get lost in the complex web of intellectual seeking that man on Earth seems to be so fond of. It is only necessary that he avail himself to an understanding that is not of an intellectual nature. And this he may do in daily meditation. It is only necessary that he raise his awareness, so that he grasps the understanding of his unity and oneness with the creation and the Creator. This we bring to man of Earth. This we offer in hopes that he will accept it.

We are grateful for those such as yourselves who would join with us and bring this truth to man on Earth at this time. However, we caution you that we have discovered that man upon this planet is difficult to teach. Therefore, it is necessary that the individual seeking to aid us in our endeavor to increase the awareness of those of this planet do it only after he has availed himself to the understanding that is necessary through his daily meditation. When he is ready to join with us in a direct effort to help those of his fellow man who seek his aid, at that time he will be aware of his readiness, for it will be apparent to him in his meditations.

Proceed then, with this in mind: that it is necessary for an individual to seek out understanding in order to achieve understanding; and it is also necessary that he be given that which he desires, if he is to achieve what he desires. It is available for all of mankind at all times. If you wish to act as an instrument in delivering what man of this planet desires, do so by preparing yourself. Do this through daily meditation.

I hope that I have been of service this evening. I am Hatonn. Adonai vasu.

Monday Meditation
March 4, 1974

(D channeling)

I … I am with you. I am in the room with you. I am Hatonn. I am come because you have called me, and I desire to be of service to you.

You desire reassurance of a personal nature. Conditioning is rather to make you more aware of our presence. When you feel the conditioning, you know that we are with you. If you maintain a communication this will be sent to you.

Conditioning also helps to reassure you.

(Inaudible) ✣

L/L Research

A report written by Carla Rueckert
March 5, 1974

I am recording this in the form of a report because I did not have the microphone on and so cannot furnish a transcription. I am writing down as much of the message I received as I can remember and noting the experience as a whole for the record. In retrospect, I feel it helped me learn about doing a better job of channeling.

Yesterday, the fourth, we had a very large group for meditation and Don was not here. Nor was R, nor was M. R and M are the now more accomplished of the new channels and Don is the oldest channel in the group and very reliable. There are many people in this group who have been getting conditioning. Eight people were here who have been getting conditioning that I am sure of. They have not yet really developed as channels. They have channeled one message each. And these were very short.

We simply did not have any microphones on. I felt that I was ready to channel, I heard or was aware of certain thoughts that came into my mind and I spoke them. There was, of course, a good deal of doubt in my mind later as to whether the thoughts were mine or whether they were actually channeled; especially, since there was not a more dependable channel there to correct me if I made an error.

What the message was about mainly was simply a greeting to everybody and a statement of how pleased Hatonn and Laitos were to be here. And that they would condition all those in the room who wished it and attempt to use each new instrument that they could use, very briefly. They didn't use anybody else but me. Although afterwards two other instruments stated that they could've spoken, but they were "chicken." It is very easy to be "chicken" because when you begin to get a thought all you get is the first, which is usually, "I am Hatonn." And unless you say that aloud, they won't go on to the next bit, unless you say it to yourself. Which is how I got up the courage in the first place, because I said it to myself and got about the first paragraph and I realized that I was going to get a message.

So, today, there was no one here for the first time in a long time and my meditation was by myself and I had been thinking to myself all day and as many times, as I believed in other people's channeling, I did have the predictable problem very much of self-doubt and so when I sat down and meditated and I was meditating I thought to myself, "Hatonn, if it really is an occurrence, I want conditioning now," and I began getting conditioning and when my jaw finally opened and that unmistakable "I," I said it. And sure enough, I got a thought and it led to another one and it led to another one, so I went on and channeled Hatonn to myself. And it was short. It said, "I am Hatonn. I am very privileged to be with you. I am pleased to see that you are meditating. I will recommend to you that you relax more because if you wish to become a channel and if you wish us to direct you there is no way for us to do that if you are misdirecting yourself."

There was a pause after for the thought to sink in and then he just said, "I leave you in the love and the light of the infinite Creator. I am Hatonn." So, I am now able to do it and I had a sense of it actually being over. I could feel that the contact had lifted and I wanted to ask a question so I said, "Hatonn, can I ask a question?" and immediately I could feel that there was presence as though a computer had come on and was kicking over or something and I said, "How can I meditate better?" And I got the thought, "Think of nothing. You are thinking of something."

End of report. ✢

Wednesday Meditation
March 6, 1974

(Carla channeling)

I am Hatonn. I greet you, my friends, in the love and the light of our infinite Creator. It is a great privilege to be with you this evening. We of the Confederation of Planets in Service of the Infinite Creator are always privileged to speak with you. We have had much difficulty in contacting this instrument as she was not in a relaxed state. However, she has become more relaxed. My brother Laitos is also here and will be conditioning each of you who desires it.

My friends, we come across the deeps of dimensions you know not to speak with you and yet you are asleep. And though you hear us you do not hear us. My friends, what you hear is truth and yet not truth. What you take in with your physical senses is only true for the illusion and, my friends, this illusion is a very small part of the creation. My friends, you come here, you come to each meeting and you sit at each meditation in an attempt to awaken from the slumber only knowing the illusion of truth. Meditation, my friends, is the great bridge to the total creation of the Father. It is your birthright, my children, all the children of the Father. All of us together are the Creation. Through meditation we can begin to become more aware of it. This is true of us, also. And this is our service to you. We encourage you to continue meditation and, my friends, we encourage you to stop yourself at each point in the illusion at which you think a thought and ask yourself how much of the truth of that thought applies to the real creation of the Father.

This instrument is tiring. I will attempt to contact another instrument and will leave this instrument at this time. I am Hatonn.

(Pause)

(Carla channeling)

I am attempting to use the instrument known as D. If she will avail herself to my contact, I will speak through her.

(Pause)

(D channeling)

I am pleased to be able to speak through this instrument. She has been very reluctant. As I was saying, you must be careful, for the traps of the illusion are hidden. And unless you are careful where you are stepping you will fall. Many of them are hidden. Many of them appear as flowers. But beware, my friends, for below the flower is the thorn, always.

I feel the instrument's thoughts are straying. Pardon me for a moment.

(Inaudible) … is good. I am pleased. Each of you, however, observe your actions. As to how they fall,

whether things that you participate [in] are adding to the illusion or erasing it. Of these words, I find it necessary to leave. This instrument is extremely fatigued. I am Hatonn. Adonai. 🌱

Friday Meditation
March 8, 1974

(Unknown channeling)

I am Hatonn. I greet you in the love and in the light of our infinite Creator. It is a great privilege once more to be able to speak to those who seek. There are not too many on this planet who seek. We of the Confederation of Planets in the Service of the Infinite Creator are here to help those who seek. It has been written in your holy works that if you seek, you shall find. We are here to help those who seek. We are here to help them find.

And what, my friends, shall we help you find? We will help you find life; life as it was intended. Life as you desire it. There is what man on Earth presumes to be life abundant upon this planet. However, this life is not acting in a manner ever intended by our Creator.

There are many problems upon the surface of your planet. All the life that is so abundant about you is reacting to the conditions that are not in harmony with the Creator's plans.

Yes, my friends, these conditions affect not only the people who dwell upon this planet, but all lifeforms. We of the Confederation in the Service of Our Infinite Creator are here to attempt to teach to those who would wish to learn how to live.

We have stated many times that there is a great advantage in living as the Creator intended.

However, there is no way for us to show you what such a life is like. It is only possible for us to show you how to live such a life. When you do this, you will then understand what the Creator planned for all of us.

I am aware that many of you are anxious to succeed with your seeking. I am aware that some of you think that your progress is all too slow. This is nothing to be concerned about. It is only necessary that the individual first desire to seek that which our Creator intended, and then, if he continues in his seeking, all of those things which he desires in his meditations will be added.

The seeking, my friends, is very important. This is of the utmost importance. There are many people upon this planet who are seeking something. However, very few are seeking what was meant for them to seek by their Creator. They are seeking things that are within the illusion that they have created. They are seeking these things because they don't know of anything else worth seeking.

There is only one thing worth seeking. There are many ways of defining it. There are many pathways to it, and there are many names for it. But, my friends, no matter how you name it, no matter how you reach it, no matter what it is that you achieve, there is only one objective. That objective is the same for each of us. It is only necessary that man realize that he has this common objective with his fellow man. Once this is realized, and once he begins to seek for this objective, he will be guided, for this is the way the creation functions.

And to what will he be guided? What, my friends, is this objective that we all seek? It is very simple. As I have said, it can be called by many names, and it can be reached by many pathways. However, it is simply a return to the awareness [of] the thinking of our Creator. This thinking has been demonstrated in the past. Guidelines have been set down for the people of this planet to follow, for they were not able to reason these pathways themselves; they were not ready to seek and actively find that common goal. But in laying down these guidelines and in showing these pathways there was a generation of misunderstanding.

For this reason, we say that it is necessary to meditate. For then and only then can you understand the true meaning of these guidelines and of these pathways that lead to our common objective. There has been much strife and much confusion upon your planet, and there continues to be much strife and much confusion. And even those who attempt to follow the examples of the teachers who have demonstrated the Creator's light do not understand, and there is confusion. All of this confusion, all of this misunderstanding, all of the strife that is occurring upon your planet, is primarily due to a lack of meditation.

We realize that we will be successful with only a relatively small percentage of those whom we contact. However, this will be sufficient for the time being. For from these seeds will grow a wider understanding of the truth for those who desire it.

At this time I am going to condition each member of this group. If you desire my contact, it is only necessary that you avail yourself to it.

(Carla channeling)

I am Hatonn. As I was saying, my friends, *(inaudible)* like a seed being planted, in the attempt to give service or information to those people of your planet who seek it. Like seeds in the ground, my friends, there is darkness. There is darkness also in the conscious and waking reality of those people of your planet who are beginning to seek, as they feel that they are awake, yet they are asleep and in darkness.

And just as people who are asleep and dreaming, while their real bodies are in their beds and safe, they may well imagine themselves killed. Such a thing does not happen; they awake and discover that reality was other than they thought.

My friends, true understanding of the true reality is like this. And how do those of us who wish to serve begin to sow the seed? We of the Confederation of Planets in the Service of the Infinite Creator can only come to you to urge you to meditate, to seek, to turn to the Creator of us all for His love and His light. That is all you can do, my friends.

And why can you do no more? Consider, my friends, that each man has a handprint uniquely his own. No one else's handprint in the whole world can match it. Consider each leaf or snowflake, and realize that there has never been a duplicated entity.

The way from this illusion—which is a tiny part of reality—to reality cannot be measured, and is as individual as your handprint. There is, however, a quality whereby the circumstances for understanding may occur. This quality is more possible to obtain in meditation, for by it the intellect, which is responsive only to the illusion about you, is stilled.

My friends, I am very pleased that you are attempting to persevere in this attempt to serve. We assure you, I and my brothers, that we are always with you, and are here to serve you, whether through an instrument such as this one, or through meditation by direct contact.

I will leave this instrument now, and continue to condition those of you who desire it. I am Hatonn.

(Don channeling)

I am Oxal. I greet you, my friends, in the love and the light of our infinite Creator. I will condition this instrument for a short period. Please be patient.

(Pause)

I am Oxal. I am with you, my friends, in the love and the light of our infinite Creator. It is a very great privilege to be able to speak to you this evening, using this instrument.

I am Oxal. My friends, this is of no consequence, for I am the Creator. Yes, my friends, you are listening to the voice of the Creator. You hear the voice of the Creator each day, my friends, as you go about your daily activities. It is only necessary to recognize it. As you meet your fellow man in your daily activities, as he speaks, then you hear the voice of your Creator. Birds singing in the trees, my friends, speak with the voice of the Creator. The very winds that blow through these trees speak to you, my friends. And this noise that you hear is the voice of the Creator, for His expressions are infinite. It is only necessary that you hear and see these expressions and then, when you hear and see them, it is then necessary that you understand them, to understand that these are the Creator.

This is what is missing upon your planet, my friends: the simple understanding that all of these things are the same thing. They are the Creator. This knowledge is self-evident. It does not require a complex analysis. It does not require that I prove to you that what I am saying is true. Truth, my friends, speaks to you. It is all about you. It is the Creator.

It is only necessary for you to recognize this, totally, with no reservation, and then you will think as the Creator thinks. For the Creator recognizes Himself, and there is no part of Himself that He does not accept, for it is Him, and He is one thing, the creation.

It is impossible to separate yourself from the creation. It is impossible to isolate yourself from the creation. You are it, and it is you. And all of its parts speak to you, saying, "Be of the creation." It is only necessary that man on Earth listen to this voice, and then understand its words. Understand and then demonstrate this understanding, and then man on Earth will take his rightful place with those of us who roam through this infinite Creation.

For this is our privilege, and this is your privilege, for we are all the same thing. We are love, and we are light. Adonai, my friends. Adonai vasu.

(S channeling)

(Inaudible). It has been hard for him to clear his mind. If he would just relax. Just sit and relax, and let it flow. I will now leave this instrument

(Don channeling)

I am now with this instrument. I am Hatonn. I am with this instrument. I am attempting to condition each of you in the room who desire my conditioning. I am attempting to help those who desire it to give to the people of this planet our thoughts. You will feel my contact. It is only necessary to relax. Allow your mind to stop. Think of nothing. It is difficult to change quickly, in the confusion that you meet during your daily activities and the intense use of the intellect that you experience. This is one of the great problems on your planet.

It is not necessary for man to use his intellect in such a manner. Everything that man desires is provided, it is only necessary that he realize his true relationship to the creation. It is only necessary that he realize the he is the creation.

And this is not done by intellectual complexities. This is done through a simple process, a very simple process of becoming aware. We call this process meditation, but it is not necessary that it be so formalized. It is only necessary that man realize that this may be done at any time. Relax and allow this awareness to be with you. I and my brothers will help you. We are here for that purpose. I am Hatonn. Adonai.

(Pause)

I am Laitos. I greet you, my friends, in the love and the light of our infinite Creator. It is my privilege to speak with your group this evening. I have been observing and listening to communications given to you by my brothers. I am Laitos, and I too send you my love and my light, and extend to you our warmest welcome. Join us, my friends; join us in light. It is all about you. There is much light in this creation. We are here to lead you into this light. We know that it is what you desire, for this you have expressed.

I will leave this instrument at this time. I am Laitos. Adonai vasu. ☙

Saturday Meditation
March 9, 1974

(Don channeling)

I am Hatonn. I greet you, my friends, in the love and the light of our infinite Creator. It is a great privilege to be with you. It is always a great privilege to be with those of this planet who are seeking.

This evening, my friends, I am going to speak on the subject of seeking. This is a very important subject. It is perhaps the most important of all subjects that could be spoken about.

Seeking, my friends, is, as we said, extremely important. First, I would like to explain why seeking is important. Seeking is a way of growing. It is, in truth, for the people of this planet at this time their only way of truly rapidly growing, growing, my friends, in a sense that is spiritual

The people of this planet at this time are almost all children, in a spiritual sense. Most of them are not at this time seeking spiritual growth. This is very important, if an individual is to rapidly grow, spiritually. All of us throughout all of space are growing, in a spiritual sense. However, none of us are growing much more rapidly than others. The reason for this growth is simply that these are the ones that are seeking.

It is written in your holy works that it is necessary to seek if you are to find. This is with reference to finding spiritual enlightenment. This is in reference to developing the awareness that is necessary for man on Earth to develop if he is to take his rightful place in the creation.

We of the Confederation of Planets in the Service of the Infinite Creator are aware that seeking is necessary if one is to get where he wishes to be, and he wishes to be at a higher state of awareness. Look about you, upon your planet. There are many conscious beings, in many forms of life. There are the animals, and birds, and the fish, and man on Earth. And each has a state of awareness. But it seems that man has the higher state of awareness. And yet we tell you that this awareness is very minimal. And the awareness of man on Earth can be raised to an awareness that he would consider godlike.

But, my friends, this is what was meant for man to have. This is what was the original concept of the Creator, that this awareness would be possessed by all of His children. This is what it is necessary to seek, if you are to find this awareness.

The reason that it is necessary to seek this awareness is that it cannot be given to you. It is something that each individual must find for himself. It is not a difficult thing to find. It is a very simple thing to find. It is only necessary that the individual go about seeking in a proper way. We are here to attempt to aid those who desire our aid in seeking our awareness, to find it. We will not attempt to confuse those whom we wish to aid with complex lectures on various problems and concepts. We will simply give to them the simplest of the Creator's ideas. For, my friends, His ideas are not complex. It is man, especially man on Earth, who has made a complex set of rules and conditions for spirituality.

The Creator's concept, my friends, is extremely simple. This we are here to bring to you. It is only necessary then that you seek an understanding of this simplicity. Then, upon understanding it, demonstrate it in your daily lives, and in your activities and associations with your fellow man. Then, my friends, the awareness that was meant for you will be yours. It is an extremely simple process. It is only necessary that, first, man on Earth seek.

Seek, my friends. This is what is necessary. This is the first step. Seek awareness. Seek the spirituality that was meant to be yours, and surely you will find it. For this is the Creator's plan, that all of His children should have this.

I am going to transfer this contact at his time, and continue to speak to you on this subject. It has been a great privilege to speak with you, using this instrument.

(Carla channeling)

I am now with this instrument. I am Hatonn. As I was saying, seeking, my friends, is extremely important. And yet, through the powers of your intellect, with the best of intentions it is possible to make it seem complicated.

There is the complication in your vision of the concept of time. And there is the complication in your vision of the concept of space. And you say, "Where, and when, may I seek? In what place may I find holy ground? And at what time may I seek the Creator?"

My friends, you are the Creator. For the Creator is you. And, my friends, as it is written in your holy works, the place whereon you stand is holy ground.

There is no complication in time, for all time is here and now. There is no complication in place, for all place is here and now.

My friends, there is naught but seeing; there is naught but the Creator. It is only necessary for you to turn inwardly, into the light, and enter the light.

These words are poor, but they lead the way to a new understanding. It is not necessary to have the most perfect meditation or the most proficient spiritual moments in order to be seeking. It is necessary only to turn your will. For, my friends, your will to seek is as important as the source.

It to good that you meditate. It is good that you appreciate those things in your illusion that you wish to appreciate. All of these things are here for your experience. It is, however, not necessary to feel that they are *(inaudible)*. Only seek.

It has been my privilege to speak with you. I leave you, here and now, everywhere at once in the creation, and at all times. We are one in love and in light. We are the Creator. Adonai. Adonai vasu.

(Don channeling)

I am Oxal. I greet you, my friends, in the love and in the light of our infinite Creator. It is a great privilege to join my brother Hatonn this evening in speaking to you through this instrument.

I am the one known as Oxal. It is my privilege to aid, as best I can, those who seek, and it is true that this is all that is necessary. It is only necessary that you seek. And then you will find. You will find all that there is. My friends, you will find the creation. And, my friends, in finding this, you will find the Creator. For they are one and the same thing.

When you meet your fellow man in your daily activities, you will recognize him for what he really is, a part of the creation, just as you are part of the creation. And the creation, my friends, is the Creator.

And then, as you look at Him and He looks at you, the Creator looks at Himself, through each pair of eyes. It is only necessary that you recognize this concept and understand it, and then your thinking and the Creator's will be the same. And you will know the meaning of love.

I hope that I have been of assistance in giving to you my concept of truth. We of the Confederation of Planets in the Service of the Infinite Creator are expressing our concept of truth, a concept that is the result of our seeking. When we look at you, we see our Creator. This is our understanding. When we look at this infinite creation, in all of its wonders and all of its vastness, in all of its splendor, we are seeing the Creator. This is our understanding. And when we look at the smallest form of life, or even an insect, we are looking at our Creator. This is our understanding. For our understanding is that the Creator is expressing Himself throughout all of the infinite manifestations that we experience. And His thought in all of these manifestations is a thought of love.

For this was the thought that created all that there is. Seek this thought, my friends. Seek this understanding, my friends. And then you will know. You will know love. For this is the Creator.

I am Oxal. I will leave this instrument at this time. My blessings upon each of you. We are all the same. We are all one. Adonai vasu.

Sunday Meditation
March 10, 1974

(Carla channeling)

(Inaudible)

Greetings, my brothers and sisters, in the love and the light of our infinite Creator. It is indeed my privilege to speak with you this evening. We apologize for having some difficulty.

I and my brothers are here only to serve you, my friends. And it is a very great pleasure to be here. We offer conditioning to those of you who desire this. We serve you, and we seek. Serving is seeking. The two words seem different: to seek and to serve. One suggests that you need something, and one suggests that you have something, for those who seek must need, and those who serve must have, to give away.

And so I would like to speak, my friends, about these two words. You are seeking and you are seeking to serve. It is a paradox, is it not, my friends? It is a paradox, as are all intellectual things. And yet it is the simple truth, that they are one thing.

In this illusion of Earth, my friends, those of your planet are *(inaudible)* as though they were supplicants: poor, needful and ever lacking those things which they need to progress. And so they go on a pilgrimage; some to gain physical security, and some to seek the spiritual in life.

But there is the concept of seeking which will garner a type of treasure that can be held, and can be shown, and can be counted. Perhaps we would call this, my friends, dealing from a position of weakness. In this illusion, my friends, it would seem possible to be weak, to be limited, and to be in need. Yet this illusion is banished by reality. And this reality is what we seek. And when we seek reality, we turn either very far inward or very far outward—another paradox, my friends—into the light. And we find that we are not dealing from a position of poverty, but that we have all that we have been seeking.

But we are indeed dealing from a position of complete strength. Because we are infinite. You, my friends, are infinite. You do not need help. You only need realization. All I can tell you, all you can learn, all that is possible in this infinite creation is abiding eternally within you. For you are one with all that there is. In the illusion, my friends, I am aware that I would be doing you a disservice if I did not realize that you have much to contend with, for the illusion is very strong. But so much of the illusion suggests to you that the illusion itself lacks spirituality because various things are various and sundry ways, and they do not suit you.

And it would seem perhaps that spirituality might consist in more manageable and more uniform things in your environment. The illusion is as evanescent as a bubble: *pop!* and it will be gone. It is as fleeting as a dream. Soon, you will awaken. It will change, as does day to night, and night to day. You need not do more than appreciate the infinity of the creation even in the tiny part which is the illusion.

And then, my friends, relax, and let the illusion float by you. Rest in the confidence of your seeking, and of your seeking to serve. For you have much to give, my friends.

At this time, I will transfer this message to another instrument.

(Don channeling)

I am now with this instrument. I am Hatonn. I am with each of you. I am with you in the love and the light of our infinite Creator. It is a privilege to be with you.

You have desired our presence, and we are with you. We are of the Confederation of Planets in the Service of the Infinite Creator. We are always with those of the people of this planet who desire our presence. This is our service to the people of this planet at this time. This is our technique of seeking. It may seen strange that we would seek through service, but this is our understanding of seeking.

It is stated in your holy works that it is necessary to seek in order to find. We have found many ways of seeking. One of these is to serve your fellow man. And this is our form of seeking at this time. We are seeking understanding—understanding of the Creator, for this is our desire. We are seeking this understanding through service, through serving our fellow man on Earth, and aiding him in his desire to understand the Creator.

And through aiding him, and fulfilling his desire, we aid ourselves in fulfilling our desire. For in doing this, not only does man on Earth perhaps learn more of this creation and the Creator, but also we; for it is a law of this creation that only through service may one be served. In serving others, we serve ourselves, as even does man on Earth. For this was the original idea that generated the entire infinite creation: the idea of mutual service, the idea of mutual understanding, and the idea of mutual love.

This we are bringing to man on Earth, an understanding of that that is within him, an understanding of that which created him, an understanding of our service and the need for his. It is unfortunate that there are so many that do not understand the true principles of this creation. We are attempting to help them realize this truth. It is within them and this is our service, to help them find what they desire to find—the realization of the thought that generated, not only them, but all that there is, and the thought that provided that all that there is act in such a way to serve all that there is.

This truth is all about you, very obvious to those who have stilled themselves for the very short time that is required to become aware of it. It is very obvious to those of us who view the creation of the Father in its original form. All of its parts act to support all of its other parts. All that sustains each of us is a gift of our Creator. All of the joys and experiences that come to us are gifts of our Creator.

It is only man upon this planet who has become lost in a complex creation of his own, with many thoughts of a complex but trivial nature that keep them very busy, in an effort to reach that which is of no value—a minor creation that will last only the shortest period of time—which has no value, once it is attained, for he will lose it, and once again return to the creation.

All of the children of the Creator throughout all of the universe, all of this infinite creation, my friends, are truly seeking only one thing, whether they realize this or not: they are seeking understanding, for this is all that is necessary. For once this understanding is accomplished, then all things are possible, for this is the way that the Creator designed it, this is the way that He provided. It is only necessary that you realize this. It is only necessary that you demonstrate, in each thought, this realization. And then, my friends, you and the Creator are one, and you and the Creator have equal power. For this is truth: each of us is the Creator.

It is very difficult for man on this planet to look about him and realize the truth for what it actually is. He has been conditioned, through his thinking and through the thoughts of others, for a very long period of time, to see things as they are given to him, rather than as they really are. They way that they really are, my friends, is extremely simple, for this is the way that was provided by the Creator.

This simplicity is within each of the children of the Creator. Each of them possess all of the knowledge that was the original creation. It is only necessary that they avail themselves to that knowledge. And this is very simple. It is done though the process of meditation.

When this is done, all the truth and beauty of the original creation become apparent. And then it will not be possible for the individual to be fooled by the illusion. He will not see his fellow man in any form but perfection, even though within the illusion he has been taught to disdain. This was not planned by the Creator. The Creator only planned that each of His creations should express itself in any way that he chose. This, my friends, is perfection. If man on Earth could only realize this, he would once more think in total harmony with the original creation. This may be done on an individual basis. It is not necessary that this be understood in an intellectual sense, or by anyone else than the individual endeavoring to reach this understanding.

This has been demonstrated upon your planet before. The man most familiar to you having demonstrated his understanding is known to you as Jesus. He made the simple realization, and then demonstrated it by his activities, this understanding. It was not necessary that he be understood by his fellow man, for it is impossible to force externally upon another individual this understanding. It is only possible that this understanding be attained from within.

But yet, this man demonstrated this understanding, pointed out a pathway, a guidepost for others, so that they too could find the original creation, and once more lead themselves from darkness to light.

For light, my friends, is eternal and infinite and real. The rest is illusion. Go within. Become aware of reality. It is within each of you.

We are here to help you find that reality. We are her to bring you our understanding and our love. This is our service. It has been a great privilege to speak with you using this instrument.

It will be a very great privilege to use each of you who desire to channel my thoughts in the very near future. It is only necessary that you avail yourself in meditation, and then each of you will, as does this instrument, receive with no difficulty each and every thought that we of the Confederation of Planets in the Service of the Infinite Creator bring to you. And then, my friends, you too will join us in His service.

I will leave this instrument at this time. It has been a very great privilege to meet with you. I am Hatonn. Adonai vasu borragus.

Monday Meditation
March 11, 1974

(Don channeling)

I am Hatonn. I greet you, my friends, in the love and the light of our infinite Creator. It is a great privilege to be with you once more. It is always a very great privilege to be with those who seek.

Man on Earth has very little understanding of his life. The life of an individual is not what he thinks that it is. Very few of those who dwell upon your planet have any understanding of life. Man upon planet Earth is concerned with a life that is limited by his waking hours, during a present physical lifetime. His plans, his desires, and his activities are governed by his awareness of this extremely limited portion of experience, what he considers his physical life.

For this reason, the plans and the objectives of those who dwell upon Earth are extremely limited, and for the most part of no value whatsoever. In order to intelligently make plans, it is necessary that one have information about future objectives. Man on Earth, for the most part, has none of this information, for he has not sought it. He is simply existing in a very limited state of awareness and reacting to what he is able to determine about this limited awareness. Those reactions result in his activities, which are from our point of view ridiculous.

We of the Confederation of Planets in the Service of the Infinite Creator are aware of a much longer span of life than is man on Earth. The span of life that we are aware of is of infinite length. For this reason, our plans and our objectives and our activities are much different from those who dwell upon this planet.

Man upon Earth is not trying to understand how to live. He is not trying to understand how to live because he is not trying to understand life. Life is extremely simple, and an understanding of life requires an extremely simple approach. Presently, man in your society upon Earth is attempting to approach what he considers to be life in an extremely complex manner. In doing this, he is making numerous plans and numerous deductions, based upon observations that are so limited that they are almost totally false.

Some of the people of your planet have some awareness of the principles that affect an individual in his true infinite state; and they are aware of the necessity to make plans for objectives that are totally outside of the very limited state that you call the physical life.

We are here to attempt to help those who are seeking a greater awareness find it. We are attempting to bring a simple teaching that will allow you to become able to make your own decisions as a result of a much greater awareness of truth [than] is presently available upon your planet.

At this time, I will speak to the limits of my ability to translate our understanding of life into your language about the realities of life.

Life is composed of two materials. One of them is what you might call consciousness. The other is light. But, my friends, consciousness is love and light is its physical manifestation. All that you are able to experience in the way of a physical universe is composed of one ingredient. This ingredient we will call light, since this word is closest to what we wish to express, and it is the only word that we have available in your language to express the basic building block of our Creator.

Originally, the Creator expressed a desire. This desire was expressed in a state of consciousness that is best described in your language using the word, love. The Creator, then, expressing desire through love, caused the creation of all matter. He caused the creation of light. This light was then formed in its infinite configurations in the infinite universe to produce all of the forms that are experienced. All of these forms, then, are molded or generated through the expression of consciousness that is love. They are composed of a fabric that is light. For this reason we greet you each evening with the statement, "in His love and His light." For this, then, encompasses all that there is: the consciousness that creates, and the fabric that is love and light.

The love that produces the configuration of light occurs in what we term various vibrations—or, using a word in your language that is not sufficient but somewhat descriptive, "frequency"—love occurs, then, in various vibrations or frequencies. These vibrations or frequencies are the result of free will. When the Creator produced this original concept the concept included the gift of freedom of choice to all of the parts that He created. Those parts are then totally free to change the original Thought. In doing so, they change what you understand to be the vibration of some portion of the original Thought.

Each of you here this evening has a vibration. This vibration is yours, and you have control over it. Your freedom of choice has created the love that manifests the light that is the fabric molded into your physical form.

This in the simplest analysis of all created forms of all of the creation. Each part of it is able to utilize its own consciousness, through the principle of freedom of choice, to vary or change the original Vibration.

The creation, therefore, continues to be self-generating, in an infinite variety. This was provided for in the original Thought of the Creator. It was provided that He might generate in an infinite way, in an infinite number of forms.

Through this use of freedom of choice, man upon planet Earth has generated many forms. Some of these forms were never envisioned by the Creator with the original Thought. However, they were allowed for, due to the principle of freedom of choice.

This is perhaps the most important principle in this creation: that each of the Creator's parts be able, throughout eternity, to select for themselves what they desire. In experimenting with this desire there have in some instances become a slight problem in straying away from thoughts and desires that would be most beneficial. In experimenting with these desires, none of the created parts have lost contact with the original desire. This has occurred in many places in this creation.

We are here at present to communicate to those who desire to find their way back to the original Thought information leading those who desire the path back along the path to the original Thought. It is necessary that we an act in such a way so as to lead only those who desire this pathway along it, therefore not violating the important principle of total freedom of choice.

As I was saying previously, each of you, as do all parts of this creation, have a particular vibration or frequency. This vibration or frequency is the only important part of your being, since it is an index of your consciousness with respect to the original Thought.

When an individual is aware of life in its infinite sense he is also aware of the benefits of matching this vibration with the vibration of the original Thought. It is our effort to match our vibration with that of the original Thought. This in the reason that we of the Confederation of Planets in the Service of the Infinite Creator are here now, for this service that we perform is a service that would be in harmony with the original Thought. This then produces in within us a vibration more harmonious to the original Thought.

We are attempting to give instructions to those of the planet Earth who would seek the instructions how to produce within themselves the vibration that is more harmonious with the original Thought. This, as I have stated before, was demonstrated upon your planet many times before by teachers. The last one of whom you are familiar was the one known to you as Jesus. He attempted to demonstrate by his activities his thinking. His thinking was in harmony, much more than those about him, with the original Thought. His vibration was, therefore, much more in harmony with the original Vibration.

For this reason he was able to work what were called miracles. However, the original Thought was that all of the parts of the consciousness that were of the original Thought should be able to generate by thought and consciousness what would be desired. The man known as Jesus desired, and therefore created, since the vibration which he generated was in harmony with the vibration which the Creator used to form the creation.

It in only necessary, then, that an individual become in harmony with the vibration that formed the creation in order for him to act within the creation as did the Creator, and as does the Creator. This was demonstrated to you by the one known to you as Jesus. Not only did he demonstrate what could be done in a very small way, but also how to think in order to do this. Unfortunately, man upon planet Earth has misinterpreted the meaning of this man's life.

At this time we wish to point out the true meaning of this man's life. It was desired that those who were aware of his thinking and his activities then follow the example, and as he did, become more in unison and in a harmonious vibration with the thought of their Creator.

We are here to bring you information and to impress upon you in a nonintellectual way during meditation the idea that [it] is necessary for you to increase the vibratory rate of your real being so that it is harmonious with the original Thought of our Creator. Our teachings will be simple, as were the teachings of the one known to you as Jesus. It is only necessary that you attempt to understand these teachings. Understand them in depth.
Understanding in depth can be done only through meditation.

And then, once these teachings are understood, it will be necessary that they be applied and that the individual so desiring to apply them demonstrate in his daily activities and in his daily thinking the concept that was the original Thought, the concept that we have spoken to you as being love. We have used this word, as I have said, because it is as close as we can come, using language, to the original Thought. However, this word is miniature compared to the original Thought. This original Thought can't be obtained in your intellect, only to a very small degree. It must be obtained in your total being, through the process of meditation.

Once this is done, and once your activities and thinking reflect this thought, your vibration will increase. At this time you will find the kingdom that has to understand simplicity. It is more to the nature of this illusion here manifesting on the surface of your planet to have a complicated and carefully controlled series of tests to perform, in order to reach a goal.

But, my friends, truth is in the opposite direction of this. As we have said earlier tonight, meditation brings to you this realization in a non-intellectual manner. But to arise from your meditation, my friends, and to demonstrate the truth that you have learned is indeed a challenge to your [spirits].

For how does one demonstrate the absolutely simple? Picture if you will, my friends, a prison, deep in the ground. There is old metal, and many rusty keys. And inside the old metal cells in this dungeon, deep underground, there are many, many ghosts, that can barely be seen. And yet they are trapped.

My friends, you are holding yourselves prisoner. Meditation allies you with the truth of freedom, with the truth of infinity. Unlock your own spirits from these dungeons by simply realizing that each intellectual thought process is a mere shade, only a ghost, and cannot harm, hurt or cause you pain. As these shades disappear, you rise from this earthly, rusty frame of mind and you are aware of perhaps a feeling of parting that was even painful, for it is difficult to let those things that trouble you go. And yet, my friends, once you are up in the sunlight, and the sun is warming you, and you can lift yourself to the infinite grace and listen for the waters of truth, you have found an avenue from meditation to demonstration.

At [those] times, my friends, that the illusion presses most strongly upon you, and in your desire for spiritual growth you ask what is the truth of this, my friends, ask yourself, "Does this problem have to do with my spiritual growth?" And, "Does it have to do with a service to aid another in spiritual growth?" My friends, if the answer is "yes," this problem is in the area I have described as the dungeon. It need only be let go, and then you need only become aware of the real creation, in its infinity, all around you, for you to have demonstrated at that moment a spiritual growth.

This Earth of yours, my friends, teems with many, many creatures. Infinite variety, and infinitely different manifestations of activity. We are all one with you. There is no possible relationship to them except unity, love and service.

I will leave you now. I am Hatonn. 🜚

Sunday Meditation
March 17, 1974

(Unknown channeling)

I am Hatonn. I greet you, my friends, in the love and in the light of our Infinite Creator. I am the one known to you as Hatonn.

(Microphone is moved. Channel says, "That doesn't sound so good, either.")

I am Hatonn. I am Hatonn. I am with this instrument. I am aware of your problems. I am Hatonn. I am Hatonn. I will condition this instrument.

(Pause)

I am Hatonn. I am once more with this instrument. I greet you, my friends, in the love and in the light of our infinite Creator. It is a very great privilege to be with you. It is always a very great privilege to be able to speak with you. I am having some difficulty but, with patience, we will succeed in establishing this contact.

There are many things that affect a contact such as this one. This instrument has learned through practice to be able to clear his mind of the thoughts that he became involved in in his normal daily activities. It is necessary, if a good contact such as this one be made, that the thoughts that concern the daily activities of the individual or any other thoughts be erased from the consciousness for the period of the contact. It is necessary to maintain as close to a totally clear mind as possible for a good contact. This may be practiced in meditation and an individual may learn to think of nothing. This is easier for some than it is for others. Some of those who are involved in activities that require the use of the intellectual mind and analysis of activities sometimes find it much more difficult to clear the mind than those who are not so encumbered with intellectual problems. However, it is possible to overcome this problem regardless of the indulgence of the intellectual mind into activities and analysis of a type that are foreign to the orientation of a totally spiritually-oriented individual. It is quite possible for those who are involved in these activities of the mind to learn to shut off these thoughts and to become aware of the thoughts that we impress upon them as a result of their desire. It is something that requires practice. The amount of practice is dependent upon the ease with which an individual can clear his mind. This varies widely with individuals. Some require little or no practice. Others require an extensive amount. It is only necessary that one learn to think of nothing in order for a contact such as this one to be effective.

This instrument has almost mastered the technique required for totally shutting down the intellectual mind, so to speak, at will. At times, he still has difficulty in doing this and for this reason we use conditioning at these times since conditioning causes a focusing, or concentration of thought upon the phenomenon of conditioning and therefore is a technique for clearing the mind, in itself. It is not necessary to use muscular control for communication of this type since the channel has mastered the ability of receiving our thoughts in a direct form.

It is unfortunate that your society is of such a nature as to generate so many intellectual activities as to create a situation where it is difficult for many of those who would wish to receive our thoughts to receive them.

We of the Confederation of Planets in the Service of the Infinite Creator are living in an atmosphere of thought that is quite pure with respect to yours. We have no need for an involvement in activities that you are concerned with and therefore may maintain an awareness of that which we wish to maintain—an awareness of the route, you might say, of our spiritual seeking. This is, at times, quite difficult to maintain when involved in the activities that are abundant on the surface of your planet and it is advised that, through continued daily meditation, a quieting of the conscious mind is possible for any individual and that this quieting and shutting down of the conscious mind will result, for any individual, in an ability to receive in a very direct manner the thoughts that we impress upon them.

We of the Confederation of Planets in the Service of the Infinite Creator are impressing these thoughts on all who desire them. It is not necessary for an individual to be able to directly channel our thoughts, as does this instrument, in order to be an effective channel of communication for our Confederation. It is necessary that there be more than one type of channel for our thoughts and we are very pleased to see activities of all forms that carry our message to those upon your planet who desire it. We, therefore, recommend that those who desire to be of service, [whether] in [your own way of] service or in [the channeling] service in which we serve, simply to practice daily meditation and to allow a natural progression in their seeking.

(Pause)

At this time, I'm going to condition each member of this group. If an awareness of nothing is maintained it should be possible for each member of this group to then become aware of my contact. I will now condition each member of this group.

(Unknown channeling)

There is a saying on your planet that goes, "All roads lead to Rome." This is a very true saying if you consider the road of life which lies before each of you. There are many questions about which road to choose, and there seem to be many considerations and many situations to which actions seem appropriate. "And," you ask yourself, "What does it mean? Where shall I go? What shall I do?"

Yet, my friends, there are lessons in every road and it is not what you encounter which marks the rate of your spiritual progress. It is rather the quality of your awareness of what you encounter. Daily meditation, my friends, encourages the shifting of the attention from the exterior illusion to the infinity within. Daily meditation, my friends. When you have questions such as I described, remember that the answers lie within you waiting to be unfolded through daily meditation.

It has been my privilege to speak with you this evening. I hope that I have been of service to you. I will leave you now. Adonai, my friends. Adonai vasu.

Monday Meditation
March 18, 1974

(Don channeling)

I am Hatonn. I am with this instrument. I greet you, my friends, in the love and the light of our infinite Creator. It is a great privilege to be with you this evening. I and my brother, known to you as Laitos, are here with you. We will condition each of you. It is only necessary that you desire our contact for you to receive it. We are here to serve you. If you will avail yourself to our contact we will attempt to use each of you as an instrument for communication. Our thoughts will be made clear to you if you simply relax and allow yourself to think of nothing. Please be patient, for in some cases it will take considerable conditioning. We will at this time attempt to use one of the other instruments in a vocal way.

As I said to you, it is only necessary for you to think of nothing and avail yourself. *(Inaudible)* analyze your thoughts *(inaudible)* enter your head.

(Carla channeling)

I am now with this instrument. I am Hatonn. It is a very great privilege to speak with you. And it is a pleasure *(inaudible)*. There is much confusion upon the surface of the Earth. And it is a privilege indeed to be communicating with those who are seeking. The light that you see during the day is in fact beauty and power. You and your brothers and I and my brothers and each individual *(inaudible)* share this reality. In meditation you come, do not bring your intellect, my friends. Drop it, put it down. It will not serve you, it will only beguile you. Relax, meditate and if you wish us to serve you it is our greatest please to be with you and help in any way that we can.

I will now attempt to contact another, if she will avail herself.

(Unknown channeling)

I am Hatonn.

(Don channeling)

I am Hatonn. I am again with this instrument. It is a great privilege to use those who desire to aid us of the Confederation of Planets in the Service of the Infinite Creator.

We realize that it is difficult to become receptive in a very short period of time to our thoughts. It is not something that is common upon this planet. However, we can assure you that anyone is capable of doing this. It is only necessary that he desire to receive that which we give to you: our understanding of the truth of the creation.

It is difficult to change from an environment which [has] little need of the form of communication which we are now practicing with this instrument. It is like learning a new language for many of those whom we attempt to contact. However, it is very simple and requires only that the individual desires the contact [and] avail himself to us in daily meditation.

There will be times when he thinks he is making no progress. But progress is not always indicated by a physical manifestation. Progress is being made regardless of the physical manifestations. All that is necessary is that meditation be practiced.

There are many different types of channels of our thoughts and of our communications. Some such as this instrument receive our thoughts directly and verbalize them immediately, as they are received. Some receive our thoughts in a conceptual manner and then repeat the thoughts at a time interval after they are received. Some are controlled, you might say, to some extent in a muscular fashion in order to reinforce their awareness and understanding of the thought.

This instrument has developed capability of utilizing speech as a form of communication of which I have spoken. This is done by availing oneself in meditation to our concepts. At this time he is using a form of communication that involves simply speaking that which we give to him. He has cleared his mind of all other thoughts and is simply being receptive to anything that is impressed upon him. It is very difficult for an individual who is familiar with the form of communication upon this line to do this in a very rapid manner for he attempts to analyze what is given to him. He attempts to formulate in his own mind things about what are being given to him. This instrument at this time is simply receptive and is simply speaking that which is given to him. This makes for a simple but effective form of communication. We will attempt to produce this in all of those who desire our contact. All that is necessary is that they desire [the] contact enough to spend time in daily meditation. It will not be necessary for them to experience the conditioning process that is common at these contacts in every session of meditation for this is not always desirable. However, there will be the muscular conditioning that goes along with the direct contact in new instruments.

We of the Confederation of Planets in the Service of the Infinite Creator have for many, many of your years attempted to contact many of the people of your planet. We have contacted many who have desired and yet have never been consciously aware of this contact. Those of you who are fortunate enough to hear the words of a channel and such as the other channels that are in relatively small abundance upon the surface of your planet are then in a tradition to become vocal channels of a direct nature rather than the indirect nature for those who have no awareness in a conscious sense of what is occurring.

We are unfortunately limited to this form of contact since conditions of thinking upon your planet at the present time require a very careful approach to your people. However, if we are successful in spreading our understanding of the truth of the creation to a great enough extent among your peoples it may be possible in the near future that we will be able to contact many of them in a more direct way. It is your part, if you desire to aid us in the service of our Creator, to help in disseminating this information to those who would desire it. It is necessary to remain in complete understanding of the prerequisites for an individual receiving that which we are giving. The prerequisite is desire.

We do not wish to bring to those of this planet who do not desire our understanding our understanding, for if something is not desired, it is the wish of the Creator that it not be given. It is the wish of our Creator that man throughout the universe get what he desires in all instances. It is sometimes difficult to understand upon your planet and within your present physical illusion that each of the individuals within the illusion are obtaining exactly what they desire. It is difficult for an individual who is in a position that he considers undesirable that he is obtaining and being rewarded with exactly what he does desire. But from our point of view, we interpret the law of the Creator to be infallible, that is, each of the individuals upon the surface of your planet are obtaining exactly what they desire.

It is necessary for an individual to become aware of much more than most of those of your planet are presently aware in order to understand that they are receiving exactly what they desire. This is a natural law of this creation. This is the reason that we of the Confederation of Planets in the Service of the Infinite Creator are so very pleased and so very content with our existence and our activities. We believe sincerely that we understand the law of desire and fulfillment thereof. For this reason we desire that which will benefit us throughout all of the illusion of time. We desire to be in unity with the creation. We desire to be of service in the creation. We desire to be an expression of our Creator's love. For this reason we serve those on your planet who desire our service. For this reason we serve in the name of our infinite Creator. This is what we desire: to fulfill the desire not only of those upon your planet but the desire of our Creator. This, then, is also our desire and in doing this we are rewarded with the fruits of our desire.

This is our understanding of the mechanism of this creation. It is a very simple mechanism. It was designed by a Creator who expressed nothing but total love. It was a plan that was infallible and is infallible. It is simply man on Earth, ignorant of the simple truth of this creation that causes the illusion that he now experiences and causes him to believe that the truth of his desires are not inevitable. This is not the truth. Man upon the planet Earth is receiving exactly what he desires.

It is only necessary that he understand how to change his desires in order for him *(inaudible)* It is only necessary for man on Earth to learn that in order to experience the truth of desire that he would desire even within the illusion. It is only necessary for him to desire love and therefore express and experience it in all of his activities.

This we bring to the people of the planet Earth: our understanding of the true workings of this creation. It is much simpler than you might expect. And yet it is much different than you might expect. At present the people of this planet are limited to a very infinitely small illusion. A tiny speck within an infinite continuum of time. And a very tiny understanding within the total and simple understanding of the expression that created them. It is unfortunate that truth has been so hidden from the people who dwell upon this planet. It is time that each of time be given the opportunity to form a desire for this truth.

We realize that [in] an endeavor to awaken the people who dwell upon your planet that there will be many difficulties for we have experienced these difficulties. And we realize that these difficulties will continue, but the only requirement is faith. For each individual will awaken. Perhaps not immediately, perhaps in what you would consider the farthest regions. However, he will awaken. And we will serve him, for that is our desire. For in serving him we serve ourselves, as we do in serving you. If you wish to join us in this service, it is only necessary that you avail yourself to the knowledge that is necessary to serve in the most efficient manner through daily meditation. It will be possible if this is done to not only express in words the desire of our Creator, but you will also be able to demonstrate this desire by your desire which will be the desire of your Creator.

I am Hatonn. It has been a privilege to speak with you this evening. I will continue to condition each of you throughout all of the time that you desire it. Through your meditations much will be revealed to you. Much will be revealed to you that can be revealed only through this process, much more than could be revealed than if we were to land upon the surface and walk up to you.

I will leave this instrument at this time. I leave each of you in the love and the light of our infinite Creator. I am Hatonn. Adonai vasu borragus. ✣

Tuesday Meditation
March 19, 1974

(Don channeling)

I am Hatonn. I greet you, my friends, in the love and the light of our infinite Creator. It is a great privilege to be with you once more. We have many here tonight who desire to contact those of us who are in the service of our infinite Creator. It is a great privilege to be with so many who have the same desire. We of the Confederation of Planets in the Service of the Infinite Creator are here to contact you in any way that we can within the limits of our understanding of the desire of the people who dwell upon this planet known as Earth.

I and my brother Laitos will at this time condition each of those of you who desire our contact. And we will speak using those of you who have obtained an awareness of our thoughts to a sufficient extent to channel them to those in the room who are desiring. I will at this time attempt to speak using one of the other instruments. If those who desire our contact will avail themselves to our contact at this time we will use each of those who have become aware of our thoughts.

(Unknown channeling)

I am Hatonn. It is a privilege to speak through this instrument. It is only a matter of availing yourself. It is only necessary that you clear all of your thoughts from your mind. I will now leave this instrument and continue to condition those who desire it.

(Carla channeling)

I am Hatonn. I am very happy to be using each new instrument. I and my brothers are most privileged to be working with you. It is our only desire to serve you in any way that we can, and to help all on the surface of your planet that we can contact who wish to be contacted. And so we are very pleased to be developing new instruments such as yourselves. And we assure you that if you desire to obtain this ability, it will come to you. You need only relax, meditate and avail yourselves to our contact. We will at any time be available to give you the thoughts of the teachings of *(inaudible)* as you desire it.

My friends, your meditations are like a kind of storing up of another energy. A charging, if you will, a raising of your potential forces. Consider this, my friends, it is indeed a service, one in which we wish to help you any we can for you to channel our thoughts directly. But, my friends, are we not all channels, always in all our aspects do we not demonstrate something? What, my friends, do you demonstrate? Look about you, my friends, look at the water as it rides along the shore, flowing freely, not choosing, but going infinitely, equally, from place to place. See the rain as it falls upon the sea; it does not choose to fall over here or over there, but it spreads equally. Consider the atmosphere, my friends, it ever flows around your poles *(inaudible)*. It equalizes itself, not selecting this or that course, but choosing them all. The Earth, my friends, *(inaudible)* but does not choose, my friends. It gives what service it has to give to those who ask. Consider that you are channels, my friends, every day, in all that you do and say. You reflect something. Take the potential that you have raised, my friends, and *(inaudible)* within you. Take it, for indeed you have it and demonstrate it as best you can, for you are already channels, yet there is a place for contacts of a direct nature *(inaudible)* such as these and many others that you have heard from the Confederation of Planets in the Service of the Infinite Creator. It is our very great pleasure to be with you. At this time I will attempt to transfer this contact to another.

(Unknown channeling)

I am Hatonn. I am now with this instrument. This instrument must try to clear his mind in order to better receive our thoughts. There are many upon your planet who will become channels. There is much work to be done. The time of the great harvest is at hand. We of the Confederation of Planets in the Service of the Infinite Creator stand ready to assist in the harvest. Soon, my friends, there will be more opportunities for you to be of service to your fellow man than you can presently offer them.

(Inaudible)

… able to serve. Able to serve through stimulating others to seek truth and thereby aiding them in their spiritual progression. This, my friends, is the greatest thing which one can do for another: to aid another in his or her spiritual evolution. I and my brothers, as we have said many times in the past, are always available to help you—this is our purpose. All that is needed is that you desire it and avail yourself. I will now attempt to use another of the new instruments that we are conditioning.

(Pause)

I am again with this instrument. I am sorry I could not get through to the one known as R. We are confident that she will …

(Inaudible)

(Don channeling)

I am with this instrument. I am Hatonn. It has been a great privilege to condition each of those of you who desire. I am at this time in a craft that is high above your dwelling place. It is a craft that we of the Confederation of Planets in the Service of the Infinite Creator use to travel from planet to planet. It is a small craft that is sometime in use for travel between planets. However, for our purposes, it is sufficient to say that it is a craft that allows us much freedom of motion. We are aware that the people of your planet have seen our craft many times without understanding our purpose for visiting the planet known as Earth. However, this is no problem. It is our purpose that our craft be seen to some extent. There are many of those who dwell upon this planet who have begun to think of our craft as what they actually are: craft from a planet other than this one. They will not be surprised to learn that the occupants of these craft have delivered messages to those on Earth who would receive them. This is the condition which has been created over the past several years. And it is the condition that is best to produce seeking among many of the people of Earth.

This is what is necessary if an individual is to realize the truth of the creation. It is necessary that he seek this truth. There will be many in the very near future who seek to find the truth of the creation. There have been many who have sought to find the truth of our craft, but they have not been rewarded with this information because their seeking has been of a nature that will result in no real gain for them. The seeking that is necessary for an individual to actually make gainful progress is seeking in the spiritual nature. We have attempted to provide an atmosphere in which seeking is a generated result of our presence. We have then attempted to provide answers, answers to seeking of a spiritual nature.

(Tape ends.) ♣

Tuesday Meditation
March 19, 1974

(Don channeling)

I am Hatonn. I greet you, my friends, in the love and in the light of our infinite Creator. It is a great privilege to be with you this evening. It is always a very great privilege to be with those who are seeking.

My friends, you are seekers. If you were not seekers you would not be here. Seeking, my friends, is the most important thing that you do at this time in your existence, and at any future or any past existence.

Why, might you ask, is seeking of such great an importance? Friends, we are all evolving. Upon your planet there are many theories of evolution. None of them are correct. Evolution takes place as a product of consciousness. Consciousness evolves several different ways, but consciousness only evolves at a rapid rate when directed by consciousness. This direction is known as seeking. There are many things that are sought by the people of your planet. However, the understanding of their own consciousness is sought by very, very few and this is what is necessary if they are to create an acceleration in their evolution, and this is what is desired by all of us who realize that the process of evolution is taking place, and what the rewards of evolvement are.

There are many problems that plague the peoples of your planet. There are problems of a political nature. There are problems of an economic nature. There are problems of an emotional nature, and many, many other problems. Some of the peoples of your planet are not affected, at all, by any of these problems, for their evolution of consciousness has removed them from a state of being affected by these type of situations. These, then, are the ones who are able to serve others, to serve others in discovering the necessity and the pleasure of seeking. They are able to serve others, for they are able to demonstrate their knowledge which they have obtained through seeking.

There is a reaction to every effect that is felt by an individual in his daily existence. The reaction that the individual experiences is dependent upon his state of evolvement. The man known to you as Jesus, the last of the great teachers upon your planet, displayed reactions to the effects of his environment quite different than those about him. His reactions were due to his own state of evolved consciousness. He was able to realize the truth of all that he experienced, and being able to do this, to truly react with intelligence and to serve his fellow man, he was recognized as one [that] could be followed. This, my friends, is the only way that is provided for the education necessary for the people of this planet to carry on their evolvement of consciousness. There is a very good reason for this. The reason, my friends, is that there is no better way to do this.

It is necessary that an individual initiate his own seeking. It is necessary that, once he has initiated his seeking, that he carry it through to a state of realization and understanding. In this way, he evolves, and in no other way, after he has reached that state where he can initiate seeking.

Many of the people upon your planet at this time have reached that state and need but little enticement to move that short distance onward to the goal which we all understand to be that which we truly desire.

At this time, I will transfer this contact to the other instrument.

(Carla channeling)

I am Hatonn. As I was saying, my friends, your seeking is most important.

It may be thought of, shall we say, as a projector of which there are two components, the aimed direction of the projector, and the force which impels that seeking upon the projector. The seeking itself is largely the directional portion of the projector. The energy which impels this seeking is the function of the unity which is present between you and the creation. There is an infinite amount of energy available to all entities at all times, and when properly directed and fully realized, there is no limit to how far one may seek. However, the degree of realization of the unity between the seeker and the creation of which he is a part varies from individual to individual, and it is through meditation that a closer and firmer realization of this unity is obtained. With the seeking carefully centered, aimed and prepared and with the energy channel opened, you embark upon your seeking.

We are aware that it is not always as simple in the doing as in the telling and we do not wish to infer that we are not aware of the difficulties of working within the illusion that you now enjoy. But, my friends, what you seek is all about you. You have walled yourself away from what you seek because, within the illusion, it seems to be a safety-making factor to have walls, physical walls, mental walls of defense, emotional limits beyond which each individual does not go. For, he wishes to be safe within his walls, and within his illusion, these walls make him safe.

But, my friends, this *is* the illusion. The reality is that you are part of the unity. There is none other than you. That which you seek is that which you are. You need only come into full realization of this unity, and that which you seek will be yours. This, my friends, is your birthright.

It is our great privilege to be attempting to alert those of your planet who wish to hear this, that this is true. We hope that these thoughts have been of service to you.

I will leave this instrument at this time. I leave you in the love and the light of our infinite Creator. Adonai, my friends. Adonai vasu.

Saturday Meditation
March 23, 1974

(Carla channeling)

I am Hatonn. I greet you, my friends, in the love and the light of our infinite Creator. It is my privilege to be with you this evening. We of the Confederation of Planets in the Service of the Infinite Creator are always privileged to be able to speak with those upon the surface of your planet who wish understanding. This is our service to the people of this Earth.

And yet, this service is indirect. It is, my friends, understanding that we feel to be the most valuable commodity that we can offer you. Our understanding has enabled us to do some things which those upon the surface of the planet upon which you now live do not [enjoy]. We can understand miraculous things, which are not miraculous at all to us, and [that] we can promise to anyone who wishes to seek are not miracles [and] may become natural things. And how do we do this? Indirectly, my friends. We wish to give a way of understanding; we do not wish to insist or to convince.

We have suggested that the way to understanding is meditation. My friends, this suggestion, in one form or another, has been before the people of your planet many, many times in the past. The great teacher, known to your people as Jesus, understood the truth of spiritual seeking and demonstrated in his daily life the spiritual seeking of which we speak.

Those of you who have wished it are receiving conditioning and we will be with you at any time to aid you in whatever way we can. Our gift and our service to you is simply our understanding of the truth. We are still seeking. We are not of the ultimate authority, nor would we ever insist upon anyone listening to what we have to say if another mode of thinking seemed more profitable. So, my friends, understanding is possible only for one person at one time. Each person is completely free at any time to choose. This is why we are indirect. We may say things to you that you may consider them in the privacy of your own thoughts and what you choose to do is completely your own idea.

This is as it should be, my friends. And what is our understanding? Our understanding, my friends, of this illusion, which is taken for the physical life upon your planet, is that it consists of a path, of a road, to be followed, and of lessons to be learned. There are as many paths as there are people, my friends, and there are no set lessons. But after a great many lessons have been met, my friends, there comes a time when all of the lessons change to a different set. And those who are ready for the change go on to a new set of lessons.

It is our understanding, my friends, that the planet known as Earth approaches the end of one set of these lessons. And thus graduation is at hand for some and not at hand for others. And that there are many people balanced very delicately between going on and repeating these lessons for another cycle or time. It is our desire, my friends, to aid those who are almost ready to graduate.

In their graduating, we have some success in the past in giving this service to other peoples in other places and times. We are hopeful of doing this same thing here. This is our fervent desire, for in our service to you lies our service to ourselves. It is by our serving you that we are able to progress upon our spiritual path. Our only hope is to be able to aid you in every way that we can.

At this time, I will attempt to condition those of you who desire it, if you will avail yourselves to my contact.

(Inaudible)

(Carla channeling)

I am Hatonn. I am again with this instrument. I will leave you at this time, my friends. I leave you in the love and the light of our infinite Creator. Seek understanding, my friends. Seek through meditation and seek to know there was a reason that the master teacher known as Jesus retreated from time to time to a place where there was silence. There was something he was seeking. Seek for the silence where there is much understanding awaiting you.

I leave you now, but I will be with you any time you desire my contact. Adonai, my friends. Adonai.

Sunday Meditation
March 24, 1974

(Unknown channeling)

I am Hatonn. I greet you, my friends, in the love and in the light of our infinite Creator. It is once more a very great privilege to be with you.

I am the one known to you as Hatonn. And yet, I am many. I identify myself to you as Hatonn, and yet, this does not mean what it means upon the surface of your planet. I am Hatonn, but what does this mean? Does it mean that I am a man, who resides elsewhere and speaks to you now using a technique you have come to know as telepathy? Or does it mean something else?

I am Hatonn. I and my brothers are with you. We are each with you. At this time and at all times, we are with you for we cannot be separated.

There is some difficulty with this contact, please be patient.

I am Hatonn. I am with this instrument. I greet you, my friends, in the love and in the light of our infinite Creator. I am sorry for the difficulty and the delay, but we have not established a very good contact. We will continue.

I was saying that I am Hatonn. I identify myself to you as the one that you know as Hatonn. However, this is for purposes of establishing a contact between you and us. We, of the planet Hatonn, are known as Hatonn. This identification is more of an address than it is an identification of a separate part of the creation. We do not recognize a separation in this creation. We only recognize unity. It is, however, convenient to have an address. That is, a system of location of part of the unity. And, for this reason, we identify ourselves as Hatonn.

At a later time my brother, Laitos, will speak to you concerning your question. At this time, I simply wish to point out that this identification is used only to make you aware of our location. We do not consider ourselves separate of yourselves or any other individual in this creation.

I will again condition this instrument for a short period, please be patient.

(Pause)

I am Hatonn. I am again with this instrument. We are sorry for the delay. We are having some difficulty. I am with you, my friends, in the love and in the light of our infinite Creator. It is a very great privilege to establish this contact. We will attempt to continue without the difficulties we were experiencing.

We of the Confederation of Planets in the Service of the Infinite Creator are always with you. We are here to serve you and we are always with you. We are here to bring to you our understanding of the truth of this creation. This truth we wish to bring to you because you desire it. This is our objective: to bring to man on Earth that which he desires. Unfortunately, we cannot bring to all of those who dwell on your planet exactly what they desire, for we do not have it to give to them. We do, however, have to give to those who desire it our understanding of the workings of this Creation.

This is what we bring to man on Earth. We are attempting to teach to those, who would accept our teaching, a very, very simple lesson. This is the lesson that is needed by all mankind throughout all the creation. This, in actuality, is all that is needed, for this lesson will then result in his knowledge of all things. We have been trying to give to man on Earth this knowledge for many of his years. We have attempted throughout what you would consider ancient times on your planet to bring to mankind, to those who would desire the knowledge, the knowledge that is necessary for experiencing all of the infinite experiences created by our Creator.

Some of those who dwell upon this planet in the past have accepted these teachings and have benefited from them. Benefited far beyond anything that could be imagined by those who are not experiencing the benefits. We have attempted for many of your years to bring to all of those who desire the teachings, the very simple teachings that allow you to know all. However, these … I will continue … I was saying … that these teachings have not been understood very well.

I am going, at this time, to tell a story, a story which illustrates some of what we are attempting to describe to you.

Upon your planet there once lived a man. This man had great material wealth and this gave him what he considered to be power, for many of his fellow men would eagerly do his bidding for a part of this wealth …

As I was saying … There was a man upon your planet who had great wealth and in this wealth, he saw much power. For his fellow men would eagerly do his bidding to share part of this wealth. And, for this reason, many of those who dwell upon this planet, known to you as Earth, require vast quantities of material wealth. And, therefore, acquire what they consider to be much power. What is not understood by those men is that in acquiring this wealth and in attempting to posses much power through this wealth that they are giving up an infinite amount of power for that which is in actuality no power at all.

The man of which I spoke, who had much wealth, used it to satisfy his desires … I am having some difficulty, please be patient.

I shall continue. This man used his wealth to satisfy his desire. And his desires were for things which he thought that he wanted and they were for things that he needed. For he saw in this wealth, not only a great happiness which would come from possessing those things that he desired and having dominion over all of his fellow men about him, but also he saw great security in that he would need not want for the rest of his days.

And, therefore, he coveted greatly his accumulation of wealth. And he had at his command everything that he desired and great status. But he lacked one thing. He lacked love. For it was not given to him by those about him and this he did not understand. And he became aware of his need for this experience that he called love and he set about to discover how to obtain it. And he questioned those about him. And asked them why he was not given love and they could not answer him for they did not know.

And he went to a wise man and offered to pay him much of his wealth if he would but tell him how to obtain love. And the wise man gave unto the rich man all that he possessed, for all that he possessed was but a pitiful small amount. And the man of great wealth accepted it, for he had long ago resolved never to turn down a gift. And he left the wise man and went to his home and pondered this gift, leaving the wise man penniless. For he had not paid the wise man. For the wise man had not told him how to find love.

And as the days passed, he returned to the wise man, for he could not understand why he had been given all that was possessed by the one who was said to be so wise. And when he asked him he was answered by the wise man who said, "It is because I have a great love for you and you desire wealth. Therefore, I give you that which I have to add to your riches, for this is what you desire."

And at that moment, the man of great wealth looked at the wise man and said, "And in turn, I, for the first time, know love." And he gave to the wise man great wealth. And in doing so, he felt an even greater love. For, for the first time, he had learned the truth of the Creator's gifts to His children. And this man was very fortunate, for he had been able to discover a way of generating love.

And yet, man on Earth continues to seek within his material illusion; continues to seek that which is of no real value, for he lacks faith. He stands upon the surface of this planet and experiences all of the gifts of his Creator. He breathes the air and smells the fragrance of the flowers and is in the company of his fellow man and finds many things provided for him. And yet, he does not understand. He does not have faith that within this creation, he has [supply]; and due to this lack of faith, he finds hardships, for he does not understand faith.

Therefore, man, in many instances, does not seek the knowledge of the wise man. But he seeks a security and a power that is not secure and is not power.

I will leave this instrument at this time. I am sorry for the extreme difficulty with this contact. I am the one known as Hatonn. Adonai vasu.

L/L Research

Thursday Meditation
March 28, 1974

(Don channeling)

I am Hatonn. I am with this instrument. I greet you, my friends, in the love and light of our infinite Creator. It is a great privilege to be with you. I and my brothers are always privileged to be with you.

I am at this time in a craft. A craft that you would call a flying saucer. This craft is in your atmosphere.

I am aware of your thoughts. This seems strange to the people of your planet. However, let me assure you that it is not at all strange.

We of the Confederation of Planets in the Service of the Infinite Creator have been for many of your years aware of many principles of reality. We are aware of these principles because we have availed ourselves to them just as the people of your planet may do.

This instrument has been able, as have been others, to become aware of our thoughts as we direct them to him. This is the normal way of communicating. The method used by the people of your planet is not at all normal. The Tower of Babel referred to in your Bible refers to the loss of ability of the people at that time to communicate with each other, using what you call telepathy. Telepathy is the normal technique for communication. It is simply that it is necessary to be in tune with the intended expression of love that created this universe to be able to use what you would call telepathy as it was intended.

We of the Confederation of Planets use this form of communication and we are able to contact any of our brothers as easily as you would use your telephone. It is something which we are quite accustomed to doing. It is as simple for us as breathing or listening or speaking is simple for you. In the illusion in which you now find yourself, you find that you are isolated from your brothers except by the medium of the illusion. It is necessary in order to communicate to express yourself verbally and then transfer through the air by means of sound waves to express to your brothers, or it is necessary to use some electrical or electronic device. In other words, there is a separation between your consciousness and other consciousness that is the illusion. The separation is illusion and is not reality.

It is possible through meditation to totally reduce the illusion that you now experience that creates the separation—an illusory separation—to what it actually is—a total illusion. We have been continuing to speak to you about meditation. We have spoken to you many times about reality and about love and about understanding. And yet, you do not seem to be able to overcome the illusion. The illusion is extremely strong. It appears as if it [is] strong to you at this time. However, the illusion to us is of no consequence. We appear to you at many times as the illusion rather than the illusion which causes your separation from your brothers on your planet. The truth, of course, is the reverse. We are reality.

How then can you experience reality? And I define reality as being the original concept of our Creator rather then its extension through the experiments of His children. We are somewhat hampered in using your language, since in order to express these concepts it is necessary to use a system which was evolved within the illusion, and which therefore has all of its basis for value within the illusion.

When speaking to you through an instrument in this manner, it necessary therefore to speak using these concepts which since they are of an illusory origin convey at least partially illusory definitions. It matters not, however, that it is impossible to intellectually communicate precisely what we are trying to convey. It is more important that we impress the need for nonintellectual communications, communications that are direct and not restrained by a system of semantics that was evolved inside a totally erroneous concept.

For this reason we have continued to speak of the necessity for meditation. We will continue to speak of this necessity since this is actually the only way that anyone upon your planet at this time can be directly aided by those of us who are here to serve. What we are most concerned with at this time is that there be definite progress by those who desire to make progress. If this is to be done with any rapidity, it will be necessary that the illusion be obliterated. This may be done by analyzing each facet of the illusion that encumbers you in your daily existence and then reducing it to its proper dimension. Its proper dimension, my friends, is that of non-existence. What is important is for one to recognize the illusion for what it is. It is important that one recognize reactions to the illusion for what they are. It is very important that one recognize the truth of the Creator's love and how it expresses itself through you. If this is done and it is augmented by daily meditation there can be an extremely rapid progress made toward joining those of us who are able to live in the light which was provided by our Creator for our enjoyment.

It is extremely important that every thought that is generated by an individual who wishes to make progress be analyzed immediately upon generation.

If this thought is a thought generated by the false illusion, then this thought should be immediately rejected. It is possible to know the value of a generated thought. This is possible by learning to maintain a continual state of meditation. There are many things that occur in your daily activity that are generated by potentials within the illusion. These are the things which must be carefully watched. The reason for the illusion, my friends, is one that man on Earth has generated. He has generated it out of desire. This illusion is useful. It is very useful for those who would wish to evolve at a very rapid rate by experiencing it and then overcoming [*i.e.* using] it while within it. Many of us who are now circling your planet would desire to have the opportunity that you have, the opportunity to be within the illusion and then through the generation of understanding overcome [*i.e.* use] the potentials of the illusion. This is a way of gaining progress spiritually and has been sought out by many of our brothers.

I cannot overemphasize the necessity of becoming able to understand the nature of the potentials within your illusion and then by self-analysis and meditation, reacting to that in a way that will express the Thought that generated us: the Thought of our Creator. This was done by the teacher whom you know as Jesus. This man recognized his position. He recognized the illusion. He understood the reason for the potentials within the illusion. And his reactions to these potentials and activities within the illusion was a reaction which was expressing the Thought of our Creator; a Thought of love.

Keep uppermost in your mind that the illusion that you experience is an illusion, that it is surrounding you for the purpose of teaching you. It can only teach you if you become aware of its teachings. It is said that, "He worked His wonders in mysterious ways." This way may seem mysterious; however, it is the way of spiritual evolvement. There are many souls experiencing the illusion in which you find yourself; however, there are few using this illusion to grow. They are not doing this other than at a subliminal level because they have not availed themselves through their seeking to a knowledge of the possibility of doing this.

Once an individual has become aware of the possibility of using the illusion in which he finds himself in your physical world for the progression of spiritual growth, it is necessary that he take the next step and use his knowledge to express, regardless of the potentials which affect him, the love and understanding of his Creator.

I have spoken at length upon this. It is extremely simple. Those of us in His service understand without saying the concepts of which I have spoken. You also understand these concepts; however, they become lost in your waking state, due to the impressions of the illusion that has been with you. It is up to you to use the knowledge that we attempt to reawaken within you in order to express the love and understanding that is within all mankind. Do this for this is what you desire. And when you do this, my friends, it will become immediately obvious to you that this is what you desire. Do it all of the time. This is possible if meditations such as this one are on a daily basis and individual meditation such as you may carry on yourselves are on a continuing and constant basis.

Retain an awareness of the truth that is within you. Do not let the illusion overcome your thinking. In the environment that you now experience, there will be continuous communications to you from others within the illusion attempting, through no fault of their own, to obliterate the memory of truth that you evoke through meditation. These must be guarded against for only in maintaining an awareness of this truth can you be of service to those who seek your aid, even though in seeking they might impress upon you conditions of the illusion that you do not wish to accept. An awareness that you maintain through meditation, however, will limit to their actual place the illusory concept, to that place which is total illusion, not reality, my friends. [The illusion is] nothingness, an invisible fabric of nothingness. Think backwards in what you consider time, say, one year. Consider all the potentials within the illusion that you have experienced in that time and how they affect you now. Think backwards five years or ten or fifteen. The illusion has no lasting effects, my friends. It dissolves. It is a fabric of nothingness. Who are you today? And why are you you, today? It is because of your thinking. It is because of your reactions to the illusion perhaps, the Creator most definitely.

Wherein lies truth, my friends? It lies in you. In your ability to express it lies your ability to serve. In your reaction to the illusion lies your ability to demonstrate your awareness and therefore your value in service. Consider this carefully, my friends. For this is how you grow.

I hope that I have been of service. I am Hatonn. Adonai vasu borragus. ☥

Tuesday Meditation
April 2, 1974

(Don channeling)

I am Hatonn. I am with the instrument. I am known to you as Hatonn. I am with you in the love and the light of our infinite Creator. It is a privilege, as always, to be with you. It is a privilege to be [with] those who seek.

There are many of our craft that have been seen in your skies, however, shortly more of our craft will be seen. For shortly it will be necessary for us to advertise our presence. This we will do. Primarily by being visible in your skies. This will alert many of your people to our presence, many who have heard of us previously, but who have not considered our presence of any importance.

There is a choice to be made very shortly, and it would be preferable if all of the people of this planet understand the choice that is to be made. It will be difficult for many of the people of this planet to understand what this choice is because it is a choice that they have not considered. They have been much too involved in their daily activities and their confusion and their desires are of a very trivial nature to be concerned with an understanding of the choice that they are very shortly to make. Whether they wish to or not, whether they understand it or not, regardless of any influence, each and every one of the people who dwell upon planet Earth will shortly make a choice. There will be no middle area. There will be those who choose to follow the path of love and light, and those who choose otherwise. This is all that is necessary.

This choice will not be made by saying, "I choose the path of love and light," or, "I do not choose it." The verbal choice will mean nothing. This choice will be measured by the individual's demonstration of his choice. This demonstration will be very easy for us of the Confederation of Planets in His Service to interpret. This choice is measured by what we term the vibratory rate of the individual. It is necessary, if an individual is to join those who make the choice of love and understanding for his rate of vibration to be above a certain minimal level. There are many now that are close to this minimum level, but due to continuing conditions of erroneous thought that prevail upon your surface, they are either fluctuating around this point or are even in some cases drifting away from the path of love and understanding. There are many whose vibratory rate at this time is sufficiently high for them to travel with no difficulty into the density of vibration that this planet is shortly to experience.

So what, my friends, is the task of groups such as this one as we of the Confederation begin to advertise our presence? Groups such as this one have the task of bringing an understanding, to those who desire it, of their alternatives. This is important at this time, very important, my friends. There is going to be a harvest, as you might call it, a harvest of souls that will shortly occur upon your planet. We are attempting to extract the greatest possible harvest from this planet. This is our mission, for we are the harvesters.

In order to be most efficient, we are attempting to create first a state of seeking among the people of this planet who desire to seek. This would be those who are close to the acceptable level of vibration. Those above this level are, of course, not of as great an interest to us since they have, you might say, already made the grade. Those far below this level unfortunately cannot be helped by us at this time. We are attempting at this time to increase by a relatively small percentage the number who will be harvested into the path of love and understanding. Even a small percentage of those who dwell upon your planet is a vast number. And this is our mission, to act through groups such as this one in order to disseminate information in such a fashion that [it] may be accepted or rejected, that it may be in a state lacking what the people of your planet choose to call proof. We offer them no concrete proof, as they have a way of expressing it. We offer them truth. This is an important function of our mission—to offer truth without proof. In this way, the motivation will, in each and every case, come from within the individual. In this way, the individual vibratory rate will be increased. An offering of proof or an impressing of this truth upon an individual in such a way that he would be forced to accept it would have no usable effect upon his vibratory rate.

This, then, my friends, is the mystery of our way of approaching your peoples. This is why groups such as this one are important: to present truth without proof, to be the second stage, you might say, of our attack. To be the commercial that follows our advertising display in your atmosphere. It will be necessary that the truth given to those who will seek in the very near future be given with great care, for it must be truth and nothing else. We have asked that members of groups such as this one spend time in meditation. For in this way and only in this way can they avail themselves of the precise truth that we offer. And only in this way can they prepare themselves to disseminate this truth to those who seek in an exactly correct and understandable way in the language of your peoples. This, my friends, is a much, much more difficult task than you might imagine. There is an unbelievable amount of confusion existing upon the surface of your planet among your peoples. Many have been confused by the numerous religions which have given partial truths and in some instances, complete falsehoods. Many of your peoples have done no thinking on matters of a spiritual nature and will have no concept of things that seem straightforward and of utmost simplicity to yourselves.

It will be a great task. And we and you will not be entirely successful. We are able to say this, for we have had experience at harvests in the past. There will not be success in a complete way in disseminating the information that we bring to the people of Earth. There will be a complete success in the harvest of which we speak. It will be difficult to bring the truth to the understanding of the peoples of this planet, However, this will be done in one way or another. It will be up to the individual and his desire to understand and desire to seek this truth to create his vibratory change, even though it may necessarily only be slight.

I am going to condition this instrument for a short period of time and then transfer this contact to another instrument.

(The contact was transferred but was inaudible.)

Wednesday Meditation
April 3, 1974

(Don channeling)

I am Hatonn. I am with you. I greet you, my friends, in the love and in the light of our infinite Creator. It is a great privilege to be with you this evening. I am the one known to you as Hatonn. I am speaking through this instrument.

I am aware at this time of certain thoughts …

(Carla channeling)

(Inaudible). There is quite a bit of difficulty with this contact but we will do the best that we can.

We wish to give a few thoughts at this time. You may remember in reading the holy work which you call the *Bible* that the master known as Jesus had a simple reaction to the upsetting type of illusion which he faced. His reaction was to inform it that it was an illusion. When he was confronted with a very stormy sea, he said "Peace. Be still." And by understanding that the difficulty was an illusion that vision caused his own reality to become peaceful and still. The ability to look at the illusion upon your planet and say to it, "Peace. Be still," is very dearly earned. We are aware, my friends, of the great efforts which a person who lives upon the surface of your planet and enjoys your illusion must make to be able to accomplish the detachment of which we speak. And yet, my friends, once this is accomplished we may suggest to you that you may find it to have been worth the effort and more than worth the effort. For reality, my friends, is a freedom that is a great joy to those who have never known what lies beyond the illusion of storm.

We are aware, my friends, that at this time those of your group who have been faithful are beginning to prepare themselves as channels in one way or another. And this gives our hearts great gladness. And we only give you this thought that there is a, "Peace. Be still," to be inserted before any information is passed in order for you as the channel to be sure that you do not say that which has not been asked. And that you say what you say in such a way that it does not infringe.

We are aware, as we said, of the great difficulties of operating in reality while in the illusion that you enjoy upon the surface of your planet. But this service of yours needs the purity of that, "Peace. Be still." It needs the detachment to listen to what is answered and it needs the ability to allow oneself to be linked to the higher, infinite mind that will answer truth. Incorrect information or information given at the wrong time may not be of service, so in the midst of our rejoicing that you are channels may we also give you this simple caution *(inaudible)*. And may we offer our service always, at any time, to help you in any way that we can. To give you our thoughts directly if you are a channel, or to speak without words informing your own thoughts so that you may speak for us.

I would like at this time to transfer this communication to the instrument known as H, if he will avail himself.

(H channeling)

I am now with this instrument. It is always an honor to avail our thoughts to any who desire. We wish to come into contact with many of your peoples of your planet. We have a great service to offer you. It is a simple service, yet it is a service which can render great benefit. In order to transcend from this illusion, there is needed an awareness and understanding which cannot be obtained through the mechanism of the illusion. This awareness can be obtained only through meditation. It is our wish to render this small service to your peoples and *(inaudible)* which we can aid you in attaining, through your meditations. In the near future, there shall be many people of your planet who shall seek information. When this opportunity, or service, is presented to you …

(Some group members arrive.)

(H channeling)

I would like to extend my greetings and love to your new arrivals. It pleases us very much to avail our thoughts to you.

I was speaking of the times that are ahead when you shall be confronted with the many opportunities to render your service to other peoples of your planet. When you are asked to be of aid, simply be grateful for it is a gift from the Creator. Service is the only means of evolving into realms or ways. Be grateful whenever you have the opportunity *(inaudible)* and if you can render proper aid to those who request, for this ability shall be obtained through your daily meditation. Be cautious as not to create any negative train of thought. When being of service you shall be asked many questions. Many questions you will not be able to offer answers [to] unless you spend time in meditation. You can relay the thoughts of the people. Infinite awareness at all times if you avail yourself. Do not become alarmed at any given situation in which we can be of service. There is nothing in all of creation to be alarmed at if you are in constant state of consciousness *(inaudible)*.

(Inaudible)

And it is our desire to help all that have this desire. We cannot contact all of these peoples at this time because many have not yet awakened. *(Inaudible)* the time will be short and they shall need information through channels such as the ones here. In order to gain a strong, shall we say, grip on the light, they will be able to evolve rapidly once making the decision.

At this time I would like to contact a different instrument. I am Hatonn.

(B channeling)

I am having difficulty. I am Hatonn. I would like to say that I am pleased to communicate with this instrument. It is very difficult to *(inaudible)*.

(Tape ends.)

Second Monday Meditation
April 8, 1974

(Unknown channeling)

I … I am … I am … I … I am … I … I am … I am … I am … I am … I am … I am … I am … I am … I am … *(inaudible)* I am … I am with the instrument. I am Oxal. I greet you, my friends, in the love and the light of our infinite Creator. I am the one known to you as Oxal. It is once more a great privilege to speak with this group. I am Oxal. I am at this time … I am at this time in a craft above your house. This craft is of a type that you *(inaudible)* this type of craft *(inaudible)* small vehicle used for short reconnaissance type of *(inaudible)*. We are at this time in position to *(inaudible)*. We are at all times available to serve, however it is impossible for us at this time to meet with you in a direct physical way. We realize that you would wish to meet with us and we wish for the same *(inaudible)*. However, at this time it is not possible for us to do this.

(Unknown channeling)

(Inaudible).

(Unknown channeling)

As new channels are developed you will find degrees of difference in communicating. This is natural, my friends. Be patient. *(Inaudible)* I am *(inaudible)* we are here to help you in any way that we can. We are here to serve your peoples, to aid your growth and development of your planet's consciousness. *(Inaudible)* it pleases … as it pleases us to have the opportunities for communicating to a small degree.

(Pause)

As I was saying, a small degree. A small degree of infinite knowledge that is in store for you as you grow with the new vibrations of your planet. We are here to offer our aid, to share our love, *(inaudible)*. I am Oxal. I shall now leave this instrument and then attempt to condition the various instruments *(inaudible)*. I am Oxal. *(Inaudible).*

(Unknown channeling)

I am Oxal. I am with this instrument.

(Unknown channeling)

I am Oxal. I am with this instrument. I am having *(inaudible)* difficulty. I am having some difficulty with this instrument. I will attempt the instrument known as D *(inaudible).*

(D channeling)

I am … I am …

(Pause)

I am Oxal. I am with the instrument. I am sorry for the delay. It is a great privilege to be with you this evening. I am the one known to you as Oxal. I am speaking through this instrument. I am of the

Confederation of Planets in the Service of the Infinite Creator. I am in a craft above your house. I am speaking to you directly from this craft. I am in this craft at this time for a particular purpose. You will become aware of this purpose as I speak to you. We of the Confederation of Planets in the Service of the Infinite Creator are here to serve. We are here to serve in more ways than one. We have primarily attempted to serve you in arousing the interest in seeking. However, shortly we must serve you in an additional way. This addition *(inaudible)* will be in a more direct way.

It will be necessary if we are to do this that you prepare yourselves for this meeting. This may be done by availing yourselves *(inaudible)* to meditation. We will not be able communicate with you unless you are able to avail yourself to our thoughts in meditation. We cannot contact you in the manner you are accustomed to using upon the surface of your planet. This would be of no avail. We do not have concepts in your language that we wish to convey; we have concepts that are not within your language. If you will avail yourself in meditation to us we will prepare for our *(inaudible)*, but this is essential.

We are going to at this time prepare each of you in a certain way. It will be obvious to you. Please be patient for a few moments.

(Pause)

(Unknown channeling)

(Inaudible). As we do this, feel the rhythm … the rhythm of your breath *(inaudible)* as it slowly becomes one with all that surrounds you. This realization is important. It is a major step towards reaching a new level of consciousness for the peoples of your planet. Only then can you begin to experience *(inaudible)* level of vibration of this planet … of this planet Earth but only if there … It is important to master the technique if we are truly communicating *(inaudible)*. All the peoples of your planet have this potential if they so desire it. We realize that it is sometimes difficult for the level of your awareness *(inaudible)* is small beginning in the realm of the creation but, my friends, *(inaudible)* if you so desire it. There are no rules that omit any one of you *(inaudible)* with the growth if any within your group *(inaudible)* begin to feel.

This road is an individual road. The growth, my friends, is a vibration which can be felt by all of the peoples around you. We of the Confederation of Planets in Service to the Infinite Creator are very concerned about the course your planet has chosen to follow. When we speak of planet we speak of the peoples of your planet for they do represent the vibration of the creative intelligence of life. My friends, if you are to survive you must grow. It is our wish to help you grow … to transcend the vibration of hate and replace it with one of love. For love is all there is, my friends. This is the mainstay of all creation. We offer it to you. You must learn to offer it to all of you … to all of those around you. Only as you begin this course will you help. Your planet, my friends, is in the midst of many changes. These changes will affect your lives in many ways. I know it is hard for you to understand, but you must trust for we do bring love.

(Tape ends.) ❧

Wednesday Meditation
April 10, 1974

(Carla channeling)

I am Laitos. I greet you, my friends, in the love and the light of our infinite Creator. I and my brothers are very privileged to be among you this evening. We will be conditioning those of you who desire it and we will be using the next few moments in order to communicate to you through the medium of silence. We are pleased with your progress and we wish especially at this time to give you an awareness of certain truths. If you will avail yourselves to our contact we will communicate with you directly. You will be able to sense our presence. I will leave this instrument at this time and we will be with you. We are also with you, we of Laitos and others who help the brothers of Hatonn, at any time you may need our services. It is our great privilege to oblige. I will leave this instrument now. Adonai.

(Carla channeling)

I am Hatonn. I greet you, my brethren, in the love and in the light of our infinite Father. We are most pleased to be with this group once more this evening. We have been watching the proceedings and we and our brothers of Laitos will continue to condition each of you that desire this conditioning. This conditioning, my friends, is not a unified phenomenon. It is a variable one, for it depends completely upon its effect on the individual who is receiving it.

The conditioning wave, my friends, is sent in a blanket wave. Some physical vehicles are attuned to accept the conditioning wave in a certain way so that it shows up immediately as certain feelings of energy. Others may not experience immediate sensation yet they too are receiving conditioning and their physical vehicles are becoming more closely attuned to the conditioning wave. There are many reasons why some people experience variations in the conditions however it is sent and it is received. There are varying lengths of time necessary in individual cases for the conditioning wave to begin to manifest in the manner recognizable within the physical illusion as conditioning, as you call it. We are, however, satisfied that the wave is doing its work as we see each individual who is seeking the conditioning making progress towards a full ability to receive the wave in its most efficient form for producing instruments. This is, of course, only given upon request.

My friends, how privileged we are to speak with you this and each time we do. We have so much to say and yet our brothers were most correct earlier in accepting the silence also as an active point for more advanced messages. We do not wish to bore you with speeches. You are in a garden at this point, my friends. In you holy works it is called the Garden of Eden and in the garden there is perfection, there is safety, there is protection—against all, against each, against every possible evil for, indeed, my friends, within the Garden of Eden there is no evil. You are in this place as you meditate, my friends, for this place is reality. This perfect garden is truly your home.

My friends, take this high place, this garden, this home, and live in it in your mind—not just in meditation, but always. Keep it close. Reach for it. Move into it. Keep it by you. Use it. Live in it. Become one with the garden, for this is your true identity and in this realization your shining beauty will give grace and happiness to many.

I am most happy to be able to use another instrument and I will at this time transfer this message to the instrument known as R. I am Hatonn.

(R channeling)

I am Hatonn. I am now with this instrument. We are always … we are always privileged to speak with this group and others such as this group in different places upon your surface. It is very rewarding to help another along on the path of love and light. Though you sometimes feel as if you are at a standstill, that you are progressing …

We are having some difficulty. There will always be times when conditions are not exactly correct for an instrument to receive our thoughts. Because of [this] we will leave this instrument at this time for she is having difficulty *(inaudible)* receive our thoughts. I am Hatonn.

(Carla channeling)

I am again with this instrument. I am sorry that I cannot use the instrument known as R at this particular time. However, in the future the conditions will ameliorate themselves as she learns to avail herself more adeptly to our contact. It is only necessary to practice and to maintain a relaxation and a lack of analysis that produces a good contact.

I will leave your physical awareness at this time though I stand sentinel above you, far above you, waiting and watching for any way in which I may be of service to those of planet Earth. Only seek our aid and we will surely be there, within the silence and within your service. It has been our privilege to speak with you this evening. I leave you in His love and His light. Farewell, my brothers. Farewell.

Friday Meditation
April 12, 1974

(Carla channeling)

I am Hatonn. I greet you, my friends, in the love and in the light of our infinite Father. It is, as always, my pleasure and privilege to speak with those who are seeking. My brother Laitos is here. He is in the room with you. He will be conditioning those of you who desire this service. My friends, we would like to take this opportunity to say a few things about desire.

Desire is a somewhat misunderstood phenomenon upon planet Earth, the misunderstanding lying principally in the feeling that one has desires about only certain sorts of objects. My friends, the term "desire" is very pale for what we are aware of as desire. The truth, my friends, is much closer to the intensity of fire. There is, however, no such word as what we are looking for and we use the word desire.

Each incident that you experience in your present activities is a result of one thing, my friends—desire. The work of past desire is brought to fruition in the present. And for the future—my friends, while in this illusion it is reasonable to speak of the illusion of the future—your desire at this time shapes your future. It is your future, my friends. You were given complete freedom of choice by an infinitely loving Creator. Give back to Him the highest desire you can be aware of.

Be aware, my friends, that there is much to transcend. There are many levels of earthly desires that may be transcended fairly rapidly by those who seek. The more esoteric intellectual desires may soon be passed by those who truly seek. Are you aware, my friends, that you may desire to be a star? Are you aware, my friends, that it is permissible to desire any and all of the understandings that you wish to know?

The shape of the path that you follow is ever towards the infinity of the circle of unity, as you reach the reality of planet, of star, of open space, of infinity itself, as you begin to become aware of how far your desire may take you towards the love of the Father, so you may turn back to the present and concentrate, my friends, concentrate upon the purity and the essence of this desire.

You wish to know, to understand and to accept the truth—the highest truth—and as you do this, my friends, you will be moving. As well as you do this so well will you move towards that which you seek, for it is desire alone that will impel you forward. Your desire, my friends. Your desire. We can only encourage you and give you food for thought.

The sun shines beautifully upon your planet, everywhere the same and yet, my friends, if you have what you call a lens the sunlight may be so focused that it will burn paper. This, my friends, is desire. Desire to know the infinite Creator in the highest way of which you are capable. We are most happy to be of service to you in this seeking at any time in any way we can. At this time I will transfer this contact. I am Hatonn.

(Pause)

(Carla channeling)

I am again with this instrument. We apologize for the delay. There was some difficulty. We will leave this instrument at this time, leaving only in the sense of vocal contact. We are with you. Seek, my friends. Seek and focus. Meditation is the focusing point. We leave you in His love and His light. Farewell my brothers. I am Hatonn.

(Unknown channeling)

I am Hatonn. I am once more with *(inaudible)* love and in the light of our *(inaudible)*. I am aware at this time of certain considerations. I am attempting to use this instrument. Please be patient. We, the Confederation who are in the service of our infinite Creator, are here, as we have said many times before, to aid the people of this planet. It is, however, impossible to aid them in a direct manner for there is nothing that we can give to them of any value *(inaudible)* to aid them in the sense that they would consider aid. We are attempting to bring to the peoples of this planet what they require. We are attempting to bring understanding. *(Inaudible)* understanding will not be very easy to give to the peoples of this planet.

(Unknown channeling)

I am Hatonn. I am now with this instrument. We are experiencing difficulty *(inaudible)* contact. *(Inaudible)*. I shall attempt to reestablish contact with the one known as *(inaudible)* instrument *(inaudible)*.

(Unknown channeling)

I am with this instrument. I am Hatonn. I will continue. Please be patient. I will continue. I was saying that it will not be very easy to bring to the people of this planet understanding. They have for many, many centuries of their time been immersed in a way of thinking that is totally incorrect. The people of this planet have given almost no consideration to the spiritual nature of creation. This is a great mistake. The creation is entirely of what you would call a spiritual nature. There is nothing else. Creation is not at all what you think it is. It appears to you to be of a certain nature but this is simply because that at this particular time your awareness is limited to the boundaries of this particular nature.

We will shortly be experiencing a much closer contact with peoples of this planet. Their understanding of us and our purpose in being here will at first be almost negligible. They will have no understanding of our objectives or our values for they do not know reality. It is going to be up to those of the groups such as this one who have been able to experience some portion of reality to convey our real purpose. This is not going to be in all cases very successful, for it requires considerable meditation and seeking in order to discover the truth of which we have so often spoke.

There are many of your peoples at this time who would meet with us with much less alarm than would have occurred at a previous time. However, these numbers are not too great and there are but very few who understand our true objectives. Nonetheless, it is going to be necessary for us to accelerate our program of contacting peoples of this planet for now the time has grown quite short and there will be certain things in the way of contacts that will now occur that could not have occurred in the past.

There shall be, however, no general proof to the peoples of this planet at large of our reality and of our purpose. We still wish to remain in a condition so as to cause seeking of those who would seek. There are many of the peoples of this planet who do not desire to seek and for this reason it is not possible for us to encroach upon their desires. There are many who would much prefer to remain within the illusion that they now enjoy. This may seem strange to members of this group but this is true and will be necessary when contacting peoples *(inaudible)* to serve only those who desire your service.

There will be many of those who dwell upon this planet who will not under any circumstances wish to be made aware of the spiritual nature of this creation and as I have said it will be necessary to be careful not to impress upon these ideas of the nature of the reality that we bring to you. This may seem a strange way of serving peoples of this planet but this is our interpretation of the wish of our Creator—that each of His children seek what he desires regardless of any other interpretation of the value of those desires. It will be important, therefore, if we are to aid and communicate with members of this group in a more direct manner for them to keep in mind the necessity for them to only aid those who seek.

I am sorry that there has been some difficulty this evening in contacting this instrument but this sometimes occurs. I will at this time leave this instrument. I am Hatonn. ☥

Saturday Meditation
April 13, 1974

(Unknown channeling)

I am Hatonn. I am with this instrument. I … I greet you, my friends, in the love and in the light of our infinite Creator. It is a great privilege to be with you once more. It is a very great privilege to speak with you. We of the Confederation of Planets in the Service of the Infinite Creator are always very privileged to be able to speak with those of the planet Earth, as you call it, who seek.

What is it that you seek? My friends, you seek understanding. And what is understanding? Understanding, my friends, is not precisely what you think it is. Understanding is not an intellectual interpretation of the creation or of its realities. It is not an emotional response to reality in what I might call the most approved fashion. Understanding is not an emotional or intellectual response to your fellow creatures. Understanding, my friends, is very, very simply understanding the demonstration of the love of your Creator. This, my friends, is understanding. This is what we of the Confederation in His service attempt to bring to you: understanding of the demonstration of His love. For this, my friends, is the understanding of all that there is. For, my friends, His love is all that there is, for this love has created all that there is. And this is what is sought by those who seek whether they are aware of it or not. They simply seek to understand His love and thereby to demonstrate it … to demonstrate it in every thought, in every word, and in every deed. Through this you may too be of service in our Creator's plan.

It has been stated that man upon planet Earth is a conscious being but that he does not understand. Some of the people of Earth have begun to understand, but it is difficult to continually demonstrate this understanding. The last great teacher known to you, the man called Jesus, was demonstrating his understanding of this truth in his life and yet he was not understood in this demonstration. He gained this understanding through meditation. This understanding may be obtained while you inhabit your present illusion through meditation. This is necessary. For this reason we continually emphasize that you avail yourself to truth through meditation. My friends, you seek understanding. Understanding is within you. You may reach this through meditation. This is very simply all that is necessary for you to know.

It might be asked by we of the Confederation of Planets then bother to communicate more than this one simple concept. My friends, it is very difficult to awaken those upon your planet who have the potential to seek. We have found that it is necessary to spark their interest using techniques that augment the basic truth which we bring to them. We have in this simple statement given you the very core, the essence, in actuality the totality of what we wish to convey to you. But we will give you more, my friends. More so that you too can serve, so that you will be equipped … equipped to help those who seek but must be led through their our pathways to the understanding of the very simple truth that we are bringing, for man on Earth is very complex and is unable, for the most part at this time, to receive this simple truth and use it.

We have for many of your years enticed those who would seek by various methods. We could have simply produced techniques for disseminating the simple truth which we just conveyed to you. My friends, this would not have been understood. Seeking must be generated within those who have the spark. The illusion in which you presently dwell is extremely strong even for those who deep within themselves desire to seek in a spiritual direction. For this reason our program has had necessarily to include many years of enticement and mystery.

We would much prefer to come directly to the point, to bring this simple truth directly to all of your peoples and then allow those who would seek it to seek it, but we understand from our experience in such matters that this produces a very shallow harvest of seekers.

If an individual is already seeking our methods sometimes appear to be rather foolish and lengthy and in many cases with little point. My friends, for those who are already seeking our methods are just that. They are unnecessary. The illusion, my friends, is very difficult to break even for those who would seek, even for those who are of a very spiritual nature. There are many, many of your peoples who are of a high spiritual desire who are within an illusion of religion or otherwise, which does not allow them to modify their thinking rapidly in order to accept such as we who attempt now to contact your planet. In order to communicate it takes much effort and much time. We will continue in our effort to arouse those who will eventually attempt to understand what we bring to those of this planet who desire to have it.

I will now transfer this contact to one of the other instruments. Please be patient.

(Carla channeling)

I …

(Side one of tape ends.)

(Carla channeling)

(Inaudible), my friends. We would like to point out to you that we are aware that each time that we speak of understanding we always link it to service. We do not wish to, shall we say, draft you into service with us. We are not attempting to sway anyone against his will nor are we attempting to choose for you the future action that you will select.

The reason that we constantly link the concept of understanding through meditation with its demonstration in service is that we are not aware that there is any other possible path upon the upward way. It is important to seek. This is the first constant. Once seeking has been established then understanding begins to impel one along the path of spiritual development.

My friends, there is a very great distance which one may travel simply growing in understanding. However, the most exalted and pure understanding is an empty shell if it is not expressed. There is a limit to how far you may go in understanding if you do not choose to express your understanding through demonstration in service. The reason for this is one of the simple laws of reality. There is balance, my friends, in all things. Each thing which seems to be one thing is the other as well. If you wish to receive you simply give. This is a law. This is why we speak of service, my friends.

Beyond the first rungs of understanding one climbs the narrow way by service. It is for this reason that we are here for by our service to you we advance ourselves in understanding. We are not aware of any other means of effectively creating a forward movement in our own understanding. We are not aware of any other way for you to increase your understanding.

Each entity that you meet is yourself turned over, the other side of you, the other side of the coin, my friends. The side you cannot see of yourself turned suddenly so you may see it; there you are. Serve your fellow man, my friends. We suggest this to you because we wish very much for you to advance along the path of spirit and because in your progression you also aid us greatly in our service to this planet at this time.

I am aware that this instrument is experiencing some difficulty with this contact. I will attempt to transfer this contact to the instrument known as R. I am Hatonn.

(Carla channeling)

I am Hatonn. I am sorry that we are continuing to have difficulty with this contact. We will leave this instrument at this time. We leave you in the love and in the light of our infinite Creator. It has been our privilege to speak with you this evening. Adonai vasu. ♣

Sunday Meditation
April 14, 1974

(Unknown channeling)

I am Hatonn. I am with the instrument. I greet you, my friends, in the love and the light of our infinite Creator. It is a great privilege to be with you this evening. I am Hatonn. I speak to you from a craft. The craft is known to your peoples as an unidentified flying object. We are seen in your skies and we are known as unidentified.

Let us consider, my friends, the meaning of identified. Identified, my friends, is something that you understand. What do you understand? Peoples of your planet believe that they understand many things. They do not understand the unidentified flying objects that are in their skies. What they do not realize is that they do not understand anything, for they have not attempted to understand anything.

Your science has created what you consider to be many marvels, but these marvels lack true understanding. These marvels of your science, as you consider them, have been given to your peoples within the past very few of your years. They have been given for a purpose. It has been part of a program that has manifested upon your planet. Up until the very recent past your planet has enjoyed but very little so-called scientific advance. Within the past one hundred of your years there has been an advance in your knowledge, what you consider to be science, of many, many thousand-fold.

This advance was not an advance brought about unaided. This advance was not from within [the] simple advance [of] the understanding of those who were progressing upon your planet. This advance was highly augmented, my friends, for a purpose. Unfortunately, this advance has included not only benefits to man on Earth but he has also used it to create many devices that are far from beneficial. We are very sorry that this has occurred but it was necessary for man on Earth to experience certain benefits of what you know as a technological nature prior to the termination of the great cycle of time through which your world has passed.

It would have been possible for the cycle to have terminated, of course, with no more advance in technology than was appreciated over one hundred of your years ago. However, this was not deemed to be as efficient a way of producing the necessary information so that all those who would attempt to seek would find the information that they sought. As strange as it may seem to you, my friends, [the] entire technological advance your civilization has experienced in the past one hundred or so years has been for the purpose of increasing the ability of those who seek new intellectual *(inaudible)* to find intellectual answers which will lead them to non-intellectual truths.

It is difficult for a society primarily intent upon maintenance of the physical body to spend much time actively seeking in a spiritual way. It is difficult for those who seek spiritual truths to find them if there is very little dissemination or publication available to you. This may seem paradoxical in that we have stated many times that meditation is the only real pathway to complete understanding. My friends, we do not wish to confuse by attempting to point out to you that your present technological systems are necessary to augment this seeking in a most satisfactory manner. We, however, do state that they do accomplish this purpose in more than one way.

There are those who have become fascinated within this illusion that they presently enjoy as they would become fascinated with the physical aspects of any illusion, regardless of its relatively technological aspects. These are the ones who cannot be greatly helped. *(Inaudible)* those who have been spared quite so much physical labor in order to simply exist upon your Earth world. It is those who have been provided with more leisure time [to] extend their seeking that we are primarily concerned with.

Many civilizations have existed upon your planet. It is true that many of these have reached great advancement prior to their destruction. It is also true that the reason for this advancement prior to their destruction was to provide the atmosphere for spiritual seeking that was not as prevalent in a more primitive environment. This is not the decision of any particular person. It is not the decision of a council. These things do not come about because of a specific plan. This comes about in a more natural way as many entities find an attraction to the experiences [that] will be generated near the end of a cycle such as this one. They are drawn into physical experience and those who are drawn into the experience are those of a more advanced nature. This includes, of course, technological as well as many other forms of previous experiences which then are reflected in their works during their present experiences within the physical.

There is a general overseeing, you might say, for each planet but this is much less controlled or directed than would be appreciated by those of your peoples who are accustomed to the careful direction of their present governments. It is then an aspect of the termination of your present cycle that you appreciate great technological advancement with respect to previous experience of your planet's inhabitants for many thousands of years. It was the same condition that created relatively great technological advancement upon the continents known as Atlantis and Lemuria.

We of the Confederation of Planets in the Service of the One Infinite Creator are here to aid those who seek. We are here also to help them understand conditions that they meet in their daily experiences. We are attempting at this time to point out to you that your present experience upon the surface of this planet is somewhat unique in the light of what we would consider normal conditions upon your planet. Normal conditions upon your planet, my friends, are not at all technological. When viewed over a period of several thousands of years you will find that people in general have been intellectually extremely unenlightened. There have been, of course, those few scholars throughout all of the experiences and ages who have been remembered and studied. We are speaking, my friends, of what you would call the man in the street. He has in your society been educated only within the past hundred of your years to any extent at all. This is unique … not common.

This was the case in the experience known to you as Atlantis. Many of those who dwelled within that experience are now returning and have returned into the physical to experience once more a termination, a change, and this time an even more grand change than that which they experienced before. It may seem that it is not too wise for such technological advance to fall upon a people whose spiritual qualities are so lacking and in this, my friends, we are in complete agreement. However, we are unable to control such matters since they are generated primarily by the desire of those who are of the Earth but who are not in physical form.

We are, however, able and willing if necessary to terminate certain totally insane actions which could conceivably be originated with respect to your nuclear weapons. Unfortunately, these weapons are of such a nature so as to endanger not only the peoples of your planet in a spiritual way, but also in a way so as to terminate their existence. It will be necessary, therefore, for an intervention to be made by those of us of the Confederation who monitor the aspects of these nuclear weapons. If such a condition manifests we of the Confederation of Planets do not wish to interfere and cannot interfere in the activities of peoples of this planet with very few exceptions. Interference of a nature to terminate such nuclear warfare is, however, within that which we will accomplish.

It is interesting to note that the decimation of information about the teachings of the [one] known to you as Jesus, the last great teacher upon your planet, are almost negligible with respect to [the] numbers of peoples aware of them for many years after his passing from your planet. It is interesting to note that at this time dissemination of his teachings are at their maximum. Unfortunately, as we have said before, his teachings are not understood even though there now exists upon your planet a communication system which will reach a very large percentage of the peoples in many, many of the areas of your planet's surface, especially those peoples who have evolved to a point where they can use their intellects to augment their natural seeking.

At this time we will attempt to transfer this contact. Please be patient.

(Tape ends.)

Sunday Meditation
April 14, 1974

(Carla channeling)

[I am Hatonn.] It is very often that these words are misunderstood for one reason or another. The difficulty, my friends, is the constant use of the intellect taught to all people who have been at all educated. There is very little spiritual training that would be most helpful in supplying a spiritual development in a growing entity. As the physical body grows, the entity within is educated upon those portions of your planet which are now receiving the aid of technological advances. This enables his intellect to grow and his body to grow. There is much lacking after these two items have become mastered

We are aware that you already feel this to be so. The question of what to do about it in your [own] existence is twofold. In the first place, what you do within your own situation, spiritually speaking, we would suggest, will be a function of one thing only and that is your understanding of the lesson which you are to learn. Each situation that you surround yourself with in general is a part of a lesson or a lesson for you. We are not referring to daily details which occur under the simple laws of chance; we are referring to the overall trend of generalized direction or general dimension of your situation. Whatever the difficulty is in this situation, the approach we would suggest spiritually is to take it, as we may predictably say, to meditation. Out of meditation, come with some understanding. Not in your life, but simply in you of the lesson of the job to be done within that situation in doing the job, in as workmanlike and cheerful a manner as your meditation has given you the ability to maintain. As you accomplish your work within that lesson, the circumstances about you will alter of their own accord.

The constant feeling of pressure from outside is an illusion, my friends. Sometimes, an extremely heavy one, but only an illusion. Your lessons will be learned from within. This is our feeling about the truth, spiritually speaking. We are aware that technology presses hard against spiritual seeking. And may seem in many ways a harsh antithesis. And yet, my friends, all things are one and so meditation on a regular basis will proceed with you as you go along the path.

The question of how to instill the type of training of the spirit to which we refer is a question that is very difficult for us to answer for you. It would be necessary to have communities centered about the great truths of the spirit. It would be necessary to have in each person and in [each] such group of people who have banded together, a spirit of understanding and seeking. It would simply be necessary to have a completely different type of environment than you have. There is much that can be done within the sanctity of your own life. Those people of like mind may provide for you, and those dependent upon you, an atmosphere conducive to spiritual growth.

In your own household, much may be done to encourage the constant awareness of the love of the infinite Creator. Where growing entities [are] aware, as their bodies and their minds mature, that their infinite and eternal spirit was real and was capable of maturing also. If there was a place they might choose to go and with no pressure or suggestion, seek their own peace and find their own truth, then the training for the spirit might be a much more possible thing for those upon your planet surface. Needless to say, my friends, we have not found rich earth for planting this idea in many places. However, you are welcome to it.

At this time, my friends, I will leave this instrument. I leave you in the Creator's love and light. Adonai, my friends. Adonai.

Monday Meditation
April 15, 1974

(Don channeling)

I am Hatonn. I am sorry, the instrument has made an error. I am Oxal. I am with the instrument. I am Oxal. I greet you, my friends, in the love and in the light of our infinite Creator. It is a great privilege to be with you this evening. I am the one known to you as Oxal. I am here with you in the room. I am Oxal, and I am here.

(The instrument is receiving conditioning at this time.)

I am Oxal. I am Oxal.

(Conditioning continues.)

I am Oxal. My friends, I great you in the love and in the light of our infinite Creator. It is a great privilege to be able to speak to you this evening using this instrument. We are having some difficulty, but it is because of his inability at this time to clear his mind. If you will please be patient, we will remedy this.

(Conditioning continues.)

I am aware of questions within this group. I am here, at this time, to attempt to answer some of these questions. We of the Confederation of Planets in the Service of the Infinite Creator are attempting to serve to the very best of our ability those who seek our service. This service will include the answering of any questions that we are able to answer.

(Conditioning continues.)

There are, at times, difficulties with an attempt to answer certain questions, for the answers are not within the limits of interpretations using your language. But there are some things that we can speak of.

(Conditioning continues.)

I … *(The recording is difficult to hear.)*

(Carla channeling)

I greet you, my friends. I am Hatonn. We are most pleased to be speaking with you this evening. We wish to state that we have been aware of this group's activities. We are aware of the difficulties of our brother in maintaining contact. We will at this time therefore give you a few small thoughts to think about while our brothers from Oxal are conditioning a channel for their use.

We would like you to consider, my friends, an island in an ocean channel far out at sea. There is no land in sight and this small rock, washed by waves, bleached by the sun with small flora and fauna growing upon it, looks out upon the world, and its limited consciousness attempts to grasp the reality as it eddies and swirls about it. The little island detects many strange things as they enter its purvey. It lives through differences in climate and feeling and mood. It experiences the seasons of its flora and its fauna and it attempts to piece together a reasonable and holistic view of its reality.

It is fixed in position, my friends, a poor small rock. The far limits, wherefrom come the waves, and the far limits to which they return, will be forever unknown to the island. The island can never know or fully understand that which appears at [its] doorstep, so to speak.

This, my friends, is a very rough and perhaps shallow example of the type of instrument the intellect is. The intellect upon your planet is very useful within the imagery for which it was made. But the attempt, my friends, to use the intellect to understand the far limits of your origin or the far limits of where you shall return again is impossible. For in the image, which your intellect works upon, you are a rock changed to one *(inaudible)*. This is not reality, nor can your intellect give you a picture of reality. Rather, my friends, in meditation seek to be the water. Seek the consciousness, the oneness, the unity, and the adventure of water. All water is inseparable. There is no separation: it flows, it is as one. And each wave that breaks upon this shore may have broken anywhere and may move to another. Let your consciousness flow like the water—not like an island—inwardly.

We are most pleased to have had this opportunity to give you these few thoughts. We will leave this instrument at this time. I leave you in the love and in the light of our infinite Creator. I am Hatonn. Adonai.

L/L Research

Tuesday Meditation
April 16, 1974

(R channeling)

In the love and in the light of our infinite Creator, I am pleased as always to be with you this evening. It is always a pleasure to be with those who desire to hear what we have to say. There is always so much to say and so little time to say it in, that given any opportunity to speak, we are glad to do so.

(Pause during conditioning.)

As I was saying … Although we do not always speak to you during the meditation, we are always with you during your meditation. We are always listening and glad to help. There are very few of your people who desire these thoughts. But we feel, in the near future, there will be many of your people, many more of your people who desire this. As we have said many times and this is just to emphasize to you the importance to you what we are saying, we will try to reach all of your peoples that we possibly can; for there will be times when people will be seeking to known why these things are happening that will be such as physical changes. We are always sending the people of Earth our love.

I will now transfer the contact to another channel. I am Hatonn.

(Carla channeling)

I am Hatonn. I am with this instrument. I apologize for our difficulties in contacting this instrument. We will attempt to use this instrument while we can as conditions are not good. It is very difficult for us to say words that have the desired effect. We wish for them to impel you or inspire you towards seeking to pique your interest and divert your attention to the subject of your own spiritual development. So many words remain simply words. We wish to effect the transformation from word to idea. Therefore, we have more to say than we can ever say and we have very, very little to say, for our truth is very simple and all we really wish to do is to propagate that truth as we understand it to you to the best of our ability to as many people as possible in the time allotted to us.

At this time, we are aware that many of those in this group are experiencing perplexities and while conditions are not serious physically for you, they are somewhat perplexing to you. And we wish to say to you today to consider that there is a duality of ways to look at the spiritual point of view. One way is the way of taking a life or death attitude towards your understanding and going after spiritual understanding as the life and death matter, as indeed it is. There is, however, a perfect opposite to this, which is equally valid and equally helpful and too little practiced, my friends, upon planet Earth. And this is simply to not worry about the meaning behind the illusionary experiences that fill each day. This seems, in a way, very shallow; however, once you have aimed yourself toward the spiritual path and have begun to discipline yourself with regular meditation, patiently and carefully kept up, the ability to take the all-important step backwards towards detachment from that which is about you in your daily life is extremely important. It may mean the difference between a great many perplexing situations and a feeling that is more often with you—that [of] the rhythm of the universe resounding recognizably in your life. When your worried mind is still and when all the ripples of worry of your daily life have stopped, then and only then, may you discern the flow and stately movement of the universal rhythms.

I am having difficulty with this instrument. I will leave this instrument at this time. I am Hatonn. ☥

Wednesday Meditation
April 17, 1974

(Unknown channeling)

I am Hatonn. I greet you in the love and in the light of our infinite Creator. I am most pleased to be speaking with you this afternoon.

I am aware of your concern at this time, and so we will speak this evening on the subject of becoming channels for aiding the Confederation of Planets in the Service of the Infinite Creator. We are aware that you desire to become channels. My brothers and I have been constantly with you and we have been pleased with progress made in your conditioning thus far. We are aware that neither the one known as E nor the one known as T is pleased over the progress he has made. My friends, there is much to be done sometimes when one begins the process of conditioning to become a channel. This does not have to do, my friends, with your basic vibration. This does not have to do with the level of awareness, except in a very general way. What it has to do with is the amount of intellectual activity which the individual who desires conditioning is allowing his brain to function with.

In the case of the instrument known as E, the amount of intellectual analyzing is considerable. The habit is very strong and each imperceptible wave of conditioning received moves such a strong habit of analysis only very slightly. The one known as T is somewhat closer to experiencing a physical manifestation of conditioning. This is due to his attempt from time to time to effectively refrain from analysis of data.

It must be understood, my friends, that to become a channel is to temporarily trust another entity with the use of one's vocal mechanism. This involves letting the control go completely and not retaining any amount of judgment over it. This is very difficult or impossible to achieve, if there is any thinking going on at all on the part of the channel. The conditioning is sent out and is deliberately intended to be effective only to those who have accepted the form of meditation which precludes analysis of thought. This, my friends, is a challenge indeed, and one which we are aware is very specialized and can be very difficult. However, my friends, there is no doubt in my mind that each of you may be instruments if you desire to become instruments. It needs only complete relaxation and a complete ability to refrain from analyzing any thoughts that you receive. It may take some time, as you know time. However, it is not only possible, but inevitable, if you continue to desire this service. We will, my friends, attempt to help you in every way that we can, as always, and we are extremely privileged to be allowed to be conditioning you.

Perhaps, my friends, we should say a few words about the possibility of being somewhat disappointed in ourselves. That is to say, that we are not disappointed at all; we are very pleased, for we can see your progress. We are, however, aware that there are disappointments you feel. We can only tell you that there is no need ever to feel disappointment in yourselves. You must have heard us say many times that there is no time but the present. Regret has to do only with the past.

We are not saying that it is not your business to live as correctly as you know how, but the time to live correctly is the present moment. A mistake made or a missed step or a simple misunderstanding later corrected, is simply a corrected error. What matters is not that you have made the error, but that you have become aware of it and corrected it. The present, with the awareness that you have known, is all that you need to consider. Waste no more time on what is gone forever than you need to learn from it. Then carry on with the life that you are living now, for, my friends, there is a great deal of each present moment that most of those upon your planet miss completely.

The ability to live fully in the present with full knowledge of what you see and hear of God's beautiful creation about you … This instrument has made an error. We will attempt to continue.

The ability to live with complete awareness of the creation of the Father about you and of the possibilities of that creation within you, is most rare and valuable.

My friends, we will leave this instrument at this time. We will be conditioning you as you meditate. We are always with you. Our love is always with you. We leave you in the love and the light of the infinite Father. I am Hatonn. Adonai vasu borragus. ♣

L/L Research

L/L Research is a subsidiary of Rock Creek Research & Development Laboratories, Inc.

P.O. Box 5195
Louisville, KY 40255-0195

www.llresearch.org

Rock Creek is a non-profit corporation dedicated to discovering and sharing information which may aid in the spiritual evolution of humankind.

ABOUT THE CONTENTS OF THIS TRANSCRIPT: This telepathic channeling has been taken from transcriptions of the weekly study and meditation meetings of the Rock Creek Research & Development Laboratories and L/L Research. It is offered in the hope that it may be useful to you. As the Confederation entities always make a point of saying, please use your discrimination and judgment in assessing this material. If something rings true to you, fine. If something does not resonate, please leave it behind, for neither we nor those of the Confederation would wish to be a stumbling block for any.

CAVEAT: This transcript is being published by L/L Research in a not yet final form. It has, however, been edited and any obvious errors have been corrected. When it is in a final form, this caveat will be removed.

© 2009 L/L Research

Friday Meditation
April 19, 1974

(Carla channeling)

I am Hatonn. I greet you in the love and in the light of our infinite Creator. It is a great pleasure and privilege to be with you this afternoon. We are very pleased to see each of you here.

(Gandolph the cat needs attention.)

Carla: This is me. Wait just a minute.

(Pause)

(Carla channeling)

I am Hatonn. I am again with this instrument. We apologize for the delay. We are always most pleased, we were saying, to be of any aid we can.

(Gandolph continues meowing. Discussion ensues as to what to do.)

Carla: Well, I'll try once more.

(Carla channeling)

I am again with this instrument. I am Hatonn. We are aware of the difficulty. We apologize for the delay. As I was saying, my friends, it is our privilege and our mission to come to the aid of all those upon your planet's surface who seek.

We would like to give you this one thought this evening, and that is that our only aid to you is to give you a concept of understanding. What you are seeking is understanding. The fire and the energy with which you seek it is drawn from within the very marrow of your eternal reality. Your true desire is to seek this understanding. This understanding, in turn, my friends, that we are attempting to aid you in becoming aware of is very, very simple. It is, in fact, unitary. There is only One.

This unity, within which the entire Creation resides, is whole, complete, unbreakable and transcendent of all illusion. Therefore, my friends, it is the most impossible thing to conceive of within the boundaries of your intellect and your consciousness within the physical. This consciousness of unity, which is your understanding described in one way, is available to you only through meditation. It is quite, quite amazing to us that those upon your surface have devised so many different ways of removing from themselves all indications of the reality, or even the possibility, of understanding. However, you are, although in the physical environment, not of it. Your choice is completely free. You may seek for this understanding even within the dense illusion which occupies your physical senses. We offer you only simple help. We offer you only simple understanding, for there is only one understanding, only one truth, only one entity: the Creator, my friends. Any attempt to work through any other understanding will be an attempt which is working within an extremely transient illusion.

My friends, we are most happy to be with you. We will condition each of you and will attempt to contact another channel and transfer this message at this time. I am Hatonn.

(Unknown channeling)

I am now with this instrument. It is pleasing to make the contact. I and my brother Laitos are here with you at this time, and will be conditioning those who desire it. We of the Confederation are pleased that so many of the peoples of your planet have begun to avail themselves to our thoughts. We have been attempting, for many of your years, to contact your peoples. Recently, our efforts have been very fruitful, and through the extension of our contact to your peoples we can shortly contact many more. It will be your privilege, in the future, that you offer your services to your peoples. There is much work to be done and you should look forward to this time as being a great opportunity to advance yourself in His service.

Many of your peoples do not comprehend that which you have come to accept. You need to grow in the confidence in order that you may be of beneficial service to these people. Many will approach you and will begin searching because of the confidence you display in the Creator. Your vibration shall rise and shall be felt by those who you come into contact with. Use what time remains to develop your confidence in His will. Your Father wishes all to join in this seeking, and all shall have the opportunity to seek, but only those who desire shall do so. It cannot be accomplished by any other individual. It is controlled by your desire.

At this time, I shall attempt to contact another channel. I am Hatonn.

(Unknown channeling)

The content of the message that we bring is often repetitive. However, this enables a new instrument to receive the thought we are using until he has sufficiently developed his ability to receive data of a more specific nature.

I would like, at this time, to transfer this contact to another instrument, if she will avail herself.

(Pause)

(Carla channeling)

I am Hatonn. I am with this instrument. We regret that we were not able to speak through the instrument known as D. However, the situation is a transient one and, in the future, we will again attempt contacting [her.]

This is nothing unusual, my friends. It is a common difficulty with the newer of the channels. We may say that it is to be considered that, when the condition-wave is given, the thoughts that are of a creative or spiritual nature will vibrate within your mind and you will feel the impulse to speak. The question of whether these creative thoughts are yours or ours is somewhat unspiritual, in that those thoughts which are of a spiritual nature are the thoughts of the Creator. As they are in me, they are in you. And as they are in you, they are in everyone, every entity of whatever plane and in whatever station in all of the realms of the Creation.

I will attempt, at this time, to contact the one known as D, if he would avail himself to our contact.

(Tape ends.)

Wednesday Meditation
April 20, 1974

(The first thirty minutes of this channeling session are mostly inaudible.)

(Don channeling)

We of the Confederation of Planets in the Service of the Infinite Creator are here to serve the people of Earth *(inaudible)*. These ways are varied. However, they seem mysterious. They seem mysterious to you. They are not mysterious to us.

(Side one of tape ends.)

(Don channeling)

I am again with the instrument. I am Hatonn. I was saying that we serve the peoples of Earth in a way that seems mysterious. However, this way, to us, is not mysterious. It is logical. It is the only way that we have of serving the people of Earth, for we bring to the people of Earth a service that they desire, but they are not consciously aware that they desire this service.

People of the planet Earth are fascinated by many things. They are fascinated by these things because they are children, truly children in the evolutionary state of this vast universe. There are some of the peoples of the planet Earth who are not as fascinated with the things of childhood, who are seeking the things that are enjoyed by those whom we might consider adults. If it is possible to serve those of Earth, then, it must first be made possible to serve the adults. For this reason, we act in a very mysterious way in order not to alarm the children while contacting the adults. The adults, as we call them, will understand our service and our message. Children will never understand. This is unfortunate, but this is [the] condition that exists upon your planet.

It is up to members of this group and the members of other groups like this one, if they desire to serve, to serve by contacting the adults of your planet. It will be of no value to attempt to serve children with the information that we have given, for they will not understand it. No matter how you phrase it or how you prepare it for them, they will not understand it. For, as you know, a child does not understand many concepts. Prepare yourself, therefore, to serve the adults. Prepare to serve them well. For, in being adults, they will require that you, also, speak as an adult.

Of course, my friends, I am speaking of the adult who is mature in a spiritual awareness. Many of your people are quite mature with respect to the planet's average maturity. They simply are unaware of the truth, of the reality of the creation in which they exist. Serve these, those who will understand. It is quiet simple for you to identify them, for they will understand, the child will not. Do not do the child a disservice by impressing upon him something that he cannot understand. Serve those who seek. Serve those who will initiate their seeking very shortly. And remember, if you are to serve those who are adult, it will be necessary that you speak with the knowledge of an adult. For this reason, it is very necessary that meditation be practiced daily. For in this way and only in this way can an individual become aware in an intellectual way of that that is necessary to give to those who seek. In no other way can he obtain this ability.

There are many upon your planet who, in a spiritual sense, have reached adulthood. However, many of these are very misinformed. They are able to act and to demonstrate a knowledge of the Creator but they are, for the most part, unaware of much that must be achieved through active seeking of truth which can be accomplished, at any time one desires, through meditation.

(Pause)

I am again with this instrument. I am sorry for the delay. I was saying that it is necessary to serve those who are seeking. It is as simple as that. It is only possible to alert those, very slightly, who are not seeking, for they simply will not seek an understanding, and this is what is necessary if the program that we of the Confederation of Planets in His Service [are following] is to be successful. How many more of the peoples of this planet are seeking now than were seeking when we initiated our program? Considerable more, my friends, considerable more. And yet, their seeking is going, for the most part, unanswered in many respects. For, there are all too few groups of this nature, groups that are able to act as goads for those who seek.

It is difficult for us to work through a group such as this one. It is difficult, but it is the only way available to us. We must rely upon those who are in the density that you now enjoy to act to aid us in the service of the infinite One. It may seem mysterious and, in some cases, unintelligent to act in such a way as do we, the Confederation. We have found, however, that this is the only method that produces a satisfactory result. That result, my friends, is simply the spiritual evolvement of a maximum number of those who will evolve.

It will always be up to those who are living upon the surface of a planet such as this one to act, to convey to their brothers that which they desire: the truth of the creation. This must be the way of truth, for it was provided for by the Creator of us all that those upon a planet such as this one would have a freedom of choice that is complete. This choice may not be influenced in a direct manner. This choice must include the only thing of importance in the universe. That, my friends, is the individual's acceptance or rejection of his Creator. This, my friends, is what this group is doing. It is aiding; aiding, not in the judgment of those of this planet, but in the judgment of their Creator, their *own* judgment, a judgment to accept His principles free from any coercion or influence, or to reject [them].

This group has made its choice, long ago. The vigor with which it acts is dependent upon a choice that it will make in the future. The effectiveness with which it will act will be dependent upon its ability to avail itself through meditation. We, the Confederation of Planets in His Service, are serving, serving those who wish to mature. For we also wish to mature. For, as it is known by the adult, the rewards of true maturity are more desirable than those of childhood.

I will leave this instrument at this time. I am Hatonn. Adonai vasu.

Sunday Meditation
April 21, 1974

(Carla channeling)

I am Philip of the Brotherhood of the Seven Rays. I am with this instrument. I am here. *(inaudible)* although my previous contact has been *(inaudible)*, this instrument has received my thoughts correctly.

As I speak to you, there is between us an ocean amount of space *(inaudible)*. My beloved brothers, you have truly bridged this chasm, this great ocean which lies between the understanding *(inaudible)* within the physical illusion, and we understand *(inaudible)* has the dilemma in understanding that we *(inaudible)*. The difficulties of communicating across this gap are formidable. And yet, my friends, as this instrument has noted, I say that it must be done and that it can be done. You are truly a shepherd. You are truly a disciple. To you, my brethren, is given a great task, but you are not left [helpless]. The ability in which you have *(inaudible)* with your contact, the One Who is All, in meditation will stand *(inaudible)*.

It is very necessary, my friends, for you to shepherd your sheep. There is information about the other side of the ocean that needs *(inaudible)* to be expressed to all those standing on the shore *(inaudible)* who are looking out to sea. What you have done, my friends, is already an aid. There is much more that you are *(inaudible)* to do and that you may do if you are willing *(inaudible)*. We will be of help to you in whatever way that we can. There are things that we can do, things that we have done, and things that we will do if you desire us to aid you.

We are aware, my friends, that you long to be on [a different] part of the shoreline that you are now on, and that you wish to be, in spirit and in truth, within the sphere of understanding in which *(inaudible)*. As we say to you, my friends, we each have our [part]. Each of us has a service to perform, and when that service is done, the next service may be *(inaudible)*.

I am having trouble with this instrument. I will leave you. I leave you *(inaudible)*. ☙

Monday Meditation
April 22, 1974

(Don channeling)

I am Hatonn. I greet you, my friends, in the love and in the light of our infinite Creator. It is a great privilege to be with you this evening as it is every evening. It is a great privilege to be able to serve those who seek and, my friends, you are seeking, and this is rare upon your planet. There are but few people upon your planet who are seeking. There are many who believe that they are seeking, but they are not seeking. They are simply going through motions and fooling themselves.

What is seeking, my friends? What is true seeking? Seeking is an attempt to understand the desires of your Creator. Seeking is an attempt to understand why you are yourself and how you may express the desire of your Creator. This, my friends, is true seeking.

There are many upon your planet who seek many things. They seek understanding, but they do not even understand that it is possible to seek the understanding of which I have spoken, an understanding, my friends, of how to express the desire of your Creator in every thought and in every deed and in every activity in which you involve yourself. This, my friends, is seeking. This, my friends, is what is necessary for an individual to become aware of if he is to make progress in a direction that he truly desires.

Most of the people of your planet at this time are not aware of their true desires. They are not aware of these desires because they have not availed themselves, through meditation, to this awareness. Avail yourself to your own desires, my friends. Do this through meditation and you will make the progress that you wish to make.

All of the people throughout all of space wish to make progress but many, many, especially upon this planet, do not understand what progress is. They are aware of many concepts of progress but most of the progress of which they are aware is quite transient, of no real value. Become aware of real progress. Become aware of what you must know in order to reunite your thinking with that of your Creator. That, my friends, is progress; the progress of understanding what you must know to, once more, think in exact harmony with the original created Consciousness. In this way, and in only this way, can you truly progress.

I will, at this time, transfer this contact to another instrument.

(Carla channeling)

I am now with this instrument. We are aware, my friends that at this time there is, within this group's consciousness a desire to be of service that is far beyond the desire of most of those upon your planet, and we can assure you, again, as we have before, that your efforts to aid those of us in the service of the infinite One are very much needed and very much valued.

My friends, as you seek to progress and as you attempt to become ever more able to shepherd those who begin to seek upon [the] planet and turn to you for aid, we ask you to be ever vigilant that your *(inaudible)* is still within the infinite Creator and within the consciousness of *(inaudible)*. The interpretation of change and event is extraordinarily different when seen, first, from the standpoint of the illusion and, second, from the standpoint of the infinite [being]. There is no difficulty in physical change from the viewpoint of the eternal *(inaudible)*. Furthermore, even within the illusion, you may have an intellectual knowledge of the fact that there will be physical change acting upon an individual, within his lifetime, which has more *(inaudible)* and which will take him from *(inaudible)*. These things are inevitable. These things are not to be feared. These things are part of a whole that is organic, natural and extremely helpful as you [cycle] through the physical illusion. Each experience that you have desired comes to pass and you learn from them. Those around you, my friends, are traveling upon similar roads. There is no exception to this truth. The present day is the point at which your *(inaudible)* may *(inaudible)*.

My friends, as you progress upon the road attending those [few] seekers who turn to you, always remember that the human viewpoint, shall we say, is not what you or what those who seek from you are truly seeking. Within meditation, my friends, *(inaudible)* reality and see all the *(inaudible)* from its true perspective.

We will now condition those *(inaudible)*. You will *(inaudible)*.

I will leave this instrument at this time. I am Hatonn.

(Don channeling)

I am Oxal. I am with this instrument. I greet you, my friends, in the love and in the light of our infinite Creator. I am Oxal. I am using control.

I am at this time in a craft speaking to you using a beam. This beam is intense enough to give to this instrument, quite clearly, the thoughts which I project.

I am going to tell you, at this time, of the sphere [of] which you have spoken which was discovered on your southeastern coastline. This sphere is a device. It is a device for control of our thought. I will explain what I am trying to give to you. This device is of a nature so as to project a thought to a point on your planet. It was not intended to be found. It was a remote amplifying device which was able to project thought. I am sorry that it has been discovered, although I seriously doubt that an examination of it will produce any knowledge of its purpose. However, there is something that can be done in the presence of this device to test its purpose.

I am going to use the instrument known as *(inaudible)* if he will avail himself.

(Unknown channeling)

(Inaudible) with this instrument. I am the one known as Oxal. I was speaking of the sphere which has been [examined] by scientists of your planet. Their examination revealed to them no *(inaudible)* as to its origin or purpose. They intend to continue their examination. It is our wish that the purpose of this sphere not be detected at this time. Your scientists, if able to [detect] its purpose would not understand or realize that the knowledge gained in improper *(inaudible)* will lead *(inaudible)* such spheres throughout your planet for transmitting thoughts to areas on your planet.

(Tape ends. Session continues on a different tape. The first part of this tape is inaudible.)

(Unknown channeling)

There are many occasions when we cannot be directly contacted *(inaudible)* and, therefore, we have placed in many areas devices which *(inaudible)* receive and relay our thoughts. It is unfortunate that this sphere has been found. *(Inaudible)* necessary to replace *(inaudible)*.

(The next few minutes are inaudible.)

(Don channeling)

I am Oxal. I am with this instrument. I will continue. I will say that this is undesirable for your government to determine the purpose of this sphere, however, we doubt that this will be possible. I …

(The rest of the tape is inaudible.)

Tuesday Meditation
April 23, 1974

(The first twenty-four minutes of this channeling session are inaudible.)

(Don channeling)

I am with this instrument. I am Hatonn. I was saying that in the future every member of this group who desires to serve those who seek this service will have the opportunity to serve. If this service is to be effective, it will be necessary to one offering service to fully qualify [to do so.] These qualifications may be obtained in only one way. It is necessary to spend time each day in meditation. There is no other way that the qualifications that will be necessary to serve your fellow man can be obtained. We speak of true service. We speak about service that will bring to those of the peoples of Earth who desire understanding the understanding which they desire. This is all that we are attempting to do, for this is all that is necessary. For once this understanding is [acquired] by an individual, he then needs nothing else. For he is, then, an integral part of the Creation in every respect. He, then, no longer is separated in an illusory way by the illusion which he and his fellow man have created for their experience. And this, my friends, is the only thing man on Earth needs, the understanding that allows him to dissolve the illusion in which he now finds himself.

(Pause)

I will transfer this contact, at this time, to one of the other instruments.

(This next thirty-seven minutes of this channeling session are inaudible.)

(Don channeling)

There are many ways to serve the people of a planet such as this one. There is only one way to serve them with what they truly desire. Even though they do not realize this, they desire understanding. There is only one way to bring to them understanding. This we of the Confederation are attempting to do at this time. You who seek to serve with us to bring this understanding to as many of the people of your planet who desire it as you are able will find that this seeking and service will bring to you much joy, as it does to us.

This understanding is not easy to bring even to those upon your planet who seek it, for there have been strong conditions impressing the thinking of most of those who are to be served. If they are to be served, they must be served with truth and this truth must be brought to them in an understanding and concise way. For this reason, it will be necessary that those who wish to serve spend much time in meditation. For, in this way, and in only this way, can an individual prepare himself to bring to his fellow man that truth that all of us desire.

Meditation will allow the individual to eliminate questions concerning the validity of the information that he receives from his thoughts. Meditation will allow the individual to become aware of reality and therefore truth. This truth will be self-evident and it will not be necessary for an instrument to seek an appraisal of that which he is able to channel or to speak. For through meditation he will know, as it is written in one of the holy books of your planet, know the truth and the truth shall make you free. Free from what? Free from the illusion, [my friends.] It is stated that you must know the truth. It is not stated that you must be told what is true and what is not true. It is stated that you must *know*. My friends, there is only one way to know; that is through meditation. This will bring you all that you desire.

I hope that I have been of service. It is sometimes difficult for a new instrument to speak using the thoughts which we project but this problem, like all others, is eradicated through meditation, for this eliminates questions of falsity or truth. It simply avails, to the individual, of the truth that is within all beings throughout Creation.

I am Hatonn. I shall leave you at this time. Adonai vasu.

Wednesday Meditation
April 24, 1974

(Unknown channeling)

I am Hatonn. I greet you, my friends, in the love and in the light of our infinite Creator. I am Hatonn. It is a great privilege, as always, to speak with you.

My friends, we wish only to speak to you very briefly this evening. We are shepherds of your flock and we see the needs of the flock. Our only desire is to aid those of the flock who seek our aid. The aid you seek, my friends, has become very much focused upon true seeking than that of most of the sheep of the flock. Therefore, what can we say to you intellectually is more and more lacking in complete satisfaction. It is for this reason, my friends, that we stress to you, even as you are gaining advancement, the continued need for more and more meditation. For, my friends, what we can give you through use of the intellect and language is a very small percentage only of what we are able to give you by direct contact—mind to mind.

We would say this to you: there is an everlasting experience that's cycled again and again within the physical illusion that you now enjoy. This experience is one of complexity. Events that happen are always events that are essentially unexplained. My friends, the unexplained sets up within your human intellect a great frustration and you seek the explanation with your intellect. But, my friends, the explanation for the cycle of experience within the physical is never within the physical.

The answer, my friends, is to be found within the spiritual consciousness. The flimsy craft of your physical intellectual ability is not designed to sail from the deep seas of spiritual reasons. Do not attempt to take it into the depths of reasons or else, I assure you, your flimsy craft will break apart and you will think that you are surely lost.

My friends, there is no loss. There is only unity. The great storm that is with this great illusion is forever stilled by the consciousness that you may obtain through your meditation. As the master known as Jesus has been quoted as saying, "Peace, be still." This statement is a statement of faith. When applied to the storm in any illusory existence, the illusory storm is bound to respond and by growing upon, "Peace, be still." This concept that the consciousness of the Creator has dominion over the consciousness of the physical illusion is truth and is, we hope, a helpful truth.

At this time, my friends, I would like to spend a period attempting to condition each of you who desires it. I will be attempting to effect some recognizable alternations in your consciousness so that you may know of my presence. My brother, Laitos, is here and will be also attempting to condition the muscles within your vocal mechanisms in such a way as to provide impulses which are recognizable. If you avail yourselves to this conditioning, we will attempt it.

I will leave this instrument at this time and will work with the conditioning. I leave you in His love and in His light and I will be available to you at any time that you avail yourselves. I am Hatonn. I hope that I have been of some assistance. Adonai.

(Pause)

(Unknown channeling)

I am again with this instrument. I am Hatonn. At this time, my friends, I will ask you if you have any questions. If there are no questions, then we will again leave this instrument. It was a privilege to be with you this evening. We leave you in the love and in the light of the infinite Father. Adonai.

(There were silent questions and the instrument was uncertain as to whether the answers were her own thoughts or whether they were those of Hatonn. An explanation follows. There was a discussion of the silent questions that were asked and the instrument and the group again meditated to try to receive the answers. The question was whether an individual could be healed of a chronic disease.)

I am Hatonn. I am again with this instrument. I apologize for the confusion. This instrument is somewhat new to our contact and has not experienced enough channeling to have the confidence of which our more advanced channels exhibit. However, we will proceed.

The subject upon which you seek information does not readily yield fruitful knowledge. However, a concept which may be helpful is as follows. You are aware upon your planet of night. This darkness is real to you within the illusion that you know as life. There is a simple physical way in which you can intellectually imagine that darkness to be only a local phenomena. The method of that understanding is to imagine that you are observing the solar system from the standpoint of the object that you call your sun.

From the standpoint of your sun, there is no night. There is no darkness. There is no lack. There is no limitation. There is only light. An enormously wasteful amount of energy, infinite, self-perpetuating and determined and a type of light that expresses itself in all directions with all of its heart and strength. The concept of darkness, lack, limitation or any petty restriction of any kind is quite foreign to the point of view of the inhabitant of the sun.

It is for this reason, my friends, that we often describe to you the love and the light as being like sunlight or some form of light. This light, this phenomena called light, is a spiritual phenomena. It is one of the two building blocks of your entire universe. Light, with no limitation of any kind, vastly [energetic] and infinite in its capacity, is the basis for all that is in a physical sense. The shaping, the creating, the molding force is the consciousness, the Thought, which we call love. Love shapes light into the vibration that we know as the physical world.

The Creator's love is completely, down to the very smallest detail, a spiritual thing. One entity made of spiritual substance can seek and love. The lack, the limitation, the darkness and the want is the creation of that most chief of the Father's creations—that being mankind.

Mankind is a creator even as his Father wished for him to be. He has created. And through his desires are things which he does not truly desire. He has invented a great many different ways to experience lack, limitation and want. This, my friends, is only true thought from the point of view of the dweller within the illusion who rotates with the planet and sees the sun go down and disappear. A simple shift in point of view, from the point of view of the planet, to the point of view of the source of light for the planet, will enable the understanding of the conditions of the planet upon which you now enjoy the physical existence to come into much clearer focus.

We are aware that this is a far more generalized statement than requested. However, there are many things [to] which [we do not] have the spiritual answers ourselves, but deal only with the illusion. The ability to change one's point of view will often banish a question and replace the question with understanding simply by the realization of a shift in point of view.

Is there, at this time, a further question?

Questioner: Are children born with the knowledge of love and understanding or do they have to be taught this concept, as Hatonn is teaching us?

I am Hatonn. I will attempt to answer your question. Children are born with a type of personality of manifestation of awareness which is their heritage of previous experiences and knowledge. This varies extensively from entity to entity. For the most part, those who are now incarnating on planet Earth have a considerable background of latent understanding because they have been called to the Earth at this time for experience involved with the ending of this cycle. Therefore, for the most part, the entities who are called children upon your planet at this time are somewhat advanced, before they are taught any lessons within the physical illusion.

However, the physical illusion is designed for further teaching. The teaching, my friends, is of two kinds. The first is the most important, especially upon your planet. That is, as you say, I see, upon your planet, "the school of hard knocks." I see this phrase. This phrase is the school which will teach children the lessons, for the most part, that they will learn.

Within this school, the most informative stance that those who wish to aid a child may take is that taken by the master known as Jesus. When asked for understanding, Jesus spoke to the best of his ability. But more importantly in this aspect of his service, he exemplified by his life that which he wished to make known. The experience of children as regards those around them is, to a great extent, built upon not what they are intellectually manifesting, but what they are manifesting by their existence. This, again, is your greatest area of teaching of any child. And that is the area of example.

Upon the planets in which the atmosphere is spiritually more centered upon seeking, the use of the intellect in aiding spiritual seeking in children would be greatly enhanced. However, the influences which are upon your planet at this time are, for the most part, quite baffling to spiritual impulses. Therefore, the most earnest and sincere attempts at teaching of spiritual concepts will be frustrating to the teacher and to the child. It is therefore recommended that when the opportunity for this type of intellectual teaching arises, the truth be spoken and that the frustrations connected in attempting to live the spiritual life within the confines of an unfriendly environment be accepted without undue disturbance or strain. It is to be expected that there will be difficulty and confusion.

Therefore, we say to you, there are three simple ways to attempt to aid. One is to be aware that children are, for the most part, already somewhat mature and that, therefore, they only need direction.

Two, that the best direction comes from the twenty-four hour a day abiding of yourself with the light of your own spiritual awareness. This is your best contribution to anyone that you meet. It is your life itself. By example, more have been aided than by any other more elaborate means.

The moment to moment existence within the physical provides you with your third form of aid to another entity. The attempt to speak the truth as you know when asked is always a good thing. We remind you that to forgive and to encourage amidst difficulties and setbacks and even failures is also a service. It is to be remembered as a principle that you are part of the infinite Father and just as you yourself, as a child spiritually, are taught that always welcomed upon whatever terms.

So in expressing yourself, you may remember that you may teach, but, always above all, accept and love on any terms. We wish that we could tell you that there is a way to ensure that a human entity will surely be aided and given the right concepts; we cannot tell you any such joyful news, my friends. We have been attempting to aid each entity upon your planet for many, many years. Some may be aided, some may not. They may be aided only when they desire it. It is within each entity to choose what he will learn and what he will not learn. All that can be done by example is to have the awareness ready to be shown to those about you.

We are sorry that we cannot give you any [more] sure method than those that we have told you about. But the Father gave us all free will: the least and the greatest are equal spiritually. Be staid in the knowledge that all things are fulfilling the purposes for which they were intended. And you have only to respond to each days' request for help to the very best of your ability and to the very furthest of your knowledge and you will have been of service to those whom you wish to serve. We hope that we have been of service to you in this matter.

Is there a further question, my friends?

(No further queries.) ❧

Thursday Meditation
April 25, 1974

(Carla channeling)

I am Hatonn. I greet you in the love and in the light of our infinite Creator. It is a great pleasure and privilege to be with you this afternoon. We are very pleased to see each of you here. I am Hatonn. I am again with this instrument. We apologize for the delay. We are always most pleased … we were saying, to be of any aid we can. I am again with this instrument. I am Hatonn. We are aware of the difficulty. We apologize for the delay.

As we were saying, my friends, it is our privilege and our mission to come to the aid of all those upon your planet's surface who seek. We would like to give you this one thought this evening and that is that our only aid to you is to give you a concept of understanding. What you are seeking is understanding. The fire and the energy with which you seek it is drawn from within the very marrow of your eternal reality. Your true desire is to seek this understanding. This understanding, in turn, my friends, that we are attempting to aid you in becoming aware of is very, very simple. It is, in fact, unitary. There is only one. This unity within which the entire Creation resides is whole, complete, unbreakable and transcendent of all illusion. There, my friends, it is the most impossible thing to conceive of within the boundaries of your intellect and your consciousness with the physical.

This consciousness of unity, which is your understanding described one way, is available to you only through meditation. It is quite, quite amazing to us that those upon your surface have devised so many different ways of removing from themselves all indications of the reality or even the possibility of understanding. However, you are, although in the physical environment, not of it. Your choice is completely free. You may seek for this understanding even within the dense illusion which occupies your physical senses. We offer you only simple help. We offer you only simple understanding for there is only one understanding, only one truth, only one entity—the Creator, my friends. Any attempt to work through any other understanding will be an attempt which is working within an extremely transient illusion.

My friends, we are most happy to be with you. We will condition each of you and will attempt to contact another channel and transfer this message at this time. I am Hatonn.

(H channeling)

I am now with this instrument. It is pleasing to make contact. I and my brother Laitos are here with you at this time and will be conditioning those who desire it. We of the Confederation are pleased that so many of the peoples of your planet have begun to avail themselves to our thought. We have been attempting for many of your years to contact your peoples. Recently, our efforts have been very fruitful. And through the extension of our contact to your peoples we can shortly contact many more. It will be your privilege in the future to offer your services to your peoples. There is much work to be done. And you should look forward to this time as being a great opportunity to advance yourself in His service.

Many of your peoples do not comprehend that which you have come to accept. You need to grow in confidence in order that you may be of beneficial service to these people. Many will approach you and will begin searching because of the *(inaudible)* new display in the Creator. Your vibration shall rise and shall be felt by those who you come into contact [with]. Use what time that remains to develop your confidence in His will. The Father wishes all to join in this seeking and all shall have the opportunity to seek. But only those who desire shall do so. It cannot be accomplished by any other individual. It is controlled by your desire.

At this time, I shall attempt to contact another instrument. I am Hatonn. The content of the message that we bring is often repetitive. However, this enables a new instrument to receive the thought for usability until he has sufficiently developed his ability to receive. There are *(inaudible)*.

I would like at this time to transfer this contact to another instrument, if she will avail herself.

(Unknown channeling)

I am Hatonn. I am with this instrument. We regret that we were not able to speak through the instrument known as D. However, the situation is a transient one and in the future we will again attempt contacting. This is nothing unusual, my friends. It is a common difficulty with the new of the channels. We may say that it is considered that when the conditioning wave is given, the thoughts that are of a creative or spiritual nature will vibrate within your mind, and you will feel the impulse to speak. The question of whether these creative thoughts are yours or ours is somewhat unspiritual in that those thoughts which are of a spiritual nature are the thoughts of the Creator. As they are in me, they are in you. And as they are in you, they are in everyone; every entity in whatever planet and in every station in all of the realms of the creation.

I will attempt, at this time, to contact the one known as D, if he will avail himself to my contact.

(Tape ends.)

Friday Meditation
April 26, 1974

(Carla channeling)

I am Hatonn. I greet you, my friends, in the love and in the light of our infinite Creator. It is a pleasure and a privilege to speak with you once again, as it is always a privilege to speak to those upon the path of seeking.

We would like to say a few words to you about this seeking, my friends, and this is, as we have said many times before, our only concern is to help you with your spiritual seeking. A great deal of activity has already taken place upon the surface of your planet and within its atmosphere by way of interaction between those of us in the Confederation of Planets in the Service of the Infinite Creator and those who dwell upon the surface of your planet. Each confrontation of whatever nature was intended in some respect or another to turn those people involved toward an attitude of seeking. In many cases, my friends, we would say the majority of cases, this attempt worked, in that whatever anomalistic phenomenon—as this instrument would put it—occurred created the alerting mechanism in that entity's mind which it was intended to create.

Our problem, my friends, is not in gaining the ability to catch the attention of the people of your planet; our difficulty is to aid them in a way that is truly consistent with all of their desires. We cannot transgress the principle of free will. This holds us in check so that we can come only as close as thought or in some isolated instances, isolated contact. More definite contact must wait until we are more definitely welcome. Therefore, what we have to offer in the way of confrontation is largely a thought value.

This is as it should be, my friends, and yet we put it to you there is a continuing difficulty, not in alerting the consciousness of men of Earth alone, but in keeping those who are alerted within the active attempt that they are making. We have seen many, many people who have gone through some sort of confrontation and gain a sense of seeking only to place it far back in the closet of their mind to be taken out at some future time. You cannot lose awareness, my friends. Yet, there is little time and it is our desire that we may help each of you who truly desire it to seek not only when there is that very day a reason for seeking, but to seek each day in a self-perpetuating way, so that your thinking is completely independent of such things as physical or thought appearances of a controversial nature which turn you toward seeking.

"Seek ye first," my friends, is written in your holy works. Seek ye first the Kingdom of Heaven. If we can lead you to this level of seeking, then we will have been able to have produced in you the capacity which you have always enjoyed for continual, life-long and productive seeking. Furthermore, once this seeking has taken its place within your life as knowledge which needs no impulse to give it the central place in your consciousness, then you are within the boundaries for a true discipleship in which you join the service of the infinite Creator. This, my friends, is a true service and we are very pleased with the progress which this group is making towards this level of seeking.

Your scientists will shortly experience a great deal of consternation, for in their physical skies they will discover a new phenomenon entered. Very few of those who are now guarding the intellectual spheres of learning in the physical upon your planet will have any idea that has any relationship to a true explanation of this phenomenon system. This will turn many minds to seeking. The physical trauma, which you have experienced from time to time, often produces this same seeking, but, my friends, it is not a lasting stimulus. The only true stimulus comes from within and can be discovered easily and always through meditation.

I am, at this time, going to spend a few minutes conditioning each of you who desires it and then I will transfer this contact to another instrument. I am Hatonn.

(Pause)

(Don channeling)

I am with this instrument. I am Hatonn. I was saying that shortly within your skies will be occurring a phenomenon which will create much interest among the peoples of your planet. This phenomenon will be looked upon as miraculous. It will be looked upon as miraculous because it will be exclusively different. It seems that within the philosophy of the peoples of your planet the miracles are reserved for those things which are considered exclusively different than that comprehended as normal. We of the Confederation do not consider anything more miraculous in this creation than anything else. The creation is a miracle in each of its infinite parts. You are shortly to experience a part that has not yet been experienced by the peoples of your planet. This new experience then will create among many of them seeking. Some will be inclined to seek in a scientific manner. Others will be inclined to seek in a spiritual manner. It will be helpful if at this time those who are inclined to seek in a spiritual sense would have available for them an avenue of intellectually attaining truth in order that they might find the pathway through meditation to a complete realization of the creation.

At this time I am going to transfer the contact to one of the other instruments.

(Pause)

(H channeling)

I am now with this instrument. I am Hatonn. I shall continue. The phenomenon [of] which we have spoken is to occur within a relatively short period of time. There is an awareness within this instrument as to predictions which have been recently brought to the instrument's knowledge. He has attempted to relate this with that which we speak. It is related, but shall be different from what your so-called psychics have predicted.

You, along with your entire system of planets, are evolving into a new sector and vibration within this creation. There shall occur many changes in the physical appearance of your system. The phenomenon shortly to occur shall be the first major change in your system. It shall be observed in your skies by all the peoples of your planet and shall be explained to your peoples through your governments in the manner which they use to explain all things. Therefore, what we attempt to say is that they shall be able and shall desire not to explain. They will have no comprehension of this. Only those who seek shall comprehend of this occurrence. It truly shall be the change, or shall I say, one of the changes in your heavens, as it is often referred to.

We generally have not given such specific information, but this occurrence is only one of many which we shall attempt to inform those who seek about. You can use this information in establishing the requested validity of our knowledge to those whom you serve. As I have said, this prediction, as you call it, is uncommon to you through our contact. It shall come to pass, as shall many other changes [about] which we shall inform those who seek, and we are happy to share our knowledge with you. When it occurs, you shall surely have no more doubts. We do not attempt to convince anyone. Those present need not be convinced, thought there still remains doubts.

I shall attempt at this time to establish contact with the instrument known as T. I am Hatonn.

(Pause)

(T channeling)

I am Hatonn. I am having difficulty with the instrument which we have attempted to contact. He is analyzing our thought. Attempt to relax and with the stimulation from our conditioning take that thought which occurs at that time and speak it, for it is truly our thought. Do not doubt. We are attempting contact. Relax. Avail yourself and speak. There is no need for fear of error. There are instruments present who will be able to correct any error and no one present would be concerned.

I shall again attempt the contact. Please relax and avail yourself. I greet you in the light and love of our infinite Creator. I wish to tell you that there is no reason to fear. I wish to tell that there …

(H channeling)

I am again with this instrument. We are pleased to have made this contact and would desire to continue through the one known as T. You can realize that your contact was broken through your analysis of the thought. Please refrain. It is necessary only to relax and say that which is impressed upon your mind. Do not search for the words, this shall come. I shall again attempt this contact. I am Hatonn.

(T channeling)

I am Hatonn. I greet you, my friends, in the love and the light of our Creator. I want to … I wish to tell you that there is no reason for you to worry that you will make a mistake. We will correct any mistakes that you make, if necessary. I am pleased that you are making this contact. I want to say that I am pleased for you. I will make contact with you again later. I am Hatonn.

(H channeling)

I am Hatonn. I am again with this instrument. We wish to express our gratitude for having been able to establish contact with another new instrument. It gives us great satisfaction to see so many within your group avail themselves to our thought. The instrument has progressed quickly through his desire. Continue to desire to be in His service and you shall become that.

I am Hatonn. I am now with this instrument. It is a privilege which you desire. At this time I shall establish contact with another instrument. I am Hatonn.

(J channeling)

I am Hatonn. I am now with this instrument. It is a privilege to be able to contact new instruments …

(Side one of tape ends.)

(T channeling)

I greet you in the light and love of our infinite Creator. I wish to say that … I am Hatonn. I wish to tell you that you are going to be all right. Please avail yourself of our contact. We will help you. We will help in your efforts to relax. This is your problem. You need to stop … You need to stop analyzing. This is … I want you to relax and avail yourself to our thought. They are ours.

I will switch this contact to another instrument now. I am Hatonn.

(Don channeling)

I am with this instrument now. I am Hatonn. I shall continue. It is difficult at times for a channel, even an experienced channel such as this one, to clear his mind totally and to refrain from analyzing the concepts that are given unto him. However, this may be done with practice. It is easier if the new instrument has had a period of time of meditation prior to attempting to receive our contact. It is difficult to come directly from one's daily activities and involvement in intellectual exercises and to reach a state of meditation and freedom from intellectual thought that is required for a good contact. With practice, however, this may be done. It will be possible if one will practice through meditation to go directly into a state of non-intellectual analysis.

This instrument is able at times to channel our thoughts very accurately. At other times, he finds it somewhat difficult to receive our contact. The problem is always the same. The problem is one of analysis and use of the intellectual mind. At this time, this instrument is not using his intellect or analyzing what we are giving unto him. He is simply repeating what is given unto him. This is what is necessary if a channel is to become a good, functioning channel. As I have stated earlier, the way to accomplish this is through meditation, a divorce of the intellect from analysis, a total freeing of one's mind of intellectual thoughts. This may be done through practice. This practice is simply meditation, a meditation in which the mind is allowed to relax and to discontinue its thoughts of that which affects you in your daily activities.

I am aware that there is some question with respect to the type of phenomenon to be observed shortly in the skies. This phenomenon will be of a radiation nature. It will be a visible radiation that will change the color and the intensity of your night sky.

I shall transfer to the instrument known as H.

(H channeling)

I am Hatonn. I am now with this instrument. We were attempting to answer the question which has [been] impressed upon us by one of the members of this group. We have said it shall be of what you consider as a source of light in your sky. It shall have a radiance different from any object presently in your skies, and it shall radiate intensely and shall have the ability to change the entire appearance of your night sky. There enters a new body into your system, which shall be visible for quite some time. It is, as we have said, an occurrence brought about by your revolution into the new vibration. Everything within your present physical world shall be changed, and when this is mentioned, it is usually considered that we mean only the planet which you now occupy. But it shall also include planets in your system and all of the heavens surrounding.

You pass into a new vibration where all shall be of great *(inaudible)* and vibrate with the new and great intensity. This intensity, or shall we say, the vibration shall be attuned directly to receive the love and awareness of the Creator. It shall not be affected by any negative vibrations, for the vibration shall not be able to be penetrated by negatives. As these changes occur, so shall your awareness. Enjoy your present situation with the awareness that through your meditation you shall be within this new level of vibration.

I have been pleased to share this information with you and I am also pleased to have established contact with the new instrument. I shall leave. I leave you in His love and His light. I am Hatonn. Adonai vasu borragus.

Saturday Meditation
April 27, 1974

(Unknown channeling)

[I am Hatonn.] *(Inaudible)*. I and my brother *(inaudible)* are here to condition each of those who desire *(inaudible)*.

At the present time there exists a condition of confusion among your people. This creates a great opportunity for those who desire to serve their brothers. An opportunity to help those who desire assistance and *(inaudible)* their lives and an opportunity to obtain a higher personal vibration. The state of confusion which now exists among your people is but a small … a small confusion compared to that which will exist in a very short time. There is much enlightenment to be obtained to efficiently give to these people the knowledge which they need, enlightenment obtainable only through meditation. So, my friends, those of you who desire our contact for the purpose of serving, it is only obtainable to those who … but one must, at the same time, meditate to attain not only our contact, but the contact of the consciousness of the creation whence all enlightenment is obtained.

I would at this time attempt to transfer this contact to another *(inaudible)*. I am Hatonn.

(Unknown channeling)

I am Hatonn. As I was saying, there is much confusion going on on your planet at this time. Those of you who are accepting the Creator's answer have found much peace in your own mind. As time progresses you will find this peace will intensify. This, my friends, is a very comforting thing in the days that are shortly upon you. I wish to stress that daily meditation be adhered to. Through meditation you will find the answers to many questions that may be brought upon you if you wish to serve. I and my brother wish to show you *(inaudible)* can help in anyway possible for a *(inaudible)*. I would like to say that much confusion will be brought to your door, but within meditation you will find the path to peace.

I will now attempt to communicate with the one known as D. I am Hatonn.

(D channeling)

I am Hatonn. As I have said, my brothers and I are with your thoughts at this time. We are here to aid in any way we can. Those of you who wish to serve your fellow [man] can do so with the aid of meditation. There is only one way in the true seeking and that is through meditation. Many of your people are in a negative state of mind, mainly because they are unaware of their own negatives. Through meditation they will see their negatives and eliminate them. Meditation, my friends, is the one true way.

I am Hatonn. I am pleased to be using this instrument. It has been difficult … *(pause)* … in contacting this instrument. I am now going to contact another instrument. I am Hatonn.

(Carla channeling)

I am now with this instrument. I am Hatonn. As I was saying, meditation is the all-important technique for you to be aware of. We give you this information very often, of this we are aware. The information is simple and in many cases may be profitably recycled so that it may serve its purpose as well when heard a second time, or a third, as the first. It is an everyday job to live a spiritual life and to keep the truths immediately before you. It is all-important to meditate and in your daily consciousness to be consciously aware for in some slight meditation at all time of the creation of the Father.

This is what meditation is designed to do. To put you, part of the creation of the Father, into direct communication with the Father, which is all that there is. The creation of the Father is all about you, my friends. This too we have said and we say it to you again. Remember it, my friends, as you go about your daily routine. If you can see something which was not made by those upon the surface of your planet, such as the clouds, the water, the vegetation or the animals, observe what you see, be it large or small. Truly observe the creation of the Father; there is much to observe. You yourself are a creation of the Father. Truly observe yourself. In this way, as well as meditation, you may become more aware of the truth of what is. The creation of the Father is all about you; meditation is within and needs only to be beckoned forth.

At this time I will attempt to contact another of the new channels. It is my great privilege to be speaking through these new channels at this time. I am Hatonn.

(Unknown channeling)

I am Hatonn. I greet you in the love and the light of the infinite Creator. I am pleased to speak through this instrument. It is still not as relaxed as he should [be]. This is causing some difficulty. He should attempt to clear his mind for the contact. This is the reason he experiences some discomfort while attempting to channel. We will further condition. I am Hatonn.

I will attempt to transfer this contact to another instrument. I am Hatonn.

(Don channeling)

I am with this instrument. I greet you once more, my friends, in the love and the light of our infinite Creator. I am the one known to you as Hatonn. It is a privilege to be speaking to you through so many new instruments. It is also a privilege to be using one of the more experienced instruments. I shall use this instrument at this time to instruct you on techniques for clearing your mind. It is a problem to receive accurately our thoughts if you analyze what you are saying. It is necessary if you are to become a fluent channel capable of speaking at a reasonable speed with clarity, that you do not look ahead or behind the word that you are speaking. Concentrate only on saying the word that you are speaking. Do not try and anticipate what is to come next, or do not try to think about what you have said, simply say the word that is given to you. This will create a fluent state of communication. The new channel is often in a state of mind that is questioning what he is saying. The new channel, in other words, is sometimes doubtful that what he is saying is being given to him by us, those of the Confederation of Planets. This is of no importance. It is only necessary that the channel learn to not think during communication; he will learn more rapidly to transmit our thoughts. It will be apparent to him after he becomes fluent in this form of communication that he is in fact channeling our thoughts, for when we are not with him he will have no flow of thought at all.

(Pause)

(Unknown channeling)

I am Hatonn.

(Side one of tape ends.)

(Unknown channeling)

As I was saying on the subject of radiation in your sky. At the proper time you will become aware, possibly from another channel. This will be explained fully and understood by those who are seeking, who choose. It is our honest wish that all of you will be ready for this.

I am very pleased with the work and progress accomplished by this group. Through further meditation you will find your talent as a channel further [enhanced] if you will return to become one with the Creator.

I will now attempt to communicate with the one known as K. I might add at this point that she relax completely, clear her mind of all thoughts and she will express *(inaudible)*. I am Hatonn.

(Unknown channeling)

(Inaudible)

(S channeling)

(Inaudible). We are sorry for the difficulty of the contact with the one *(inaudible)*. We would say to clear all of these thoughts from your mind and feel within *(inaudible)* and let the thoughts being impressed flow freely without analyzing. We assure you that with time and meditation, it will begin to flow more freely. It is only a matter of time, a time that is only a part of your *(inaudible)*. So do not concern, we will *(inaudible)*.

I … I would like to speak to you on the subject of radiation through your skies.

(Pause)

This instrument is not willing to speak on the subject. He is very unsure. I would like to transfer this contact to the one known as Don. I am Hatonn.

(Don channeling)

I am with this instrument. I am Hatonn. I am sorry that I have had difficulty in speaking through the instrument known as S. The problem of transmitting specific information through an instrument is sometimes quite difficult, for the instrument lacks confidence and therefore is unwilling to speak using the thoughts that are given to him. It will be necessary, however, if each new instrument is to become fully usable, that he become confident in his ability to channel our thoughts. This confidence will be of great importance in the future. It will be necessary, therefore, to attempt once more to channel this information through the instrument known as S, if he will avail himself to our contact. I can assure him that if an error is made that it will be corrected through one or more of the other instruments. It is unfortunate that it is necessary to channel information of a nature that is specifically on a subject other than the philosophical concepts that are given to you and the truth of the creation that you are with, but at times this will be necessary.

Once more I say that for this reason it would be of aid to not only we of the Confederation, but of aid to the instrument known as S to attempt to channel what is given to him. Please be patient while we attempt to contact this instrument.

(S channeling)

I am with this instrument. *(Pause)*. It is a matter of [confidence], of obtaining a high enough vibratory rate to be, shall we say, eligible to experience such [a virbration] as I have mentioned. For unless the instrument's vibratory rate is of sufficient, shall we say, harmony with that of the *(inaudible)* it would be [inadvisable]. The instruments which we use to create these are of a specific vibration. To observe them might not be within range of that [vibration]. Through these *(inaudible)* much awareness will be given and information which will be of great value in serving those who are now in a state of much confusion.

There is very much truth we have to give to you. The time for when you will need this knowledge is of insufficient … time for one to obtain it only through meditation. So the *(inaudible)* [Saturn] Council has decided to use either of its *(inaudible)* knowledge.

There is no other way of obtaining a higher vibration except for meditation and service. Through meditation one obtains a method to serve. I am pleased that this instrument … I … I am pleased with the progress of this instrument. We are very pleased with the progress of all of you who channel. Their progress is very rapid compared to that of previous … experiments. We have found a new method recently for developing channels. It expedites rapidly the awareness of these few to our condition and contact. It also contains much less of the physical condition which is to be of benefit to most.

I will at this time leave you. I will *(inaudible)*. I am Hatonn of the Confederation of Planets in the Service of our Creator. Adonai vasu borragus. ✤

Monday Meditation
April 29, 1974

(Unknown channeling)

I am Hatonn. I greet you, my friends, in the love and the light of our infinite Creator. It is a privilege to speak once more with this group even though there are very few present this evening. I and my brothers are always ready to serve those who seek. We can appreciate that it is not possible for the entire group to meet each day for this would work some hardships upon many of those who are seeking.

I am aware of certain questions that I will attempt to answer at this time. I am at this time going to speak of a phenomenon known to you as channeling. Channeling, my friends, is something that is available to all but not sought by all. It is necessary that an individual truly desire to become a vocal channel in order to do so. This, my friends, is the most important of all of the factors involved in channeling: that the individual who is to be a channel desire to be one. This desire also governs the ability of a channel to channel different types of messages and different contacts.

There is, on occasion, doubt about the validity of this form of contact in many of the minds of those who have become channels. This doubt acts upon their desire to channel the information which we give to them. Their desire, let's say, therefore brings about a lesser ability to channel and [those] upon your planet understand but very, very little about the action of desire.

But, my friends, we can assure you that Creator intended that all of His children be able to have exactly what they desire at all times. Man on Earth, as we have said before, is at this time experiencing exactly what he desires to experience. This is always the case. What is necessary if man is to desire what he desires ultimately is for him to understand his ultimate objective. Man on Earth is very confused about his desires. For this reason he experiences things that he apparently does not desire, but, my friends, we can assure you that if he truly did not desire these experiences they would not come to him.

This is very difficult for the people of your planet to understand. It can be only understood if they spend time in meditation for within them is the truth of this statement and all others. It is necessary if one is to experience his ultimate desires for him to reach his ultimate thinking through meditation. We realize that this cannot be done instantaneously or in what you would consider a very short amount of time. But, my friends, we are attempting to point out to you the pathway to controlling your thinking so that your experiences will conform with desires that are what you will discover that you desire at a later time.

Man on Earth experiences many things and many effects that he never dreamed that he really desires. However, things that he experiences that he thinks that he does not desire he actually desires. The intellect is a very poor tool when not augmented in its abilities through meditation. An intellectual appraisal of one's desires is far shortsighted with respect to one's actual desires. Become aware of your true thinking through meditation.

There are many effects upon your planet at this time. There are many thoughts generated by the peoples of your planet. These thoughts are generated due to their desire to generate them. The effects upon your planet are effects that are a product of these thoughts. It should be possible for you to follow the reason which will even intellectually lead you to a discovery of the action of desire.

We of the Confederation of Planets in the Service of the Infinite Creator desire one thing: we desire to be of service in the love and in the light of our infinite Creator. This is the original Thought. This is the Thought of our infinite Creator: to serve all of His parts so as to bring to them in each and every instance that which they desire. The experiences that accompany such desire are experiences that are free from any problem or difficulty that could be imagined.

There are many people on your planet at this time in what we consider to be a state of absolute confusion. The answers that they actually seek are answers of infinite simplicity. Unfortunately, they have fabricated a system of thinking so complex that a return to the simplicity of which I speak is very difficult. This, my friends, is all that is really necessary: a return to the simplest form of understanding. A return to the simplicity of the love that generates all of us. This may be done by anyone at any time. We recommend that this be done through the use of meditation.

At this time I will transfer this contact.

(E channeling)

(Inaudible)

(Unknown channeling)

I am Hatonn. I am with this instrument. I am having difficulty with the instrument known as E. I will use this instrument *(inaudible)*.

There will be a sign given to you. This is going to be necessary. It is at this time appropriate. The sign will occur within the week. It will be quite obvious. And at that time its purpose will be revealed. This is highly unusual, but is necessary at this time. We do not attempt to influence peoples of this planet too greatly, however, some influence is necessary or we could accomplish nothing at all. We realize that the members of this group understand that it is necessary to proceed as we do with caution in bringing our message to the people of this planet for there are many of the people upon this planet who do not desire this message and for this reason they must not be upset. However, the time is growing short and it will be necessary for many, many more of those for those who would seek our information to have it made available for them. For this reason there will be a contact of sorts made which will be self-explanatory.

At this time I will continue using the instrument known as Carla.

(Carla channeling)

(Inaudible). We are sorry for the delay with this instrument. The instrument was not in a sufficiently relaxed state of meditation and found it impossible to discern our thoughts. The contact remains difficult, however, we will attempt to proceed if the instrument stays relaxed and avails herself to our contact. We will attempt to strengthen this contact if you will *(inaudible)* not a sign, my friends, that will mean the same thing to all people *(inaudible)*.

The concept of a sign is always the concept of a common event which has a special meaning to a few select people and so this will be. However, there will be much clarity about the event in your minds as *(inaudible)*. This is out of our hands completely. We merely observe that it will occur. We would not be able to inaugurate such infringement. However, there are forces who work for the Creator who are within the vibration of your planet and whose home has been here. These entities have worked with us and do work with us and it is through their action that the physical plane will be affected. We will, however, be lending certain meaning to the event we have spoken of.

My friends, to speak to you in this manner is unfortunately to enter into the area of the intellectual and the explanatory. Truth does not reside here and, indeed, where truth resides there will never be the need for any sign. Your true desire is for this truth. So be it that a sign will come to you. But remember that faith is transcendent to any phenomenon of the physical illusion. Open yourself to the truth through meditation until you have begun to find faith and then, my friends, continue. For in that dimension called faith or love or understanding or truth lies that which you truly desire.

I will re-contact the instrument known as Don at this point.

(Don channeling)

I am with this instrument. I am Hatonn. I am going to leave you, but before leaving I would like to reemphasize that what is about to come to you is no more than you have already experienced. It is simply different. There are an infinite number of experiences. You have in your present illusion experienced a small number. Many of the people of your planet have labeled events as miraculous. My friends, you are surrounded by the miraculous. There is nothing but a miracle—a miracle created by our Creator. Does it take another one to awaken those who seek? Do not they see that which surrounds them? Become aware of your illusion. The illusion, my friends, is within your thinking. Destroy that and become aware of the love that has brought about the miracle that you have always experienced.

I shall leave you at this time. I am the one known as Hatonn. Adonai, my friends. Adonai vasu.

Tuesday Meditation
April 30, 1974

(Carla channeling)

I am Hatonn. I greet you, my friends, in the love and the light of our infinite Creator. I am pleased to be with you at this time. We are aware that there is a question and we will attempt to give you a few thoughts on the subject of service. Service, my friends, is a concept which is very difficult to express to the people of your planet for it is a spiritual concept of such a nature that it baffles the intellect. However, we will attempt to speak of it in such a way that you may more readily understand what service is.

The most difficult thing to accept about service is the fact that you cannot give service. There is no way to give service. Service, my friends, must be taken. There is a natural law which governs the absolute free will of each developing particle of consciousness in the universe. Each entity upon your planet, my friends, who enjoys physical human consciousness at this time has a complete universe to himself through which nothing can come without his expressed approval. Many, many things seem to come into the universes of each of those entities within the physical which these entities do not expressly desire. However, my friends, in truth that which comes into each entity's environment is what he has desired. Nothing else may enter. Therefore, there is no way to give service to an entity. There is only the ability of each entity to request and accept service from another entity. Therefore, my friends, those of you who have begun seeking and are now attempting to learn how to serve may discover more and more the difficulties of service.

However, my friends, we may encourage you in the following manner. Consider the tree which produces fruit. The tree spends much time, much love, and much care and all of its energy, in producing the edible fruit which it then offers to any who would desire to take the fruit. This is its service and, my friends, it may be that one tree goes through an entire cycle without benefiting any entities and instead of having been of service the tree has been unable to give of its fruit. But, my friends, the tree dos not become discouraged for it knows several things. Even with its limited consciousness it knows that after rest it will be ready again to be of service and it knows that even though the fruit withers and drops to the ground that the seeds within it may produce for many, many years to come other fruit trees and other fruit and an endless amount of service.

My friends, what we are attempting to tell you is that it is not possible to know within the physical illusion precisely what your short-term objectives of service may [be]. However, my friends, it is sufficient to your spiritual advancement that you be ready to serve by abiding within the light of a spiritual consciousness and that you respond to any request for service whomever it comes from. The abiding within spirit that you do by constant meditation is of the greatest service. We suggest that you think within yourself of your knowledge of the meaning of the past five years of your life. My friends, do the events not come into clearer focus after a longer period of time has detached you from the illusions of the moment? What is meant will occur by the techniques with which you meet each day. You will begin more and more to fill your consciousness with the environment that you truly desire within spiritual consciousness. Do not fear that you will not be of service. Only be ready to be of service, for you will surely be asked if you are ready to serve.

I hope that these few comments have been of aid. At this time I will leave this instrument and will attempt to condition those in the room who desire it. I am Hatonn.

(Unknown channeling)

I am Hatonn. I am now with this instrument. I would like to speak for a moment on the *(inaudible)* of desire. The greatest desire which one may have is to be of service. The proper manner in which to desire to serve is to desire to serve at any opportunity to any entity which requests this service. There shall be many opportunities for each of you to serve. There is no special service, for all service is special. The ability to serve can be found through meditation and once found it is the privilege of the finder to utilize it for the benefit of all.

In your daily functions you shall often wonder as to the path of service which you desire to find. Do not wonder in this way for if you truly desire to serve your path shall be given unto you. If you desire to serve walk the path and do not walk the last part of the path without fully walking the first. You cannot bring about that which is to come without experiencing that which comes before. Patience is required of each entity in order to be of service, for in your service you shall experience much which will try your patience. *(Inaudible)* patience to faith and faith to attempt to fulfill yourself with the love of the Father as He intends to do so for you and act only what this love requests. Nothing else is needed in order to serve.

Your greatest service is your love for all of the creation. Love any part and you love all, but love all and you shall love any part. Do not separate the two for there is *(inaudible)*. Do not refuse your service to anyone that desires it, and if your desire is to serve you surely shall *(inaudible)* do so. Be aware truly of your desires before you shall receive these desires and you must be aware that this shall come about and if it is a desire which you have had through patience *(inaudible)* you may not enjoy the experience of the desire.

I shall leave this instrument at this time and attempt to contact the one known as J. I am Hatonn.

(J channeling)

(Inaudible)

(Unknown channeling)

I am Hatonn. I am again with this instrument. I would like to conclude this message with this thought. If you truly desire to serve do not be concerned as to how you may serve. Concern yourself only with developing your awareness through meditation and your opportunities shall be presented to you. You need not search in order to serve. Your service shall be sought. In the short time remaining develop your ability to serve if this is your desire.

I shall leave you now. I leave you in the love and in the light of our infinite Creator. I am *(inaudible)*. Adonai vasu borragus. ☥

Wednesday Meditation
May 1, 1974

(Carla channeling)

I am Hatonn. I greet you once again, my friends, in the love and in the light of our infinite Creator. I am the one known to you as Hatonn. While I am speaking through this instrument my brothers will be conditioning each of you.

My friends, we would like to speak with you this evening on the subject of the physical illusion. This illusion is very difficult to comprehend from within the illusion for like a dream it often defies identification from within itself. However, when one wakes up from a dream, one is aware that one has dreamed. And when this segment of your infinite and eternal journey has been completed you will be aware of that which is known as life. You will be aware that this life is an illusion, the illusion of the physical.

My friends, we are here to aid those who seek and we have been with you greatly in these past days for you have sought our help and we have responded. There has been much communicated to you in a direct way. We will continue to be with you and at this time we only wish to remind you through this channel that each of you dwells in a physical illusion. My friends, the concept of personality is highly respected within the illusion. However, my friends, consider for yourself what function personality truly has when seen in a spiritual light. As one sees the world from the standpoint of the Creator, and one sees what is real and what is not real, one sees that the personality is completely involved with the illusion and that no part of personality as such is involved in the spiritual consciousness.

A tree, my friends, may not have personality for it is a part of the real creation. What it has is an awareness of the Creator's law and the Creator's love and as it receives and gives love it obeys the law of service. There is no personality necessary in order to express the Creator's love.

My friends, man has been given free will by his infinite Father and therefore man also is a creator. And man creates many, many things within the illusion. These things separate him from other entities and from the true creation. One of the most effective of these separating devices is the device of the building up of personality. To be involved in personality is to be involved in the illusion, my friends.

In order to determine how to be of service and in order to receive and to reflect the love and the light of the infinite Father it is only necessary to meditate and through that meditation seek to serve. The ability to withdraw from consideration of personality is an ability that will enable you to seek much more efficiently within the realm of service for it is not nearly as effective to serve an entity while responding to personality as it is to serve an entity while conscious of that entity only as a perfect child of a perfect Father. All is one, my friends. There is no personality necessary for all is in unity and all is in love.

At this time I will contact the one known as *(inaudible)* and continue this communication. I am Hatonn.

(Unknown channeling)

I am *(inaudible)*. I am with this instrument. There has been great concern amongst the members of your group about the acceptance of our information. This has become evident to us. And we are concerned before those who are presently confused. We have stated many times that each must choose for himself that which he wishes to do and what path he wishes to take. There is no possible means of convincing anyone of the truth of our information. This must be accepted by each entity alone through their own intellect. We are aware of great tensions which are being presented and as this instrument has expressed, the increasing vibration is affecting the consciousness of all you. As this vibration increases, the negative conditions within your consciousness shall begin to stir, for they are being repelled by the higher vibration. But the vibration presently is causing these negative thoughts to enter the awareness of each entity. This is as it should be, for that which you contain within yourself which is of a negative nature must be decided upon by each entity and each entity must choose how to rid himself of this negative.

Many people on your planet shall not be able to cope with this new vibration for within them remains great negative awareness which when vibrated by the new vibration shall overcome the entity's consciousness in the entity's inability to properly judge the situations presented to him. We have mentioned the increase in the vibration many times. And as this vibration draws near all activity upon it shall increase and before passing totally into the influence of the new vibration all negative vibrations shall be dispensed.

This is beginning to occur and shall rapidly grow in its occurrence. It is only the will of the thought which works through this increased vibration and therefore any activity not in harmony within you shall be repelled by the vibration. If each entity affected by the vibration chooses to allow these negative vibrations to be repelled and turn to seeking they shall obtain the existence within the new vibration. Yet we are aware that many shall despair due to the intensity caused by the increased vibrations. In the days to come you shall see more vividly the manifestation of this high vibration. As we say, all things shall greatly increase and by choosing to seek this vibration shall amplify your own.

We wish to see all of your peoples begin to seek, yet we aware that all do not choose to do so at this time. There is no way we can be of a [service] to those who do not desire and though we feel sorry for these entities we cannot aid them for it would not be the Father's will that we educate anyone through imposing upon them our aid. They must request this aid and turn to seeking through meditation. We greatly look forward to the day when we can come into direct contact with your peoples and render our services as this vibration increases and your planet's consciousness increases. This shall be attained. It will give us great joy to do this for we have much to offer which can only be offered through direct contact. Continue your seeking if it is your *(inaudible)* and you shall all be splendid and a beauty of all Creation.

These times which shall be the test of your people should be looked forward to and appreciated for it is truly a great gift from the Creator and through this gift you attain a higher spiritual awareness. I am sorry for the delay. I have spoken about the increased vibration which your planetary system is rapidly passing into. Your system is presently within a close distance of this vibration. Its effect is presently being felt and shall be felt greater as the system draws near. Be aware of the increase in vibration for it shall cause a great increase in your spiritual vibration and also within your physical awareness. It shall cause one to make rapid decisions as their intellect increases in activity. Be aware of this fact and do not allow your intellect to become overactive in any negative thoughts.

I shall leave this instrument at this time and return this contact to the one known as Carla. I am Hatonn.

(Carla channeling)

As we look down upon your planet we can see it in all its beauty, my friends. The planet known as Earth has an extremely beautiful appearance. It seems perfect and indeed, it is perfect. It is the desires of those who seek to look with their intellects far too closely that produce the many, many concepts of imperfection with which your planet abounds.

We will attempt to speak a very brief amount *(inaudible)* using the instrument known as E in order that she may develop, as she desires to. We are aware that there is some difficulty, however, we assure this instrument that it is only necessary to meditate, think of nothing, and when the impulse to speak comes, speak up with what is on your mind and you will be speaking our thoughts. We will now attempt to contact the instrument known as E if she will avail herself to our contact.

(E channeling)

(Inaudible) I am Hatonn.

(Carla channeling)

I am again with this instrument. We are very pleased that we have been able to contact the one known as E. This is the most important event for a new instrument, the recognition of our contact. Once this has been accomplished it is simply a matter of constant effort in availing oneself to this contact. It will become more and more easy to receive our thoughts.

We are very pleased that we have been able to make so many new contacts from your group. It is a great privilege to work through all of you. We join with you in what we hope will be the most successful mission during this cycle span. I hope that I have been of some service. I will leave you at this time. I leave you in the love and in the light of our infinite Creator. Adonai, my friends. I am Hatonn.

Thursday Meditation
May 2, 1974

(Carla channeling)

I am Hatonn. I greet you, my friends, in the love and in the light of our infinite Creator. I am pleased to be with you this evening. My friends, we have come to a place in dealing with the information which we give to your group where we are aware that there are a certain intensification of difficulties. There is a reason for this time of difficulty. You must have thought to yourself lately that a slight intensification of difficulty seems to be occurring among those who are seeking within the group. The reason for this, my friends, is very simple. The whole mission that we of the Confederation of Planets in Service to the Infinite Creator have here is simply the alerting of those of you upon the planet's surface who wish this alerting of the knowledge of the true pathway of spiritual seeking. Once you have been alerted, my friends, to the fact that your physical existence is the environment that you have chosen in order to learn, you will after that begin to experience a certain cycle of testing. As you learn more about the spiritual path you will find a way to either demonstrate that knowledge or to refrain from demonstrating that knowledge.

When we have alerted you to the possibility of accelerating your spiritual progress then you have the opportunity to take these tests and on a conscious level be aware that you are being tested by your higher self. Each of those in your group who is honestly seeking is now at a stage of seeking in which he has learned to a certain extent in a spiritual manner it is in the nature of this environment that this new knowledge be tested. It is in actuality an occasion to rejoice for each demonstration of the way of the Father raises your vibration that much closer to your original perfect vibration.

We are afraid that we must tell you what we have learned about ourselves is also true of each of you. We have found that in each entity who seeks within the physical illusion for wisdom there is one great villain who steals all of the truth, all of the progress, and all of the awareness that he can from each of us. Who is this villain, my friends?

You may look and look for this villain but I must tell you you may not go very far before you find him, for this villain is yourself. There is a type of specific illusion which is termed personality which has to do with the physical illusion which is given by the Father the power of creation. And this so-called personality creates many, many ideas and concepts and false realities which sometimes very effectively baffle the attempt of the spirit to maintain contact with the One Who is All.

It is not a difficult thing to recognize the workings of this illusory self. It is somewhat difficult to inhibit the actions of this personality. The constant attempt to remain to some degree in a meditative state will be of great help to you in attempting to meet these tests. It is only necessary to continue to seek. It may seem difficult and, indeed, it is difficult. And yet, my friends, it is difficult no matter what road you choose. The rewards of the spiritual seeking, however, are somewhat more worth the difficulty.

We send to you our love as channels for the love of the Creator. We are His and you are His. We are all one. We are one mind and one being. Do not let yourself separate you from yourself. There is much to rejoice in and we rejoice in being able to attempt to serve you at this time. I will condition each of you now. I will communicate with you in a direct manner. I will leave this instrument at this time. I am Hatonn.

Sunday Meditation
May 5, 1974

(Unknown channeling)

I am Hatonn. I am with this instrument. I am the one known to you as Hatonn. I greet you in the love and in the light of our one infinite Creator. I am aware of the instrument known as Carla as to her concept of the source of the thoughts which she channels. This is a personal message. We of the Confederation of Planets in the Service of the Infinite Creator are here to serve you. We do this in giving to you certain thoughts that are generated within us. My friends, these thoughts are also generated within you.

If you consider the source of your thoughts producing the messages that are said to be from the Confederation is within yourself, then you are correct. However, you are also correct if you consider the source of these messages to be Confederation of Planets in the Service of the Infinite Creator. There is confusion among those of the people of your planet who act as channels for that which we bring to the people of your planet. We are real, as real as yourselves. Our methods of communicating with the people of your planet are varied. In some instances, there are thoughts that are given to you from us. However, these thoughts are then your thoughts for they were given to you to keep. And they were given to you by yourself, for we are you and you are we. There is only one consciousness. There is no separation.

We are here on your planet and we are part of your consciousness for we are a part of the Creation's consciousness. It is impossible to separate anything in this creation from anything else except in an illusory manner. Therefore, if an instrument believes that he has himself generated the thoughts which he channels, then he is correct, he has generated them. If he believes that they have been generated by us, then he is correct, we have generated them. But, my friends, both of these have been generated by the same consciousness. Which of these thoughts is then to be considered valid: a thought generated by the instrument or that thought generated by us or a thought generated by some other [origin]?

All thoughts, my friends, are valid. There is no such thing as a thought that is not a valid thought. The only question, my friends, is whether the thought that you are aware of is a thought that you would wish to use for your own edification. There is much for each instrument who channels [the] Creator's thoughts to learn. There is much for those who listen to these thoughts to learn. For these thoughts carry within them not only the apparent meanings but many other meanings, for each individual that becomes aware of these thoughts becomes aware of a meaning for himself. And each individual uses each thought is his own particular way. And yet, each of these individuals and each of these individual's thoughts are part of the same thing.

And so we have conditions of an infinite entity communicating through its parts to its parts and evolving through this process and yet its parts in many instances do not become aware consciously of the reality of their condition of being in unity with each of the other parts and therefore consciously create the separation which is erroneous.

We of the Confederation of Planets are here, for we know we are here. For we, like you, cannot be anyplace else, for here is the Creation. The Creation is totally unified. And here, my friends, here is all places and in all times. It is only necessary to become aware of your real nature, of your identification for you to merge with reality. It is not what you conceive it to be in your present state of understanding. It is all places and one place. It is all things and one thing. It is all times and one time. There is no separation. There is a single consciousness. All separations are illusory. If we speak of being from elsewhere, we speak to you using terms that are appropriate to your illusion. There is no possibility of separating our thoughts from your thoughts except in the illusory manner that is practiced by many of those who dwell upon this particular planet.

I will leave this instrument at this time. I hope I have been of service. I am Hatonn. Adonai *(inaudible)*.

Wednesday Meditation
May 8, 1974

(Carla channeling)

I am Hatonn. I greet you, my friends, in the love and the light of our infinite Creator. I am most pleased to be speaking with you again today. My friends, I wish to greet each of you and to give you our comfort, insofar as we may do this.

We are aware that there are continuing questions upon your minds, and that there are questions that you would like to ask. We will attempt to answer some of these.

First, we would like to speak of the technique for dealing with the physical illusion, which is called meditation. We have spoken of this many times, and yet there is always another facet …

(A telephone call interrupts the session.)

(Carla channeling)

As I was saying, there is always another facet to be explored which sheds light, in a new way, upon a clouded area of your seeking.

Meditation, my friends, is a much more basic, and much more general technique than you may think. It is not part of a daily life, my friends. It is the beginning of a completely new life. It is a replacement. The two types of life, that is, that not in meditation and that in meditation, are two completely different vibrations. The reason for this is that, one, the normal physical existence dwells and deals completely within the illusion. The meditation is an attempt to contact your original identity, the consciousness of the all. This consciousness is a much different reality, a transcendent reality to that of the illusion. We might even call it *the* reality were it not for the fact that we know that there are transcendent states to any reality until such time as we are truly aware of unity with all that there is. This is a higher state than we have yet achieved, and we, too, are seeking towards it.

My friends, to dwell in the higher reality is an experience transcendent to your illusion. It sheds its own light upon your life as you return to the illusion. It is necessary, when dealing with the illusion, to refrain from attempting to discern your own desires within the illusion. It is important to take questions [into] meditation, for there is a purpose to your life which is not to be discerned within the illusion, but only while you are in contact with your true reality within the All.

Turn towards your true consciousness in meditation. When there are pressures, doubts and difficulties, turn to meditation. When there continue to be these, continue to turn to meditation. There will come, in time, a simple awareness of what is required and there will be, at that time, the ability and the tools with which to do it.

The Creator, and that part of the Creator which is you in your true form, have provided you with each day, and each need is taken care of along the path which you are intending to go. Trust to this and seek to know the *(inaudible)* through meditation, my friends.

At this time, I will transfer this contact to another instrument. I am Hatonn.

(Don channeling)

I am Hatonn. I am with this instrument. I will speak using this instrument.

(Pause)

I will continue. I am sorry for the delay. I was speaking on the subject of meditation.

(Pause)

My friends, meditation brings about a simple result. It brings about an awareness.

(Pause)

Sorry for the delay. We are having some difficulty. I will attempt to transfer this contact to another instrument.

(Carla channeling)

My friends, we are also aware that there is a *(inaudible)* which helps, in general, but not specifically so. We find it difficult to communicate helpful knowledge at this time. However, we will say this: the key to a knowledge of the path ahead is a knowledge of yourself.

It has been said by your Holy Book that not all those who are called are [saviors.] My friends, this we have found within the mind of this instrument, but we have not found this understood correctly. In truth, my friends, each of those called is chosen. The call that is felt is a true one. But, my friends, you, yourself will *(inaudible)* your service, not simply in your state before birth when you are aware of the true reality of what you desire, and within this illusion you must become aware and look *(inaudible)*, and then you must chose. You must know yourself, and then you will see the choice is to seek, and you have already done this.

After that choice, my friends, it is always clear, very soon, that your way is a way of service, and then your choice becomes cloudy for it is very difficult to know what your service is. And yet, my friends, do not fear for you will be of service if you so desire. You have been called, and it is up to you to chose each step how you will be of service. Each of you, my friends, has his own talents and his own way of being of service. These ways are many, as many as there are people. It is not *(inaudible)* the physical illusion …

(Tape ends.)

Saturday Meditation
May 11, 1974

(Don channeling)

I am Hatonn. I greet you in the love and the light of our infinite Creator. It is a great privilege to speak with this group once more. I and my brother Laitos are here. We shall condition each member of this group who desires our conditioning. You will feel our presence.

I am aware of a question. I will attempt to speak through this instrument to answer the question which has been asked. There are many ways to meditate. There is, however, only one true form of meditation. It is necessary, if meditation is to be effective, that the intellectual mind be allowed to cease functioning, for this acts as a type of interference to realizing and understanding that is within all beings. In order to do this it is necessary to learn how. There are many, many techniques employed in this practice. It is extremely simple for those who have mastered it and seemingly very difficult for those who are still attempting to master it.

There are certain necessary steps if one is to rapidly master this process. It is necessary, it seems, for the individual to be in an atmosphere free from outside distractions. This is of great aid in initially attempting to master the art of meditation. It is also necessary that the individual maintain a posture in which the spine is approximately vertical. The body should be comfortable, but not relaxed in a position so that the spine is not vertical. This, perhaps, is the most important aspect in mastering the art of meditation: that the spine be maintained in a vertical position. Once a comfortable position has been assumed with an erect position of the spine, it is then necessary that the mind be allowed to slowly discontinue its thoughts. This may be done by focusing the thought upon one object, or upon the center of the forehead, or by simply allowing intellectual thoughts to leave the mind.

As this process continues, there will be a cessation slowly of the awareness of the physical body. This state should be maintained for a reasonable period of time. This period of time is dependent upon the desire of the individual performing the meditation. However, the benefits of meditation will become obvious to the practitioner and therefore his length of meditation will depend completely upon his own desires. There are many benefits from the process of meditation. It is up to the individual to discover them for himself, for they are beyond communication in terms of your language.

We of the Confederation of Planets are bringing to the people of Earth a simple message and simple instructions. We bring you these simple messages and these simple instructions since these are the only things that are needed at this time by the people of the planet Earth. There is but one lesson to be learned. It is the lesson of awareness. We find the people of this planet are blind, for they cannot see. We find they are crippled, since they cannot move. We find they are dumb, because they do not understand. And each of these maladies is a result of one disease, a disease very easily remedied, a remedy which we bring and offer the people of this planet, a simple remedy which can be practiced and administered to all. A simple remedy of meditation, to open the eyes, to free the spirit, to unlock the mind so that man of Earth may regain his normal abilities.

At this time I will leave you. I leave you in the love and the light of our Creator. Return to the knowledge that is yours as provided by your Creator. It is available at any time, it is available at any place. It is only necessary that you reach out and accept it. I will leave you, my friends. I am Hatonn. Adonai vasu. ☥

Sunday Meditation
May 12, 1974

(Don channeling)

I am Hatonn. I greet you in the love and the light of our infinite Creator. It is a great privilege to once more be with this group. It is seldom that we are able to contact those who are seeking upon the surface of this planet. There are not too many of those people of this planet who are seeking at this time. We have spoken many times to this group and to other groups about the importance of seeking, but we feel that this is not fully understood. And for this reason we will speak this evening on the subject of seeking.

It has been written in your holy works that it is necessary to seek in order to find. We are going to instruct in methods of seeking and we are going to tell you what you may expect to find. The method of seeking which we have spoken of has *(inaudible)* be the only recommended by us is the method of meditation. There are many forms of seeking, many intellectual forms of seeking, many practitioners of seeking. My friends, there is much to be gained through meditation that can be gained in no other way. We do not disapprove of seeking in the form of reading different manuscripts and materials. This is of a beneficial nature. However, there is no way, to our knowledge, to arrive at the goals that one [who] is truly seeking desires, unless he spends considerable time in meditation.

Meditation is what you might consider to be a strange phenomena. It does not at first seem that the individual is making progress when he avails himself to that which he desires through meditation. My friends, this is not correct—progress is always made when an individual meditates. If an individual is able to clear his conscious mind of thoughts and to relax while maintaining the spine in a vertical position, he is able to open his mind to much, much more than his normal awareness allows.

Upon your planet at this time there exists many states of awareness. The awareness of the population of your planet is quite varied. There is an awareness of an extremely low level among many of your peoples and there is awareness of extremely high level among a few of your peoples. The awareness of which I speak is an awareness of truth. Truth, my friends, being simply defined as that which is the same regardless of who is aware of it. Truth, my friends, is the same for you as it is for us. It is the same for the Creator as it is for you or us. Truth, my friends, is an absolute.

The understanding of this absolute is variable. Some of the peoples of your planet have a vague or shaded understanding, others have a much clearer understanding. Truth, my friends, is extremely simple and requires no intellectual analysis. It is simple and within each of the Creator's children. The differences that are encountered among the peoples of your planet with respect to their understanding of this truth is due primarily and almost exclusively [to] one thing. It is due to their meditations, whether these meditations occurred in this particular experience or incarnation or whether they occurred at a previous time and were carried over into the present experience.

The Creator intended for His children to experience what they desired in every instance. He did not assume that His children would desire something that they would not wish to experience. In other words, it was assumed, you might say, that the individualized consciousness *(inaudible)* as created would act in what you would consider to be an intelligent manner and experience desires which would lead to the enjoyment of the creation envisioned by the original Thought. We find the condition upon this planet quite divergent from this plan. We find that man upon Earth has suffered many aberrations as a result of his lack of understanding of his ability and the original Thought of his creation. We suggest that as an individual is experiencing something which he does not wish to experience that he is experiencing this due to his ignorance. This ignorance is a product of his lack of communication with the original Thought and this lack of communication is simply due to a lack of meditation. In other words, my friends, many of the people of this planet have cut themselves off from the understanding that was given them by their Creator by ignoring the necessity of maintaining this contact.

Man on Earth has generated an illusion of false values so strong that he finds it almost impossible to return to the simplicity of the original Thought that generated it. This thought, of course, is one which we will attempt to express by using the word in your language which most closely approximates the expression. That word, my friends, is, of course, love. It is unnecessary to complicate your thinking in any way other than to express the simple love of your Creator. If this is done and the understanding is augmented through daily meditation, the system of values that is illusory and has been generated by many of your years of erroneous thinking and has been impressed upon the minds of the people of your planet because of their acceptance of these thoughts will become meaningless, and the only true meaning remaining in your consciousness will be the simple acceptance of the love of your Creator. For I suggest to you to join with your brothers of the Confederation of Planets in the Service of the Infinite One in rejecting all concepts other than that concept given to them by their Creator. Remove from your thinking everything but this love. Do this through daily meditation and then you will know the joy that we in His service know. For this, my friends, is the creation: the joy of knowing and expressing the love of our Creator.

It has been a great privilege in speaking to this group this evening. I am at this time in direct contact with this instrument. It is very simple to maintain contact with this instrument. There is only one thing that allows me to make this contact. It is necessary, my friends, that the instrument desire the contact. If this desire is what we might call an absolute desire, this contact may be established in a perfectly fluent condition. Adonai, my friends. I am Hatonn. Adonai vasu. ☥

Monday Meditation
May 13, 1974

(Inaudible) our messages can be of an expanded consciousness … This instrument is tiring and I will now attempt to transfer this contact.

(Don channeling)

I am with this instrument. I am again attempting to condition each of you. I am also attempting to contact another of the newer instruments if he will avail himself to my contact.

(Pause)

I am once more with this instrument. I am Hatonn. I am sorry we are having difficulty. I will attempt to use another of the new instruments. Please avail yourself to my contact. I will speak by giving thoughts to you. Do not be afraid of making errors. I will use this instrument to correct any error that might be made. I am Hatonn. Please avail yourself to my contact.

(Unknown channeling)

I am Hatonn.

(Don channeling)

It is a very simple process. However, it does require some practice. This instrument has learned to go ahead and speak with the thoughts that we give him. He has also learned to clear his mind to almost a one hundred percent extent. This varies somehow—this instrument has made an error—this varies somewhat depending upon the conditions that are surrounding him. At this time the conditions are quite good and he is receiving my thoughts almost in a word for word fashion, since I am familiar with your language and am also able to transmit the words that I wish for the instrument to speak.

In the case that you are now witnessing, the instrument is receiving the words that I wish for him to speak. In some other instances when I am using this instrument, I use him by giving him concepts and allow him to verbalize these concepts using words that he chooses.

Each one of these techniques has its own merit. This one is extremely valuable in communicating information of a specific nature. It does require, however, a greater degree of control of the environment. In other words, the conditions for reception for my thoughts at this time are quite good and this instrument is able to repeat word for word what I am giving to him. This is a very high quality contact and it is possible to have just as high a quality contact with each of you here in the room. It is only necessary that you learn like this instrument has to clear your mind of thoughts. It is a little trick that must be practiced. You practice this through daily meditation and also through use of the channeling technique. You will not arrive at the fluidity that this instrument has arrived at without practice in doing so. For this reason, we recommend that you simply relax and allow us of the Confederation of Planets in the Service of the Infinite Creator to impress upon your thinking our thoughts. And then as these thoughts enter your mind, instead of analyzing them, simply repeat them.

The analysis that you make of what you are doing is detrimental to the type of communication that we are making. This instrument is doing very little analysis of what we are giving him at this time. He too, in the beginning of his channeling, had some difficulty because he analyzed at that time what he was saying. For this reason, it took a great amount of time to transmit a thought through him and there was but very little success in using this form of communication which requires no muscular control at all and is a technique, as I have said, that gives to you our thoughts in a verbal fashion as we arrange the words.

I am going at this time to tell a little story to you in order to allow you to focus your thinking on that which is necessary for you to focus it upon in order to very simply receive our thoughts. This story has to do with a small child. This small child listens to its parents, and its parents spoke to it. The child, before listening to its parents, could not speak, but after listening to its parents, it could speak quite fluently. However, the child was totally unaware of the process by which it learned to speak. It simply was there and it simply learned to speak.

This is the process we are using. Not to say that you are as a little child, that is the problem. If you were as a little child, we could speak through you with no difficulty. The problem is that you are not as a little child. We recommend that you think of yourself as you would of a little child and relax and know nothing. In this way you will very rapidly learn. This is what is necessary if you are to very rapidly learn to channel our thoughts. The child, you see, has no knowledge of what it is supposed to do, it simply speaks. This is how it is possible for you to learn to do this rapidly.

We have found that some peoples about your planet learn much more easily than others. We found peoples in a technological society such as yours sometime require great effort because they have learned to question quite carefully everything that is presented them. If you do not question what we are attempting to do, but simply relax and let it happen, it will happen.

I hope that I have been of assistance in attempting to strengthen our contact. I will again at this time try to speak through one of the newer instruments.

(Unknown channeling)

I am once again with this instrument.

(Inaudible)

We are aware of the activities of your group, as we are aware of the activities of all of the people on your planet. We are here to be of service to you. We bring our love.

(Tape ends.)

Tuesday Meditation
May 14, 1974

Group question: Who were the UFOs that picked up Betty and Barney Hill, as told in *The Interrupted Journey*? Were they evil, or to be feared? Do evil planets attempt to invade Earth?

(Carla channeling)

I am Hatonn. I am aware of your question. *(Inaudible)*. It is a privilege to be able to attempt to answer your question *(inaudible)* our emotional reaction to them, for they are the Creator's children to us, and we wish only to help them, as we wish only to help you. We are, unfortunately, unable to help them at this time. Therefore, we are content to wait until such time as they require our aid.

Meanwhile, regard them with the love of the Creator for all of His created beings. To be afraid of such entities as you have called invaders is to be afraid of yourself, my friends. And it is not needed to be afraid of anything or anyone.

I am aware that this does not satisfy your questions very well, and I will attempt to use this instrument for a more specific answer, although she will find it somewhat difficult, because there must be more control used to which she is not used at this time.

The entities of which you have spoken were friendly. They were a scientific expedition which had good intentions, but their knowledge of life-forms on this planet was lacking. They had no intentions to commit any sort of infringement. They had been cautioned by the Confederation that it was best to refrain from investigating in areas populated by people.

They wished only to collect specimens of the fauna of some parts of the planet and to gain data about the predominant life-forms.

They did not attack then. They will not attack you. Their intentions are positive. They are aware of our presence. Their presence is not a harbinger of any sort of enemy.

As to other invading visitors, they are only all the barriers and possibilities. There are many, many myriads of populations throughout the cosmos. Many of them are extremely advanced, and a few of them are not only advanced but also of a nature which you might call evil.

The Creator is at the end of your path. Your faith is far stronger, if you indeed realize it, than any evil. Remember this, my friends. It is completely within your power, through meditation, to gain the love of the Creator that conquers all lack, limitation and … But, my friends, be aware that the only true nature of evil is separation from the Creator. It cannot touch you if you maintain your contact with the One who is All. Nothing from the outside may come in to harm. From the universe of truth and understanding you may show love and light upon all who come into your view.

Do not fear, my friends. There is nothing to fear but fear. This has been said before upon your planet, and it is quite true. Never waste time in fear or in hatred or in anger, for it is only another opportunity at such a time to experience and to demonstrate the love and the light of the infinite Creator.

I am the one known as Hatonn. I hope that I have been able to answer your question. Are there any further questions?

Questioner: Hatonn, can you give us a specific reason why we can't meet you face to face?

I am Hatonn. I am with the instrument. I will meet you face to face on the day you enter the Kingdom of Heaven. You may do this at any time. It is doubtful that you will do it while in the body. If you do achieve this state, then whether you are in the body or not, you would be instantly able to speak with me on any level you desired. At that point you would recognize me as your brother. No more, my friend, and no less. I am afraid that one cannot fulfill the burden of influencing one or any of your people by appearing within your vibration while your consciousness is as it is now.

You are very far from having a negative reaction, and we are pleased and privileged to have your fellowship and acquaintance in this work. But, my friends, I am only as you are.

We will proceed to the next question.

Questioner: What about sex? Is it better to be a monk if you are on the spiritual path?

My friends, the subject of the physical illusion has always been a difficult one, and your question about what you call sex is an area which has a great deal of trauma associated with it.

We can only tell you that you are a free agent. You have incarnated into a physical vehicle. This physical vehicle is designed in order to offer you various experiences which you need for your progress spiritually. Due to the fact that each one is sovereign unto himself, being a free child of the Creator, each man therefore will have come to this incarnation with a peculiar and unique set of needs, which his excursion into the physical illusion will satisfy. To some people, the experience of sexuality is extremely important. To some people, there is little or no need for this particular type of activity. The rather large number of people who have lined up on one side or another of this question, and others like unto it, are reasoning about an infinite situation. There is only one answer for each person.

My friends, the sexuality is neither good nor evil. Your physical body is neither good nor evil. Sexual activity, as such, is neither good nor evil. The natural activities upon your planet are part of the Creator's plan. Were it not part of the Creator's plan that man should have sexuality, then man would not have sexuality. It exists simply as an opportunity. It is completely under the control of each individual as to the use to which he puts this opportunity.

There is a simple progression for those on your plane. We have noticed that you are aware that many of your Earthly masters on your planet were not particularly interested in the experience gained within the province of human desire. This is due to the fact that the Earthly plane is experienced first in a relatively gross or material state, a state which yields great strength, great sexuality, and a great deal of aggressive emotion.

The progression towards the next density of experience is one which more and more experiences an abiding within spirit, and a detachment from the needs of the material part of the self. In extreme cases, this has meant that there will be no activity of a physical nature at all for a certain person.

However, we must point out to you that this state is not arrived at by a person who decides to become holy by imposing such restrictions upon himself. This state is properly attained as a natural result and an involuntary occurrence upon achieving a completely transcendent state.

There are many, many seekers. Many of these seekers are in many, many different places. We are aware that much good may be accomplished by the correct mating of two individuals in mind, body and soul. Again, this is not a necessary path to take. There are a thousand paths to take. Each individual finds what is proper for him. To find a proper path, one may meditate, as we have said so many times. Simply meditate.

We are aware that this is a subject of confusion. But, my friends, it is simple. There are opportunities, and you are a discerning entity who seeks to understand.

Seek, and ye shall find. These are true words. Seek through meditation.

Have you a further question?

Questioner: Yes, I have one more. The soul does not sleep *(inaudible)*. What does it do when the body is asleep?

I am Hatonn. I am aware of your question. At night, my friends, you truly come alive. Many, many upon your planet only rise in consciousness in their sleep. There is a desperate starvation upon your planet. It is the starvation of the spirits that have forgotten how to contact their Creator. During sleep, my friends, your spirit involuntarily goes directly into the real universe, and breathes and lives and radiates the joy of the Creator.

Were it not for this unconscious activity of the spirit of many of those upon the surface of the planet, they would be unable to continue their existence in the physical body.

In fact, this is the reason for the amount of sleep that is needed upon this planet. It is necessary in order to give enough food to the spirit. In the case of those who through meditation have found a conscious contact with the Creator, they may find that less sleep may be adequate.

Questioner: Yes. Can you still remember on awakening?

All is remembered, my friends. Nothing is forgotten. There will be much remembering of much that we seem to have forgotten when we leave this chemical vehicle and this heavy illusion.

Are there any more questions?

Questioner: No.

If that is so then I will leave you now, my friends. It has been my pleasure to serve you. I hope that I have been able to communicate with you. I leave you in the love and the light of our infinite Creator. I am Hatonn. Adonai.

Wednesday Meditation
May 15, 1974

(Carla channeling)

I am Hatonn. I greet you, my friends, in the love and the light of our infinite Creator. It is indeed a pleasure to be speaking with you again this evening. I am here, far above you. You cannot see us, my friends, at this time, for the distance is too great.

We are here, and we abide with you, for, my friends, we are your brothers, and we wish to share with you our understanding. This evening we would like to urge you to seek that understanding with more single-mindedness than you have been propounding and expressing recently.

My friends, as we are privy to your spiritual conversation, we listen to much of what you say, and when you avail yourself to our thoughts, you listen to what we have to say. We hope that the exchange is beneficial to you as well as to us.

My friends, your minds are stayed far, far too strongly upon those illusory goals of the intellect which your conscious awareness makes such advanced company of. These intellectual pretensions, my friends, are no kind of advanced company to be in. Their group name is complexity, and, my friends, understanding is simple.

Let us examine this concept. Understanding, my friends, is simple. It is unitary. It is not logical. It is not intellectual. It is not necessary that you understand understanding. It is not necessary that anyone around you understand what you are understanding.

It is necessary only for you to seek the understanding of the true creation within, and this we will attempt to give you in a simple way. With the intellect and with words, my friends, we can only approximate understanding to you. And your attempts to examine it on an intellectual level can only be a type of subterfuge, camouflage and misdirection. You must not depend upon the tools of the physical illusion in order to build for yourself your bridge to eternity, for that which is of the illusion will vanish and be no more before you are able to cross that bridge.

Let go of the preconceptions which are imbedded deep in your intellectual mind. Allow yourself simply to seek, and then to have faith in the seeking. What you seek is simple. The creation is simple. There is only one understanding which we can offer you, my friends, and that is that the creation is one great Being. The creation is you; the creation is me; the creation is all that ever was and ever will be. The creation, my friends, is the Creator. As you look into the eyes of another upon your planet, you are looking at the Creator. As he looks at you, my friends, he also is looking at the Creator.

If you may achieve this simple understanding, then and only then you may live in harmony with the understanding of the Creator, Who created each portion of His creation in order that it may be of service to every other portion of the creation.

This is our understanding. This is our simple understanding: all is one. We cannot speak to you in any complex manner, for we do not have a complex statement. We sincerely hope that you may heed our caution, and allow that portion of yourself which is stored with the knowledge of all of the creation to come into life within you. Allow it to do so by exposing it to the love and the light of the Creator through meditation.

Seek, my friends. Seek understanding, and through meditation, understanding will be given.

At this time I will condition each of you who desires it, and I will attempt to transfer this contact to one of the new instruments, to continue this message for a time. I will leave this instrument now, and will condition each of you who desires it. I am Hatonn.

(T channeling)

(Inaudible)

Thursday Meditation
May 16, 1974

(Carla channeling)

I greet you, my friends, in the love and the light of our infinite Creator. I am the one known to you as Hatonn. I and my brother Laitos are here to serve you, and we are with you in the room. My brother will be giving conditioning to each of you who desires it as we proceed with this message. We are most privileged to be speaking with you this evening.

We would like to give you a thought upon the nature of the spiritual path. Consider for yourself, my friends, the nature of your interior universe. How much of your thinking is involved with striving, attaining and grasping at things within the physical illusion? What fire consumes you? What greed or envy or base desire have you allowed to continue to have power over your thinking? And then, my friends, what portion of your thinking is clear, calm, motionless, humble, unassuming, and content?

I do not need to tell you which portion of your interior universe is more correctly called the spiritual part. The truth of the universe is a very simple truth. Correctly understood and practiced, it eliminates the striving for selfhood within the physical illusion. It eliminates it because it offers a more rewarding reality along the spiritual path.

The reason, my friends, that you have not completely become one with the spiritual path is not because you have not been trying. Do not cause yourself anxiety. It is simply, my friends, that the illusion under which you labor is extremely strong upon your planet, and there is a good deal of constant and faithful meditation and discipline to be achieved before the final breakthrough can come, and you may be free of your selfhood within the illusion.

Without that selfhood, my friends, without that which upon the part of the planet which you live is termed ego, you may achieve all things, in the name of the Creator. For having no limitation of self, you may give for all men, and to all men.

It is a matter of knowing whom you serve, my friends. As you go through your daily existence, therefore, we suggest to you that you contemplate, when it may serve you to do so, that which is called water. Water, my friends, is the humblest and weakest of all substances. It abides in the lowest places. It constantly seeks a level. It is ashamed to go nowhere, but flows where every opportunity takes it. My friends, water may wear away the hardest substances, for it is far stronger in its weakness than rigid substances can ever be.

Be like the water, my friends. Upon the spiritual path that you are seeking to follow, seek the nature of water.

I wish to continue this contact but to transfer it to the instrument known as R. We will condition him for a brief period, and then we will attempt to transfer this contact. I will leave this instrument. I am Hatonn.

(R channeling)

I am now with this instrument. Seek, my friends, to become the water—still and pure. It has been said that life is as a vast ocean, and we very often cause waves through our actions and our thoughts.

Through self-discipline it is possible to wear away through this action those qualities about yourself that would be considered undesirable. Through lack of control of your actions and thoughts, great storms will arise. Your thought, my friends, is that which creates tides and waves. See your thoughts as waves. The waves that you create have a vast effect upon the rest of the body of water.

The waves which cleanse and wash away are also those which erode. By directing your thought, you direct the waves, and become, with you, as you seek them to be.

Consider then, my friends, the water, like unto yourself; consider, then, your thoughts, like unto the waves, and that which directs the water.

I would at this time attempt to continue this communication through the instrument known as T.

(T channeling)

I am Hatonn. I am now with this instrument.

(Inaudible)

(E channeling)

As I was saying, like the spirit, water flows quietly along its path, until it reaches an obstacle. It then must go around or over the obstacle. In going around or over an obstacle, it will erode the obstacle. Then the obstacle is no more, and the spirit or water is free of that obstacle.

The movement of the water is like thought or actions, in that the thought … the movement of the water is like thought or action.

I will continue this contact with another instrument. I am Hatonn.

(Carla channeling)

I am again with this instrument. I am Hatonn. I and my brother Laitos have been most privileged to have been able to serve you this evening. We hope that we have been able to aid you in your seeking.

I am aware that there is a question. It will be somewhat difficult to use this instrument to answer this question. Therefore, we would prefer to await another opportunity to use a different instrument for this particular question. Is that satisfactory with the person who desires to know the answer to this question?

Questioner: It's OK to wait, but could you try to answer the part of it that you can through this instrument, and then I'll ask it again of another instrument? I want to know whether it is harmful or helpful to use drugs, especially for intellectual purposes.

I am Hatonn. I am again with this instrument. We will attempt to communicate through this instrument upon this question.

The use of any outside or external stimulus has no appreciable effect upon your internal spirit. The center of the problem of which you speak is not the fact that these foreign substances do or do not transfer parts of your vibratory makeup into novel spaces. Various external influences have various effects. By the use of these, the type of awareness that may be achieved through meditation can be achieved. The difficulty, as we have said, lies in the fact that these substances are external, and do not come under the will of you, the individual who is seeking.

It may be acceptable therapeutic measure, to increase one's faith in the reality of the spiritual path, to experience such a state by means of such an outside stimulus. However, the use of internalizing effects, such as meditation and service, wherein your will makes its own contact with the Creator and the creation, is a far more realistic way of entering upon the spiritual path.

It is important in the extreme that you be living within yourself, at the center …

(Doorbell rings.)

(Pause)

(Carla channeling)

I apologize for the difficulty. We may continue.

We were saying—in order that you may experience the reality of the Father's creation, it is important that you be able to achieve the awareness of that creation from within your own spirit. The use of outside agents simply puts you in places which you are not ready to comprehend or make use of. True seeking is inner seeking. To be able to give, it is best to refrain from taking. It is far better to achieve an awareness of the creation through meditation than through the use of any external agent.

There is not any more harm or acceptability for the use of any drug or material over any other. We have observed simply that they all lie outside the control of your inner self, and are therefore not a part of your spiritual world.

We are aware that this instrument is becoming fatigued. She is not used to this much control. Therefore, we would be privileged to speak using another instrument at a later time, if you will ask your question again.

May we answer you further?

Questioner:

(No further queries.)

I will leave you now, my friends. I am very pleased to be speaking through the new instruments. It is a great pleasure to my brother Laitos and to myself to be working with you and with your group. Blessings upon you. I leave you in the love and the light of our infinite Creator. I am Hatonn. Adonai.

L/L Research

Friday Meditation
May 17, 1974

(Unknown channeling)

I am Hatonn. I greet you, my friends, in the love and the light of the infinite Father. I am the one known to you as Hatonn and it is my pleasure to speak with you once again.

I am very, very pleased to greet each of you. I and my brother will be conditioning you as I speak, using this instrument.

My friends, it is very interesting to us who have come here to aid these of you upon the surface of your planet who seek, to notice the constant and widespread misapprehensions under which your people labor, with regard to the idea of normalcy.

There are many things which are looked upon within your physical illusion as being quite normal, which to us, my friends, look quite abnormal. And as we patiently search among the people of your planet, we find very few whose actions we would call normal. It is as though the people of planet Earth are all mysteriously prey to some widespread emotional disorder.

We did not understand this when we first came, and our first attempts to communicate with your people suffered much because of this misunderstanding. We have come to understand much more. And now, we can see the strong and ever-present cause of this widespread aberration of the peoples of this planet.

There is an abnormality which has been developing through many, many of your generations, which has been building through many, many of your generations, until now what is in truth normal has become unheard-of, and its place completely overtaken by that which is complete illusion. You, my friends, having accepted the illusion, have simply reacted to what seems to be reality. The fault is certainly not your own, within this particular physical experience.

However, it has happened. But, my friends, were there not hope that you might be able to reestablish contact with reality, and thereby return to a normal state of awareness with regard to the creation, we would not be here. We have come because those who have the potential for using our aid have desired our aid. We are here to serve you. We are here to encourage you. And we are here to attempt to give you our understanding of the creation of the Father.

You must realize, my friends, that although we cannot lay any blame at the feet of those people of your planet who do not understand, we can lay the blame at our own feet. For, my friends, we are each of you, and we have, through our free will, created this illusion. Your pain has been created by us, and we feel that pain very deeply. It is our strong desire to enable you to become able to have clear sight of what is real.

The very few people upon your planet who see reality are often thought to be quite insane. My friends, one must not attempt to understand what we are giving on the level of language. Go within, my friends, and meditate. For knowledge of reality will come only from within. Accept nothing on blind faith, but accept everything that is of good report. Allow all paradoxes to remain so. Accept much, and reject nothing.

Go within, my friends, for within you lies reality.

I wish to transfer this contact at this time to the instrument known as Don. We are aware that there are certain reservations. However, if he will avail himself, we would like to speak through him.

(Don channeling)

I am with this instrument. I am Hatonn. Please be patient while I condition the instrument.

There are many ways, my friends, of gaining what you seek. However, what you seek now will change. It will change as you seek it, for this is the nature of seeking. For as you seek, you find, and as you find, you understand. And as you understand, you continue in seeking, but at a different level.

So do not attempt to understand that which at present seems to be beyond you. Simply go within, and you will be led to an understanding that will place you upon a new plateau, from which you will be able to view much, much more of reality.

Seeking, my friends, is not a direct attempt to understand each intellectual question which crosses your mind. Seeking is the attempt to known one's Creator. There will be in your seeking an unfoldment of understanding. Each step will show itself to you. When it does, raise yourself upon it, so that you may find the next one.

We bring to man of Earth understanding, and yet we cannot speak to him and cause him to understand. We cannot communicate through channels this understanding. We can only point out directions for his seeking. For it will be necessary for him to change his point of view, and to change it, he must understand; and to understand, he must seek.

There will be many paradoxes in your seeking, for this is the nature of seeking. But as you continue, these will dissolve, for you will reach a new plateau, and a new understanding. And the seeming paradox that you have bypassed will appear in its true light.

Meditation, my friends, is the only method of which we know to allow an individual to rapidly form this new basis for his understanding. For this is not dependent upon preconceptions. It is not dependent upon the definitions of a language that was never intended for spiritual seeking.

Redefine that which you experience. Redefine it through your seeking, and through your growing awareness of the creation and our Creator. And then, my friends, you will not question, for you will know. For you will have grown in your understanding.

It is sometimes frustrating to be unable to find answers to those questions that seem paramount and directly in the path of your seeking. But these too will fade as you pass them by and become more and more aware of the single truth that permeates all things and answers all questions.

We will continue to aid you in any way that we can, but primarily we will point out to you the wonders and the joy of the creation that you experience. And we will attempt to bring to you an understanding that will grow with each day, an understanding that will be a result of your meditation.

I will leave you at this time. I hope that I have been of service. It has been a great privilege speaking to you. I am Hatonn. Adonai vasu.

Saturday Meditation
May 18, 1974

(Carla channeling)

I greet you, my friends, in the love and the light of our infinite Creator. I am Hatonn. It is a privilege for me to meet with you this evening, as always.

I am aware that you wish to know something about the confrontation between a combatant from another planet than your own and two of your people. We will attempt to explain through this instrument, however, we are having a certain amount of difficulty with this contact, and patience on your parts will be required, for this instrument is resisting the amount of control that is necessary for projecting more closely the information we must project.

This type of communication is not the completely controlled type of communication of which we have spoken in the past. However, the concepts which we are sending are considerably more restricted in their interpretation, and therefore, we must keep a much closer amount of control over the consciousness and the mechanism which is producing the message. This amount of control is still somewhat difficult for this instrument to accept. However, we have been conditioning her while we have been talking, and we believe that we have a somewhat improved contact at this point.

The Pascagoula landing, my friends, was, as far as we are aware, not a completely isolated instance. However, it is the only instance which has been delivered into the hands of public knowledge. On the other hand, although it is not the only landing of that particular group of alien individuals, it is one of the very few.

These peoples are members of a type of combatant group. There is not the idea of the soldiering or war as you know it. However, it is the closest interpretation which your language and the use of this instrument will permit. These people were interested simply as passersby in the phenomena which they saw, and, not having strong enough leadership, they decided to take a closer look. There was no intention of any harm intended at all.

It is doubtful that this type of craft and this particular group of beings will cease passing this particular area of space, for several reasons, none of which are in any way connected with the planet on whose surface you now reside. Therefore, you may again discover some evidence of such a contact. But we assure you that it is merely a rare, scattered, and unharmful confrontation.

Do you have a further question?

Questioner: Were the people who came from the spacecraft people or robots?

These were beings with consciousness and individuality. They were, however, not precisely of the nature which you would call human. You are not at this time aware of the possibilities that exist in the creation. However, these people are not robots.

Questioner: Can you give me some idea of what you meant by combatants?

There is a great deal of difficulty in working out of the language of your culture in explaining another culture, especially an alien culture. I am attempting to give to this instrument an idea of the structure of thinking upon the planet from which these people come. I am giving her the name but she does not seem able to understand it. However, the structure is somewhat more totally conscious of illusion than your own world structure. Each of the projects and difficulties of learning within a density somewhat comparable to yours results in an externally expressed series of movements which eliminates for these people the need for inner fears and doubts. By the structuring of the illusion, they so recognize it and deal with it in a highly stylized fashion. They have a good record of advancement along the spiritual path, using this technique. The closest that this instrument can come to explaining the concept she has been given is probably the concept of a few people's ambitions. They go, therefore, a far distance to take part in a game which has much of the mental characteristics of war, but which is entirely mental.

Due to the type of structure which these people have obtained throughout many generations of this discipline, the outcome of this combat will be final, just and completely acceptable to each who has depended upon the combatants of each different opinion.

These people are progressing along a different path than yours, and this is true throughout the infinite creation. But they are progressing towards the same goal that we all share.

Have you a further question?

Questioner: With respect to progress, what would be their relative progress and understanding with respect to this planet's general progress?

I am afraid that it is difficult in the extreme to state where a relatively stable, progressive culture lies, in comparison to the somewhat uneven picture which is represented on planet Earth. The potential which is within very many of those upon the planet Earth is somewhat, shall we say, more advanced than the basic vibratory level of the planet …

Carla: I can't get that. They're telling me a name, but I can't get that.

(Carla channeling)

However, the average vibration upon that alien planet is far more advanced than the lower average of those upon planet Earth who stubbornly sleep. We are afraid that as those of Earth have much potential, so they also have little time to translate their potential, so they also have little time to translate their potential into the actuality that they in truth can deserve and have.

Both planets are within the same basic vibration. And the planet upon which you enjoy physical existence is far more advanced through its cycle within this particular vibration.

Is there another question?

Questioner: What type of sensory equipment do these individuals have? Do they see, hear and communicate like we do?

No. They are aware. The material which covers them is aware of more than all of the physical senses upon this planet are aware of, in unison.

Questioner: What do you mean by the material which covers?

You would call it skin.

(Transcript ends.)

Sunday Meditation
May 19, 1974

(Carla channeling)

I am Hatonn. I greet you, beloved brethren, in the love and in the light of our infinite Creator. I am the one known to you as Hatonn. I am far, far above you, in what you would call a craft. We are here, my friends, to aid you in that which you seek to accomplish. It is our great, great privilege to be with this group this evening, and we greet each of you.

We are aware that there are questions upon your minds, and we will not speak at great length before beginning the questioning. However, we would like to say a few words about service, my friends.

The many attempts which each of you makes to give service to others is more successful than you know. The simple turning of the self from the seeking for sensation in self to the seeking towards service gives the seeker the ability that he seeks.

However, my friends, if you wish to improve and expand your service, we can only suggest to you that you turn within, away from all sensation, and towards meditation. There is no power without you. There is nothing that you can smell or taste or experience in the physical that can cause harm or give aid. The power that you seek is the power of the reality of the love and the light of our infinite Creator, and it lies within. Go within, my friends. Meditate. Seek that which you desire, and it will come to you.

At this time, I wish to transfer this contact to one of the other instruments. I am Hatonn.

(H channeling)

I am now with this instrument. I was speaking of service. We are aware that those present desire to serve. This is a true and worthy desire, and we find there can be no greater desire. For, as we have often said, a service performed by any entity towards another is also service towards that entity. For as we comprehend, the creation is but one thing. That is this creation is love, and is the manifestation of the Creator. And within it exists no separation. Therefore, any service rendered unto the creation, in any portion of it, is also service to oneself.

I am aware of the presence of those who are experiencing their first exposure to our contact. We also are aware of their great service, which they render in the name of the Creator. It pleases us that your path has led to union with ours, for we serve the same purpose. We wish to serve in the name of the Creator. And this Creator can only be explained as love.

We are aware that there exist many questions, and we will at this time attempt to transfer this contact to another instrument who shall be capable of answering questions. I am Hatonn.

(Pause)

(H channeling)

I am Hatonn. I am again with this instrument. Pardon me for the delay. We are experiencing some difficulty in contacting the instrument known as Don. Please be patient, for we feel that in order for your questions to be answered, we shall establish contact with the one known as Don. Please be patient while I again attempt this contact. I am Hatonn.

(Pause)

(H channeling)

I am again with this instrument. We find that we are unable to establish contact with the instrument at this time. We are aware that there exist many questions, and would desire to attempt to continue through this instrument. This may be slightly difficult, and require a great amount of conditioning. Yet at this time we will attempt to answer an question you desire to ask.

(There is a short conversation in which it is advised that questions be asked verbally.)

I am Hatonn. We are aware that there are questions being asked within your thoughts. Yet this instrument is having difficulty in receiving our thoughts due to not being aware of the question, and fearing somewhat [to err] in answering. We would suggest that you would attempt to verbally ask a question, and we shall attempt to answer through this or another instrument. I am Hatonn.

Questioner: What level are you on? Have you been on our level? Will we attain your level? How far are you from the final destination?

We shall attempt to answer this question. Through our experiences within this creation, we have found that there exist an infinite experience, which is to be experienced by all entities. We of the Confederation of Planets in the Service of the Infinite Creator have experienced the type of physical illusion which you now find yourselves experiencing. This, as we refer to it, illusion that you are presently in is culminating in what we call its present cycle. The entity asking this question is truly aware of that which he considers the second coming of the master teacher, Jesus. These times truly are here, and these times are within the will of the Creator, the times for graduation into a higher spiritual awareness for those who would desire it.

We have experienced this same, shall we say, trial, and we sought the truth of creation through meditation. We attained a higher rate of vibration within our spiritual being through this meditation, and evolved to a greater awareness than that which can be attained within this illusion.

We of the Confederation are truly aware of the difficulties which you encounter, for as we have stated, we also have experienced your physical illusion. Our, as you say, level of existence is one of what you would consider spiritual. It is much higher evolved than that which you are presently in, yet the question of the attainment of the ultimate source, or shall we say, union with the Creator, to us at this time we cannot answer. For we have not evolved into realms higher than the one we presently occupy. Yet we are truly aware of their existence, for in our travels throughout this creation, we have come upon experiences and entities who were able to avail to us truths of even a higher awareness. And they have availed to us the thought of infinite levels of awareness on the path to total union with the Creator.

There is much within this creation that we do not comprehend, and there is much that you do not comprehend. Yet, we have experienced your present existence, and do have the understanding and realization of a higher awareness. We do not claim to be an ultimate source of information. We are capable of committing error. And I would like to say that, in your experiences, if you encounter any entity who exclaims that he can commit no error, you should truly known that this entity has erred in that judgment, for only the Creator can function without error.

And it is our mission at this time to aid the peoples of your planet in seeking the union with the Creator from within through meditation. For if you can truly gain this union, then you can …

(Side one of tape ends.)

(H channeling)

Are there any more questions? I will attempt to transfer this contact to another instrument, and continue to answer questions.

(Carla channeling)

I am Hatonn. I am with this instrument. Are there further questions?

Questioner: What is life like on your planet, as compared to our life?

Life on our planet at one time was much like that upon planet Earth. However, at this time our entire population of sentient beings has developed a singular desire. This desire began as a simple seeking for understanding, and has developed into a completely unitary and combined ability of each brother of the planet known as Hatonn. The combination is so strong that we are able to do many, many things. Feeling and being as one, we are now seeking as one, and as our seeking has led us forward, we have found our way to be pointed directly at service, ever expanding service, service to all parts of the creation.

And as our service has been needed, whereas before we were not capable of discovering the means to perform this service, we became able to perform the service that we came to see as our service.

In this manner, we have developed abilities which you may call miraculous. We have the ability to transcend what you know as time and space. We have access in a conscious manner to knowledge of which you have access only during meditation, in a subconscious manner.

The freedoms which we enjoy, my friends, are there because we have begun to see that we are all one. Realization is all that is between planet Earth and the planet Hatonn. On your planet as on our planet, each blade of grass is alive with the knowledge of the Creator. The winds sing His praises. Trees shout for joy in the creation of our infinite Father. If you are not able to see the Creator, my friends, it is a matter of seeking, and seeking, and continued seeking. And then, my friends, you will begin to realize and to understand that the creation of the Father is all around you.

Planet Earth, my friends, is indeed a lovely planet. It will soon be vibrating in a vibratory manner which is far more associated with realization of the Father's creation. Begin to realize, and move with your planet, as we moved with ours. There is only that which is in your mind, and within your consciousness, and within your faith, between the pain, the lack, and the limitation which you experience and the complete freedom which is our vibration we experience.

We invite you to join us, my friends. Seek, and ye shall find.

Are there further questions?

Questioner: The service you perform with Earth—does this same service extend to other planets? If so, can you give us some idea of how many, and their levels of consciousness?

We have aided many other planets within the same general vibratory level. The aid is given to this level by us because we are, shall we say, at the next level of awareness, and are best able to communicate to those people who wish to enter into understanding which we share.

We have dealt with many planets who are beginning a new phase of vibration. We have aided many a graduating class, and we have done so successfully. We have also failed, not once, but several times. It is completely possible for us to fail, because we wish to fail if it be the will of the people of the planet we are attempting to aid.

We come because we feel the desire that brings us here. And we give what aid we can to those who wish it. Our thoughts are available to all who desire them. However, we attempt to do this in such a way that no individual is ever in a position where he cannot accept or deny our thinking as he so pleases. Those who are vibrating within the level that will appreciate the information that we give surely recognizes that which is truth.

At the present time, we are far behind where we had hoped to be at this point while helping planet Earth. We had hoped to have been much more successful at reaching the people of this planet. It is possible that there will be a smaller graduation than we had hoped.

However, my friends, it is our greatest pleasure to be working with those of you, however many or however few, who are seeking. It is only necessary to seek, and the spiritual path shall roll behind you, and open before you. And what you desire shall be yours.

Have you further questions?

(No further queries.)

Carla: Hatonn says goodbye.

Thursday Meditation
May 23, 1974

(Don channeling)

I am Hatonn. I greet you, my friends, in the love and the light of our infinite Creator. It is a very great privilege to speak with this group this evening, as it is to speak each evening that you assemble. We of the Confederation, as we have stated many times before, are here to serve you each and every time that you avail yourself to our service. It is always a very great privilege to speak to those who seek. Seeking, my friends, takes place in many and varied ways. What is important is the seeking, not its definition or its appearance. When an individual begins to seek, he will find. What he will find will seem to be different with respect to others who also seek, in many instances. However, it will only apparently be different, for they will be finding the same thing. For, my friends, there is in truth only one thing to find and that is the love and the understanding of our Creator.

Tonight as you attend the meeting that you are planning, you will hear words spoken by another seeker. These words will be understood by some who hear them and they will not be understood by others. And yet, this is always the case upon your planet. It matters not, however, whether they are understood or not, for the much more important aspect is that those who came to listen came because they were seeking understanding. And this action itself is much more important than the intellectual understanding that they are attempting to find.

We of the Confederation of Planets in the Service of the Infinite Creator have spoken to you many times about the value of meditation. This, my friends, is of utmost value, since it leads you not to an intellectual understanding but a spiritual understanding. It is, shall I say, only of a transient value in indicating your attempts at seeking. This intellectual understanding, which is sought and found by many of those who dwell upon your planet, is an indication of your progress along the path toward a total spiritual understanding. It in itself is of no real value for what you find in these endeavors to understand within the limit of your illusion and within the limits of your intellectual mind is so very, very limited as to be of no real practical value.

We do not wish to state that type of endeavor is totally useless and should not be practiced, for some benefit is derived in an endeavor to seek. But, my friends, we do say that in your seeking it is much more important that you realize the truth of the creation of the Father through a much more direct method, a method that is not relegated to the biases of the intellect, a direct and simple understanding through meditation of the total love of the Creator of us all.

This, my friends, is all that is necessary: simply know this love and reflect it. Know it in a total sense. Do not attempt to understand it; embrace it through meditation. And then you must reflect it in your daily existence.

I have been using this instrument rapidly, for he desired speed of communication, knowing that the time available was short. This in some cases reduces the clarity of the instrument's contact. However, this contact was within a satisfactory range for understanding. I will leave this instrument at this time. I am Hatonn.

(Pause)

I am Hatonn. I am once more with this instrument. I am sorry for the interruption. We will continue. We were speaking to you about the value of intellectual knowledge and understanding. My friends, there is no understanding within the intellect. The understanding that you seek can be found only within a much, much greater mind than that that you understand [with] your present intellectual mind. There is a very simple way to reach the understanding that you seek. This very simple way is also the very best way. It is through the process of meditation. We have said this to you many, many times and this is truth. Meditate and it will become obvious that this is the understanding that you seek.

There is no system of arrangement of words that are presently in your language which can define adequately the creation in your creation. There is no system of words which can tell what you will reach through the simple process of meditation. It is understandable that it seems at times that this process is not fruitful. My friends, this is the only fruitful process in which you engage. Spend as much time as you can in availing yourself to truth through meditation. We know that this is what you desire. If we did not know this, we would not give to you this information.

We will leave you at this time. Adonai, my friends. Adonai vasu. ☥

Friday Meditation
May 24, 1974

(Carla channeling)

I am Hatonn. I greet you in the love and the light of our infinite Creator. I am one with each of you. It is my privilege to *(inaudible)* with you and it is my privilege to speak through this instrument.

I am aware that there is a question about what you call a UFO sighting. We are not aware of more than one sighting. We find in the mind of this instrument that a sighting has been had by one of you, with which we did not have a part. We do not know without consulting records what it was that you saw. However, we assume that you would be interested in knowing of the one which we are aware. The patterns which were drawn in the sky were drawn by a member of the Confederation of Planets in the Service of Our infinite Creator. We indulged ourselves at that particular time and for the general purpose of sending a reason *(inaudible)*. It is very seldom that this situation is possible. A specific type of attitude must have been nurtured over a fairly long period of time in most cases. However, the attitude of accepted *(inaudible)* was present, and so we sent a reason *(inaudible)*.

Are there any questions?

Questioner: How about the other two people that saw it *(inaudible)*?

Within these two persons this sight was a neutral experience. It had no negative or infringing nature because there was no type of message which was sent forth to either of them. Having nothing to attach this phenomena to, they were able to experience it without either positive or negative reaction. This is acceptable to us.

Questioner: How high *(inaudible)*?

The craft of my brother was a larger craft than the one upon which we normally dwell, although it is not as large as a carrier craft and does not have *(inaudible)* intergalactic capabilities. It could be *(inaudible)* to be. I am having difficulty transmitting numbers. I will transmit the size by means of comparison. This ship was approximately the size of more than one football field. It was above the level of atmosphere at the fringes of space. I am afraid I cannot tell you the specific distance. This instrument is having much difficulty receiving numbers.

Questioner: Was it more than twenty miles?

It was at the place where there is no shield from radiation.

Questioner: Was there any meaning in the patterns *(inaudible)*.

They were intended to be obvious and to indicate to you only that your brothers—intelligent, sentient and very close to you—were sending greetings to you. Other than this the movements were not symbolic, but was intended simply to be an obviously non-natural movement.

We wish that we could indulge ourselves and express our great joy at all times in greeting each of you. We would do this and more, my friends, for we feel very much joy at being able to share with you our understanding and our very existence in the Father's creation. We have not, however, found that this is possible, so must send our greetings, our love, and our aid to you from the creation to your creation by these [ways and means] until such time that we can be true brothers and experience the joy of the Father's creation together in all its freedom.

As to symbols, my friends, symbols are what you understand them to be. There are no arbitrary symbols. The true symbol is that which is most real, just as the sun is often a symbol. When the circle is seen as symbol, the circle is a representation of the sun. And the sun is [thought of as] a beautiful example of the unity of the creation, the light and the love of the reality of the center of the universe. What you see as a symbol may mean this or that. The only importance in any symbol is that it points you toward your center and toward the center of the creation. And this can be done by any symbol, by any task, as long as you turn within. If you saw a symbol in our motion or in any other phenomena around you, then, my friends, turn within and allow that which is merely symbolic to become reality.

Are there further questions?

Questioner: Is there normally physical *(inaudible)*.

We were in a normal condition when you saw us. However, we have several normal conditions, only one of which is visible within this particular universe. We normally operate in another of our normal conditions due to the fact, as we said, it is not usually an acceptable thing to do to greet man on Earth directly due to our possible infringing upon the free will of those upon planet Earth.

Questioner: What is the probability of meeting with me if I were to sever *(inaudible)* and totally isolate *(inaudible)*?

We are not able to say. It would be necessary for you to simply attempt such a thing. There are many *(inaudible)* which cannot be evaluated on supposition, promises or hope. There are many things that you cannot know until they have been experienced. It is very rare that each question of such an articulated desire come into being correctly. However, it has been done. We cannot speak nor be doubtful, for we do not know how these *(inaudible)* will be settled for any particular situation. You are, of course, aware that you are attempting to meet yourself. This may be of some help to you in preparation for such a successful confrontation.

Questioner: Could you expand *(inaudible)*?

My friends, it is all too often that it is thought of man on Earth that we of the teaching realm are some extremely wise and distant and almost god-like beings. Others picture us as somewhat overbearing and clever *(inaudible)* who are the advanced representatives of an invading civilization. We know these things, my friends. We know them all too well. They do not grieve us unnecessarily. We are aware of the difficulty which the heavy illusion of Earth gives even to the most earnest seeker. But, my friends, we are not distant wise men. Nor are we advanced representatives and diplomats. We are you. And you are we. If you can understand that you have not met any who is not you, then you can begin to understand that when you meet us you will be meeting yourself.

The infinite progression of this understanding is at the heart of the ability to say as you approach the level of spiritual seeking at which you will graduate into a higher level of understanding you become more able to see that you are meeting yourself. Without this understanding you will never be able to meet us. But in order to obtain this understanding it is necessary to meet each individual that you meet with the love, the infinite compassion, and understanding with which you would meet yourself. It is an extremely freeing type of realization, my friends, for in actuality it is fairly easy to meet yourself.

Concentrate then as you meet others upon meeting them in truth as completely whole and perfect individuals in the reality of yourself. Not yourself as a person, but yourself as the creation. We have said this in many different ways, my friends, but we observe that it is extremely easy for those of you who are seeking to concentrate very much upon an abstract mental state and to become somewhat lax about the delicacy and the excellence of his attitudes in regard to those of his own species which he meets every day. It is easier to speak of meditation than of service to those who to you do not seem to be very much like you. My friends, they are like you. In fact, they are you. And we are you and you are we and we are all the creation.

As you begin to approach understanding and practice of this most difficult understanding, you become more capable of an actual meeting with us. It is not the only requirement, my friends. There are difficulties not only with yourself, but with each of those who are with you. There is difficulty that must be centered and dissipated having to do with the unified feeling of any group so that all is completely as one within a group if the group is to meet with us. We cannot specify the needs to be met. We cannot even give our opinion as to whether such a meeting would prove helpful, for this opinion would vary depending upon the group, the time, the place and the understanding. However, we are with you and it is a pleasure to be here.

Have you further questions?

Questioner: This is a question that you probably won't answer, for the same reason that you may fear infringing upon the free will of the people *(inaudible)*. I have read in several—from several different sources that the transition that the Earth will go through will be [from mixed vibrations], will be somewhere in the neighborhood of 150 years. If this figure is anywhere near correct, the question is will we possibly see this transition all the way through in this incarnation, or will it be necessary that we reincarnate *(inaudible)*? Or can you answer this with a blanket statement? *(Inaudible).*

Your understanding of the end of the cycle is not …

(Side one of tape ends.)

(Carla channeling)

… the change from the physical state before the end of the cycle. Your ultimate destination is an individual matter and a blanket statement cannot be made. It is advisable in your experience that you concentrate as you have been doing upon your spiritual journey for you have managed to pull yourself very definitely off of the descent *(inaudible)* and into the right direction.

You have chosen right, my friends, each of you have. And whereas before it is entirely possible it would have been necessary for you to return for another cycle of learning, you have earned for yourself a strong chance of being part of the so-called graduation class. There is much awaiting you, my friends, and we call for you to join us. This is your opportunity; you are making use of it. My friends, continue, continue and continue. You have much to do, I assure you.

Have you other questions?

(Pause)

In that case, my friends, I will leave you now, reminding you that we are here to aid you and serve you. If you wish our aid, our conditioning, or our thoughts, simply avail yourselves to us through meditation for it is our privilege to be with you at any time you call for us.

Please, my friends, remember that all is ultimately without being for intellectual expression, that all abides within love and light. Instead of allowing yourself to be washed away into intellectual shallow waters, imagine yourself standing on the beach with the sun pouring down. Imagine how the gentle breezes calm you and cool you. And let the warm sun take any ache or pain from you. The love and the light of the infinite Father is like the beam of light and warmth of light. If you bask in it, my friends, there is the end to questions and the beginning of true comfort.

Nevertheless, we are also aware that there are simple needs that those of the planet Earth do have. We are aware that you need to grasp them with the feeling of your mind and to turn them over and over and to this purpose we have trained channels of assistance so that when you have questions as you seek, you learn from a direct communication and ask those questions that cause you wonder. We welcome your questions and we attempt to answer any question.

I hope that I have been of service today. I and my brothers are most happy to have been with you. I leave you in the love and the light of our infinite Creator. I am Hatonn. Adonai vasu. ♣

Saturday Meditation
May 25, 1974

(Carla channeling)

Greetings, my friends. I am Hatonn. I greet you in the love and the light of our infinite Creator. We are privileged to be speaking with you and we will be conditioning you. It has been extremely difficult to make this contact for this instrument is not very relaxed. However, we will attempt to speak only very briefly.

My friends, we would like to say a few words about the nature of the physical illusion. At the time at which each of you incarnated, my friends, each of you was aware that certain lessons, hitherto unlearned, were to be the goals for achievement of this incarnation. If it seems to you, my friends, that your entire incarnation within this illusion has been a series of difficulties of one particular type, then you are almost certainly aware in some manner of one of your lessons. As you can see, these lessons are not to be avoided. They are to be learned.

Further, we must point out to you that when a confrontation in such a lesson has been achieved, that which separates you from understanding it is most often your own thinking. Your conscious thinking processes are quite capable of being self-destructive in the sense that they may aid you to avoid the lesson that you wish in reality to learn. Therefore, my friends, as you approach a lesson, we suggest that if it is possible to achieve a temporary abeyance of the conscious, analytical processes, then, my friends, you may return to the problem with a much clearer mentality, ready to learn what you came to this experience to learn, rather than only to avoid what you came to learn.

We know how difficult it is to achieve the meditative state at all times, for we have been where you are and we are aware of that particular type of illusion that you call physical. We urge you, therefore, to depend on meditation of a formal kind. Then to attempt a semi-meditative state, and by this, my friends, to simply achieve a state of attention also so that your destructive impulses are not free to completely clog your mind and keep you from learning the lessons you came to learn.

We would like to contact each of the other instruments. However, we are aware that there is some difficulty. We will at this time, however, attempt to contact the instrument known as Don.

(Don channeling)

I am Hatonn. I will condition the instrument, please be patient. I will continue. I was speaking of your attitudes toward what you experience in the physical illusion. I find your reactions to what you have experienced in your illusion are reactions based upon an unbound faith. This is normal upon your planet. The reactions to experience in almost every case are based upon an intellectual understanding of your present illusion. This understanding is totally false. It is necessary to construct a totally new base for understanding. This new base should be one which communicates with truth. It is only possible to construct this through meditation.

We observe the people upon your planet, we observe their conditions and their reactions to experience. Their reactions are totally different from ours, or from any people who are aware of the nature of the illusion they are experiencing. It is a very difficult problem for the people who have not become enlightened as to the true nature of their existence to break out of the responses that they have assimilated during their present experience. However, this not only should be done, it must be done if one is to make full use of the experience. And this can only be done, as far as we are aware, through the process of meditation.

This process will provide you with answers to all of your questions. You have at this time many questions, but, my friends, even these questions will lose their meanings as you avail yourself to truth through meditation. For you will find that the answers which you sought are no longer meaningful. You will construct an entirely new system of thinking, and entirely new awareness, an entirely new understanding. This is necessary if true progress is to be made.

Do not react to conditions within the illusion that you experience simply because this reaction is assumed to be valid. Avail yourself to truth through meditation and then you will understand each and every experience that is brought to you.

Are there any questions at this time?

Questioner: Hatonn, do you mean daily *(inaudible)* very little experiences, or do you mean *(inaudible)* experiences?

Every experience.

Questioner: Will you know when you break out of the illusion?

Yes.

Questioner: *(Inaudible)*.

Yes. I shall continue. The master teacher known to you are Jesus was able through meditation to become aware of truth. His reactions to experience were of such a nature to cause much concern among those who were aware of his reactions. They did not understand his reactions to the illusion for his reactions were based upon his understanding of truth. This understanding allowed him to act directly as an emissary of this creation. Acting in accord with the laws of his Creator, he was able to fulfill the desires with many he came in contact.

His reaction to this experience is but partially known to the peoples of your world at present, but this will serve as an example. His reaction was one of love. It was a reaction of love that was in no regard whatsoever to the nature of the experience. This love was not necessarily expressed in the way that it is expressed by the people in your particular illusion, for it is not understood. For this reason, this man was hated by many and love by many, many more. His expression of love was very pure in nature. It was not in the same sense as the emotional love that your peoples express in an attempt to indicate their conception of love. It was a simple demonstration of total concern for the fulfillment of the desire of his fellow man. His awareness of this desire was greater than the awareness of those whom he served. For this reason, they did not understand his expression of love. This man attempted to fulfill their real desires. The people whom he attempted to serve were unable for the most part to understand that he was serving their real desires.

These desires, my friends, were simply to grow in a spiritual sense. It was not possible for this man to provide fulfillment of this desire for spiritual growth without apparently seeming to provide that which those whom he served did not actually desire. For this reason, there was little understanding of his service by any but those whom were directly aided in a physical way. He considered the spiritual growth of an individual of much greater importance than his physical well-being, which is a very correct analogy. For this reason his actions at times seemed in divergence with the love and understanding that he brought to those whom he served.

Meditation erases these false illusions under which the peoples of this planet are forced by their own thinking to *(inaudible)*. Spend time in meditation and become aware of reality. There are but a few simple concepts that are necessary to understand. These can be understood quite simply in meditation. We have spoken many times through instruments such as this one about these simple concepts: the eradication of the personal ego and the desire for anything but service. This, my friends, if thoroughly understood and practiced, will result in immediate dissolution of the illusion under which you serve. And then you may serve directly in the light of your Creator, for this is His service, this is our service, this is the original Thought. This is the original creation; each part serving all of the other parts, asking nothing, and expecting nothing and therefore receiving everything.

It has been said in many ways by many of the masters who have lived within your illusion and have understood. And yet it is so very difficult for man on Earth to understand. Very difficult for him to understand, my friends, as long as he does not avail himself to the true understanding of this through the process of meditation. Through this process, my friends, the words which you now hear become meaning and you no longer question, for this meaning is truth and it is for you. And you then are aware of the reality, the beauty, and the love that has been yours throughout all time.

Open your minds and your hearts to this awareness. Do it through meditation. This is the only way that we know that this may be accomplished. When you have become aware of this simple concept you will have no more questions. You will not wonder as to your accomplishment of this awareness because this awareness will be self-evident. You will no longer question the motives of your fellow man. You will no longer fear the actions of your fellow man. You will simply project the love of your Creator for all of Its parts, for you will be all of these parts. And you will be aware of your unity with all of these parts. You will not be understood, my friends, but it will make no difference, for you will understand. You will not be loved, my friends, but this will make no difference, for you will love. You will feel the vibrations, they will merge with the creation. Your spirit will sense in harmony with all that you experience.

I am Hatonn. I will leave this instrument at this time. It has been a great privilege to convey to you the understanding that is there for you to accept. You seek it, my friends. We instruct. We instruct a simple method of acceptance. Adonai. Adonai vasu. ♣

Sunday Meditation
May 26, 1974

(Carla channeling)

I greet you in the love and in the light of our infinite Creator. I am the one known to you as Hatonn. My brothers and I are in a craft far above your planet. We are very, very privileged to be speaking with you at this time. And we greet each of you.

My brother Laitos will be conditioning each of you who desires it as I speak.

I wonder this evening, my friends, if you have allowed yourself during this day to rest in the enormous ocean of love which is yours if you realize it to be yours. Have you allowed yourself to soak up the infinite light and love of your Creator during this day? Or, my friends, has it been a day during which you felt some lack of this love in which you felt that you were separated from the sunlight and the warmth of life?

We are aware that the very nature of the physical illusion is such that the individual who is enjoying this illusion experiences many sensations of seeming separation and lack of love. My friends, we can only tell you that this is an illusion. If you allow yourself through meditation to seek reality, you will quickly discover the vast and limitless ocean of love which bathes the entire creation of the Father. There is nothing but this love. Not only is it all about you, but, my friends, it is you in that each fiber of your soul and your physical being is composed of love and light.

Due to this heavy sense of illusion, my friends, it is very possible for you to experience the pain of this lack. It is often intensified in its negative effect by an accompanying belief in the reality of what you know as time. When you experience illusory lack, it is also very easy to further assume that this lack will be for a certain amount of time which seems to be extremely long.

My friends, within meditation make contact with the timeless, the infinite, the eternal truth of creation. Discover love and light of the Creator. It is all about and if you are able to make contact it may flow to you and through you so that you are lifted upward along the spiritual path and are finally free of the illusion.

These experiences are necessary to you, my friends. They are simply your means of spiritually growing while you enjoy the physical experience. However, you need not be limited by the difficulties of this illusory existence. While you are learning you may also go within, my friends, and speed your learning considerably by contact with all that there is.

I would like to transfer this contact at this time to the one known as T if he would avail himself.

Sunday Meditation, May 26, 1974

(T channeling)

I am with this instrument. *(Inaudible)* that you do not cope adequately and that you are making inadequate progress. All peoples of your Earth are *(inaudible)*. All peoples of your Earth live daily problems which are solvable in meditation. All problems can be taken to meditation—small problems and large problems.

Most people who meditate think not to bother with small, day-to-day difficulties and will not take them to meditation. All answers are *(inaudible)*. While most day-to-day difficulties are not really worth bothering with, it is necessary that you exist from day-to-day. Meditation will help you in every way. *(Inaudible)*.

(Don channeling)

I am with this instrument. I am Hatonn. I will condition the instrument for a short period.

(Pause)

I was speaking my friends, of the importance of meditation. It is difficult for those of your planet to fully comprehend the need and the results that may be obtained in respect to meditation. It is very difficult to understand how this simple process could bring to you everything that you desire. The peoples of your planet have believed for the most part for many, many centuries of their time that knowledge is knowledge obtained through the five physical senses. My friends, the knowledge that you presently have is of absolutely no value. The knowledge that you will gain in reading or in studying or through any learning process will have only one value. That single value will be to make you aware of the need for meditation.

We have said to you many times that all truth lies within. We have said to you many times that you may find this truth through the process of meditation. My friends, we cannot overemphasize this simple truth. The most educated of the peoples of your planet know nothing of truth if they have not availed themselves to it in meditation. My friends, there is no intellectual awareness of the truth of this creation. It is all something else, something much more basic. It is an awareness that transcends any ability to rationalize or to comprehend in an intellectual manner. There is no way to transmit this awareness through the senses that you possess to comprehend your illusion. The illusion that has been fabricated by the peoples of this planet is far from the truth. Any endeavor to comprehend truth through the use of any part of this illusion is totally of no value.

We have attempted, speaking through channels such as this one, to make you aware of the possibility of awareness. This is all that we can do. We can instruct on the method of achieving this awareness. We can tell you that this is what you desire. But only you my friends, can find it. You and you alone must make the step—simple step of meditation of each day to arrive at the awareness that you desire.

I will now transfer this contact to another of the instruments. Please be patient while I establish the contact.

(Carla channeling)

I am attempting to contact the instrument known as E. We are having a certain amount of difficulty due to a slight interference due to the instrument's analysis of our thoughts. If this instrument will avail herself we will again attempt to speak using her.

(E channeling)

I am now with this instrument. I would like to say she should try to relax and avail herself. It is a very great privilege to make contact with this instrument. *(Inaudible)*. It has been a very great privilege to make contact. I am Hatonn.

(Don channeling)

I am with this instrument. I am Hatonn. I will continue using this instrument. I am sorry that we mere unable to make satisfactory contact with this instrument known as E. As I was saying, it is difficult to maintain contact if the instrument attempts to analyze thoughts which we give to the instrument. It is a simple process to learn, to simply repeat what we impress upon the mind of the instrument. If this simple process is maintained, then a communication will flow as smoothly and simply as it does now.

The problem we believe, is that the instrument is unsure and therefore afraid of making an error. We are using this instrument now and it is unafraid of making an error for he knows that if an error is made it will be corrected, for we do not allow an error to be made that is incorrect. It will facilitate the ability of a new instrument to channel our thoughts if the instrument will simply communicate what is impressed upon them with no analysis and with no fear of causing error.

(Pause)

I have just allowed this instrument to pause for a period of time to demonstrate to him and to the others in this room that when we are not transmitting a thought to the instrument, he receives no thought. This instrument was aware of receiving no thought for a period of time during which he did not channel.

I am aware of certain questions that have been raised by members of this group and will attempt to answer them at this time. All members of this group who so desire will benefit from our conditioning and will be able to receive our thoughts as clearly and as concisely as any other member of this group. It requires only that the individual avail himself each day in meditation. He will in a short period be able to receive and to channel our thoughts just as does this instrument.

There are several different [ways] of initially receiving our contact. The way that is experienced by the instrument is dependent on his susceptibility to each particular technique. The technique of contact will therefore be somewhat different for each instrument. It is utmost that the instrument totally relax in meditation and allow his mind to become blank if at all possible. This will facilitate greatly our ability to contact the instrument. Each one of the members of this group will receive our conditioning. It is only necessary that you desire it. You will become aware of it in a physical way.

At this time I will leave this group. It has been a great privilege to be with you and it is always a very great privilege to bring to those of the planet Earth that which they desire. That single [thing] that man throughout all of the creation desires—understanding of his Creator so that he may travel more swiftly along the path to the love and understanding that has created him. I am Hatonn. I will leave you at this time. Adonai vasu. ❦

Monday Meditation
May 27, 1974

(Carla channeling)

[I am Hatonn.] I greet you, my friends, in the love and the light of our infinite Father. It is our privilege to speak with you again this evening. It is always our pleasure to aid those who are seeking understanding. We will be with each of you and will condition each of you who desires it.

My friends, as we experience this present awareness of shared fellowship with you our hearts are very light. We are, as you would say, very happy to be speaking with you. My friends, we are always very happy. We suggest that you look around yourselves and inquire of yourself as to what portion of your creation seems to be always at peace or happy. You will find, my friends, that it is the creation of the Father that remains in equilibrium while the creation of man of Earth has many unhappy phases.

It is for this reason, my friends, that existence in a more remote area causes one to experience more peace of mind. This is a natural consequence of additional amounts of exposure to the creation of the Father. This creation may be seen at its most accessible in less populated places, my friends. But, in reality, it is all around you no matter where you may be. It begins with yourself. Through meditation you may remain constantly in contact with the real creation. You may feel the equilibrium of the Father's creation and you may, as are we, be happy, as you call it.

This happiness is simply the awareness that you are a part of all that there is. It is a simple awareness and defies definition of any kind. It is only in the creation of man on Earth that individuals require definitions. Definitions and distinctions and disassociations are all separations from the Creator's plan of unity. And if the following [of those] will inevitably cause what you know as unhappiness, allow yourself through meditation [to be] aware of the true creation.

We can only suggest this. We cannot speak in such a way as to demonstrate this truth. It is completely up to you. We can tell you of advantages to be gained in meditation and we can change you towards obtaining a stronger contact with reality. But, my friends, you are a free creation, an entity with a mind and will completely sovereign. It is totally within your province of choice as to what you wish to do with [each] succeeding moment of your conscious awareness within this incarnation.

We are aware that you are seeking, for you are here now. We can encourage you, urge you, and challenge you to seek through meditation that each time that you may consider doing so in formal groups such as this one, in smaller groups in your home, or very short periods simply taken throughout the day, minute by minute, as needed, all of these techniques of meditation will avail you, my friends, and we very strongly invite you to experience the creation of the Father to the farthest which …

(Side one of tape ends.)

(Carla channeling)

Grasp it, mold it and it will allow itself to be grasped and molded according to your highest aspirations. There is no end, or limit to what you may accomplish by use of your true and eternal spirit.

What you obtain in the physical illusion is yours for a very short time. But, my friends, the strides that you are able to make within the purview of your spiritual path will last throughout eternity. You will never need to take these steps again.

It is indeed my pleasure to be speaking with you. I would like to transfer this contact to another instrument at this time. I am Hatonn.

(Don channeling)

I am Hatonn. I am with this instrument. It is a great privilege to use this instrument as it is all of the developed instruments of this group. We of the Confederation of Planets in the Service of the Infinite Creator are here to serve. This we will do to the very limit of our ability. Our ability is limited only by the people of planet Earth.

We are limited due to their desire. Many of the people of this planet are not yet ready to understand what we are attempting to bring. For this reason it is necessary to act in such a way so that those who desire our service receive our service and those who do not are not made aware of our presence. For this reason, it is necessary to communicate in this fashion in such a way so that our words may be accepted or rejected.

Many of those who are now seeking are accepting our words. They are following our instructions. In following these instructions, they are finding that which they are seeking. We simply intend to lend a helping hand to those on Earth who seek. Who seek in the direction of their Creator. We will very gladly aid any of those who seek. Our thoughts may be received by any who sincerely seek. All that is necessary is that they avail themselves in meditation.

There is much to be gained through the process of meditation. This, my friends, is the only important thing that you will do during your incarnation. For all of the fruits of meditation that you receive will be the project of this simple effort. Effort to find how to serve, find technique of serving your fellow man is simple. It is done in meditation. This was demonstrated by the master teacher known to you as Jesus. His service to his fellow man on the planet Earth was very great. It is a service that continues even to this day even though this man was poorly understood it is still understood that he was acting in the name of a loving Creator. He discovered through meditation the way in which he would serve his follow man.

This we offer to the people of Earth, instructions so that they may also discover their service and how to perform it simply through the process of daily meditation. Spend time, my friends, in meditation. In this way and in only this way will you realize the truth of the creation and understand in the fullest sense its workings and your parts in those workings. This, my friends, will result in a state of ecstasy which we cannot describe. We can only point out that is possible to reach such a condition and that this may be achieved through daily meditation.

At this time I will leave this instrument. It has been a great privilege to be with you this evening. I am Hatonn. Adonai vasu. Adonai vasu. ☥

Tuesday Meditation
May 28, 1974

(Carla channeling)

I am Hatonn. I greet you, my friends, in the love and in the light of our infinite Creator. It is my privilege to speak with you.

I am aware of your question. The fear of, as you say, being possessed is a somewhat over-generalized fear. We may assure you that you have nothing to fear if you are under a certain amount of correct understanding as to the nature of what you know as possession.

There are basically two types of so-called possession. The first type is extremely rare, but [does] occasionally occur and can be dealt with specifically. The second type is extremely common and can be dealt with quite specifically.

The first type of possession is the so-called actual possession of one sentient being's physical vehicle by the consciousness of another individual. Whether the possessing individual be in the physical or removed from the physical is of no consequence; possession is the same phenomena. The reason for the possession is simply opportunity and a possessing entity who desires to take such an opportunity. This type of possession is extremely rare for two reasons. First, there are not a great many possessing entities who are seeking an opportunity to enter a vehicle not their own. Also, the dissociation of consciousness that is required in order to provide a reasonable opportunity must be somewhat extreme and reliable. The difficulties connected with great changes such as becoming an adult in the physical sense may [make] an entity given to dissociation more vulnerable to such dissociation. It is only in cases of extreme dissociation that the opportunity for a possessing entity to come in is available.

Once such a condition has been understood, it can be treated. It requires only that the condition be recognized and that appropriate measures be used in order to alert the consciousness of the entity who has been pushed aside by the possessing entity. The entity who has been pushed aside has a sovereign right to the physical vehicle from which he has been temporarily removed. Depending upon the type of culture and normal usage which the original entity has been accustomed to, the alerting mechanism or ritual designed to attract his attention will somewhat vary. Within some cultures, certain religious rituals are observed. Once the original entity whose physical vehicle it is has been alerted the entity need only assert correct and rightful ownership of the physical vehicle and it will be necessary for the possessing entity to depart.

The second type of possession is much, much more common. It is as common as the first type is rare. This type of possession is the possession of the balanced individual consciousness by certain portions of that same consciousness. There are many, many phases of your desire with which you came to this incarnation. It is the great lesson of your ancient teachers that you must know yourself. It is your job in whatever way you choose to discover who you are, what you desire from this experience, and how you desire to prosecute these desires. When your desires are not recognized by yourself, when you have overlooked a portion of your total self and are therefore not attempting to learn those things which you came to learn, these portions of yourself which are then frustrated may become somehow loosened from their integrated place within your consciousness and they may attempt to attract your attention in ways you do not understand. They may attract your attention by causing pain. This always attracts attention while the person is conscious of physical programs.

And very often, when there are persons of the consciousness that have not been heard they then became heard in this way. This is possession by self. You may be possessed as a result of negative or positive emotion. However, my friends, due to the type of experience which you seek to learn within this vibration and due to the type of group illusion which the people of your planet labor under, for the most part these are types of experiences of a negative appearance. They may be treated by understanding. The more that you can discover what lies behind pain the more you may remove the pain.

In truth, there is no such thing as any sort of difficulty such as you have spoken of. It is all, shall we say, in your mind. Therefore, it is necessary to investigate your mind. There you will find your possessing and by understanding the message which is being brought to you by these subconscious means you may redirect your thought unto a more positive and upward path. It is sometimes the work of *(inaudible)*.

You have demonstrated patience already and this is a prime qualification for study, for in this path of spiritual gain, my friends, it is important to go slowly enough so that you may assimilate, learn, demonstrate and become one with each piece of new information. To go more quickly than your true understanding can take you is to become unbalanced and prey to a great deal of confusion. Meditate and seek to understand yourself, for within your mind is all that there is.

At this time I would like to attempt to transfer this contract to another instrument. I am Hatonn.

(Pause)

(Carla channeling)

I am Hatonn. I am again with this instrument. My friends, we wished to communicate through the instrument known as Don because we wished to use a word for word type of communication which this instrument is somewhat reluctant to attempt. There is some difficulty with this instrument and therefore we request that you wait if you can, [until] a later time [for] this message. Is that satisfactory to you? Are there further questions which this instrument may attempt to answer?

Questioner: What do you mean by dissociation?

The instrument had this word within her vocabulary and although it is not entirely correct, it seemed closer to the concept which we gave than any other. By that word we intended to convey the concept of the certain unit of individualized consciousness that for some reason had such a mismatching within its own vibration that it temporarily was not able to function as a unified portion of consciousness.

Questioner: You said to take your problems to meditation. Do you mean to sit and think on the problem all through the meditation or do you ask and then clear your mind?

Neither. It is not necessary to ask for any information in meditation. Nor is it necessary to concentrate on any problem. Meditation is not a specifier or a prescription technique. Meditation is the transfer of your consciousness from the phase of existence which lies within the perimeters of your physical illusion to the phase of consciousness which lies within the perimeters of the love and the light of the infinite Creator.

It is a transfer from that person of your soul within a physical vehicle to that totality of soul which is your individualized consciousness within the total consciousness of the Father. This contact gives one a general and non-analyzable understanding. When problems are seen in the light of this understanding it is most often the case that they will evaporate naturally and as dew evaporates. It is not that the dew is unreal. It is simply that it is one state within a perfectly reasonable and constructive cycle which gives life and nourishment to part of the natural creation.

Your problems are part of the cycle of your physical existence. Given room to mature and evaporate, they will do so. They are not to be despised, nor are they to be given more importance than they deserve. Meditation simply gives one the awareness that this view of that which you call problems is so. There are methods for obtaining a more complete view of what you yourself think about any specific problem. However, these attempts at self-knowledge are intellectual and analytical and are not of as much use as simple meditation, in our opinion.

Our path is what we truly believe to be a useful one. However, if the path of analysis of problems, specifically and individually, appears to hold more chance for advancement to you, we urge you to do that. We are aware that there are thousands and millions of paths to be followed and that we encourage what seems to us to be the straightest. This does not negate the fact that at the end of each and every path lies the Creator.

We do not have a great deal to say about any attempts at problem-solving on a more material plane. It is not our way. We are aware that there are techniques that may be used and these techniques have been described by many upon your planet.

My friends, it is such a pleasure to speak with you and to serve you in way that we can. We are so pleased to speak with you and we are so pleased at all times to be in contact with you. We send you the love and the light of the Creator at all times. We will leave you at this time if there are no more questions. We leave you in the love and in the light of our infinite Creator. I am Hatonn. Adonai vasu.

Friday Meditation
May 31, 1974

(Don channeling)

[I am Hatonn.] I greet you, my friends, in the love and the light of our infinite Creator. It is a great privilege once more to meet with this group. We of the Confederation of Planets in the Service of the Infinite Creator are always privileged to meet with those who desire our services.

Desire, my friends, is the key to what you receive. If you desire it, you shall receive it. This was the Creator's plan, a plan in which all of His parts would receive exactly what they desire. My friends, often in the illusion which you now experience it seems that you do not acquire what you desire. In fact, exactly the opposite seems to be the case in many, many instances. It is a paradox, it seems, that such a statement should be made and that such apparent results of desire are manifested. And yet, we state without exception, that man receives exactly what he desires.

Perhaps, my friends, you do not understand desire. Perhaps, my friends, this understanding is not within the intellectual mind. Perhaps it will be necessary to spend time in meditation to become aware of your real desire. For, my friends, there is much, much more of you and of the creation than you presently appreciate with your intellectual abilities in your present illusion.

We have stated many, many times that it is necessary to meditate if one is to evolve from one's present state of understanding to that which he desires. We have used the word, desire, in several ways and yet we are very limited for we cannot use the language of your people to express the truth of the mechanics of these comments. They are, I can assure you, extremely simple, but much, much broader and much, much farther reaching and much, much more elementary than that which you appreciate in your present limited state.

Creation, my friends, operates on a very simple method. It is up to man to learn what he has forgotten. The knowledge of those principles, like the principles, is not complete. And it is not an intellectual understanding, it is a simple knowing, a simple knowing that is within all of the Creator's children. This knowing, when fully appreciated, is simply a part of the individual just as all his senses are a part. It is not possible to intellectually understand the physical senses that make you aware of your illusion and your surroundings. It is only possible to utilize and know that they are part of your consciousness.

Expand this awareness, expand this consciousness. Become in a state of knowing so that you understand your desires, so that you understand how you may desire something that is more along the path that you will eventually choose.

Friday Meditation, May 31, 1974

It is very difficult for the peoples of this planet to give up their illusion, to give up the preconceived knowledge of what they believe to be cause and effect. However, my friends, this is not reality. This is illusion, born of illusion. It is a simple product of the complexity that man upon this planet has generated. Join with us in divorcing your thinking from such complexities and become aware of what has created you, everything that you experience and everything that is thought. Become aware of your Creator. Become aware of His desire and when you know this desire, you will know your own, for you and your Creator are one. And you are one with all of His parts and therefore all of your fellow beings throughout all of the creation.

When you know His desire you will feel it. There will be no more confusion, there will be no more questions. You will have found what you have sought—you will have found love. For this is the desire of your Creator: that all of His parts express and experience the love that created you. This may be found simply, in meditation.

No amount of seeking within the intellectual concepts of your people, no amount of planning or careful interpretation of the written or spoken word, will lead you to the simple truth. It is you and it is all about you. It expresses itself in every living thing. It expresses itself constantly and unceasingly. It shouts at you from every blade of grass and from every animal and bird, from all of your fellow beings in a terrific crescendo of love.

And yet man upon Earth is blind and is deaf to these sights and these sounds. And all that is necessary is that you become aware, my friends, develop an awareness to see your creation, to understand your Creator, and to understand His love. Do this, my friends, by simply availing yourself to Him. Meditation will provide this; nothing else is necessary.

I at this time will transfer this contact to one of the others. I am Hatonn.

(H channeling)

I am Hatonn. I am now with this instrument. I will desire to continue upon the same subject. The people of your planet, though many are not aware of it, all desire the love of the Creator. Through each *(inaudible)* experiences there is formed within their intellect, their, shall we say, version of this love. Through experiences within this illusion are greatly presented to you for a purpose of, shall we say, testing, your seeking of this love. All within your illusion has been greatly affected by these fallacies of your society and the true love and the true concepts of the Creator cannot be gained through utilizing the portions of this illusion.

We have stated many times that the true means of seeking is love. It is meditation. For through meditation you may realize the simple truth of this love which is given by the Creator. And within your illusion all has become, shall we say, the opposite of simplicity. There exists great confusion, the confusion brings about *(inaudible)*. No matter how further *(inaudible)* the desire to find the love of the Creator, this shall not be true *(inaudible)* without daily practice of meditation.

There have been many great teachers who have come from our realm of existence to attempt to teach to your people the true method of seeking this love. Every *(inaudible)* of these great teachings have been greatly misunderstood. Their lives were missions of peace. Yet their teachings were either not accepted or translated, shall we say, through your intellect. The teachers have all said to seek within—that it is to be considered the Kingdom of Heaven. But your peoples, by allowing the confusion of this illusion to penetrate their intellect, have not understood the simplicity of these teachings: to turn within through meditation.

We can present—correction—we cannot present to you *(inaudible)* this concept. To us it does seem to be very simple. Learn and practice meditation, and all knowledge which is in you shall be given you through your seeking. Do not allow the great confusion that exists upon your planet to base your knowledge of life *(inaudible)*.

I will at this time attempt to make contact with another instrument.

(Carla channeling)

I am Hatonn. I am now with this instrument. I will conclude, my friends, this evening by giving you, shall we say, one parting thought, for indeed we are invaded and we are battling, seeking to conquer this planet by love. We wish to give you this parting shot of thinking to take with you into your daily life.

What do you seek, my friends? This is our question to you. What indeed do you seek? If you can describe what you are seeking we are afraid, my friends, that you are still within the material illusion. You are seeking reflections of reality. Remember that that whom you truly seek is not material or illusory, but is real and eternal. The master which was known to you as Jesus had very much the same difficulty when he was recognized as a ruler. It was for the most part as the ruler of a material world. However, he had no desire for a material kingdom. He worked only to accomplish the Kingdom of Heaven. This place lies before each of you in this room. You may ask yourself what is it that you seek and know you that this is the most important question that we can offer you as a signpost within your own thinking to guide you to this path that leads to the Kingdom of Heaven. As you meditate, you will be seeking. What will you seek? That which you will seek, my friends, you will surely find.

It has been a great pleasure and a great privilege to speak using these instruments. I will leave you at this time. I am Hatonn. Adonai.

Saturday Meditation
June 1, 1974

(Don channeling)

I am Hatonn. I greet you, my friends, in the love and the light of our infinite Creator. It is a great privilege to once more be with this group. At this time I am in a craft far above your place of dwelling. I am at this time able, however, to monitor your thoughts. This, my friends, might seem to some of your peoples to be an infringement. But I can assure you that it is not. Our capabilities of knowing the thinking of the peoples of the planet Earth are not designed in any may to infringe upon either their thinking or their activities. We do not consider the knowledge of the thoughts of others to be an infringement for we see these thoughts as our own. We see these thoughts as the thoughts of the Creator.

My friends, it may seem to you that thinking of the nature other than one of love and brotherhood might be a thought generated not of our Creator. My friends, this is not possible. All thought that is generated is generated by the Creator. All things that are generated are generated by the Creator. My friends, He is all things and is in all places. And all of the consciousness and all of the thought that exists is the thought of our Creator. His infinite number of parts all have free will, and all may generate in any way they choose. And all of His parts communicate with all of the creation, in His entire and infinite sense.

We are not attempting to change the thinking of our Creator. We are only attempting to bring His ideas to some of the more isolated parts for their inspection and appraisal. Isolated parts, I say, my friends. And why should we consider these parts to be isolated? We consider them isolated, my friends, because from our point of view they have chosen to wander far from the concept that we have found that permeates most of the parts of the creation with which we are familiar. We find, my friends, that man upon planet Earth in his experiences and experiments has become isolated in his thinking and has divorced it from that to which we are accustomed in the vast reaches of creation which we have experienced.

We find man on planet Earth to be an aberration, an aberration in thinking, in experiment, and in present experience. If the Creator, as represented by His parts upon planet Earth, wishes to experience and experiment in the manner of man on Earth, then this is exactly what we wish for Him to do. For He is us and we are Him. And we realize that this is a privilege, a privilege of this being that is all of us.

And yet we believe that in this isolation some of His parts have grown tired of the experiences of man on Earth and they are now seeking an experience more closely allied with what we have found to be normal, in that it is what we find in our experiences and investigations through a very large portion of this infinite creation. So we are here to monitor the thoughts of the Creator on planet Earth, and to discover those who seek to reunite more closely with His original Thought—a Thought of total love.

We are here to advertise, to advertise the possibility of a simple return to this thought, to contact as best we can those of His parts who now wish to move away from the experiment within your Earthly illusion, the experiment which has carried man of Earth far from the original Thought into an experience that is even unwanted by those who have generated it.

Yes, my friends, we know your thoughts for you and we are the same; exactly the same, my friends, for we are one and the same thing. We are not joined in something that you in your present form can reach out and touch, or something that you could even see. But we are nonetheless joined as is everything in the creation, joined by that single force that created you, joined by that single force that has generated all that there is. We have called it love, but this is inadequate for this is a word in your language expressing emotions and reactions that you experience in your illusion. And yet, we must use it. We must use it until you avail yourself to its total meaning.

And this you may do, my friends, quite simply, as we have said many times, through daily meditation. And then those of His parts who are now locked within an illusion, an illusion created of a need for experience to desire for experience, will begin to free themselves, will begin to change their desires, and will begin once more to become aware of love, not the interpretation of man of Earth, but in its true meaning, in its infinite and all-embracing sense. And then, my friends, you and we will be much, much more closely allied. For you will know our thoughts as well

(Carla channeling)

I am Hatonn. I am with this instrument. I urge you, my friends, to remember what we have brought to you. The next time that you are, shall we say, backed into a corner by the circumstances which prevail within the illusion of your physical existence, remember what you have learned and do not forget what you have worked so hard to obtain. You will choose at any time to alter your needs and desires from within the physical illusion to your being within the creation of the Father.

As long as your objectives lie within this physical illusion it will be necessary for you to be subject to the laws which prevail within this illusion. If your desires can be altered by the application of what you are learning and are lifted into the creation of the infinite One, then, my friends, you may have a great deal more ability to remove yourself from the corners which the illusion seems to back you into.

You have chosen to come into this illusion, my friends, because you thought that you needed the experiences which you could gain here. If you now feel that you would enjoy ceasing to experience the physical illusion with its troubles and difficulties, and beginning to experience that which you desire in spirit, you have only to alter your desires and, my friends, in time you will find what you desire to have come about.

If you will be patient with me I would like to contact our developing new instrument. At this time I would like to transfer this contact to the instrument known as E.

(Unknown channeling)

I am with this instrument. I am Hatonn. I have spoken to you this evening on several matters. However, in closing I would like to state that there is only one thing of great importance for you to consider at this time. That is your personal preparation for service. You are to serve your fellow man, and therefore it is necessary that you prepare yourselves for this service. This, of course, my friends, is done in meditation.

We cannot over-emphasize the importance of meditation. Through this technique you will receive answers to all of your questions. It is difficult to realize this, but this is true. All of your questions can be reduced to an extremely simple concept. This you can become aware of in meditation. Once this has been done you will be ready to serve, just as others have served and are now serving upon your planet. Follow their example, spend time in meditation. Qualify yourself to reach out to your fellow man and lead him from the darkness of confusion that he is experiencing back into the light that he desires.

I will leave you at this time. I am Hatonn. Adonai. Adonai. ♣

Sunday Meditation
June 2, 1974

(Unknown channeling)

I am Hatonn. I greet you, my friends, in the love and in the light of our infinite Creator. It is a great privilege to speak with this group this evening. I am presently in a craft which you would call a flying saucer. This instrument is able to receive my thoughts. He is simply receiving what I give to him and repeating the message to you. This is not difficult to do. This may be accomplished by any of the peoples of planet Earth who desire it. We of the Confederation of Planets in the Service of the Infinite Creator are here to serve man on Earth. We have been here for many of your years and we will continue to contact those of the people of planet Earth who desire it. We are at this time totally familiar with your language and all of your concepts. We are giving information to this instrument and he in his own words is relaying it to you.

I am at this time going to transfer this contact to one of the other instruments. I am Hatonn.

(Carla channeling)

I am now with this instrument. I am Hatonn. My friends, as you come here tonight I am aware that whatever differences in thinking you may experience there is one thing which you all have in common. You are all seeking the truth, my friends. You are all seeking understanding. You are all seeking reality. The seeking, my friends, has brought you here and your desire for knowledge has brought us to you. We are here to aid you in any way that we can in giving you what you seek.

My friends, there are as many different paths to your common goal as there are individuals and we cannot give you any final words, for our message cannot be expressed directly. We can only act as guideposts to point you in the direction of that which you so desire. We can only tell you to the best of our own limited knowledge that in our opinion the direction in which the truth lies is within your own being, my friends.

We encourage you to begin to meditate and then to continue in this practice. Allow the practice of meditation, my friends, to inform you of its own value to you. Only from within can that which we are suggesting that you seek be found. We can only suggest. I say we have limited knowledge, my friends. This is so and yet we are aware of very much more of reality than are you as you dwell within your physical illusion on planet Earth. It is our experience as …

(Pause)

I am sorry, there was difficulty. We will continue. As members of the Confederation of Planets in the Service of the Infinite Creator, we have experienced many times that the most efficient way to begin to obtain the truth, the knowledge, and the realization that you seek is to go within and to seek contact with reality through meditation, to seek contact with that which is infinite, that which is love and light.

At this time, my friends, I will attempt to transfer this contact to another instrument. I am Hatonn.

(Unknown channeling)

I am now with this instrument. We are aware that there are those present who are experiencing for the first time with our information. As we have stated, we have come to your planet to offer our services for we are aware that your planet is presently at the culminating point of the cycle which it is in. There is to come great changes to all phases of what you would consider your world. We have through our seeking gained great knowledge and are aware of information which will be of great aid to the peoples of your planet during this period of, shall we say, trial. We at this time do not wish to deeply go into the facts which we have to present for we have in our contact with your people realized that the intellect which you possess can accept only small segments of our information at any given time and this information must be analyzed before you can receive, shall we say, a higher form of information. And when we say you must analyze the information, we do not mean that you can analyze all that is happening around you by the use of your intellect. Yet, as your peoples are locked within this illusion, they must analyze in order to accept their experiences.

If it is the desire of those newcomers present to, shall we say, look into what we have to offer, we would suggest that you attempt to practice a daily period of meditation. For this is our greatest service—offering to those who would desire our knowledge and instruction, or shall we say, suggestion, the practice of meditation. Through meditation you may gain what you would refer to as a spiritual awareness. This awareness goes much beyond what is capable of your physical intellect and it is the most valuable portion of information we have to present. For without meditation, there can be gained no true understanding of the Creation.

You, presently, are living upon a planet and this planet, we find, to be in a great state of confusion. And in order to transcend this confusion it is necessary that you not use the information and intellect contained within this world. There can be no other means other than meditation to gain a proper understanding. As the great master whom you would refer to as Jesus, spoke many times, "The kingdom of heaven lies within." And by this he means within your being. Turn within yourself through the use of meditation and you slowly shall find the truth of what we wish to present and what many great teachers have also attempted to present to your peoples.

It cannot be expected that you gain great realizations in short periods of time, for meditation is a process of learning and all that you learn must come, shall we say, from the beginning and slowly develop to the climax. Yet, if you wish to consider a climax, we are not aware of that climax, for we are not to be considered as an ultimate source of information. We are fortunate enough to have experienced what you presently are experiencing and chose to seek the truth through meditation. Through this seeking we have evolved into a higher understanding. This understanding we wish to share with you. There is no means and we would not desire to avail our information to anyone who would not desire to accept it. We wish only to serve your peoples and to help them realize the love, which is all that is contained within this Creation.

I would like at this time to attempt to establish contact with another instrument. I am Hatonn.

(Unknown channeling)

I am Hatonn. I am now with this instrument. I shall continue. We have spoken many times of the great lessons which are to be obtained through your meditations. The first and the greatest of all is that of love and what can be obtained through this love. Through love you receive all your faith and through your faith, your desires to serve the Creator in which way that you have chosen. When looked upon in the right manner there is no other force in your universe that can possess more teachings for your effort. It is within this means that you are to share with the others the knowledge of the Creator and of His creation. You shall learn and come to a more great understanding of all creation. We wish to stress the importance of your meditations, be they solemn or a group meditation such as this. For one, you may gain the knowledge in which you seek to serve and the other, the knowledge of the Creator to serve.

I shall at this time leave you. I leave you in the love and in the light of our infinite Creator. Adonai my brothers. Adonai vasu borragus. ☙

Sunday Meditation
June 2, 1974

(Unknown channeling)

I am Hatonn. I greet you, my friends, once more in the love and the light of our infinite Creator. It is a great privilege to be with you this evening. It is a great privilege to meet with you any time that you desire our contact. We of the planet Hatonn are here to serve you. Avail yourself of our service. You desire it and we bring it with love and a deep desire to serve all of those of the planet Earth who would avail themselves.

We are going to at this time establish contact with the newer channels of this group in hopes that they will generate proficiency. At this time I will transfer this contact. I am Hatonn.

(Unknown channeling)

I am now with this instrument. We wish to express our joy in the progress of such new instruments as this one. I wish to speak to you tonight upon a matter in which *(inaudible)* may be *(inaudible)* assistance to those new instruments who may desire our aid in the progress of their channeling. We have oftentimes *(inaudible)* that your progress increases with the [volume] of your desire. Through your desire you obtain the knowledge with which to guide you through the trials in which all instruments who choose to serve the Creator must serve. For you see, the road is always difficult but through your meditation you are given the strength with which you are to bear these trials and yet with each trial you gain further faith and further knowledge of the Creator.

It is somewhat a difficult task to devote individual attention to all of those who desire it at this point. Therefore, we have developed new devices in which, once developed in awareness of your desire, we may share with you our love at any time you so desire. We wish to express our love for all the peoples of your planet and our desire to serve you. All who wish this desire, the choice is in the individual, for it is said and it is true that every being on your Earth is of their own free will [and] can make of their lives what they may.

I would like to at this time attempt to condition those new instruments in this room at this time if it be of their desire. I might add that it's *(inaudible)* to say do not be afraid to say this thought for the thought you may have is often mistaken as being of the fault. Do not have fear of mistakes for it is a common occurrence in the lives of all the beings of your planet and also, I might add, it's the fault in which all of God's children may *(inaudible)*.

I shall at this time attempt to condition those who may desire. I am Hatonn.

(Unknown channeling)

I am Hatonn. I am now with this instrument. It is indeed a great honor to be with again a new instrument. I would now like to proceed upon the subject of inspiration. Inspiration is indeed what takes almost all things you obtain to come true.

I have experienced some difficulty with this instrument. I will now continue. As you go about your life on your planet there is indeed a great illusion.

(Unknown channeling)

I am Hatonn. I am again with this instrument. I should like to continue. I was speaking of your need for inspiration for it is the inspiration in which you need to bring about the will to desire the knowledge or whatever you may seek in the name of the Creator, for it is when it is used as a service of the Creator a most worthy power of suggestion that can be offered. We wish to convey a short message pertaining to the development of these, shall I say, cosmic powers. Through your meditation may we gain much knowledge. We wish to stress the need not only for your group meditation, which is good for the development of your intellect, but we also must stress your need for silent meditation for it is within this that you gain the knowledge in which is needed for your daily life in the service of the Creator.

I would like at this time to make contact with any entity who will avail themselves. I am Hatonn.

(Unknown channeling)

I am Hatonn. I am again with this instrument. I will *(inaudible)* on the subject of influences. You as a person living on your planet are subject to many influences. We in some way hope to bring about small things that will help influence your mind as to the power of the infinite Creator. But at the same time we do not wish to get, as you say, carried away. I and my brothers only wish to make it possible for you and those of you that wish to know to have certain information at your disposal. It is indeed a great honor for us to be able to do this. I and my brothers are extremely proud of the great number of you who are making themselves available. I sincerely hope that in the near future it will be possible to give better messages to those who have not experienced channeling for *(inaudible)*.

I am aware of the uncertainness in the ones … one known as G. I will at this time attempt to establish contact with her if she desires. I would like to say to her that she relax completely. I am Hatonn.

(Pause)

I am experiencing trouble in establishing contact so I would at this time like to close. It has been a very great honor to talk to some of the new channels. I am Hatonn. ✣

Wednesday Meditation
June 5, 1974

(Unknown channeling)

[I am Hatonn.] We are sorry, *(inaudible)* spend a short time in [silent] meditation before we made verbal contact. I wish to express great feelings of progress which we wish to share with you. We are most pleased to see the efforts of such group meditations, for it is through the knowledge necessary for your effort [comes through yourself] in which our most valued *(inaudible)* for you shall learn the steps you need take so that you may devote your life to the service of the Creator and through your group meditation this is possible. We wish to state that all entities which desire our presence and our guidance shall receive it and [we] wish to express the progress gained as most satisfactory. We are most pleased with the progress of your group and are doing everything possible to help this progress.

I shall like at this time to switch contact to another instrument. I am Hatonn.

(Long pause)

(Unknown channeling)

I am now with this instrument *(inaudible)*. We wish to extend to you the greetings of all of your brothers in the Confederation, in the love and in the light of our infinite Creator. We are most pleased to see the forming of a new meditation group. We feel that the development of this group *(inaudible)* to those who you shall render your services to. We of the Confederation of Planets in the Service of the Infinite Creator desire to serve in whatever way we may the peoples of your planet. We cannot avail our services to any entity who would not desire it. We wish, as we have said, to serve all of your peoples yet we are aware that all shall not accept and we shall serve those who would desire.

Our service is, shall we say, of *(inaudible)* compared to the service you may render unto yourself, and this service is the daily practice of meditation. For through meditation you may attain the knowledge which shall be greatly needed in the coming times upon your planet. We are most pleased to have been given the opportunity to aid your peoples and it pleases us to see such great numbers within recent period of time accept what we wish to offer. We have offered our services to many planets in many regions of this creation. Your planet is not the first we have come to. We have expressed before that we of the Confederation are not of an ultimate source of knowledge, and yet we do have, shall we say, the capability of error. For we ourselves are also experiencing this creation. Though we exist within a higher realm of awareness there exist many beyond our own. We are aware of your present situation for we have experienced that which you experience at this time and we *(inaudible)*, shall we say, of the next realm desire to aid you in achieving the awareness which we have achieved through our meditation.

I would at this time desire to establish contact with another instrument. I am Hatonn.

(Unknown channeling)

I am Hatonn. I am again with this instrument and wish to add, shall I say, a line to the *(inaudible)* of many dwelling in this room at this time. For we are aware of your actions and aware of your desires. [For once chosen a path] in which to serve the Creator, for we are constantly within, trying to aid in any way possible. We are aware of your desires as we can see them, the desires of your [love] and of your mind. Those desires of love are truly the desires in which you are to gain knowledge and gain a higher [vibration]. We have often stressed many times that the negative activity oftentimes enters [reality] with confusion on the part of the desires of love you wish to explore. For unless your desires are truly of love and not of *(inaudible)* you wish to *(inaudible)* for there is a difference between what is right and what you wish to believe is right. For you shall seek this and have sought knowledge through the meditation *(inaudible)* in this [room].

We must stress that the road to further knowledge cannot be sought in this [way], for we realize that man was created in the Creator's image, and which entitles him to a free will, one with which to choose the path he has to go and the speed in which he has to take. For it is the free choice of all entities on your planet. This is why, my brothers, we have higher [levels] and some have stronger desires to reach the higher levels faster than others. We can, shall I say, let it be *(inaudible)* for what is learned shall be learned at their own rate of learning.

I wish to at this time to attempt to condition new channels, if it so desired, *(inaudible)*. I shall now attempt to move this contact. I am Hatonn.

(Unknown channeling)

(Inaudible). We are aware that it is your desire to [convince] and that we were as you are now. Desires of this progression through *(inaudible)*. My friends, this is a proper desire and insomuch as you have desire, it shall be given to you. Free choice. For each moment that you desire what is true, you are in communion with many, many souls filled with light and joy and [ecstasy]. We have only one question to give you, my friends. The path of progress is *(inaudible)*. There is very, very little that you may not learn [from]. We are not talking about directions that may be necessary with circumstances, but *(inaudible)* we are talking about intellectual being. Intellectual being, my friends, has been our specialty and for many years we have proffered to those who are seeking, and it has served as a guidepost to introduce many to that which they are seeking. No [backgrounds]; what we offer you with words is merely an arrow painted on a sign. It is you who must walk the road, it is you who must seek, the *(inaudible)* that you are seeking. We are not going to stop talking to you, my friends, indeed not, but the importance of your portion of the contact becomes more and more paramount as you draw closer to union with us. Therefore, my friends, seek from these fields that which you desire, seek for your wellsprings of faith and hope and love. For we are waiting in great company to rejoice each time you find a little bit more of your birthright.

At this time I wish again to attempt to contact another instrument. I am Hatonn.

(Unknown channeling)

I am again with this instrument. We are sorry for *(inaudible)* which have been experienced this evening. There exists some difficulty in establishing contact. We wish not to lengthen this session and would like to state without any offence towards any entity present that we are aware of the purpose for the formation of this group. Its purpose is, as you might say, proper and beneficial to all members of your group. We do not wish to dwell on this, for it is within the minds of those who desire this … what we speak of. It is your choice as to the means of achieving this desire.

I would like to attempt to establish, shall we say, our final contact for this evening with the instrument known as Don. I am Hatonn.

(Don channeling)

I am with this instrument. I am Hatonn. I am with you, my friends, in the love and in the light of our infinite Creator. It is a privilege to be able to use so many instruments for communications. We have, for many of your years, attempted through groups on your planet to establish contact with as many of the peoples of Earth as would desire our contact and as would serve with us in bringing, to those who desired it, our knowledge of this creation. We have much to offer man on Earth, but it is necessary first that he desire it and then it is necessary that he accept it. Unfortunately, many of the people either do not recognize the value or need for that which we bring. This saddens us, but if it is not their desire, then we do not wish to bring it to them.

Questioner: Hatonn, I have a question.

(Don channeling)

I am aware of your question. It is a privilege to give to you that which you desire. We of the Confederation are brothers to all of mankind throughout all the creation. This is unchangeable since we, and all of our brothers throughout all of creation, are in truth one and we must serve them as we serve ourselves and we must understand their desires as we understand our own. Man on Earth has many needs, but his real and only need is understanding. For when man, at any place in this infinite creation, understands then he has no more needs. Our Creator, Father of us all, intended that all of His children should demonstrate the love that He expressed in creating. In demonstrating this love, they would in return benefit by receiving exactly and completely what they deserved. Man upon planet Earth has lost an awareness of this simple concept and has become confused. It is difficult to give to man on Earth the simple understanding that he needs, for he has lost this deep within his consciousness. For this reason we have requested those who hear us to avail themselves to the knowledge that is within them through meditation so that they might return to the knowledge and the love and the understanding that created them and once more live and benefit in the light that is theirs.

There are at this time many of our craft surrounding your planet. They're here for only one purpose, to serve their brothers. Whether or not this service will be accepted is dependent only upon man upon Earth. Whether or not he desires to accept this service, it is available to him. It is only necessary that he become aware of his desire. It is only necessary that he become aware of himself. Man upon Earth has lost an awareness of reality. He is living on a planet that supports his every need and yet he has lost sight of this reality. An atmosphere surrounds him, each breath supports his life. Food abundantly grows on the surface of the plant and he is supported and yet upon Earth man has forgotten simple services provided him by the creation and has through his unbalanced desired arrived at a position of total ignorance at how he is in actuality a simple child of an infinite creation.

It is not necessary for man to seek for himself sustenance. It is only necessary that he seek understanding and seek to serve and then the gifts of the Creator are reflected upon him. For this was within the original Thought that created all that exists. Man upon Earth has lost an awareness of these simple ideas. Return to this awareness through meditation and then man will once more retake his rightful position, a position of love as provided for by his Creator.

There are many things that man on Earth can seek. There are many pathways down which he can seek. There are many goals for him to generate within his thinking. And yet, after he seeks down all these pathways, after he succeeds in reaching all of these goals, he simple finds that there was only one worth seeking and worth reaching. This goal, my friends, is the understanding [of] that love that created him. An understanding that he has always had which is within him because it is within all men throughout all of the creation. We of the Confederation of Planets in the Service of the Infinite Creator are simply here to direct man on Earth inward, to show him where lies his goal. It lies, my friends, in the same place for all men. Whether he be limited to the surface of a planet such as yours, or whether he be with us or elsewhere in an infinite and totally benevolent creation of love.

I will leave this instrument at this time. I am Hatonn. Adonai vasu borragus. ♣

Wednesday Meditation
June 5, 1974

(Unknown channeling)

I am Hatonn. I am with this instrument. It is a privilege once more to be with *(inaudible)*. I greet you, my friends, in the love and the light of our infinite Creator. It is a great privilege, as always, to contact this group. We are aware of the question which has been asked and we will attempt to transfer this contact to the instrument known as Carla in order to fulfill this request. We must be patient.

(Carla channeling)

I am Hatonn. This instrument seems somewhat reluctant to speak on this subject, however, we are attempting to achieve a contact that will make it possible for her to trust our thoughts on this subject. If you will be patient, we will need some time.

The man of which you spoke is a somewhat rare type of entity. He is among those who have chosen to incarnate upon the surface in order to be of some aid to those upon the surface of this planet. Much of what he is able to do is dependent upon those areas of awareness which he has brought into this incarnation upon this planet. It would not be possible for this person to be used as a type of channel were he not what you might call a somewhat advanced being. He is telling the truth about each of his experiences and there are those within the Confederation who have given to him certain access to certain thoughts, which lead him to be able to exercise his natural gifts in such a way that he is able to aid your people.

This is a sort of experiment, my friends. There are many such experiments. There are many, many contacts. These contacts differ. Some contacts, such as the one of which we are speaking, are very ambitious and some seem to be not so ambitious. However, it is a great aid to us to be able to make contact with many instruments, for each channel has an untold effect upon his environment.

I am attempting to continue, however, due to the amount of control we must use with this type of contact and due to the fatigue of the instrument we are finding it increasingly difficult to maintain a satisfactory contact. Therefore, we will attempt to continue through another instrument.

(Unknown channeling)

I am again with this instrument. I am Hatonn. It is difficult, at times, to express what is about to happen in a way that it may be understood. This would be necessary if an understanding of this man were to be appreciated. We, of the Confederation of Planets in the Service of the Infinite Creator, are aware of his activities and his abilities, which your people consider miraculous. I am sorry that it is not possible *(inaudible)*. However, as I have stated through the other instrument, there are many experiments taking place upon the surface. This is but one. There is a program now in progress to awaken the peoples of your planet to their rightful heritage. There are many facets to this program. There are many of those of us from elsewhere in the Creation who are involved in doing this. It is very difficult to progress in an exact and direct way and certain things must be brought to your people in a very small amount of your time. This is the only possibility for them at this time. We will, in the future, attempt to give you a greater understanding in this area of your seeking. However, this is difficult at this particular time. We will leave at this time. Adonai vasu borragus.

Thursday Meditation
June 6, 1974

(Carla channeling)

I am Hatonn. I greet you, my brothers, in the love and in the light of our infinite Creator. I am most pleased to greet each of you this evening. It is a privilege to be speaking with this group of seekers. My friends, it is a very pleasing circumstance to us to notice that your paths have all crossed for this meeting.

We have been aware of your desire to serve for, in some cases, a considerable length of time as you know. No one can know better than some of you here tonight that our mission on planet Earth has not been as successful as we had hoped. The harvest is coming, my friends, it is coming very quickly. And the harvest will be somewhat smaller than we had ever hoped. And in this fact we experienced a degree of sadness for we attempted to the best of our ability to alert all of those on the planet known as Earth who could hear to the possibility of a higher existence. And in many, many cases this information was not recognized or desired. You, too, from attempting to express the thoughts of the Creator have often found this to be so. And I am aware of the great sadness that you too feel.

My friends, although this call bides within us all, let us not spend more time than is necessary to accept this experience for there is a great deal to do for the ones who have not rejected the higher experience.

There will be many who still seek and some who flounder *(inaudible)* and there is much that ones who are aware of truth can do to encourage those who are seeking towards a path that will lead them into the real creation.

True progress, my friends, is without the dimension of time and without the dimension of space. That which you do for one, you do for all. And as you meditate, my friends, your meditation is the totality of what you can offer. Do not be discouraged, but continue in your seeking and through daily meditation keep yourself grounded well in the creation of the Father, for we have much to do yet and it is our greatest privilege to share with you our thoughts. We may be of much help, my friends, never doubt that.

I would like to condition others of this group who desire for a period. And then I will transfer this contact to another instrument if he will avail himself. I am Hatonn.

(Unknown channeling)

I am *(inaudible)* a great honor to be with you through these group meditations. You will find *(inaudible)*. I and my brothers are *(inaudible)*. I will at this time transfer to another instrument. I am Hatonn.

(Carla channeling)

We are having some difficulty, my friends, contacting the instrument known as R. If she will avail herself to our contact, we will attempt to communicate a brief message through her. I am Hatonn.

(Pause)

I am again with this instrument. I am Hatonn. I will leave you now, my friends. I leave with a thought. The thought is one of love, my friends. The simple and eternal question is always, "What is love?" Love is all, my friends. He is love. Be one with love and allow the divine love of the Creator to flow through you. In this way, my friends, you know the ecstasy that comes with being one with [all] that there is.

I leave you in the love and in the light of our infinite Creator. I am Hatonn. Adonai.

Thursday Meditation
June 6, 1974

(Unknown channeling)

(Inaudible) in my presence. I am a new teacher to this instrument and *(inaudible)*. I have also this evening which you would say is many miles away *(inaudible)*.

I would like to say but a few words; that there will be many teachers that will come to you. There will be many different kinds of channels. There will be some who can see the future, *(inaudible)*. And there will be more than one teacher who *(inaudible)*. And you will know the difference of the vibration and *(inaudible)*.

It is remarkable and unusual and delightful to see, I would say, the younger generation interested in our thoughts. But again, if you really think that, haven't you always known this? But at times when you do *(inaudible)*. We know if you feel *(inaudible)* … It is in your actions and it is the way you say you feel. And the way *(inaudible)*. The way you help and the way you do help *(inaudible)*. You all must work and the work is not easy. And it will not be done for you, but you will be guided as we always try to do. You will be given suggestions, as one of your words—a hint—of a means. And sometimes *(inaudible)*. And what one can figure out himself. To do something yourself *(inaudible)*.

(Inaudible)

I will not speak any longer because I know that you must be weary. But if *(inaudible)* will avail himself, Deltron would like to speak for just a brief moment. I leave you with this thought in mind: all there is, you are. My love. I am Nona.

(Unknown channeling)

(Inaudible) in the radiance and love of the infinite One. I am known as Deltron. I am fairly new with this speaker. I have been here for some time and I have been observing classes of students that my brother Hatonn is working with. I have found communication with your people interesting and delightful. I have not spoken through an Earth instrument until a few months ago when I spoke through this instrument for the first time. I told him, at this time, I was not of this galaxy. I am from another galaxy entirely different from this planet's.

I and many of my brothers have answered the call to come and assist the people of Earth. We have been up to now merely observing and learning the techniques of contacting the Earth people. Some of our observations are very interesting. We find your people still devoting a great deal of their time to elaborate ritual, to the building of fabulous houses. We find your people searching in all directions for that which they call the light of their Creator.

My friends, there is a story upon your planet. I believe it is referred to as the search for the bluebird of happiness. In this search, an individual was seeking happiness and much to his own surprise he did not find happiness until he looked in his own backyard.

My children, this is the truth of your searching. Search no further than yourself because your Creator has endowed you with all you will ever need. It is there for you to find. It is found in sincere searching through love for yourself and for your fellow man. It is found *(inaudible)* within yourself. It is found through consideration, compassion and the reflection of love and understanding to those about you. You are well on your way and there are many more to guide and direct you. It is up to you to open your heart and to reflect that radiant light, that loving presence that is within you today.

I believe I have spoken long enough this evening and I shall extend to each one of you the love, the understanding, and the warmest blessings from myself and from my brothers. May each of you walk in the light of that radiant light. Fill yourselves with light [from] those of us.

I am Deltron. I [bid] each of you go in peace and be of good cheer in the days to come. Vasu. Vasu, my friends.

Friday Meditation
June 7, 1974

(Carla channeling)

I am Hatonn. I greet you, friends, in the Creator's light and love. It is a great privilege to speak with you this evening. I am aware of your questions. Although we are capable, as members of the Confederation, of perceiving and understanding the *(inaudible)* thoughts of those upon your planet, we are reluctant to attempt to explain certain of these thoughts. The intention of the *(inaudible)* personality, as we would call it, is to achieve understanding of some aspect of your illusion which the entity is experiencing in a waking state which is causing him confusion. By means of alternate representation of the waking illusion, the sleeping individual is able to, shall we say, come to terms with the illusion. This is sometimes a lengthy process and the dream recurs unchanging as the understanding that is needed is acquired.

To explain what the symbols of a dream mean before the waking personality is ready to understand the dream may not be helpful. Therefore, we will not comment upon the dream of which you spoke except to indicate that it is a normal and ongoing pretense *(inaudible)* of the individual of whom you speak to attempt to understand the natural processes which occur within the physical illusion, especially within the context of time. I am sorry that I cannot satisfy your curiosity. And most specifically, however, it is my privilege to have been able to answer you as best as I could.

My friends, this evening I would like to say a few words about the concept of death. Why do I bring this up, my friends? It seems the proper time to ask you to hold it as clearly as you can as a concept of a real and specific context within your imagination. Imagine your own death, my friends. Imagine each death and dismal corridor of pain and difficulty and lack of faith *(inaudible)*. Imagine all the evil, the negativity, the limitations. Imagine it all, my friends. Allow it to build and build and build until you have a big and towering mountain of death and destruction.

What are you looking at, my friends? What are you imagining? What are you afraid of? What do you know about death, my friends? You have been exposed to much information. It is now that the time has come to begin to absorb this information. What do you know about negativity, my friends? Do you then run for death? There are many on your planet who do. Instead of being involved in the cycle which is of the day, they are involved in the glory of the cycle which may be described as of the night. They sincerely hope for death, either of a searching concern or because they are aware that things will be better to grasp their beginning after the physical death.

But what do you know, my friends? As you meditate what pours forth from within your soul? Are you not aware that which is light and dark which is darkness? That which is life and which is death is merely part of the infinite cycle of an eternal and unchanging creation. A creation which has neither life nor death, my friends, neither dark or light, but is all things, is all cycles, not unmatched and resolved in unity and love. Facing darknesses, my friends, you have nothing to lose but the fear that is holding you within a prison of your own choosing within your mind.

I will attempt now to transfer this contact to another instrument. I am Hatonn.

(Unknown channeling)

I am Hatonn. I am now with this instrument. We would like to, at this time, to speak with you upon the subject of love as experienced by the people of your planet. We have expressed many times that those upon your planet do not truly realize the concept of love. *(Inaudible)* attempt to define the concept *(inaudible)*. Yet we find that it is the only word to express that which will *(inaudible)*.

(Inaudible)

I shall leave you at this time in the love and the light of our infinite Creator. Adonai vasu borragus.

Saturday Meditation
June 8, 1974

(Don channeling)

I am Hatonn. I greet you, my friends, in the love and light of our infinite Creator. It is a great privilege to be with this group once more. It is always a great privilege for those of us in the Confederation of Planets in the Service of the Infinite Creator to speak to those of planet Earth who desire our services.

We are here to attempt to aid man on Earth, but in order to aid him he must desire this aid, for this is our understanding of the Creator's plan and the Creator's desires: that man, wherever or whoever he may me, should receive exactly and totally what he desires. We have been for many of your years attempting to aid the people of this planet. We have been required by our understanding of our Creator's principle to remain in hiding, for we cannot serve one individual and at the same time do a disservice to his neighbor by proving within his own mind that we exist, for many of those of planet Earth at this time do not desire to believe in or have proof of our existence. For this reason we find it necessary to speak to those who seek through channels such as this one. We find it necessary to give to those who seek that which they seek in such a way that they for themselves may appraise its value and accept or reject on their own terms those thoughts that we bring, and being our understanding of the reality of the creation in which all of us exist.

Man upon Earth is conscious and intelligent and yet for the most part he is unaware of reality. He is unaware of the simple reality that he is capable of sensing with his physical senses. In addition, he is unaware of the much greater reality that lies outside the boundaries of his physical senses. For the most part, man on Earth has neglected the beauty and the order of the creation that surrounds him. He neglects notice of his total support by this creation. He neglects noticing that he breathes the atmosphere without which his physical body could not exist. He neglects perceiving that he partakes of the food that is amply supplied by the Creator.

My friends, man on Earth has come to look at these things as being provided by his own technology and devices. He has become very shortsighted in appreciation of the creation. He does not understand the true meaning of the simple and beautiful life that surrounds him. He does not appreciate its generation and regeneration. He learned that the very atmosphere that he breathes is cycled through the plant life to be regenerated to support him and his fellow beings and creatures. And yet this seems to the vast majority of those who dwell upon this planet to be an exercise in technology rather than one in theology.

And there is no awareness of the Creator's plan to provide for His children, to provide for their very desire and to provide a state of perfection. Man on

Earth has lost the awareness that is rightfully his. And why, my friends, has he lost this awareness? He has lost this because he has focused his attention upon devices and inventions of his own. He has become hypnotized by his playthings and his ideas. He is but a child in his mind.

And all of this may be very simply remedied, and man can once more return to an appreciation of reality rather than an appreciation of the very false illusion created by his mind. All that is necessary, my friends, is that he individually avail himself to this appreciation of reality through the process of meditation, for this process stills his active conscious mind which is continually seeking stimulus within the very false illusion developed over so many centuries of time upon planet Earth. And very rapidly then he can return to an appreciation of the reality in the functioning of the real creation.

That is the only reality that surrounds the reality of the love generated by his creation which in turn generated himself and all of the beings and all of the animal life and all of the bird life and all of the fishes in the sea and all of the vegetation, all of the planets, all of the stars, and all of the systems that surround us. My friends, your illusion is very complex. It is meaningless, your cities, your political systems, your concept of science, your concept of philosophy, they are all complex. They require great intellectual ability to encompass them, and yet they are nothing compared to the one simple Thought of your Creator who created you and all of the real creation: the simple Thought of absolute love.

This, my friends, is what man on Earth must return to if he is to know reality: this simple Thought of absolute love, a Thought of total unity with all his brothers regardless of how they might express themselves or whom they might be, for this is the original Thought of your Creator.

Your creation supports you. It was designed in thought by your Creator to support and to provide you with all of your desires. It was the Thought of your Creator that each part of this creation should serve all other parts, for this is the Thought of absolute love, the Thought of total service. When man on Earth is once more able to realize this Thought and then express it in every aspect he then will know his creation, for he will be at one with this Thought and this love.

Seek this understanding through meditation, for all rewards are within. Move backward to the simplicity that is the creation. Still the conscious mind and become aware of love.

At this time I will transfer this contact to another instrument. I am known to you as Hatonn.

(Carla channeling)

I am now with this instrument. I am Hatonn. Meditation, my friends, is one word with one concept we project over and over. We do this for a simple reason: it is the best fruit that we have to give you, for all that we can do, my friends, is to point you in the direction of that which you are seeking. We can only point you in the direction of your inner self, for your inner self is one, truly one, with the Creator, and you are a creation.

My friends, we are aware that *(inaudible)*. There are various expressions of what you would call happiness. My friends, this happiness seems to be something that is sought as being of great importance upon your planet. We ask you, my friends, if you look at this happiness that you may gain through use of the cycles and polarity of your physical manifestation, if you can in any way compare this so-called happiness with the experience of being one with an unchanging creation of love.

There are two paths, my friends. There are two kinds of happiness, my friends, the happiness within the illusion that you know of as the physical illusion that you now enjoy, and happiness known only as understanding. One can only seek one's choice of these two.

The effects of the seeking is to present one with what one desires. So we urge you, my friends, to be very careful as to what you are truly seeking. Do you seek within this illusion which shifts and is so changeable? Or do you seek for reality? Only meditate, my friends, and you will be seeking in the direction of the reality you seek.

I would like to speak briefly through a newer instrument. I will condition each of you who desires it and will at this time attempt to contact the instrument known as R.

(Pause)

I am Hatonn. I am having some difficulty in contacting the instrument known as R. We find this difficulty often when the new instrument has not availed himself for use as an instrument. Too often when the reason *(inaudible)*. There is nothing to be concerned about. If it is again desired to be of service, my *(inaudible)* friend, it is only necessary to begin to avail himself in the regular manner and new ability will become fluent in a very short time.

We will now attempt to contact the instrument known as T, if he will avail himself.

(T channeling)

I am Hatonn. I am now with this instrument. It is a pleasure to be with this instrument. This instrument is also experiencing some difficulty in relaxing *(inaudible)*.

We would at this time [like] to say a few words about *(inaudible)*.

Will now attempt to transfer this contact to the one known as E.

(E channeling)

(Inaudible)

(Tape ends.)

Sunday Meditation
June 9, 1974

(Don channeling)

I am Hatonn. I greet you, my friends, in the love and in the light of our infinite Creator. It is a privilege once more to be with this group. We of the Confederation of Planets in the Service of the Infinite Creator are always ready to serve those who seek and desire our services. At this time I and my brother Laitos will condition each of you and then we shall attempt to use each of you who desire our service as an instrument.

I am at this time going to contact the instrument known as Carla.

(Carla channeling)

I am with this instrument. I am very happy to speak with you. It is *(inaudible)* to join our services to yourself. We wish to assure that the service of channeling will be one which is very valuable in your immediate days to come. It is not *(inaudible)* that you will be asked specific questions by many who seek, although this will certainly be true. It is also that this contact will give you confidence and with this confidence you may the more carefully carry on your own program of seeking in such a way that you will recognize that which is there for you to do, for you to know, and for you to be aware. Much of the attempt which is initially made by those who begin seeking to discover their inner selves is such a confused attempt that it must be simply guided into another attempt. Therefore, many questions which you will receive will have very little meaning to you in light of your contact with the knowledge and understanding of the One Who is All.

That which you say under those circumstances must *(inaudible)* a very careful line. You must not give false information; you must not be discouraging. You must be encouraging and somehow understanding within the light of that which you know to be true. In many cases, my friends, this will entail an answer that is not an answer, which may temporarily confuse the person you are attempting to help in which you will not be what you as your previous illusory self would have answered. In this contact with us it is good, therefore, in your service in two ways. First, in giving specific answers to specific questions which have an answer which can be given. And second, in giving you confidence as a channel for the thoughts of the original creation so that you are able to speak as its servant rather than as your own limited earthly self.

There is much in this work ahead of you which the world will not understand. And this, my friends, is precisely the difficulty. Because the world does not understand, my friends, we are here. For it is seeking to understand and we hear its cry. The service that you are performing is truly, truly an important one. Have faith that your seeking is in the direction of progress and continue, my friends, if you desire. We are very, very grateful to you for your attempts to serve and we welcome you to our company.

I would like to speak further and to contact the instrument known as T at this time. I am Hatonn.

(T channeling)

I am Hatonn. I am now with this instrument. I wish to continue as saying, as I said before, many people will not understand what you will tell them. Your daily contacts will at a time in the near future provide a very fertile field for the dissemination of information. Many people will ask questions, my friends. This may not seem very likely in the present, but I assure you that the situation will change to a large degree. Many people will ask questions. More than likely in many instances after you have answered their questions, they will not believe you. They will not believe what you have told them. Again, this is to be expected and to be prepared for it. It is not something to be discouraged about, my friends. They will in their own good time come to understand and accept what you say or what someone else tells them. Your attempts at service in this manner will bear much fruit either immediately or in the future. So prepare yourself, my friends. Prepare yourself through daily meditations. Prepare yourself through group meetings such as this.

I will now attempt to transfer this contact to the one known as B. I am Hatonn.

(B channeling)

I am Hatonn. I am now with this instrument. I wish to continue *(inaudible)*. Through your daily meditations you will be supplied with many answers to questions that will shortly be asked you. I and my brother Laitos will be at your disposal at any time that you wish to communicate with us. It is our sincere hope that through more meditation the newer channels of this group will be able to take on, as you say, more *(inaudible)*. I and my brothers are very pleased at the progress made by this new channel.

In the days that follow, many hardships will come to the planet known as Earth. I and my brothers will try to answer all the questions that are put to us. On many occasions you will find that some questions asked again [and] again. Many people that *(inaudible)*. I will repeat. Many people known as friends will not believe the message that some of the channels will try to *(inaudible)*. It is not the duty, so to speak, of these channels to only look to friends at a time like this. Many, many people will be questioning and there are not enough channels to meet with all. Through the developing *(inaudible)* instruments, people will be guided to you with questions and *(inaudible)*. I am sure that all who dedicate *(inaudible)* will find great inspiration through their channeling.

I at this time will try to communicate with the one known as E. I am Hatonn.

(E channeling)

I am Hatonn. I greet you once again. Meditation is very important for all channels. There will be new information given during meditation. New channels should meditate as much as they can in order to understand new information that will be given. *(Inaudible)*. Stay in meditation as long as you can in order to acquire understanding.

At this time I will again contact the channel known as Don. I am Hatonn.

(Don channeling)

I am with this instrument. I am Hatonn. It is a privilege to be able to speak through each of the instruments present this evening. As I have stated, meditation is of utmost importance. Meditation will allow you to become totally aware of the concepts which we bring to you. These concepts are very simple, but they cannot be communicated effectively with words alone. When you become aware of these concepts in their total nature, there will be a transformation in your thinking, a transformation that you presently desire. If you did not desire this you would not be seeking it. This transformation is necessary if you are to be totally effective in serving with us our Creator.

This transformation has seen demonstrated to you at a previous time upon your planet. The last teacher with whom you are familiar who so demonstrated this transformation of thought was known to you as Jesus. This man lived and acted quite simply. However, this thinking was unique. This thinking was recognized by those around him as being unique. It was also recognized as being correct by many of those who were aware of it. We wish to bring to you that which you seek—that transformation of thought that has been demonstrated so clearly to [you] by this man. My friends, you may obtain this transformation through meditation. It is of the awareness. Spend time in meditation. Spend time to become aware of that which is already yours—a total knowledge of the love and the understanding of our Creator. This is all that is necessary for you to serve in your fullest capacity.

It has been a great privilege to bring to you these thoughts. It is always a very great privilege to serve those who seek. We bring to you the answers to all of your questions. I am aware of your question. It is very good to seek in all directions. There is much to be gained from these activities. However, meditation is in all cases of primary importance. I am at this time attempting to answer this question. Seeking takes many forms and many expressions.

(Pause)

I am with this instrument. I am Oxal. I am using control. It will be necessary to use control. I am aware of this question. I am sorry but it is impossible at this time to answer this question. I am Oxal.

(Pause)

I am Hatonn. I am once more with this instrument. It has been a privilege to speak with this group this evening. I am sorry that we have not been totally capable of fulfilling your immediate desires. However, all things come to those who wait. I shall transfer this contact for my departure to the one known as Carla.

(Carla channeling)

I am Hatonn. I am now with this instrument. I am having some amount of difficulty with this instrument. If you will please be patient we will condition her for a short period.

There are pieces of information that are of importance and there are pieces of information that are not. As we told you before, there are many times in which questions must be turned away. Wisdom is a rather lonely matter, my friends. You must accept this truth as you acquire the burden of wisdom. That which you know you are to be careful of, for what you know in the real creation has power. And that which you desire is all of the direction which that power will be aimed at. But have faith, my friends, in what you know and what you are learning. And feed your faith and your understanding through meditation. The farther that you go along this path, my friends, the more meaningful you will find this simple statement: meditate. It begins as a simple process and little by little it becomes the way in which you live. Observe it, my friends, as you progress along your own spiritual path.

It has been a great privilege to speak using each of you. We are most honored and we hope that we have been able to be of some aid to you. We are with you always. We leave you only seemingly as we leave this instrument. We leave you in the love and in the light of the One Who is All. I am Hatonn. Adonai. Adonai. ❧

Thursday Meditation
June 11, 1974

(Don channeling)

I am Hatonn. I greet you, my friends, in the love and in the light of our infinite Creator. It is once more a great privilege to be with this group. It is always a very great privilege to be with this group. We of the Confederation of Planets, as we have said, are here to serve those who seek.

There are more people upon this planet seeking than there have been in the past. However, many are quite confused in their attempts to seek and there is a need at this time for many more channels such as this one who can receive directly the thoughts that so many of the people of this planet are now seeking. We are attempting at this time to generate greater numbers of proficient vocal channels who can receive our thoughts quite readily. This requires daily meditation. This is all that is required: daily meditation. It is assumed, of course, that as this daily meditation is performed there is a desire for our contact.

We have been contacting people of planet Earth for many, many of your years. We have been contacting at intervals of thousands of years those who sought our aid. It is time for many of the people of this planet to be contacted for many now have the understanding and the desire to seek something outside the physical illusion that has for so many years involved the thinking of those of this planet.

The process we are stimulating is one which is self-generating. As more and more of those who desire our contact receive it and pass it on to others, then those who receive this passed-on information will they themselves be able to reach a state of thinking and understanding sufficiently in tune, shall I say, with our vibrations in order to receive our contact.

For this, my friends, is how contacts work. It is first necessary, if the entity is to be able to receive our contact, for him to become of a certain vibration as a result of his thinking. This is greatly speeded by involvement in groups such as this. And then it is finally done through meditation.

In other words, the verbal communications given to the entity by the channels such as this one create a system of thought and a desire for spiritual awareness that raises his vibration. Through meditation he is able to attune his thinking to those of us who serve planet Earth. He then can receive and repeat what we give to him, in order to regenerate, from its beginning, the process of teaching and of instructing others who will follow in the same path. Through this technique there will be many more of the peoples of the planet Earth made aware of the truth and the love that is theirs, as it is the will of their Creator.

We of the Confederation of Planets in the Service of the Infinite Creator are very sorry that we cannot step upon your soil and teach those of your people who desire our service, but, my friends, as we have said before, this would be a very great disservice to those who do not desire our service at this time. And we are afraid we would have little effect in bringing understanding even to those who desire it, for understanding, my friends, comes from within. We can only guide. We can only suggest. We are attempting to do this in such a way so that the seeking of the individual will be stimulated to turning his thinking inward, inward to that single source of love and understanding, the Creator that is part of us all, part of everything that exists, for everything that exists, my friends, is the Creator.

We are very privileged to have those of you who join with us in this great service at this time in the history of your planet. For, my friends, this is a very great time, a great transitional period in which many of the Earth's people will be raised from their state of confusion to a simple understanding: the love of their Creator.

It has been a great privilege to speak to you through this instrument. At this time I will transfer this contact to another instrument. I am Hatonn.

(Tape ends.)

Friday Meditation
June 12, 1974

(Carla channeling)

I am Hatonn. I am now with this instrument. It is a pleasure to be able to use this instrument. As I was saying, my friends, for your meditations we suggest that you may be able to experience *(inaudible)*.

Within the illusion, my friends, there are many obstacles. The illusion, in fact, is designed to produce the obstacles which will deliver unto you the choices which you desire for learning how to be of greater service to others. The lessons of this density, my friends, are lessons of service to others. And each obstacle is an opportunity which is a *(inaudible)* within the illusion think it is difficulty. Each obstacle is your opportunity to grow. *(Inaudible).*

There is much to learn and you, my friends, are just *(inaudible)* on the path. That which you have gone through up until now is the beginning without which we *(inaudible)*. With that which lies ahead is a new chapter. It will be a unique experience for you, my friends. It will be a difficult experience in some ways. Yet it will be a uniquely designed opportunity to be very rapidly progressed along the path of seeking and service.

I am aware that there is not precisely a question, but a thought within this group, and I would respond in this manner. It may be of the nature of a beneficial experience to you to open these meetings at a certain time to those who are not specifically of the Confederation of Planets in the Service of the Infinite Creator. We would not suggest this to an introductory group because it is necessary for those who listen to contact *(inaudible)* the astral plane that they have a firm grasp of objective reality. The personalities with whom you might make contact can be very informative and interesting to you. However, they are not free of the density which you are also now within and therefore their information will be to an extent subjectively different than objectively *(inaudible)*, simply because they will be under the same illusion which you *(inaudible)*.

Therefore, it cannot be recommended that a meeting be opened up to such entities when the group is not totally aware of the creation of the Father. We do not feel that you can gain a great deal of spiritual information from them. However, there is one aspect which *(inaudible)* and that is, my friends, the beginning of an understanding of just how miraculous and vast the universe is. The number of portions of the creation which exist upon a planet such as this one is actually infinite. However, you might perhaps best understand what we intend to tell you if we *(inaudible)* and individualized portions of consciousness which are the Creator. This piece of understanding is extremely helpful in its own way in that it begins to give this illusion its proper place within your thinking. *(Inaudible).*

I would like to move to another channel after a brief period of conditioning for each of you who desires it. I am Hatonn.

(H channeling)

I am now with this instrument. I would wish to speak to you upon the subject of what you would consider to be *(inaudible)*. We hope that in our communications that many times there shall be needed by all a total confidence and acceptance of the world of the Creator. This total confidence is to be considered *(inaudible)*. There are *(inaudible)* of aiding the growth of your planet. The one that we suggest that you utilize mostly and the one which is most beneficial to you is your meditation. In your periods of meditation you shall attain knowledge which is not directly impressed upon your intellect, yet when you face situations in your daily life this knowledge shall penetrate from within your being and shall function through you. This knowledge and this growth brings about your faith which is so greatly needed.

There is also a need of enabling your faith which you contain within your intellect. The intellectual faith is also quite valuable and is also a need to your meditation. The growth of this intellectual faith comes about by your understanding. Each difficulty or each situation which you experience contains truth and within this illusion the truth of each situation is very difficult to find by utilizing your thoughts. Allow the intellect to be guided by meditation and it shall be able to find the great lessons which lie in *(inaudible)*.

In many circumstances the situation will try greatly your confidence in the world of your Creator. You shall experience times when you shall question His word and wonder to yourself if it is *(inaudible)*. This is normal in your growth for your intellect does continue to operate and we find this the path of the intellect of your people. Yet, each time you question, turn to your meditation. Meditate upon this question and the awareness and the answer which is needed shall come to you. In this way the intellect is aided, for seeing the truth and finding the answers in meditation, it gives you the intellectual knowledge of faith.

You realize that [you] may seek the guidance when you see it and in many circumstances you shall see it within your life come about. *(Inaudible)* but do not allow the intellect to be your only means of prayer for it is *(inaudible)*. The great necessity [is] that you seek the guidance in all situations through meditation. We of the Confederation of Planets in the Service of the Infinite Creator are pleased to have the opportunity to serve the peoples of your planet. And it is most gratifying to us to see so many individuals who have desired to aid in our service to your people.

This group and many like it upon your planet shall shortly be prepared to render great service to all of the people. We wish shortly to indulge upon lessons of a higher knowledge which shall be of great aid. And we are pleased to see the formation of this group and of others like it for it is our intention to avail this knowledge through these groups.

The knowledge of which we speak would be at this time, shall we say, too intense for beginners upon the path of seeking. But as we stated earlier this evening you are well established upon the path to begin *(inaudible)*. Yet the path shall express throughout *(inaudible)*. This path shall only culminate when you attain a true meaning of the Creator. We welcome you for we also follow the path you have chosen and we wish to aid you. So we are aware of your needs upon this planet.

I wish at this time to attempt to transfer this contact to another instrument. I am Hatonn.

(B channeling)

I am now with this instrument. It is a great honor to once again to have this chance to speak through this instrument. I and my brothers are now in the room with you. I am now going to *(inaudible)* each of you. I would now like to speak on the subject of … I am having trouble with this instrument. I shall rephrase the sentence. I would now like to speak on the subject of loyalty to others of your peoples.

As one goes about his life on the planet Earth, he develops many loyalties to people and family. This loyalty is very important if evolved as perfect mentally and partially *(inaudible)*. Although many times on your planet this loyalty is taken advantage of, while one reaches a higher vibration, he is made more aware, so to speak, of the appreciation that one has for loyalty. It is very important that you carry through. Although there are times when I am sure everyone in this group will be faithful, no loyalty will be part of this. I will prove this *(inaudible)*.

I am very, very privileged at being able to speak with this group. It was indeed a great honor to once again speak through this channel. I will attempt to communicate at this time with another instrument. I am Hatonn.

(T channeling)

(Inaudible)

I will now attempt to transfer this communication. I am Hatonn.

(E channeling)

Greetings once again, my friends. I would like to *(inaudible)*.

(Inaudible)

(Tape ends.)

Thursday Meditation
June 13, 1974

(Carla channeling)

I am Hatonn. I greet you, my friends, in the love and the light of our infinite Creator. It is as always a great pleasure to speak with you. My brothers and I are here to aid you in any way that we can and to send you our thoughts and the love and the light of the One Who is All. We are aware that you have questions at this time. We are aware that you wish to know if we are, as you say, robots. No, my friends, we who are speaking to you are individualized portions of consciousness in the same mode of being as are you. The robots or computers that you became acquainted with in your reading about Uri Geller are not of the same type as what you know as robots or computers. It is more simple than it sounds, my friends. The Confederation is a unity of thought and of mind, my friends. There are many *(inaudible)* and types of entities who dwell within this creation who wish to be of service to others and who have joined as brothers in this Confederation to serve the Creator, each in his own way.

The system which this Confederation uses for communication is not a simple computer as you know it but a construct in a timeless dimension of thought. The thoughts of the Creator which those of the Confederation wish to program and the destination intended for these thoughts can be given instantaneously and delivered instantaneously. There are other abilities that go with this communications system. The limitations of this system are those of your letters. We speak to you as though by telephone and you can answer and we can adjust our information to adapt to yours. The communications which Geller received were only capable of being given within certain preset parameters. If the answer had not been prepared it could not be given.

We are within your time dimension. We are here on a special mission. We are the teaching *(inaudible)* of a very vast Confederation. The complexity of this Confederation is only an illusion, as each one of us, by means of our awareness, is constantly and completely aware of the ongoing attitudes and progress of each of the other portions of the Confederation. We do this by achieving, through mediation, our awareness of unity with each other, as we are one in the Creator.

We are speaking to you in person because we do not wish to convince you of physical phenomena but to guide your seeking. It is upon your shoulders that a certain carefully arranged service will fall. This service can only be performed by those who have been apprenticed for some time to the discipline of meditation and to the thoughts of the Creator, which only become understood through meditation. The type of contact which occurred with Uri Gellar occurred precisely because these people, in spite of being extremely and unusually positive and powerful individuals, could not seem to be contacted by the means of meditation. Therefore, because these entities had a mission to perform, they were contacted in a more gross and material manner.

I am aware of another question at this time. I am aware that this instrument wishes to know why the meditation group has become smaller. Watch out. Do not be naive. There are cycles in all things. You have sent out one harvest and this harvest is beginning to give its service to others. In time there will be another season and you will prepare for the further harvest. Meanwhile, that service which you perform is simply to abide in your understanding and to leave the door open for such meditations.

I am aware that there is another question. Do you wish to ask it?

Questioner: Yes. Several times in the past you have spoken upon … of tests that will be for members of this group *(inaudible)* to give us an opportunity to prove our newfound awareness. Are these to be individual tests or are they just to come as one huge test, one large test?

These will be individual for the present.

Questioner: I have a question. This dreadful fear that I have. Is it real or not?

Fear is always an illusion. What can happen to you? You can die. That is a birth. You can *(inaudible)*. Debt is a kind of death.

Questioner: This fear I have is *(inaudible)*.

Carla: I didn't hear you *(inaudible)*.

Questioner: This fear that I have … is it a test?

(Inaudible) friend, do not look to your fear for your test but look behind the fear, for there is a mistaken idea which is causing this fear. This is the test.

Questioner: *(Inaudible)*.

The happening may be swayed by your thinking. It is extremely helpful to project peaceful and optimistic views of the future to replace traumatic visions, for what will happen, will happen, and there is no need to fear.

My friend, we do not feel that it is desirable for us to inform you as to the future. The test is in your own mind. It is your tool. You may use it but you should not let it use you. If a thought is not one which is designed to help yourself or another then it is somewhat suspect. If it is a negative amount of help to yourself or someone else then it is definitely not a desirable thought. These thoughts are yours. They surround you. They are real. They exist within the etheric realms of your planet. That which you think remains with you and predicts to a certain extent your future. Adjust your thinking and you adjust your future. This is why we advise you again and again to spend your days in awareness of the creation of the Father for there is nothing but love in the true creation and your present awareness of this will guide you into calmer waters.

This, then, is the test and we hope that we have guided you in how to meet it. We offer you these ideas hoping they will help you. They are indicative of our methods. We too must meditate to retain contact with that we know to be truth.

I would like at this time to exercise the newer channels and to give a short message to each. I will attempt to transfer this contact to the instrument known as E, if she will avail herself to my contact.

(E channeling)

I am Hatonn. Greetings once again, my friends. It is indeed a pleasure to use the newer channel. Once again may I say to use your time wisely *(inaudible)* your understanding of the creation. During your daily activity keep in mind the creation as it exists all around you *(inaudible)* just as below. Secure yourself in the love of the Creator and all is well.

I will transfer now to the one known as T.

(T channeling)

I am Hatonn, and am now with this instrument. I wish to *(inaudible)* goes without saying *(inaudible)* must *(inaudible)* meditation if possible these should be at somewhat regular intervals. Secondly, my friends, if at all possible try to set aside times that are somewhat devoid of *(inaudible)*.

(Side one of tape ends.)

(T channeling)

(Inaudible) this channel will in the near future begin to develop enough confidence to challenge us *(inaudible)* questions *(inaudible)* this after all will be one of the primary functions or services I should say as a channel and *(inaudible)* questions *(inaudible)* my friends *(inaudible)* great opportunity for service. I would now transfer this contact to the one known as Carla. I am Hatonn.

(Carla channeling)

I am with this instrument. I am Hatonn. What is your question?

Questioner: Last night at the group meditation everyone experienced after meditation was over a very high state of … a very … the situation was very … a very high energy. Does this mean that your messages came through at a greater intensity *(inaudible)* a better understanding *(inaudible)* because of our seeking or because of our place and our seeking at this time?

I am aware of what you are asking. The energy which you are aware of was the sum of the desire of each person present plus the state of awareness of each person present toward the other people present. This awareness of each other in that particular group was somewhat more unified than several other groups and this increased the energy as well as a fairly unified group desire to obtain information. However, this high energy level does not indicate that you have learned what is spoken. It only indicates a desire to meditate and to learn. Other desires can intervene. We desire for certain types of information as opposed to simply rewards of the Creator. It is a somewhat self-limiting desire since it eliminates some of the more advanced information. This is somewhat ironic, as you would say, because the very desire to obtain the so-called higher information can prevent obtaining higher information due to an incorrect assumption as to the nature of higher information.

The most appropriate way to ensure understanding what is said in an unusually high energy meeting is to allow it to leak over into your everyday thinking during the time following the meditation and if you do this you will discover a way to put this teaching into demonstration. At this point you will begin understanding in a true sense, for that which is not demonstrated is not understood. This is not to say that the high level of energy which you experience is not valuable. It is very valuable, but it must be, like any other power, guided carefully or its power can be dissipated or wrongly used. Guidance comes from listening rather than predicting.

We are attempting to gain a somewhat more stable contact, if you will be patient. We have been here, my friends, many times in the past and we have attempted to give to those upon your planet the specific type of information which many seek but we have discovered that it is an infringement rather than a service in the balance of time. Therefore, higher information, if you may picture it as having any particular characteristic, is characterized by less of a physical specificity and more of a mystical or paradoxical nature. There are abilities within some of the newer channels which will begin to be developed as they gain confidence in delivering these higher messages. They will be people who will be capable of speaking in a more abstract manner. We are satisfied that there are many in groups such as yours and others who will be very capable at this task and will give a very valuable service to more advanced grades of students in the future.

Have I answered your question adequately?

Questioner: Yes. Thank you.

I am regretful that it is such a scattered answer but you were dealing with a somewhat multiple experience, if we may say that within the framework of unity.

Questioner: I have one more question. I would like to ask this question if I may *(inaudible)*.

Carla: *(Inaudible)*. You're not going to believe this *(inaudible)*! All I see is a frog. I can't possibly channel a frog. Wait a minute. Let me see if I can follow it, OK?

(Carla channeling)

I am sorry for the levity, my friends. Consider the state of a simple frog. This frog is suddenly one day thrust into the wet wonderland which is his home. He is almost transparent when he moves with many others of his kind and evades many enemies. Gradually he attains shape, color, discovers that he can make sound *(inaudible)* and that he can take life and give it. He discovers that his consciousness is flooded with many thousands of images daily, that he has great power in his hands, and that he has a fate which he must follow. One day the frog is no more, for its body is no longer inhabited and it sinks back into the bottom of the pond from which it originated.

This frog is a very important person to himself. His awareness is very central and that which he loves and that which he dislikes are very real to him. But, my friends, we who are of the type of entity which you call human are aware that a frog is a frog. Who is right, my friends? We would like to point out the frog is correct, that you are correct, and that both of you are incorrect, for the nature of both is consciousness—consciousness which comes from one source and which is going ultimately to its own source. There is no beginning and no end. There is only the unity, the freedom of *(inaudible)* and the joy of reunion. Any other opinion of self or meaning of consciousness is quite real but is unreal.

There is always much you may do to be of service. There are always lessons to learn. There is a reality to illusion, but, my friends, remember the frog. You are a prince to yourself and your right and your wrong are extremely important and that which you love and that which you dislike are very real to you. But you are only a *(inaudible)* and there is much hope. Allow your consciousness to rise into the light which created you and ultimately the questions will be answered for you will know that you are where you are and who you are and that all is well.

I would like to transfer this contact to the instrument known as T, if he will avail himself to my contact.

(T channeling)

I am Hatonn. *(Inaudible)*.

(Unknown channeling)

I am now with this instrument. I was speaking of service and we are aware …

(Carla channeling)

I am Hatonn. I greet you once more, my friends, in the love and in the light of our infinite Creator. It is a great privilege to be able to be attempting to aid you in your seeking. We are aware of your questions and we will attempt to answer them.

The acquisition of understanding is not the phenomenon which you think it is, my friends. The acquisition of understanding is part and parcel of something much more basic. It does not come before this basic quality but rather is a result of this basic quality. One can only acquire understanding to the level at which his desire has led him.

Desire, my friends, is also not what you think it is. Desire is a great deal more than you think it is. The desire of a man is the man. It is his directional movement. This motion is the expression of his basic consciousness and is the most basic thing about him.

Now, your question is not answered by these facts, but they are necessary facts to understand before we can give you an answer. What one desires, my friends, and the purity of that desire, becomes and is the individual once he is aware that this is true. The man who is centered within his desire becomes whole and unified. This life, my friends, is a whole, it is one thing: an interconnected galaxy of time and space and meaning. Nothing may be untwined from anything else, for all is one. There is no strain or confusion in his life for he is aware at all time of who he is. He is the one who desires that which he desires. He is a seeker after truth. He is on a path. That which the path offers to him is what he is looking at, is what he is learning, and is what he is demonstrating. If he discovers that he has not followed all of his steps he learns from this discovery and never leaves the pattern of his desire.

You may, if you like, compare this self-aware existence with a knitted garment. Each stitch is interconnected with each other stitch. As it comes off the needles it is held safely in place.

My friends, the attempt to analyze one's life by means of external and intellectual concepts is much like removing one's stitches from the needles. It is very easy for them to get misplaced or temporarily lost and it may take some time for these stitches to be properly discovered again and put back into pattern. Therefore, it is much better to do without this intellectual picking. It is much better to simply accept one's existence and realize at all times who one is and what one is seeking. If one can do this it matters not whether one is sick or well or whether one is rich or poor for these things are minor details having little to do with the purpose for which your life has been dedicated.

The seeking which led you to this meeting also leads you to each item of information which you obtain. My friends, if your seeking is not ready to absorb this information then you will not demonstrate this information and you will therefore not have this information. It will not be your information. That which is not seen through you is not within you. There is indeed the possibility of what this channel sometimes calls cosmic indigestion. However, this is not the fault of the information or the fault of the entity who is not completely ready to demonstrate this information. It is simply a slight mismatching of information and it makes no difference to the seeking.

The true difficulty which you experienced was due to your intellectual efforts to analyze and to predict items which were beyond your intellectual ability. There are many things which one may think and man is a creator. Man creates many, many thoughts and, my friends, he lives with these thoughts. These thoughts are his thoughts. He does not create them to fly away. He creates them to surround him and they surround him more and more as he thinks upon the same thoughts. If you wish to have a certain thought about you, then think it, my friends. If the thought which you are entertaining is not full of faith, hope, charity, love and concern for the spiritual welfare of your fellow man then you may put those thoughts aside and you will not be responsible for their generation.

If you could be in the dimension which immediately follows yours along the scales of planes you would see your thoughts, my friends. You would see your emotions. You would discover for yourself how very undesirable it is to surround yourself with those things which cause fear, sickness, pain and lack. My friends, you would see the great strides that can be made by the constant generation of thoughts of the Creator. The intellect cannot understand these matters and for this reason we had you meditate to make you more conscious of the Creator's thoughts. We can only approximate with words what we are attempting to tell you and that is that your difficulties are due to your own ability to create by intellectual thought that which you feel that you desire intellectually but in truth certainly do not desire. Concentrate upon your desires, my friends. Do not be afraid of any information but only know who you are and what you desire.

We send you our love and our light, for we are one with you. We send you all of the creation, for we are one with the creation. We send you great beauty. Galaxies of bursting stars. We send you many thoughts and many dreams and great ecstasy. All of these things are in the creations of the Father and they are yours, my friends. We hope that we have been able to be of service. We urge you to lift up your heart, for there is much to rejoice concerning.

I am desirous at this time of speaking for a time with each of you, if you will avail yourself to my contact. I will attempt to contact at this time the instrument known as T. I am Hatonn.

(T channeling)

I am Hatonn. I am now with this instrument. My friend, I would like to say *(inaudible)* to you concern. The instrument has confused himself through *(inaudible)* attempts to analyze. My friends, I wish only at this time to exercise the new instruments. This is a common method or technique with new instruments. We send our thoughts on a rather basic level. The instruments should not concern themselves at first with the message they are receiving. No amount of analyzing by an instrument will make his message any more meaningful or profound, my friends. Merely relax and avail yourself to our contact. We will do the rest, my friends. It is not really a complicated thing receiving our thoughts. Our thoughts come to *(inaudible)* quite easily to some people on your planet who have never before consciously thought of our contact. This ease owes to their ability to totally relax their body and mind, thus becoming very receptive and merely repeating what they see and what they hear in their mind. I will now attempt to make contact with the instrument known as *(inaudible)*. I am Hatonn.

(Tape ends.) ♣

Friday Meditation
June 21, 1974

(Unknown channeling)

(Inaudible) our infinite Creator. It is once more a great privilege to be with you. This evening I will attempt to condition each of you if you will avail yourself.

(Carla channeling)

(Inaudible). I am with this instrument. Again, my friends, I greet you in the love and in the light of our one infinite Creator. I express to you my feeling of great privilege to be allowed to condition you and to … speak with you at this time using these instruments. My friends, I would speak to you for a few minutes about your meditations. Although we have been over this material many times we approach it again, my friends. That which we have to tell you is, in itself, very simple. All we can do is vary the approach which is used in explaining it. We would like to look at this time at the aspect of meditation in which your feeling about the activity of meditation is demonstrated.

How do you picture that which you do in meditation, my friends? How do you measure your gains? With what instrument are you grading yourself? We are afraid, my friends, that it is the inevitable habit of those upon planet Earth to demand a type of grading system even for those things which do not lie within the grading systems you have available. That which is measured is inevitably that which is lost, my friends. What you measure is what has been expended. And in mediation, my friends, nothing is expended. Meditation is a becoming … a becoming aware of that which already is in a timeless fashion. One cannot grade it for it is entirely a living activity. Not living, my friends, in the sense of this illusion but living in the sense that eternity lives. It is beyond that which you may know as judging.

To the human mind, my friends, that which you see about you as progress could be compared to a great coral reef. You observe that which has been left behind by previous effort, that which in fact is a pile of used physical vehicles. You can see this. You can measure it and this comforts you, but my friends, meditation is an opposite process. Free yourself from the desire to measure your progress in meditation. Free yourself from the fetters of your own systems of measurement for that which you are desiring is measureless and limitless, my friends. Simply allow yourself to seek and to accept through meditation the contact with the Creator of us all. That is your duty as a portion of this creation.

I would like to continue to condition each of you and at this time I will attempt to continue this contact through another instrument. I am Hatonn.

(Unknown channeling)

I am Hatonn. I am now with this instrument. My friends, the subject of meditation, as we said earlier, has been gone over many times. While the benefits that you receive from meditation are with you and need no measurement, your daily, shall we say habits, necessities, need to be honored so that you can find time for your meditation. This, my friends, is the greatest value of repetition on our part concerning the need to meditate. Do not allow any more than absolutely necessary your daily activities to encroach upon your mediation. Your daily activities may at times be of such a nature that you have to set aside temporarily your meditation. This is … this is your choice, my friends. Try to order your daily life so that *(inaudible)*. Each day as you continue to meditate it will seem to become easier to—again, to use your phrase—to fit your meditation *(inaudible)* to your *(inaudible)* schedule. My friends, this is due to the fact that your awareness, your, shall we say, sense of values is shifting. The realization that through your meditation all problems, questions will be answered *(inaudible)*.

So, my friends, do not hold any recriminations toward yourself if you are unable to adhere to your meditation, but, my friends, *(inaudible)*. It would seem to some that this is likened to forming a habit, but not really because a habit is usually something that *(inaudible)* necessarily *(inaudible)* derived benefit from. I will now attempt to transfer this contact to another instrument. I am Hatonn.

(Unknown channeling)

I am Hatonn. I am with this instrument. Meditation, my friends, will provide you the access to the door through which you must pass to find all of the creation that is about you. This is what we are attempting to bring to those on Earth who will avail themselves to truth. We are trying to lead them to that doorway through which they must pass in order to experience all of the benefits of their creation. It is a very simple process. Avail yourself to meditation and you will surely find the doorway. It is there for all peoples throughout all of the creation, in all places at all times. It is only necessary that they attune their thinking with that of their Creator. This may be done in meditation. Seek and ye shall find it has been written. What ye shall find is more, much more, than you could ever imagine. Find it. Find it through mediation. It is there waiting. I will leave you at this time. I am Hatonn. Adonai vasu.

Saturday Meditation
June 22, 1974

(Inaudible)

(Unknown channeling)

I greet you, my friends, in the love and in the light of our infinite Creator. I am once more with you. I and my brothers are here. Here to serve you. We will serve you for a period of time now during your meditation. All that is necessary is that you avail yourselves to our company.

(Carla channeling)

I am Hatonn. I am now with this instrument. I greet you again, my friends, in the love and the light of the One Who is infinite. As you continue upon your path of seeking, my friends, you will find that even in group meditation there will be profound silence, for with those who have obtained direct contact with us there are many concepts which may best be presented within the silence. We have been expressing to you at this time certain thoughts having to do with service. You are aware that we are here to serve you, my friends. Have you considered the way in which we offer that service? That which we offer is left, as it were, my friends, upon your doorstep. We do not remain to discover whether you will take our gift within your dwelling places, nor do we check the uses to which you put it. We do not come bowing to you, my friends, and we do not come requesting that you bow to us. We are here to serve you. We are here to serve ourselves. There is no inequality between us. There is no separation between us. We are here and we are you. We give at the same time that we take. There is no difference. The entire experience is service.

As you allow yourself to rest within the silence then accept these thoughts which in language are such halting phrases for, my friends, you are beginning to find that your desire to serve is growing and sharpening. We are aware of this. We can assure you that there will be a great plenty of work for you to accomplish in the service of the infinite Creator. All that is necessary is a continued seeking toward the source of light and love which is within each of you.

We will pause again, my friends, and we will speak to you within the silence and after a period we will transfer this contact. I am Hatonn.

(Unknown channeling)

(Inaudible) be more aware of what we speak in the silence *(inaudible)*. There is trouble with this instrument. *(Inaudible)*. What we said before, my friends—you should not try to measure *(inaudible)* transfer this contact *(inaudible)*. I am Hatonn.

(Unknown channeling)

(Mostly inaudible)

I am Hatonn. *(Inaudible)* once more, my friends, in His love and His light. *(Inaudible)* meditation …

(inaudible) meditation is good for each individual entity. It is also good for the *(inaudible)*. A period of silence *(inaudible)* meditation. *(Inaudible)* individual … This instrument is very unsure. *(Inaudible)* each individual entity to relax and *(inaudible)* and flow of energy *(inaudible)* able *(inaudible)* individual entity to receive our thoughts *(inaudible)* and reflect, shall we say, putting away our thoughts *(inaudible)*. It strengthens the entity's desire to meditate in order to receive our thoughts. *(Inaudible)* meditation to allow that entity a better opportunity to meditate and pick up our thoughts.

We are having difficulty with this instrument. She is *(inaudible)* unsure. I am Hatonn. I will leave this instrument now. *(Inaudible)*.

(Carla channeling)

I am Teal'onn. This is not quite right. I am Fillonn. I wish to only break in for a moment. I am new to this channel. I am new to this group. I'm new to this planet. I am only learning how to deal with this planet. I am studying under those of Hatonn. I am with the Confederation of Planets in the Service of the Infinite Creator. I am here to offer what I can offer of that which I am to that which you are. I am here to give to you all of the aid which I possess, of which I possess none, for I am a channel as transparent as sunlight. I only serve to focus the light of the Creator so that another who is seeking may spot this light in a world of murky shadows.

My friends, I do not know very much about you yet. I am only learning. I wish to say to you with all my heart, my friends, look up. Pay attention, my friends. Every day, every breath is fantastic. Don't lose time, my friends. Don't lose consciousness. That which you are experiencing is precious unto you. Horde it and be aware of it. You are experiencing physical existence. This is very precious, my friends. You will not find such intensity possible in other forms of existence. You will not find the ability to experience with such rapidity and such purity those things which you call emotions. Each moment is a moment of adventure and magic. My friends, look up. Pay attention. Do not let these things go by you. Allow yourself to experience each thing that is yours. Allow those things known as emotions within you to mature so that each emotion, my friends, is as pure and true as a living color.

Each emotion, my friends, is indeed like a living color. It may be clear or it may be murky. Those upon your planet seem to be somewhat murky in their emotions. They are attempting to purify their emotions for they are truly the things that survive. They are not actually emotions but you know them as emotions. They are the colors of the spectrum of light. They are consciousness. They are all the Creator. And to experience truly these colors or emotions is to experience truly the Creator, which is the sum of all which there is.

Each expression which you feel may be purified to its complete end or final form. That master known as Jesus upon your planet is a master among many but one whom you are all aware of, I believe. This master had a great ability to experience in a purified form the emotions of which his waking consciousness became aware. You also may do this, my friends, and I urge you to attempt to follow the teaching of the one who is known to you as Jesus. This man maintained an inner contact with his infinite Father and he experienced each moment for that moment and thereby was able to absorb and use the experience which was his reason of coming. He left an example for you to follow. Many others have done the same.

It has been a great privilege to meet you. I am hopeful that I will be able to speak with you again. I hope that in some small way I have been able to share a thought which may be helpful with you. My blessings upon each of you. I will leave you now. I am Teronn. Farewell and love, my brothers.

(Side one of tape ends.) ❧

Sunday Meditation
June 23, 1974

(Carla channeling)

I am Hatonn. I am with you once again, my friends, in the love and the light of our infinite Creator. We are surrounded by love. You are surrounded by the same love and that which flows between us makes us one. We are here, my friends, in your skies at this time to speak with those upon your planet who desire to hear our voices. We sing an anthem of praise to the Creator. We offer the rejoicing and the ecstasy of all of these portions of reality in hopes that the light we share may reflect upon you and that we may see reflected back a growing awakening of the light and the portion of reality which deals with each of you. This is a somewhat stately and slow-moving task. We have not been hasty, my friends. We have observed that which we have attempted and we have in many cases altered our methods. We have tried many new ways as time passed upon your planet and we are progressing in our program in such a way that we hope to give you the most completely efficient display of that which we have to give you and that we *(inaudible)*.

And what do we have to give you, my friends? We have to give you most of all a door. Only a doorway. Only a suggestion. We have to give you the suggestion of another world. Another complete reality. A reality that transcends this reality, that includes this reality, that explains this reality, that will completely outlast this reality and to which reality you will repair after this brief experience upon the earth plane.

We can give you this suggestion of eternity. We can offer you our suggestions as to how to approach this doorway. We have spoken many times of meditation. This is the most efficient way of approaching this door, the desire within you to go through the door and that alone will lead you through. Meditation, my friends, creates the possibility of nearing the door.

What do we have to give you? We have to give you something that you are seeking. It is only important to those who are already aware that they do not have what they are seeking. This is our great difficulty in speaking with you. We can only speak to those who already know that there is something to speak about. To those people to whom reality within the illusion is acceptable, our words will be nothing and less than nothing. To those people who are seeking our words will find a place. Our words will become your words, my friends, as you seek. For as you seek you will find, and as you are seeking upon the same path which we have trod, our thoughts and your thoughts will become as one and we will vibrate in harmony.

What do you seek? You are already aware of the very seed of that which you seek. What are you going to do to seek it? My friends, we suggest that you look at your meditation as the seed which is growing in the rich soil of your physical existence. It will bear fruit within your existence. And the fragrance and the beauty which meditation sheds throughout the illusion will last far beyond the illusory flower, for the gifts of this fruit last forever.

Allow the seed of meditation to be endlessly nurtured within each day and, my friends, that which you need to do to bloom will come to you. The fruit which you need to supply to be of service to others will be possible for you to produce. The energy which you need to grow and flourish will be yours and when you need rest there will be time for rest for once you are committed to the gentle cycles of eternity the physical illusion very quietly falls into place.

We are most pleased to be speaking with you. We would like to transfer this contact at this time. I am Hatonn.

(Carla channeling)

I am Hatonn. I am again with this instrument. I am very happy to be with you and to be able to speak with you. At this time I will ask if there are any questions.

Questioner: *(Inaudible).*

I am reluctant to speak ahead of the time appointed. All will be well. You must work for this is a matter of free will. Do you understand?

Questioner: *(Inaudible).*

Carla: I'm just not getting anything except a contact point. The contact is just strong. They just … they're sending light.

Questioner: *(Inaudible).*

You would understand this section as headquarters. We are a field organization. The activities of our united peoples are manifold and varied and we have recourse to a central organism which is somewhat like a computer but which does not become classified as an inanimate object in your system of understanding as it is at present. This computer-like entity is made of thought and is dimensionless, thus unifying that which is somewhat diverse. This means that instructions may be set in … in a more specific way than by contacts such as this one. This computer-like entity has powers within the realm of mass. We are not operating under this type of *(inaudible)*. We may work in time *(inaudible)*. We may speak flexibly *(inaudible)*. We have different jobs to do. There are conditions under which activities of the central organization and we in the field may merge. These conditions are very stringent.

As to why those particular people were chosen we can explain it best by telling you that we were looking for people of a specific type of vibration. These were people who have been intended for his particular experience at this particular time. The one known as Uri is an exceptional and rare person in that he is not native to this planet except for his inclination. His powers are only a small part of that which he had awareness of previous to this excursion into this density.

Andrija Puharich is a person who has worked within this planet's influence in other incarnations. His progress through several incarnations along the path of service has been very steady. He has desired to be of service on a planetary level through several lifetimes and he will be true to this desire. For this reason we have asked that he be the keeper of this small *(inaudible)*.

What they have seen is a result of who they are. The fact that their vibrations *(inaudible)* and that they are not either one able to relax and meditate is somewhat regrettable, not because of our convenience but because there is much comfort to the spirit to be found within meditation. When one is weary *(inaudible)* without meditation discomfort is somewhat *(inaudible)*.

Do we have further questions?

Questioner: What is the purpose of your *(inaudible)*?

The one who questions knows this answer. It is an advertisement. We are aware that this thought is already within your mind. An advertisement that cannot be proven but an advertisement that has increased in specificity from previous advertisements. We mentioned earlier that we [are] experimenting, trying new things, attempting to spread our message in each and every way that we can think of that does not revoke the unalterable law of free will. You are already aware of the procedure by which doubt may be maintained even though the power of the one known as Uri cannot be disproven. By the same token it cannot be identified.

Questioner: *(Inaudible).*

We seek power. We find it in your atmosphere. We do not mine or disturb the ecology of your atmosphere but we are recharged, as it were. It may be that this landing will not occur as planned or will occur in an altered form for we are not experiencing the degree of acceptance that we had hoped. It is possible for us to accomplish our goal at a slower rate but quite nearly invisible. This may be chosen as a better path.

Questioner: *(Inaudible).*

My friends, be of good faith. We cannot speak to you directly on this matter. Bring the wisdom that is within you and you will discover the true answer to your question.

Are there any other questions?

(No further queries.)

My brothers, as I found you so I leave you: surrounded by love, made totally one by light. I am the one known to you as Hatonn. Adonai, my friends.

Saturday Meditation
June 29, 1974

(T channeling)

[I am Hatonn.] Greetings, my friends, in the love and the light of the infinite Creator. It is a pleasure to once again be with you, my friends. We are in a craft high above your planet. We come to you this evening with a few words that you may call advice.

We are here, my friends, to assist you in any way possible. It is only necessary, my friends, for you to avail yourself. The best method, of course, to avail yourself to our help, to our thoughts is through meditation. Meditation opens the doorway—the doorway that leads to truth. The truth you seek will be realized by all of you in time *(inaudible)*. Some members of your group are active in their seeking. Others not so active. But all, my friends, are seeking *(inaudible)* and will eventually arrive at the same realizations.

Do not concern yourselves that one or another member of your group seems to, shall we say, stray away just a little. Many peoples of your Earth will soon not begin to seek, but rather quicken the rate of their seeking or change the direction of their seeking. Many peoples now seem to be actively engaged in seeking only physical experience. And many of these, my friends, are so very close to the turning point where they will turn inward and begin to seek. It will be a fact, my friends, that many of these people once they have begun to seek will be exposed to some small degree of knowledge. And will in fact turn away and at least for the moment not accept what they have been exposed to.

This will come to you and to others members of your group as disappointment to you, my friends. But, always [look] ahead—not backward. Look ahead at the new souls who will be seeking. Look only to the ones, my friends, who are interested, who are actively seeking. The others will come back. Allow no negative, or as little as possible, to block your path of your service because of people who seemingly reject what *(inaudible)*.

This seems to be on your Earth plane a large reason for, shall we say, *(inaudible)* in many things that your peoples attempt to do. This is their doting [on] their failures and to a great degree ignoring their successes. This *(inaudible)* … This is nothing other than negative thinking. Actively employ the positive, my friends. Squeeze out as much as possible the negative in your thinking and also in your spiritual seeking, and your spiritual consciousness. Meditation may relinquish, it is the answer, my friends, to this problem. Meditation may answer you in subtle ways *(inaudible)*.

I would now like to attempt to transfer this contact to another instrument. I am *(inaudible)*.

(Carla channeling)

I am Hatonn. I am now with this instrument. As I saying, we request that you attempt at all times [to] concentrate your energy on those positive forces within your thinking in order that as you attempt to perform your service to the Creator, you may perform a true service and avoid infringing upon that very service by negativity. It is to be remembered, my friends, that service to others is service to oneself. Notice that we do not say that service to others is like unto service to oneself. There is no similarity between others and ourselves—there is identity. There is completion and unity. Therefore, that which is felt of a negative nature towards a sheep of the flock is felt towards oneself, and is felt towards the Creator. This enters the service which you [are] attempting to give to yourself and to the Creator through service to another and causes a blot or a stain upon the perfect service you would have performed. It must be remembered that each person is a completely free entity whose independence must in no way be shaken and yet whose identity remains one with you.

It is necessary to walk with the feet of each whom you wish to serve. It is necessary to look through this man's eyes. And it is necessary to observe precisely what this person is observing. At that time, my friends, you are capable of accepting this person's oneness with you on an intellectual *(inaudible)* level. On the level of *(inaudible)* spirituality there is no need for such detailed understanding. To be one with another person, with a planet, with a rock, with a tree, or with a star, it would all be equally possible. But, you wish your service and so we speak to you upon the identification of yourself with the person whom you serve.

(The message is interrupted.)

I am Hatonn. I am sorry for delay. I will continue.

The question then, my friends, is how to understand in a true and final way the identity between yourself and each one whom you serve. There is no intellectual way to do this, my friends. Within the holy work which [was] recorded following the actions of the master known to you as Jesus lies very revealing passages upon this subject. The master known to you as Jesus said that any [one] who fed a hungry man or clothed a naked one, or visited those in prison or helped the widows and orphans had done this for this master's sake. For even as they had done this to the least of his brothers, they had done it unto him.

We are aware that is almost impossible for the human mind while entrapped in the chemical illusion to truly believe that other men are identical to yourself. Thus, it is far more possible through faith that you may begin to understand that each man whom you wish to serve is the Creator. In a higher source, you and they can merge and it is this seed which we suggest that you develop in your understanding. We will have great need of your understanding in the days to come. It is important that you do not deal in any negative way with those who would request answers to questions. Therefore, we hope that you will take these thoughts and allow them to grow as you meditate.

Negativity is a type of power. It has many, many manifestations. Those religions which you know of as Oriental or Eastern personify these negative impulses in many beautiful shapes of gods and goddesses. While you who are dwelling within, as you would call it, Western culture, can think of negative manifestations in the terms of Satan and demons. Modern science with its intellectual explanations has derived a great multitude of [physiological] phrases and descriptions for these negative manifestations. All of these manifestations are indications that those who are aware of them are under the illusion that they are not one with the Creator. They are all expressions of separation and isolation. There is only one true positive method of polarization. It may go by many different names, but [you] may identify it because of its simple unity, that which is sought being union with the Creator. Under whatever name you may find this, you may be sure that within this path lies positivity.

At this time I will attempt to transfer this contact. I am Hatonn.

(Don channeling)

I am with the instrument. I am Hatonn. I will continue using this instrument. It is a privilege to be able to use all of the instruments who are present. It is not often that we are able [to use] all present as instruments for the communications of our thoughts.

We of the Confederation of Planets in the Service of the Infinite Creator are very, very privileged to be working with those who are upon the surface aware of their need to serve their fellow man. This awareness, my friends, is a very natural thing. It is an awareness that is a product of maintained contact with reality. Many of the peoples of your planet at this time are not aware of the need for service. My friends, this is the way that Creation is designed. It is designed so that each part of it should provide a service, a freely given service to support all of the rest of the Creation. It is only necessary to look about you to realize this, to realize that all parts are performing a service.

Even though your service may seem to be extremely small, it is, I can assure you, as great as the largest service that you can think of. For service, my friends, is service, regardless of how you interpret it. A blade of grass performs a service. It performs its service to the very limit of its ability. And yet its service is a great as the service of a tree which is many times, many, many times the size the tiny blade of grass. For the tree is also performing [to] the limit of its ability its service.

All that is necessary, my friends, is for you to recognize that this is what is occurring in the Creation that surrounds you. All that is necessary is for you to recognize how to perform the service that you may give. All that is necessary for you to realize this is for you to become aware as simply as the blade of grass, or as the tree has become aware to serve, simply by being, being in a way we have expressed as being in meditation. For through this process you will understand and you will serve, for this you have always intended to do just as every other part of the creation of the Father. It is only when man forgets his real creation's purpose that he becomes isolated and lost and unable to avail himself of the love that is given to him by all of the rest of the Creation. Become aware of your service. Become aware of your purpose. Do this through meditation and you will awaken. You will awaken to the ecstasy that was meant to be experienced by each part of this infinite creation.

It has been a great privilege speaking with you this evening. I shall leave this group at this time. I am known to you as Hatonn. It has been my service to speak using these instruments this evening. We shall use the other instruments at another time. Adonai. Adonai vasu.

Tuesday Meditation
July 2, 1974

(Carla channeling)

I am with this instrument. I am Hatonn. We are sorry to have difficulty contacting this instrument. We find that this instrument's attentions are not evenly concentrated within the meditative state and we suggest that she allow her mind to become unified within one vibration. This instrument is somewhat fatigued. However, we have been conditioning her while we have [been] speaking. We believe that we may now proceed.

That which you are speaking of is not the phenomena which you are waiting for. There is another one of a more local nature. There was a sign available for you on the night in mention which some of you saw. The general and gradual effect within the night sky will be accomplished over a period of time. And you will have no doubt of its progress because those of your technology, which you call scientists, will speak, offering explanations of the subject as its progress occurs more and more within the night sky.

It is a very difficult thing to communicate specific information. We communicated several pieces of information to you which in some cases were somewhat confused. However, there was an occurrence in the night sky upon the night we mentioned at the changing of the season. And if you will remain aware of comments from those who are called scientists, you will discover the gradual effect in the night sky of which you are searching.

Have you any other questions regarding this or on any other subject?

Questioner:

(Inaudible)

The question is, rather, why all do not acquire these powers. We are not being facetious. All of you have so many powers due to the fantastic amount of energy in your body, not of a physical nature, not of light nature, that you are capable of phenomena far, far greater than anything Uri Geller can do. Uri himself only vaguely remembers what he can do. I am afraid that due to the extreme isolation which marked the illusion chosen by those of your planet you can remember nothing for the most part of the birthright of your energy.

Those who, after watching Uri, are able to demonstrate a certain amount of power, are simply remembering how reality works. It is not an intellectual process. It is a direct process. It is a process of consciousness. As each tiny portion of the universe is made of light, molded and shaped by consciousness or love, consciousness directed can mold light into new forms. This is direct use of energy. This should be the norm.

In a very mild way, Uri can demonstrate what is normal to us. Those who watch him and who duplicate his demonstration have simply allowed themselves to fully remember that portion of their normal ability. Your thought is more powerful than any physical illusion. Thus it is said in your holy works that faith can move mountains. Faith is in consciousness whereas a mountain is that which consciousness has molded and can unmold at will. The strange and unusual thing is to watch man upon Earth go through a long process of analysis and technological tool-using in order to do what is a very fundamental and simple job.

Does that answer your question?

Questioner:

(Inaudible)

Continue in meditation. There is a long road, not long in time but in sacrifice, of that which is illusion. It is entirely within your grasp depending upon your desire to become capable of moving mountains. There is much of the illusion that must be shed. And in many cases this is too painful for the entity to accept. However, if the entity accepts those things which must be done, the entity will discover that she is a person who can move mountains.

Is there another question?

Questioner:

(Inaudible)

My friends, I wish to say to you tonight a word or two concerning your vulnerability. We know how easy it is to become used to anything and so cease feeling the miraculous side of it. It is possible to do that with both the positive and negative feelings. And because of the difficulty of life within the physical illusion, the ability to be invulnerable is highly prized upon your planet.

(Tape ends.)

Wednesday Meditation
July 3, 1974

(H channeling)

(Inaudible)

(Carla channeling)

I am now with this instrument. I am Hatonn. I greet you once again, my friends. It is my privilege and pleasure to be here for it is our greatest pleasure to serve those of you who are seeking the truth.

I would like to tell you a little story about a person who was much like each of you. His thoughts were as your thoughts, and in his, as you would say, work-a-day world he was neither perfectly good nor perfectly evil, but somewhere in the middle, attempting to do the best that he could. This man carried about his ankle a ball and chain, as you call it, a heavy weight attached with an unbreakable lock. And everywhere he went, he had to take infinite pains to make each step. This man spent … many years carrying—this instrument has made an error. We will attempt to continue. This person spent many years attached to his ball and chain. He grew accustomed to it and he thought that it was a normal situation. One day he discovered some information that interested him. It was information on how to remove that particular type of ball and chain from his ankle. He followed the instructions, not perfectly, but acceptably and the ball and chain became lighter and this caused him to become interested in the instructions. And as he practiced the instructions, his ball and chain gradually disappeared.

My friends, your physical bodies and your personal sense of self which you call ego is a ball and chain to you, making your infinite spirit to take great pains in order to move about. You, whose birthright is freedom, have to crawl about on the sides of … using mechanical conveyances when within you is freedom to be anywhere at anytime. We offer you some simple instructions on how to lighten and remove the hampering limitations of your ball and chain. This set of instructions has to do with meditation. In meditation, my friends, you are separating the sense of body and the sense of ego from the sense of consciousness. And you are freeing your consciousness to be at one with the source of love and light that is the infinite Creator. Only through meditation and its allied pursuits can you remove your own need of this ball and chain.

We do not speak unkindly of this ball and chain because it is necessary for you at this time. You have chosen, you have chosen these limitations in order that you may bring yourself face to face with lessons of the universe. You are learning lessons of love and patience and of understanding. If you are not learning them, then you will have another chance at the same lessons at a future time. And you will meet that lesson until you have learned it. There is no failing in this type of school. In this planetary school, one simply continues in the same grade until one has learned all the lessons. There is no sense of failing, there is only a sense of graduation when one had learned all of the lessons of one cycle.

Each of you is within his own cycles, and the lessons are necessary and good. But, my friends, you may speed your trip to graduation very, very much by the use of meditation. Through meditation you make contact with the infinity of understanding which lies within the consciousness of the Creator. When you come back to the limitation of your physical body and personality you are carrying with you an infinite amount of understanding which you may choose to put to use.

Therefore, we urge you to meditate, as always. We especially wished to speak upon meditation for we are aware that we are speaking to a new person. What we have to say is quite simple. No matter how many or how few times you hear us speak, you will find that we are offering that which we understand to be understanding. And the greatest tool towards bringing you freedom of understanding is meditation.

I would like to transfer this contact again. I am Hatonn.

(T channeling)

I am Hatonn. I am now with this instrument. I will say, my friends, that lessons learned and knowledge gained during your meditation has to be applied in your daily life. This is your choice. Meditation alone will give you the awareness you need to adjust your daily activities or habits, to [gain] a finer appreciation of your own and the peoples you meet and the needs of these people. But, my friends, an active attempt at application to your daily situations is necessary, lest your conscious mind stray too far from the lessons and the awareness that you began to acquire in your meditations.

Each person that *(inaudible)* sets up a, shall I say, a field of action and interaction between you and yourself. We are saddened to say that in many instances upon your planet Earth, this field contains very much negativity. To learn to recognize when one is either acting or reacting in a negative way is one of the great benefits of your meditations. To know this and then to make the attempt to adjusts one's conscious behavior to a more positive way of acting is the best possible [way] to bring all aspects, both physical and spiritual, as close to one as your present awareness will allow.

This is very difficult to do at times because upon your planet in your physical illusion the natural reaction to negativity is negativity. And this, my friends, makes participating in it only create more negativity. To counter negativity with a positive attitude tends to at least equalize the negativity if not overcome it a little.

So, my friends, do not contribute more negative thought and action to your physical illusion. Always to the degree that is possible exude positive thoughts, thoughts of love for every situation. *(Inaudible)*. Love consciously directed at another person or a particular situation is doubly positive, my friends, simply because not only is the love itself involved but the, shall I say, the positive thought that caused the emanation of that love for the particular situation. So the love is compounded, my friends, when you send it to your fellow peoples *(inaudible)*.

I would like to at this time to attempt to transfer this contact to another instrument. I am Hatonn.

(E channeling)

(Inaudible)

(Carla channeling)

I am Telonn. I have spoken through this instrument before. I greet you in the love and in the light of our infinite Creator. I am privileged to speak with you. I am fairly new to speaking in groups such as yours. I have much to learn. I want to tell you that I have much to learn. I want you to know that I am as you. I am such as you. Those of us who are here from Telonn are such as you. And although the circumstances do vary within various groups of the Confederation of Planets in the Service of the Infinite Creator, the truth that we are basically such as you remains the same.

We are upon a planet. We have stepped across one blockage that you have yet to achieve. But there are many steps ahead of us. We are looking back and holding out our hands so that you may step over that blockage with as much ease as you possibly can. We wish to help you. We wish to share with you what we have. But we are not infallible. We can only communicate that which we think is truth. We suggest that you take nothing for granted in what we say. We suggest that you try what we suggest and see for yourself. It should not take very long for you to discover whether you think we may have something.

We are here to express the Creator's love and light. His consciousness, His understanding, His wisdom is love. That is all. We are not here to exact any promises or to make any demands. Only to be of service. Each choice is up to you completely.

This is what I wished to say to say to you. It has been a privilege. I will leave you. I leave you in the love and in the light of our infinite Creator. I am Telonn. Adonai vasu.

(H channeling)

I am Oxal. *(Inaudible)* in the love and the light of our infinite Creator. I am experiencing difficulty with this contact with …

I have desired to establish contact with this group this evening so that I may …

(Inaudible) ☙

Sunday Meditation
July 14, 1974

(Unknown channeling)

[I am Hatonn.] We greet you in the love and in the light. It is a great privilege to be with you this evening. It is a great privilege to be with you [at] any and all occasions when you find time to prevail yourselves in our thoughts.

We of the Confederation of Planets in the Service of the Infinite Creator are always with you. This seems strange to you that we would be at all times with you. But this, my friends, is the case. Your awareness of the illusion is such that you do not understand the real properties of that principle that you understand as time. You are that principle that you understand as space. My friends, it is possible for you to be in one place or all places at the same instance. For, my friends, in truth there is only one instance and that instance is the one that you are experiencing. There is an illusion of past and an illusion of future. However, my friends, you exist only in the present. The other illusions are never *(inaudible)*.

In this present it is possible for you to be in constant contact with all you so desire [at this time.] For this reason the Confederation of Planets in the Service of our Infinite Creator are at all times in touch with those whom we serve. It does not require a portion of what you know as time to make the contact that you desire. You have the contact at all times. It is constantly with you. All that it requires is your desire to initiate the conditions such as has this channel. Simply by desiring he has *(inaudible)* received that which he desires. Our aim in understanding *(inaudible)*. This instrument has become able to receive and then transmit our thoughts at any time he so desires. He has done this through practicing daily meditation. His desire that he be of service to his fellow man in channeling our thoughts has created his ability to do so.

We are here to aid any of those of this planet who desire to serve others, to serve peoples who dwell upon this planet. We will serve by giving to those who will meditate our understanding, our understanding of the law of *(inaudible)* given to all men by their Creator.

At this time I will *(inaudible)* of another instrument.

(Pause)

(Unknown channeling)

I am now with this instrument. I am Hatonn.

That which we wish to give you, my friends, is that which you are seeking. And the weapons that we have to use are few. We can speak to you when you meditate, through intellectually sent words, and through direct contact.

Perhaps we should say a word or two about that which we are attempting to help you with. Understanding is a term which is very ambiguous. It is very general. It is a term which does not specify what the content of understanding is. We wish to explain that understanding includes understanding of each and every portion of the Creation of all that you can see, feel, touch, imagine or comprehend. Understanding is unitary. Understanding is light. Understanding is direct awareness of love.

Consider your planet, my friends, as it moves in its orbit. It can be seen to be a complete and unitary orb. It can be understood as an entity for it is light and it is love. Let us approach closer. We may now differentiate. There are different physical shapes and sizes of objects which we may call air and land and ocean. And we may understand each of these things to be a direct awareness of love, the love of the Creator, Who created these things. We move again closer. We stand upon the surface of this [world] and we see that it is irregularly shaped and that it is covered with all manner of living things and that they are doing many, many different things and thinking many, many different thoughts. And we can see that there are many things to understand upon this planet. And we see that this understanding is, in essence, still one thing. For each of these is a direct example of the love, the original Thought of love, of the Father of us all.

Understanding is unitary. It does not change, it does not [evolve] within the definitions of changing and [evolving] within that which you are witnessing. It merely presents to that person who now understands the awareness of that which he is observing is love. It is this which we are attempting to give to you: a unitary understanding of the love and the light of the infinite Creator. You may understand what you will. The world is for you to understand. You may understand to the extent that you are able to imagine. As you meditate, allow your thoughts to rise upward into the vibration of that which is love and light, so that you become one with the original Thought of the Creator. It is to this that we point you.

I would like to transfer this contact at this time. I will leave this instrument. I am Hatonn.

(Pause)

(Unknown channeling)

I am Hatonn. I am now with this instrument. *(Inaudible).*

(Unknown channeling)

(Inaudible)

(Unknown channeling)

I am Hatonn. I greet you in the love and in the light of our infinite Creator. I greet you in fire, in wind, and with the forces of your planet which also greet you. I am at this time not too far from you. I am far above you, and yet I greet you within your heart. For I am all things and I am you. It is my privilege to speak with you this evening. I am aware that you are seeking the truth.

How hard are you working my friends to live the best life? Are you attacking each moment as if you could wrest out of it spiritual awareness and happy results? This is indeed the approved mode of operation upon your planet, and it is difficult for you who are within the physical illusion to avoid approaching the illusion with this attitude of active competition against an alien environment. My friends, as long as you retain this consciousness that you must exact from an alien universe that which is yours, you will have struggle and difficulty.

Question yourself as to who it was that accomplished the so-called miracles that occurred within the experience of the master known to you as Jesus. Remember that according to your holy works he did not take credit for this working of miracles, but instead gave full credit to the Creator Who was within him and did the work for him. My friends, this is a great secret. It is a simple change in point of view, but it is centrally important to your understanding of that which is about you. You do not live your life, my friends, any more than I live my life. You look over your shoulder and the Creator lives your life. Your consciousness and you learn but if you let that which is within you, which you may call a spark of the Creator, do that which is to be done, all things will come to you naturally that belong to you. My friends, if you were to be completely, unalterably contented, then your existence would then … this illusion would not be very useful to you.

The point of view of which we are speaking certainly does not give one a perfect contentment. What it does give to one is a means for a *(inaudible)* each crisis may be accepted, dealt with, and dropped away, in such a manner that those who see you may learn by your example that it is possible to live in an illumined fashion.

As you meditate, my friends, clarify within yourselves that which you seek and allow yourselves to become aware at this time of the unity of all that is about you, with yourself. Allow yourself to become aware that your environment is one of unity and that that which you seek is completely within yourself. And allow the peace which follows upon this awareness to expand throughout your conscious mind.

We wish to give you understanding, my friends. This understanding is very simple and it cannot be attacked, nor can life itself be attacked. It comes naturally, without pride, humbly, easy to accept and easy to forget. Yet this understanding, my friends, may lift each of you into the presence wherein you may lift yourself as have we. We do not tell you this in a sense of great pride and achievement, for we are aware that we are simply a step ahead on the path. We tell you this because we wish you to know that this path leads upward and that it is possible to follow it. Accept this understanding, as it becomes natural to you, not before. But we hope that we may, through you and others like you, share this understanding with as many as possible.

I would like to transfer this contact at this time. I am Hatonn.

(Inaudible)

(Tape ends.)

Tuesday Meditation
July 23 1974

(Unknown channeling)

I am Hatonn. I greet you, my friends, in the love and in the love of our infinite Creator. It is once more a great privilege to speak to you. As always, we of the Confederation are privileged to be of service to those who seek our service. We are here in great numbers and yet at this time our service is sought but very little. This somewhat saddens us, for we had hoped that more of those of your planet would have initiated a seeking outside of their illusion. It will soon be time, my friends, for them to experience a catalyst which may in some instances *(inaudible)* their seeking.

My friends, in truth, the only reason for the illusion that you now experience is to act as a catalyst, to act in such a way as to generate a condition which helps the individual to initiate a spiritual seeking. It might seem strange that you should go through such an unusual experience only for the purpose of stimulating your spiritual seeking. However, this, in fact, is true. Each of you in his daily experience is acted upon in many ways. The actions and experiences that you feel cause changes in your attitude, cause reactions which you interpret and identify as emotion. All of this, my friends, is for a specific purpose and you have chosen to experience your present illusion in order to achieve this purpose. The purpose, my friends, is the evolution of your spirit. You dwell within a *(inaudible)*. This is a *(inaudible)* an illusory culture *(inaudible)* identified by the very few.

Yes, my friends, as you know, only the very few of those who now dwell upon your planet are now aware of the purpose of their existence. They have not reached in their conscious evolution that salient point of transition, from that point which causes a great, great acceleration in their evolution in the spiritual sense. That point at which they become consciously aware and then upon becoming consciously aware of their existence in its *(inaudible)* begin to utilize the conscious manner for those experiences that are to teach them, use that *(inaudible)* in an efficient manner in order to accelerate and stimulate, by their own efforts, their spiritual *(inaudible)*.

I ask each of you here tonight to question yourselves, for this you desire. The individual shall ask this *(inaudible)* transition, from blind reaction to the catalytic nature of mind *(inaudible)* to conscious and full utilization of such lessons, or, "Am I yet in that period of transition?" My friends, each of you will draw your own conclusion. It is very difficult living within a society such as yours. *(Inaudible)* primarily to the gratification of the physical within the illusion, to separate this thinking from such folly and to seek that which is not transient.

My friends, I am with this instrument this evening to help you realize the importance of first totally understanding yourself, and then generating the discipline itself that is necessary to maximize the effectiveness of the experiences that are now creating the pathway of your spiritual *(inaudible)*. We have spoken to you many times about the nature of this [bridge,] about the total unity that permeates all men and all things that is the Creator, that is the Creator. Of this you are consciously aware. But, my friends, this knowledge must be constantly put to use within this *(inaudible)*. In order to do this it is necessary to spend time each day in meditation. It is necessary to be aware of your reaction, to be aware of your emotions. My friends, it is necessary for you to be aware. To be aware, my friends, is to know yourself. To first know yourself, this is the initiation of awareness. With this knowledge you then can begin your climb for those things which are the expressions of our *(inaudible)*. Only then, my friends, can you effectively apply this knowledge. It is harder to do this, my friends. It is very necessary that you spend time in meditation.

(Pause)

I am sorry. The instrument was analyzing the communication. He will have left at this time clearly his mind. I shall attempt to continue. Please be patient.

As I was saying, self-awareness is of the utmost importance. My friends, each action, each thought, each … each word that you say is of utmost importance, for this, my friends, is what is you in expression. And what is you in expression to those about you … is of very great importance, for, my friends, this is the reason for experiencing the illusion.

Many of the people of your planet have experienced that illusion that you now experience many, many times, and yet they are experiencing and will experience it again and again. And they learn, but they learn by the blind action from the experiences that befall them. And this then changes their attitude, holds their consciousness, evolves their spirit, but this evolution is not accompanied by being conscious, [and living a] purposeful life but the action of the illusion. They simply evolve. They do not stimulate the true knowledge [that] this evolves.

Become aware of what is happening. Become aware of how you are growing, growing and understanding. And then with this awareness, know your thoughts. Know your thoughts by *(inaudible)*. Accelerate your evolution in the direction that you desire. This, my friends is the great turning point. This, my friends is a place long awaited. Mark it well. Utilize this information. Discipline your thinking. Create your own evolution. This is the difference, my friends, between mastership and simple growth of spirit. And what creates this difference? No matter how you may express it, there is one, and only one, thing that will allow you to totally and completely know your own *(inaudible)*, to totally and completely make this transition from emotional reaction, from a blind and stumbling reaction to your environment to a controlled and sincere seeking path.

My friends, the only thing that will allow you to do this is meditation. Daily meditation will create the foundation necessary and then, my friends, each of you will grow at such a fantastic rate that it will be beyond even your own *(inaudible)* that you *(inaudible)* attained beyond anything that you *(inaudible)*. Spiritual growth, my friends, is the function of the individual. It is not given to you. It is something that you must find. It is something that you have always had, but it must be uncovered. This must be done through your own activities, through your own understanding. We are able to provide only the guideposts, only the simple instructions, only a helping hand. It is you that must, through your own efforts and perseverance, uncover particle by particle that truth that permeates. By only yourselves in all of this creation may this be done at any rate that you desire. Your desire, my friends, is *(inaudible)*.

We extend to you a helping hand. We implore you to take it. Develop your awareness. Know your own *(inaudible)* eliminate the personal biases which have been generated by experiences in your rather unusual illusion. We establish our … the single truth that is all things. This is the simple process followed by all of those who have attained the enlightenment that causes them to be known as masters. This is the simple process followed by the one known to you as Jesus. This simple process has [been] spelled out to you in many, many ways, many writings in your holy works, and in many other ways, and yet this simple process seems to be very difficult to acquire.

My friends, the only thing that limits your application in this process is your desire to apply.

Meditate. Know the magnitude of your desire and then know yourself. Express the love and understanding of our infinite Creator. This can only be done if you first continue yourself. Continue yourself through self-knowledge. Continue yourself through this infinite love. Continue yourself through the meditation that is so necessary to [come] to the conscious state, totally one with the infinite Thought that is all things. When you do, my friends, you will know you have done for you will experience an ecstasy beyond, beyond anything that you have known.

(Pause)

At this time I will leave this instrument. I am Hatonn. It has been a great, great privilege to speak with this group this evening. This message this evening has been a slightly more personal message. It is hoped that it has been *(inaudible)* and instructed it is hoped that each of you will climb *(inaudible)* to be in your personal secret that has been *(inaudible)*. My friends, I will say once more, each of you has this desire. If you did not have this desire you would not have received this message. I shall leave this instrument at this time. I am Hatonn. Adonai vasu *(inaudible)*.

(Unknown channeling)

I am Hatonn. I return to you very briefly because I wish to speak to one who questions. We wish to emphasize that that person who is attempting to give service to others need not worry as to recognizing the service that is to be performed. As we have stated earlier this evening it is necessary primarily to remove all doubt within yourself as to the identity of yourself. You must by some method realize that you are fragmenting your precious consciousness when you desire more than one thing. And, my friends, there are very few upon your planet who do not desire more than one thing. It is necessary only [to] desire to be in the presence of the Creator and to know His love. If that desire is perfect within you, you will be of enormous service. You cannot help being of enormous service if you are aware of your identity in seeking. Only seek to know the Father and you will pour forth the fruits of this knowledge as readily as the sun gives light.

Indeed, my friends, your problem in truth is and will be not what your service will be, but whether you are capable of accepting each service. Remember to yourself that the master known as Jesus had his chance to pass the terrible pain of death by, and after deliberation he chose to accept that heavy service. The service itself was quite obvious to him. He had a choice as to whether or not he should take it as he was quite aware of the service. So it always is with you, my friends, if you are aware of your spiritual seeking and are not fragmenting that consciousness which is your very identity by desiring various objects within the illusion.

Seek to know the Father and your service will follow very naturally. Service cannot be given by you, my friends. You will have nothing to do with any service that you give. You are a channel for the Father. It is necessary only to keep yourself open, and the love and the light that is needed by others will flow through you. You cannot adjust, interpenetrate or confuse the service of the Father. You can only channel it thorough your physical being. You can only let it shine out of your eyes and let it flow through your fingers. Each of you will find yourself very much placed before your service. You will know it and it will be your choice whether or not to accept it. Have no fear that you must do this or do that in order to be of service to know the Father. And those sheep which are in need of the light which you have will be drawn to you irresistibly. We can give you no dogma or creed for each person's path is different, being the culmination of all that he has is known and remembered for many, many lifetimes. But each person's path, my friends, has one single end and it is to that end that you may look through meditation to know the Father's love and light and to prepare yourself always for the service that will be yours, and that is yours now.

Be aware, my friends, that you are already serving. Each of you in this room has served, is serving, and will serve. We are not talking at this time to those who are not of service already. We are speaking to those who are already seriously seeking. And so we give encouragement. We give you our support and our love and our light. We are with you always. Know this, my friends. Never doubt it. Call upon us and we will be there to bless each of you. I hope that this has also been a help to you who seek. I will leave you. I am the one known as Hatonn. Adonai.

(Pause)

(Unknown channeling)

I am with the instrument. I greet you, my friends, in the love and in the light of our infinite Creator. It is a very great privilege to speak with you this evening. However, I will speak *(inaudible)*.

My friends, this evening I have one thing, one thing of which to remind you.

(Tape ends.)

Sunday Meditation
July 28, 1974

(Unknown channeling)

[I am Hatonn.] … and gives both great beauty and sweet smell, so as you open to that primary Thought which created you, you blossom within. I come, shall we say, with a watering can. I come to encourage your growth in the spirit, my friends. I urge you through your meditation neither to add nor to subtract. It is very easy to make demands of yourself and to attempt to accomplish goals through meditation. It is also an extremely likely happening that you will at some time attempt to remove some part of that which you are through your meditation.

We do not speak against these practices. They are simply outside of our interest. They are among the many, many choices which you have within your physical illusion, but there is one choice which is outside of the illusion and that choice, my friends, is the choice to seek your Creator. This is the choice that ultimately transcends illusion. And within this choice there is neither addition nor subtraction, but an opening precisely as you are now accomplishing, not even really aware that this is the heart of your seeking.

In your daily meditations, both in groups and alone, sit in meditation without thought of what you wish to accomplish. Only open in the direction of that which you are seeking. Imagine that this mortal physical body is a door which you may go through. Each of you will go through this door. It is not difficult to imagine this. It is called upon your planet, death. There is a certain joy connected for those who understand these things, with the idea of going through the door of the physical death. My friends, within you there are many such doors. They are opened and you transcend each shell when the experience for which it is provided is no longer necessary. If you truly seek to open yourself to the innermost core of all of these shells, your journey will be immeasurably quickened, so that you may at last become one with that which you seek.

That which you seek, my friends, is unimaginable. We can call it a thought, we can call it an impulse. You have the word consciousness in your language. In some dim way this concept of consciousness is correct. The source of all consciousness is the Creator. We are all a part of this consciousness. This consciousness is infinite. And in its infinity it yet remains a gloriously illuminating source of light, perfect light and love within each of the Creator's children.

That which you seek, then, rests within yourselves. The separation is within yourselves. This separation is not evil. This separation is functional. Your consciousness has been given you by all consciousness so that you may individually seek and find the beauty and the understanding which is the Creator. And all that is necessary, my friends, is that you do so. Open yourself and allow yourself to unfold inwardly so that you may blossom, not as you would at some particularly difficult time. Choose that as your higher self would choose. We speak to you on this subject at this time because we are aware of your questions.

This instrument is having a certain amount of difficulty maintaining contact as she is not aware of this information.

(Pause)

We will continue.

We simply wish to emphasize that in our experience it has been found that the attempt to decide what to do, even at the most spiritual level, will become a negative experience, although it requires additional amounts of patience. This is precisely the reason why these difficult situations arise. Patience is necessary in order to maintain the ability to keep contact through meditation with one's higher self. Circumstances which require the application of patience are designed to instruct one in patience. The answers that you are seeking will evolve with a naturalness which may be sudden but which will be able to be experienced without the negative effects of having imposed an arbitrary decision upon your higher self.

Mankind lives on this little ball, multiplies, and his kind are many. Upon his planet he considers himself a highly unusual being and master of all he surveys. Man is indeed master of all he surveys, if he is master of himself. This, my friends, has been in many cases misunderstood. To be master of yourself does not mean the ability to control, according to arbitrary decisions, that which you think and do. To be master of oneself is to know one's reality. This mastery is given, my friends, from within, through the gentle and passionless unfolding. And yet, my friends, there is no greater passion than the blazing desire which fills the heart of those who seek to know, to really know, the presence, the love, and the light of the Father.

I give you a paradox, my friends. There is nothing else to give you while I am speaking any language. But at this time I will maintain silence for a period while I condition each of you who desires it. After this period of conditioning, I will attempt to contact another instrument. I am Hatonn.

(Inaudible)

(Unknown channeling)

I am Laitos. I greet you, my friends, in the love and in the light of the One Who is All. I am very privileged to be with you. I am here to aid the brothers of Hatonn. It is my special privilege to be of service to those who desire to become instruments and join the service of the Creator in this way. I will be attempting to condition the one known as B1. I will also condition the one known as S, the one known as B2, the one known as M. I will attempt to make you aware of my presence in this room.

My blessings to each of you. I will be with you at any moment that you desire my presence, for this is my chosen specialty. If you take five minutes and you call for me, I will be there. At any time you can go into a light enough meditation so that you may call for this contact. I will, if you wish, attempt to bring you a conditioning wave. There are many ways of feeling this conditioning wave. However, the one thing that is common is that each of you will doubt. Accept this, my friends. Go right ahead and doubt. But if you wish to serve as an instrument, simply continue availing yourself, and it will not be long before you are able to register our contact and relay our thoughts to those who would wish to know them. It is indeed my privilege to be with you. I thank you for allowing me to speak.

I leave you, but only the sound of my voice is leaving you. Any five minutes that you wish to speak with me, I promise you I will be there. It does not take a great solemn meditation to begin to become a channel, for we are most eager to speak with you. And it is your seeking, more than any other characteristic, which creates the correct vibration for us to able to make contact.

I am Laitos. I leave you in love and in light. Adonai, my friends.

(Tape ends.)

Tuesday Meditation
July 30, 1974

(Unknown channeling)

I am Hatonn. I greet you, my friends, in the love and in the light of our infinite Creator. It is once more a great privilege to meet with this group. We, of the Confederation of Planets in the Service of the Infinite Creator, are always ready to serve those upon planet Earth who seek our service. It is a very great privilege to give this service to those who seek it. And, my friends, this is our entire purpose at this time, to offer to those who seek that which they seek.

There is, my friends, only one thing worth seeking. Nothing else is of any value. And that one thing, of course, is understanding; an understanding of your Creator's Thought. My friends, this is the only thing that lasts. Anything else that you might seek will be transitory and will vanish with time. When man realizes that this is his true objective, then he has made that great turning point in his development. We are here to aid those who have turned the corner, so to speak, turned the corner toward their ultimate goal, that goal of reuniting with their Creator.

People of planet Earth at this time seek many things, and yet how many of these things will last, last past the limits of their present physical life experience? Very few, my friends. Those few that will last are all of an identical nature. They are of a nature to be an increase in awareness, an increase of awareness of their Creator. We are here to help those who desire this increase of awareness find it.

We will help in many ways. There are many routes to this awareness, but each of these pathways is very similar. We are here this evening for a specific purpose. At this time, we wish to instruct this group on specific techniques of arriving at that which they seek. It is known that a group is limited by the understanding of the least of the group. The material that is given during a group meeting must always be tailored to the understanding of, shall we say, the newest of the group. For this reason, this evening we will begin on somewhat more of an advanced level, for this group we find to be quite advanced in its understanding.

This understanding, my friends, has nothing to do with your intellectual understanding, your ability to manipulate ideas, or propositions. This understanding, my friends, of which we speak, is your basic agent. It is much more than an intellectual idea. It is your awareness, which totally transcends all intellect and creates all of your present fallacies with respect to your fellow man.

This evening, my friends, with this instrument, we will speak to you at a somewhat higher level than we have in the past, in an effort to bring each of you that which you seek: a technique, my friends, of continuing to develop your awareness at a most satisfactory rate.

At this time my brother Oxal will speak for a short period through another instrument. At that time we will return to this instrument. Please be patient while I condition the other instrument.

(Pause)

(Inaudible)

(Unknown channeling)

Greetings, my friends, in the love and the light of the one infinite Creator. It is indeed a privilege to have the opportunity to speak with you for a short period this evening. We of the Federation *(inaudible)*. To be available to those who seek the understanding of the Creator and his *(inaudible)* as our brother Hatonn has mentioned we are aware that at this time that those present are, shall we say, at a level of awareness which shall allow our information to *(inaudible)*.

(Unknown channeling)

I am with this instrument. I am Hatonn. I will continue. I was saying that this evening we will bring to you certain ideas which are of a slightly more advanced level.

First, my friends, let us clear our minds as best we possibly can of all thoughts that you may have concerning your daily lives. My friends, let these thoughts of your daily lives drift away, for these are very transient thoughts. These thoughts will be gone in a few days. Let them go now. Let the influence that your material environment has upon your thinking, leave you. Let your mind be clear. Let it be as a child. Do not attempt to understand, do not attempt to understand, my friends, and then you will know. For you cannot understand by a process of trying. You must understand by a process of knowing. Do not try to come to a conclusion. Do not try to analyze. Do not try to utilize past experiences. Simply allow your mind to become clear.

When this is accomplished, my friends—and we are aware that you may not be able to accomplish this immediately but you may practice this at a later time—when you have done this, my friends, when you have allowed your mind to become clear, to become receptive and as a small child, then, my friends, become aware of yourself. Nothing else matters, simply yourself. Do not think about your thinking. Do not analyze yourself. Do not use the intellectual mind. Simply become aware of your own being. Allow this awareness to grow, to grow from a very clear and unfettered mind. Become aware of yourself and nothing else. Think of nothing else, my friends. Become aware of only yourself surrounded by nothing.

Try this now, my friends. Allow all other thoughts to escape, to be released, to no longer remain in your conscious mind. When you have done this, become aware of yourself, only yourself. Let this awareness of yourself expand. Let your own being expand. Let it move outward in all directions. Let it encompass all of infinity. Let it then know that it, in an infinitely expanded state, is all that there is. It is one in the same with every other thing, with every other experience, with every other particle, in this entire infinite creation. Nothing, my friends, is excluded. Know that you and all are one single being. Do not try to understand this. Simply practice these three simple steps. Clear your mind. Become aware of yourself, and then expand. Feel yourself expanding infinitely, until you touch every other particle in this creation. Then, my friends, you will know your true nature, for this is your true nature.

In the illusion that you now experience, man has been conditioned to think of himself as a separate or isolated being. This bias creates within you certain vibrations of thought which are unlike those vibrations that created you. We have given an exercise, an exercise in expanding awareness, so that you may change those vibrations of thought which have been brought about within your present illusion, so that you may return to that vibration that created you. That vibration is reality.

It is a very simple process, my friends. It does not require great knowledge. It does not require any knowledge. It simply requires knowing your true relationship with everything else that exists in this infinite creation. If you can accomplish these three simple steps, you will then be one with your Creator. Meditation and continued practice of this exercise will very greatly increase your awareness. You must know, my friends, that this oneness exists, that this oneness is. You cannot know this with the intellectual mind for it is very inferior to it. It is heavily biased within the illusion and will not be of great service to you in this undertaking.

It will be necessary that you spend some time first allowing your mind to become clear, then allowing the self-awareness to develop, and then allowing this awareness, this self, to expand—the all-important step, my friends. Feel yourself expanding in all directions, expanding infinitely in all directions, so that you encompass everything that there is. So that it is you and you are it. When you have accomplished this, you will no longer be able to identify anything that exists as anything but yourself. This identification will not be intellectual. You will not have to tell yourself this. It will be a simple reality, a reality that you experience automatically. As you breathe the air about you automatically you will experience this unity with every one and every thing that you meet.

And then, my friends, you will be known as a master, for this is all that is necessary to attain this dignity. This was all that was necessary as the man known to you as Jesus. He was aware of his relationship to the creation. He was aware that he and all were one. Each of you here tonight can accomplish this awareness very quickly, for you already have it within you. All that is necessary is that you practice, through meditation, this simple exercise necessary for cleansing from you the illusion which has temporarily created a condition of, shall we say, loss or misunderstanding. Your meditation, my friends, and the practice of this exercise will rapidly bring you into true focus out of the effect of the minor aberrations of thinking that have been impressed upon you in your present illusion.

Remember these steps well. Clear the mind. Become aware of yourself, and then expand. Expand infinitely and be one. If this is practiced in daily meditation you will no longer question. You will no longer question anything or any condition, for you will know, for you will be with that knowledge that has created you and is the creation. A very simple knowledge, my friends. It has been called by the people of your planet a knowledge of love. A knowledge of a love that is so intense that it is beyond expression in your language. This you will know. This you will experience. With this experience of infinite love you will then be able to serve. You will then be able to serve in a very, very great way. You will be able to bring to your brothers that which they truly desire. There will be in the very near future many of the peoples of planet earth developing this awareness. We are here to aid them in this development.

My friends, your illusion is heavily with you. And yet it is with you for a purpose. You have desired this experience. You have desired this test. You have desired these conditions. All of these conditions are for the purpose of your growth, just as they are for the purpose of the growth of all other entities within your illusion. You may now grow very rapidly. It is dependent only on your desire. We are aware of your true desire, for we are aware, quite simply, of the desire of all of the people of the planet. It is printed upon them as it is upon the cover of a book. It is as easily distinguishable as the coloring of the various lights that adorn your Christmas tree. There is a radiation from every individual that makes it impossible for those who are aware of this to mistake this desire, for it is color within this radiation. We have brought to you what is very obvious as to be your desire. We are very privileged to be able to do this, for, my friends, to do this is our desire.

We extend to you our infinite love as we extended to ourselves for we and you and all that there is is the same: one infinite, loving, totally loving Creator. Become aware of your reality. Become aware of your true nature. Become aware of your identity. This awareness will be total. You will very shortly attain. The speed at which you attain is only governed by your desire. Seek, my friends, and ye shall find. Everything awaits you. Those who you will serve, await you. This is your purpose. This is the only reason that you have selected your present experience. Shortly you will know, or shortly you will understand.

I will leave this instrument at this time. It has been a great privilege to speak with you this evening. I am Hatonn but I am also you. For you and I and everything else in this entire infinite creation are one thing. Adonai, my friends, Adonai vasu.

(Unknown channeling)

I am Hatonn. I greet you in the love and in the light of the One Who is All. It is my privilege to speak to you very briefly. It is my special privilege to condition those who desire to be instruments. I will be conditioning each of you. I would like to tell each of you what a pleasure it is to experience the vibration in this group at this time. The Earth, in general, emits a somewhat more dark painting, shall I say, in its vibration, and the experience of your vibration together is a very light spot in comparison to the surrounding darkness. It is as though it were night and as we look down we see two flickering campfires, but for the most part, no source of light. We greet the light as we see it and we are most pleased to be speaking with you.

My friends, I wish to say to you, be aware of yourself. As you learn each lesson attempt to remain enough aware of what you are doing and what you desire that the activity of meditation does not become separate from you. Meditation, my friends, shall not be something that you do if you wish to go on with anything. Meditation *is* you. I am sure that you are already aware that there are lions that guard the temple of understanding. You have become aware of several things already. We are not speaking with those who are beginning on the path. You have become aware already that outer experience is illusion and that reality lies within. And after you are aware of this, my friends, did the lions not harm you whenever you slipped and behaved as though you were not aware of this knowledge? We became aware that it was necessary to demonstrate the perfect love which you have become aware of. And since that time, my friends, have you not been painfully aware of the times when the lions turned on you when you demonstrated that which was not love? Now you stand at another initiation. There are many more. This one is an important one. It is a large step *(inaudible)*.

(Tape ends.)

Tuesday Meditation
August 6, 1974

(Unknown channeling)

… in the love and the light of our Creator. It is a very great privilege to *(inaudible)*. We of the Confederation of Planets in Service of the One Creator …

(Inaudible)

(Unknown channeling)

I am Hatonn, I greet you, my friends, in the love and the light of the One Creator … It is a very great privilege to speak to this group, to those who have arrived … I am what you apparently would call from the planet Hatonn. I am not in a physical body such as yours. I communicate through this instrument by thought. He receives my thoughts, so that they are part of him. To you, I have [chosen] to operate what you know as the flying saucers, the UFO's. However, I am not in a physical body at this time. But you have consented to be the physical body known as my brothers … our existence in the physical body as you … it will be quite physical to you … We are nonetheless the same. We regardless of less density who existed are all quite the same.

We of the planet Hatonn are here for a purpose, a very singular purpose. Like our brothers, we are here to serve the people of the planet Earth … primarily to service to awareness of the people to earth. We are here to help those who desire our aid to increase their awareness, which is our purpose. For this reason, we are constantly available to those who desire our service. At this time, our friends, at this time …

(Unknown channeling)

I am now with this instrument. I am Hatonn. I *(inaudible)*. I wish to speak through this instrument, and while this instrument is speaking, my brother, the one known as Laitos, will be conditioning each of you who desires that service. We are aware that within your thinking there are many shades of differences and that you are fascinated with the idea of the various steps you must take in order to proceed on the path. We are aware that you have a desire to understand the various categories of experience, the various densities, that you have a desire for naming that which you will begin to understand. We did not understand these things when we first came here, but we have become more sophisticated in the ways of your planet through the years we have spent within this sector of time and space. We know your people better than we used to, and we know the desire of your people for their categories to be named.

This instrument is almost reluctant to speak this to you due to the fact that her thinking has been upon these very thoughts. But we can assure her that this is not her fault but ours. These thoughts are true thoughts but we *(inaudible)*. My friends, we can only tell you that the very idea of density and category and the colors of the rainbow, each of those categorical functions that the human mind so values, is a trap and a delusion in the spiritual sense. We cannot put it any more gently and have you understand what we mean. You have to understand that your categories are occupants of this illusion which you now enjoy, which you have enjoyed since your physical birth and which you will cease enjoying upon your physical death. There is absolutely no harm in understanding the categories with which you must cope within the illusion. However, to allow this to seep into that which you know as your spiritual form is to allow a crippling influence, a halting and blinding influence, to encroach upon your search for the source of life within you.

Our understanding, my friends, is that all things are one. Nothing could be simpler than this understanding. To ask for ramifications, categories, colors of the rainbows, densities or any other list of characteristics is to attempt to impose illusion on reality. Reality is not a process, reality does not change. That which is light, simply is. It is neither active nor passive. It occupies no paradoxes. The beginning and the ending are disunity. At the end of the physical lies all eternity, and yet, eternity implies a process, an endless process.

My friends, this is true, for there are many other lessons to be learned, many other categories to be understood, as you grow closer and closer to that which is your beginning and your end. For it is our understanding that there is a point at which eternity itself is no more. And in the eyes of one who truly understands, one simply becomes that which is. Becoming is done. The circle is complete. Unity is truly known. It is possible to move closer and closer to this understanding through meditation. We are pleased with this group in that its group desire is aimed largely towards an understanding of the metaphysical. Therefore, we may give you information such as this. It is our desire that we are able to give philosophical information. For information such as this is of the higher type, whereas information on such things as density and other categorical questions are lesser in their importance to your spiritual journey.

I am going to attempt the transfer of this *(inaudible)* to one of the other channels. I am Hatonn.

(Unknown channeling)

I am Hatonn. I am with the instrument. I greet you, my friends, in the love and in the light *(inaudible)*. It is a privilege to be with you. I have been listening during your meeting, not only the words but through the instruments and our brother Hatonn, but also to the thoughts [emanating] here this evening. It is very interesting to those of us who are here to serve to find the thinking in groups such as this one evolving as a result of the efforts of our Confederation. We are here for this purpose, to create an evolution in thinking.

My friends, you are at the turning point [in] the evolution of your thinking. It is very easy for you to successfully negotiate this [change]. In turn, an almost *(inaudible)* that is generated by the people of your planet. *(Inaudible)*. And friends, when I say almost no intentional *(inaudible)*, I am referring to what you might consider to be a fantastic multitude of thoughts, the thoughts generated by this society in which you exist, thoughts that you might label as political, economic, business, social *(inaudible)* thoughts. These, my friends, are all the same things. These, my friends, represent more than you are. Friends, we consider these to be very specialized, to be a very singular process having to do with *(inaudible)*. You might *(inaudible)* the evolution of consciousness. *(Inaudible)* does not matter what you find. It is simply a return to the thinking that created you with the simple Thought of total love expressed by the Creator. This, my friends, is true thinking, to get from where people of your planet *(inaudible)* to this side *(inaudible)*, but it may only be done within the limits of our knowledge by one process. It may only be done by the process of meditation, simple, daily meditation. Meditation at the *(inaudible)*, a myriad of confused thoughts and ideas, a society in which you *(inaudible)*, in your conscious lives, and allows them to be replaced with a single Thought of your Creator, a Thought of total and absolute love, a Thought so complete, so total, and so pure that it and it alone was able to create this entire *(inaudible)*. A Thought so powerful, my friends, that it was generated through selves in every other [planet].

My friends, this is what we consider, thinking this through. This was also our objective, for we are still *(inaudible)*. We think it's absolute in its most purest form is thought *(inaudible)*. It is a very simple task, very complex it seems, for man to follow. Complex, my friends, because it is difficult for you to return to simplicity, to the thought patterns with the purest suggestion. With this Thought, all things are one, for it asks to accomplish all things, even the complexities you experience with *(inaudible)* are accomplished by this Thought as it expresses itself in an infinite and variable acts, and yet we direct you back, back to the way in its various experiences the reality and purity of the simplicity, the simplicity of pure and total love *(inaudible)*, pure and total love that is every thought every *(inaudible)*.

All that is necessary is for you to return to this understanding, eradicate any experience *(inaudible)* in the simplicity of love … Unity *(inaudible)* and you will know all things and you will be all things. You are all things … you are limited only by your desire. All that is necessary to practice *(inaudible)* meditation, elimination, cleansing, new birth, transition in thinking of nothing, in thinking of something, requires no special *(inaudible)*, no special instructions. All that is required is *(inaudible)* all of unity is desired. We are here to instruct because of your desire. You will find your path because of your desire.

I am [Hatonn]. I have been privileged to speak with you this evening. I leave in the love and the light of the *(inaudible)*. Adonai *(inaudible)*. ☥

Tuesday Meditation
August 6, 1974

(Unknown channeling)

I am Hatonn. I greet you, my friends, once more in the love and the light of our infinite Creator. It is a great privilege to be here *(inaudible)*. I am of the eternal being from the planet Hatonn *(inaudible)* physical body such as yours *(inaudible)* our thoughts *(inaudible)* our thoughts *(inaudible)*.

(Carla channeling)

I am now with this instrument. I am Hatonn. Again I greet you. I wish to speak through this instrument and while this instrument is speaking, my brother, the one known to you as [Laitos] will condition each of you who desires *(inaudible)*.

We are aware that within your thinking there are many shades of difference and that you are fascinated with the idea, with the various steps which you must take in order to proceed on the path. We are aware that you have a desire to understand the various categories of experience, the various densities that you have a desire for mainly that which you [now] *(inaudible)* begin to understand. We did not understand these things when we first came here. But we have become more sophisticated in the ways of your planet through the years that we have spent within this sector of time and space. We know your people better than we used to and we know of the desire of your people for their categories to be named.

This instrument is almost reluctant to speak this to you due to *(inaudible)*, for her thinking has been upon these very thoughts. We can assure her that this is not her fault but ours. These thoughts are *(inaudible)* but we are *(inaudible)*. My friends, we can only tell you that the very idea of density and category, the colors of the rainbow, each of the categorical functions which the human mind so values, is a trap and an illusion in the spiritual sense. We cannot put it any more gently and have you understand what we mean.

You must understand, my friends, that all categories are occupants of this illusion which you now enjoy, which you have enjoyed since your physical birth, which you will cease enjoying upon your physical death. There is absolutely no harm in understanding the categories with which you must cope in the illusion. However, to allow this to sink into that which you know as your spiritual path is to allow a crippling influence, a haunting and blinding influence to encroach upon your search for the source of light within you.

Our understanding, my friends, is that all things are one. Nothing could be simpler than this understanding. To ask for one of the patients, categories, followers of the rainbow, densities, or any other mist or characteristics is to attempt to impose illusion on reality. Reality is not a process. Reality does not change. That which is light simply is. It is neither active nor passive. It occupies no paradoxes. The beginning and the ending are this unity. At the end of the physical lies all eternity. And yet eternity implies a process, an endless process. My friends, this is true for there are many other lessons to be learned, many other categories to be understood as you grow closer and closer to that which is your beginning and your end. But it is our understanding that there is a point at which eternity itself is no more and in the eyes of one who truly understands one simply becomes that which is. Becoming is done. The circle is complete. The unity is truly known.

It is possible to move closer and closer to this understanding through meditation. We are pleased with this group in that its group desire is aimed largely towards an understanding of the metaphysical. Therefore, we may give you information such as this. It is our desire that we are able to give for the *(inaudible)* information. For information such as this is of the higher type. For information on such things as density and other categorical questions are lesser in their importance to your spiritual journey.

I am going to attempt to transfer this contact to one of the other channelers. I am Hatonn.

(Pause)

(Unknown channeling)

I am with the instrument. I greet you, my friends, in the love and in the light of our infinite Creator. It is a privilege to be with you. *(Inaudible)* not only *(inaudible)* but also the thoughts of each of you here this evening. It is very interesting to those of us who are here to serve to find the thinking in groups such as this one, as a result of the efforts of our Confederation. We are here for this purpose. *(Inaudible)* illusion *(inaudible)*. My friends, you are *(inaudible)* the evolution of your kind.

It is very easy for you to successfully negotiate for this eternity. A turn from almost no *(inaudible)* that it generated by the people of your planet. To *(inaudible)*, my friends, when I say almost no *(inaudible)* I am referring to what you might consider to be a fantastic multitude of thoughts, thoughts generated by the society in which you exist *(inaudible)* business, social, scientific, historical. These, my friends, are all the same thoughts. These, my friends, represent *(inaudible)*. My friends, you consider to be the very special *(inaudible)*.

(Inaudible) the evolution of consciousness really does not matter *(inaudible)*. It is simply a return to the thinking of the Creator. A simple Thought, total love expressed by *(inaudible)*. This, my friends, is true *(inaudible)* and yet and where the people of your planet *(inaudible)* but it may only be done within the limits of *(inaudible)* by your *(inaudible)* process. It can only be done by the process of meditation. It is simple *(inaudible)* a meditation that erases the myriad of confused thoughts *(inaudible)* this society that *(inaudible)* allows them to be replaced *(inaudible)* the same thoughts of your Creator *(inaudible)* of total and absolute love, a Thought so complete, so total and so pure that it and it alone is able to create this entire *(inaudible)*. A Thought so powerful *(inaudible)* that it is generated *(inaudible)* in every other thing *(inaudible)*. My friends, this is what you are concerned with, making this *(inaudible)*. This is also *(inaudible)* for we are still *(inaudible)* we think is absolute *(inaudible)*.

It is a very simple task, very complex *(inaudible)* complex, my friends, for it is difficult *(inaudible)* to return to simplicity. For *(inaudible)* is the purest simplicity. And with this thought *(inaudible)* all things *(inaudible)* for it has *(inaudible)* even the complexities that you experience within society are acknowledged by this Thought as it expressed itself in an infinite *(inaudible)* and yet we directly find *(inaudible)* various experiences the reality and purity of the simplicity, the simplicity of *(inaudible)* pure and total love that is every thought of your being. All that is necessary is for you to return to this *(inaudible)* any experience *(inaudible)* the simplicity *(inaudible)*.

All that is necessary is the practice of daily meditation. The elimination of transitory, rebirth, transition, thinking *(inaudible)* thinking *(inaudible)* requires no special *(inaudible)*. All that is required is desire, all *(inaudible)* is desire. We are here to inspire *(inaudible)* the desire. *(Inaudible)*.

Adonai, my friends. *(Inaudible)*.

(Tape ends.)

Saturday Meditation
September 21, 1974

(Don channeling)

[I am Hatonn.] I greet you, my friends, in the love and the light of our infinite Creator. It is a very great privilege to be with you once more.

I am aware that it sometimes seems that very little is accomplished in your seeking, but, my friends, this is far from true. Your seeking, my friends, is the most important activity in which you engage. There is nothing that you do, no thought that you make that is more important or necessary than the simple seeking for understanding, understanding the reality and the truth [of] the Creation of the Father.

Many, many of those around you are not seeking what they truly desire to seek. They are experiencing their present world, but they are not seeking outside its limitations. And this, my friends, is what they must do if they are to be successful in fulfilling their real desires. For whether man on Earth consciously understands or has no knowledge of his real desire to seek, it still is [his own] desire [among all peoples, in all places,] desire that you might call subliminal, a bias, a potential that is always with him and yet, in your present society, is submerged in a very large percentage of the cases. For in your present societies, creations [of] man on Earth have taken place [of] the creations of the Father in his thinking and in his seeking. For this reason, the abilities and the skills derived from seeking within this illusion are illusory skills *(inaudible)* pertaining only to those very, very transient qualities [which] exist for the short span of [this millennium] and then fade into the endless stream [of time] that stretches through infinity, regardless of [your present awareness.]

Some of those who now dwell upon your planet are seeking a greater reality. They are seeking in a spiritual direction. They are seeking to understand, understand those qualities that are not transient, those qualities that are [the Creation,] and in so doing, they are not only [attaining] a difference of understanding but are progressing toward those abilities that lie within the realm of spirit rather than that which is illusory.

We of the Confederation of Planets in the Service of the Infinite Creator are here for only one real purpose. This purpose is to aid those of our brothers upon planet Earth to find their real objective and then to aid [them] in [reaching] [it]. There is only one way to accomplish this *(inaudible)*. That way is that those of you who so desire [to] progress, progress [with] that real objective that is within all [men], simply do so—to first availing yourself to truth in meditation, and then applying this in your daily [activities].

It is very difficult to become a reflection, it seems, of total perfection. My friends, this is an illusion in itself. For you are already total [perfection.] It is only necessary that you realize this. For the Creator of us all has created nothing but [perfection.] Any discrepancy of your *(inaudible)* from this is an illusion brought about by the individual. All that is necessary is that you realize your [total unity with the] Creator [in this Creation.] Realize this through your daily meditation, and then express it. Express it in every thought and in every deed and you will have found precisely what you seek. [It is] a very simple formula, my friends, and one might ask if this simplicity is so [evident,] why is it not [practiced?] My friends, there is only one reason for this. That reason, my friends, is that the individual, not so doing, has allowed the illusion in which he presently finds himself to become real. This supposed reality occurs only if an individual allows it. There is a very simple process—a very, very simple process [which] will enable [you] to maintain a very simple [and correct tenet] toward the illusion [that surrounds you.]

As we have said many times, my friends, this process is *(inaudible)*. [If] you find yourself influenced in your daily activities in a way other than that which would conform to the thought of your Creator, it is simply due to insufficient meditation. [We will] suggest, then, that if you truly wish to progress at an accelerated rate that you should perform periods of daily meditation sufficient to dissolve and maintain in this state *(inaudible)*, the effects, the seeming negative [catalyst] that acts upon your awareness within your daily meditations. Maintain a constant awareness [of] the truth [of] reality [of the] Creation of the Father. Do this through meditation. Increase your periods of meditation, if necessary. Several periods, daily, are sometimes [to be desired.]

If you were not seeking, my friends, we could not tell you this for our aid must be *(inaudible)* and if you were not seeking, my friends, we could not suggest so strongly that you avail yourself to reality [with] continuing periods of meditation until you reflect the love and total understanding of that which created [you,] the Creator of us all, the total [and infinite] completely [pure Thought] of love. This has been demonstrated on your planet in the past, and yet it is not understood, and yet this reason for lack of understanding is always the same, an insufficient or total absence of meditation.

We, of the Confederation of Planets in the Service of the Infinite Creator, are here and will continue to serve your people *(inaudible)* to serve those who seek. We have ultimate patience in doing this. Patience, my friends, is very necessary *(inaudible)* seeking *(inaudible)*.

At this time, I will transfer this contact to another instrument.

(Carla channeling)

I am now with this instrument. I am Hatonn. I am aware that there are questions in your minds, and I would like to take this opportunity to answer them if you wish to ask them. Do you have any questions?

(No queries.)

In that case, my friends, I will speak with you concerning a question which, in a general way, is in several of your minds, at this time.

You have had wonder as to why the Confederation of Planets wishes to serve the Creator by the means of coming to planet Earth and talking to groups such as yours. We can certainly understand how puzzling this must look, for within the density that you now enjoy, the approach would not be used due to the fact that it would not cause a certain change within the group which you intended to aid. However, my friends, you may, perhaps, gain some understanding of our actions if you will consider that it has been, within the history of your people, a frequent custom for those who are somewhat of an advanced nature, relatively, reaching out to aid a more primitive or less sophisticated citizen or group of people who are just on the threshold of entering the more sophisticated environment. We may add, my friends, that most of the attempts that have been made by those known as missionaries, social groups sent by the government, and others, and with a very low success rate. We hope, my friends, that our basic success rate in aiding you is higher and this is the reason that we do not come among you and attempt to force you to understand that which we are telling you.

You see, my friends, you are at the beginning of a truly new age. The vibrations are being made new at this time, and those who embody within themselves the consciousness of great beings will become that which they know and that which they are, and we desire to bring each of you who is seeking into this new vibration, content to fulfill your own great destiny in the new age. We have made the step. We exist within this environment, at this time, and we know of the help that, what you might call, a cheering team can do for you, and so we cheer you along. We urge you to, shall we say, do your technique, do your homework so that you may be what you desire to be. These things do not happen by accident, they happen by desire. That desire must originate within you. We are attempting to stimulate the desire which is already within you. There is much joy and much beauty in constant presence of the Father of us all very apparent within the new vibration. The new vibration is love, as is the old vibration and yet, my friends, the truth of love becomes a little more obvious with the higher vibrations.

Through meditation, my friends, you may begin to see the heart of love in all the clumsy actions of all those who enter your atmosphere in your daily activities. There may be a great deal of difficulty. There may be misspent time and mistaken words and yet, my friends, each action and each desire is, in truth, a manifestation of love, shadowed and twisted sometimes, for man is also a creator and can cause the shape of love to change. Yet, the heart of all action is love. Know this in your inmost self and then you cannot be touched by that illusion which attempts to strike you. The freedom that this gives you to give forth love in its original state, at all times, to all people is a very precious gift, we think. This is why the Confederation is here. We are all here, many, many of us, from different planets, from different vibrations, from various densities, in many circumstances, yet we all work together, for we all have come to know the Creator and we all wish to be of service to Him, and that alone is enough for us.

We only wish to help you. We are one of many who wish to help you. We are here always, in words, if you may find a channel, and without words, if you desire our presence. We are always with you to lend our vibrations to your meditation, if you so desire.

At this time, my friends, I would like to give conditioning to each of those present who desires it. I will leave this instrument. I am Hatonn.

(Pause)

(Carla channeling)

I am again with this instrument. I will leave you now, my friends. It has been a great privilege to be with you. I am so glad to have been able to share this meeting with you. I hope that our words have been of some aid to you. I leave you in His love and in His light. I am Hatonn. Adonai. Adonai vasu. ☥

L/L Research

L/L Research is a subsidiary of Rock Creek Research & Development Laboratories, Inc.

P.O. Box 5195
Louisville, KY 40255-0195

www.llresearch.org

Rock Creek is a non-profit corporation dedicated to discovering and sharing information which may aid in the spiritual evolution of humankind.

ABOUT THE CONTENTS OF THIS TRANSCRIPT: This telepathic channeling has been taken from transcriptions of the weekly study and meditation meetings of the Rock Creek Research & Development Laboratories and L/L Research. It is offered in the hope that it may be useful to you. As the Confederation entities always make a point of saying, please use your discrimination and judgment in assessing this material. If something rings true to you, fine. If something does not resonate, please leave it behind, for neither we nor those of the Confederation would wish to be a stumbling block for any.

CAVEAT: This transcript is being published by L/L Research in a not yet final form. It has, however, been edited and any obvious errors have been corrected. When it is in a final form, this caveat will be removed.

© 2009 L/L Research

Sunday Meditation
September 22, 1974

(Don channeling)

… *(inaudible)*. I will transfer this contact at this time *(inaudible)*.

(Carla channeling)

I am Hatonn. I am now with this instrument. When we say that we know those whom we wish to help and those whom we do not wish to help, we do not speak of knowledge in your sense, and, therefore, that which we say to you concerning your progress as channels is prone to misunderstanding and even error. And yet, the fact remains that there is a flock and those of you who have the calling must be shepherds to that flock. And it is true that there are those who wish to be of the flock and that there are those who do not wish to be of the flock. And we say to each of you who is a channel, your inner eye is unclouded. It is only your outer eye which becomes confused and which sees mists and quicksand. Therefore, in your work, which is a good service, use your inner eye for that alone will serve you as you do the will of the Father.

Before me, as we are here together, each of you sits bathed in [light] and from inside each of you I have the privilege of perceiving your desire to be of service. That this fountain may run clear and sweet is our chief concern. For that which is through you is of the Father, and each of you are his channels.

What can we say to you to encourage you that you have not [already] heard? Does it seem to you, perhaps, my friends, that in your service you are forever to be stunted and thwarted and always misunderstood? I can think of many things to say to you, many words, many thoughts, all of which are true, all of which would be kindly and encouraging, but, my friends, for you I will share with you that which is of another level of understanding. For within service, as within all things, there are many levels of comprehension.

As you desire to go forth and serve, therefore, know this, that you must be prepared to give away all that you have to give. You must be prepared to walk away and not look back. For there is nothing that you can do for your Creator, but *everything*. It is a hard lesson and people have, always, the illusion [with which] to [part] within this [lesson] and they say, "Everything? Not everything!" But, my friends, everything must belong to the Creator. This is hard and yet, if you may realize this [fact] within your own [thinking,] your service will become such a thing as I cannot possibly describe.

There is an inevitable blooming of every [plant] and each tree will bear fruit in its time. The fruit of your service is a long time coming. For you have worked towards this moment for a long time to your way of thinking and as you approach this time, you have achieved many lessons, but the final fruits [come] only after the fruit has [dropped] from the plant which gave it life. Do not [take] these words in intellectual [ingestion], attempting to [coddle] an understanding from their specific [meaning,] for we are speaking not of the physical, but of that which is spiritual. Do not think in terms of the visible, for service is invisible. All those things which are visible, in reality, are invisible, [eternal] and completely without *(inaudible)*, for they are all one thing. They are all the Creator. Everything must be given to the Creator because the Creator is [everything.]

This massive indifference that you find may be turned, in an instant, my friends, by the service of your own thinking from a neutrality to a glorious joy. The indifference, the difficulties, the hindrances of service are part of an illusion which is not yours to understand. For, my friends, it is not understandable. It is simply yours to experience. This service begins within your heart which is completely empty and open for you have given all that you have to the Creator. And in return, my friends, the Creator has come into this empty and open place. The Creator has filled your essence with His love and His light and you have become a true channel, able to illuminate each moment with love.

Your service will come. As you desire, it shall be. You may, therefore, prepare and having prepared you may lie down in rest, content with the [glory] shining around you.

There is another entity who desires to speak with this group. Therefore, I will leave this instrument at this time in order to make room for my brother. I leave you in the love and the light of our infinite Creator. I am known to you as Hatonn. Adonai.

(Don channeling)

I am Oxal. I am with this instrument. I greet you, my friends, in the love and the light of our infinite Creator. It is a very great privilege *(inaudible)*.

(The rest of this side of the tape is inaudible.)

(Side one of tape ends.)

(Don channeling)

[I am Hatonn.] … it is more important or necessary than the simple seed for understanding, understanding the reality and the truth of the creation of the Father. Many, many of those around are not seeking what they truly desire to seek. They are experiencing their present world, but they are not seeking outside its limitations. And this, my friends, is what they must do if they are to be successful in fulfilling their real desires. For *(inaudible)* honor, consciously understand *(inaudible)*, but a real desire to seek, it still is. *(Inaudible)* desire that you might call subliminal, a bias, a potential that *(inaudible)*, and yet in your present society is submerged. A very large percentage of the *(inaudible)*, for in your present society, creations of man on Earth have taken place the creations of the Father *(inaudible)* for this reason the abilities and the skills derived from seeking within this illusion are the necessary skills *(inaudible)* pertaining only to those very, very transient qualities which exist for a short span *(inaudible)*, and then fade into the endless *(inaudible)* of time, and stretches to infinity, regardless of your present awareness.

Some of those who now dwell upon your planet are now seeking a greater reality. They are seeking in a spiritual direction. They are seeking to understand, understand those qualities which are not transient, those qualities that are the Creator, and in so doing they are not only attaining gifts of understanding, but are progressing towards those authorities that are allowed in the realm of the spirit, or rather in that which is *(inaudible)*.

We of the Confederation of Planets in the Service of the Infinite Creator, are here for only one real purpose; this purpose is to aid those of our brothers on planet Earth to find their real objective, and then to aid them in reaching it. There is only one way to accomplish this, and that way is that those of you who so desire progress, progress *(inaudible)*. Simply do so by first availing yourself *(inaudible)* to meditation and then applying this in your daily activities.

It is very difficult to become a reflection, it seems, of *(inaudible)* perfection. My friends, this is an illusion in itself, for you are already *(inaudible.* It is only necessary that you realize this, for the Creator of us all has created nothing but perfection. Any discrepancy or variation from this is an illusion brought about by the individual. All that is necessary is that you realize *(inaudible)* the Creator in the creation *(inaudible)*. Realize this in your daily meditation and then express it. Express it in every thought and every deed, and you will have found precisely what you seek; a very simple formula, my friends. And one might ask if this simplicity is so evident why is it not *(inaudible)*. My friends, there is only one reason for this. That reason, my friends, is that the individual, in not so doing, has allowed the illusion which he presently finds himself to become real. The supposed reality occurs only if the individual allows it.

It is a very simple process, a very, very simple process, my friends, and *(inaudible)* able to maintain a very simple and *(inaudible)*. For the illusion *(inaudible)*, as we have said many times, my friends, this process *(inaudible)* you find yourself influenced in your daily activities in a way other than that which conforms to the thoughts of your Creator *(inaudible)* insufficient. We suggest then, that if you truly wish to progress at an accelerated rate, that you perform periods of daily meditation sufficient to dissolve and maintain in the state of this illusion the effects, the seeming negative *(inaudible)* awareness within your daily activities. Maintain a constant awareness, the truth of reality, the creation of the Father. Do this through meditation. Increase your periods of meditation if necessary; several periods daily are sometimes *(inaudible)* you are not seeking, my friends, *(inaudible)*, and if you were not seeking, my friends, we would not suggest so strongly to avail yourself to continued periods of meditation until you *(inaudible)* for love *(inaudible)* total understanding *(inaudible)* completely pure of thought, of love. This has been demonstrated on your planet many times and yet it is not understood, and yet this reason from a lack of understanding *(inaudible)* is always *(inaudible)* and insufficient *(inaudible)* lapses of meditation.

We of the Confederation of Planets in the Service of the Infinite Creator, are here and will continue to serve your people. *(Inaudible)* serve those who seek. We have *(inaudible)*. Patience, my friends, is very necessary in seeking along this *(inaudible)*.

At this time, I will transfer this contact *(inaudible)*.

(Carla channeling)

I am now with this instrument. I am Hatonn. I am aware that there are questions in your minds and I would like to take this opportunity to answer them, if you wish to ask them. Do you have any questions?

(No queries.)

In that case, my friends, I will speak with you concerning a question which, in a general way, is in several of your minds at this time. You have had wonder as to why the Confederation of Planets wishes to serve the Creator by means of coming to planet Earth and talking to groups such as yours. We can certainly understand how puzzling this must look, for within the density which you now enjoy, the approach would not be used, due to the fact that it would not cause a certain change within the group which you intended to aid. However, my friends, you may perhaps gain some understanding of our actions if you will consider that it has been within the history of your people a frequent custom of those who are somewhat of an advanced nature, relatively, reaching out to aid a more primitive, or less sophisticated citizen, or group of people, who are on the threshold of entering a more sophisticated environment. We may add, my friends, that most of the attempts that have been made by those known as missionaries, social groups, sent by the government and others, [end] with a very low success rate. We hope, my friends, that our basic success rate in aiding you is higher, and this is the reason that we do not come among you and attempt to force you to understand that which we are telling you.

You see, my friends, you are at the beginning of a truly new age. The vibrations are being made new at this time and those who embody within themselves the consciousness of great beings will become that which they know and they … which they are. And we desire to bring each of you who is seeking into this new vibration, content to fulfill your own great destiny in the new age.

We have made the step. We exist within this environment at this time and we know of the help that what you might call a cheering team can do for you, and so we cheer you along. We urge you to, shall we say, do your technique, do your homework so that you may be what you desire to be. These things do not happen by accident. They happen by desire. That desire must originate within you. We are attempting to stimulate the desire that is already within you.

There is much joy and much beauty and the constant presence of the Father of us all very apparent of the new vibration. The new vibration is love, as is the old vibration. And yet, my friends, the truth of love becomes a little more obvious with the higher vibrations. Through meditation, my friends, you may begin to see the heart of love in all the clumsy actions of all those who enter your atmosphere in your daily activities. There may be a great deal of difficulty. There may be misspent time and mistaken words, and yet, my friends, each action and each desire is, in truth, a manifestation of love, shadowed and twisted sometimes, for man is also a creator and can cause the shape of love to change.

Yet the heart of all action is love. Know this within your inmost self and then you cannot be touched by that illusion which attempts to strike you. The freedom that this gives you to give forth love in its original state at all times to all people is a *(inaudible)*, we think. This is why the Confederation is here; we are all here, many, many of us from different planets, from different vibrations, from various densities, in many circumstances, yet we all work together for we have all come to know the Creator and we all wish to be of service to Him, and that alone is enough for us.

We only wish to help you. We are one of many who wish to help you. We are here always; in words, if you may find a channel, and without words if you desire our presence. We are always with you to lend our vibrations to your mediation if you so desire.

At this time, my friends, I would like to give conditioning to each of those present who desires it. I will leave this instrument. I am Hatonn.

(Pause)

I am again with this instrument. I will leave you now, my friends. It has been a great privilege to be with you. I am so glad to have been able to share this meeting with you. I hope that our words have been of some aid to you. I leave you in His love and in His light. I am Hatonn. Adonai. Adonai vasu.

Friday Meditation
October 4, 1974

(Unknown channeling)

I am Hatonn. I greet you in the love and in the light of our infinite Creator. It is a great privilege to once more meet with this group. We, the Confederation of Planets in the Service of our Infinite Creator, are here, as we have stated many times, to aid those of the people of Earth who would seek our aid. I am aware that many of the peoples of this planet are not inclined to seek our aid. Many of the peoples of this planet are not inclined to seek anything beyond the illusion that now fascinates them. Many of these peoples believe that they are experiencing the most real portion of their existence. They also believe that there is nothing to seek of any value beyond their present illusion. This is quite erroneous. They do not realize that they are presently experiencing the illusion in which they find themselves because of their desire to limit to this form their experience. They do not realize that they are experiencing an insignificantly small portion of that which they might experience.

At this time, I will attempt to transfer this contact to the instrument known as T.

(T channeling)

It is a pleasure once again to use this instrument. We are with you, my friends, at this time to help you. We are *(inaudible)* of seeking *(inaudible)* in every way that we can. There are many ways that we can aid. We wish it were possible that we could help you more than we are able, but it is not allowed that we would interfere with your free choosing of the path that you will follow. We, however, can and do bring you the greatest and *(inaudible)* matter, the only really necessary aid that you need in your seeking. And that, of course, my friends, is your meditation. Practice it daily and the benefits will be beyond *(inaudible)*. It should become a way of life with you. We are pleased that so many in your group are practicing daily meditation. We encourage all to continue to do so.

I will now attempt to contact the instrument known as E. I am Hatonn.

(E channeling)

I am Hatonn. I am pleased to be with this instrument once again.

(Pause)

(Carla channeling)

I am now with this instrument. I am Hatonn. I am sorry for the delay. These do sometimes occur and we suggest that simple relaxation and lack of intellectual taking thought will always gradually make it possible for the new instrument to gain confidence in availing themselves of channeled information.

We were speaking, my friends, of the many, many inhabitants of planet Earth whom we cannot serve at this time for they do not wish our service. Why is this, my friends? What is it that has brought you to this meeting and has left others with no desire to seek and to know the truth? What is the great choice-maker? My friends, it is not an easy concept to understand, the concept which answers these questions, however, it is an extremely simple concept. What you know of as energy or consciousness or love is extremely wider spread in its definition than you can imagine. The vibration level which forms the density which you now enjoy, has a lower and an upper limit. There are infinite varieties of vibration within this finite vibration level. And those who are at present upon this planet are existing within many, many of these various vibratory levels.

Within the lower vibratory levels, my friends, there will be an excess of certain types of energy, which express themselves in aggressive and energetic action. These types of actions are often seen among those very people who do not wish our aid. Gradually, one begins to use up, or shall I say, transmute some of this expression of energy and another type of energy begins to manifest, for energy is never destroyed, as you already know.

The higher levels of energy have a somewhat less physically energetic aspect and the intellectual aspects of vibration are begun to be experienced. After a certain amount of experience within these vibrations, the energy manifested in these vibrations is used up or, shall I say, transmuted again to a higher level of energy. The catalyst for this transmutation of energy in all cases is either experience or meditation. Experience is an extremely sure but somewhat slow-moving type of catalyst. The transmutation of your vibratory level from the lower to the higher forms of vibration will be one with the movement of the unitary mind of all of those upon this planet.

It is possible to speed your progress within this vibration by means of contacting the creation that is within you. And it is this that we have been attempting to guide you to. Each of you, my friends, is attracted to that which we have to give you because you have in the past managed to accumulate enough experience within this vibration that you are vibrating at the level at which your desires are attempting to satisfy themselves by moving into the higher vibrations of spiritual seeking. You have traveled far, my friends. It has been a long journey. You have an infinity of traveling to do yet, I assure you, but, my friends, the lessons are good. We are indeed sorry that we cannot be of aid to those who have not desired such aid. They will desire this aid in good time, my friends, and we or our brothers will be there to aid them for this is the plan of the Creator.

I am at this time going to attempt again to contact the instrument known as E. I wish only to exercise with this channel. I am Hatonn.

(E channeling)

This channel does question about the personality. She has *(inaudible)*. This channel *(inaudible)*. We spoke of *(inaudible)* the entity *(inaudible)*. It has been a pleasure using this channel. I will leave you now. I am Hatonn. *(Inaudible).*

L/L Research

Sunday Meditation
October 13, 1974

(Don channeling)

I am Hatonn. I greet you, my friends, in the love and in the light of our infinite Creator. It is a very great privilege to once more be with this group. I am speaking through this instrument from a craft high above your house. It is a craft known to you as a flying saucer. Yes, my friends, we are here and we are very close. Yet you cannot see us. Your instruments cannot see us. The radar or other devices detecting us are not useful in *(inaudible)*. Yet we are here. There are millions surrounding your planet, surrounding it with one purpose in mind: to bring to you understanding. Friends, this is something that we can only offer. It is necessary for man on Earth to reach out and take it, for understanding must always come from within. We cannot bring it to you and force it into you as a food. We can only stimulate your seeking through suggestion, through teachings such as we are performing now so that you through your own understanding can once more find the light that is within all men throughout all this creation.

It is a very great privilege to be able to perform this service for the people of Earth, for this is the only service that is of any real importance. For, my friends, everything that you seek is in the direction of this understanding—total, complete understanding of the truth and love of your Creator, the Creator of us all. This is what men in all places and at all times are seeking. Whether they realize this or not, this is what they seek. So, my friends, tonight we will speak to you about understanding. We will speak to you about reality. We will speak to you about what we have to do.

It is often said upon your planet that it is difficult to understand the meaning of life. However, my friends, it is not difficult to understand the meaning of life if you avail yourselves of this understanding through meditation. This meaning will not come to you in words, my friends. You will not be able to explain it in so many sentences or paragraphs. But you will begin to understand this meaning. You will begin to obtain an awareness of it. When this awareness has reached its fullness, you will then be with your Creator, the Creator of us all. And the understanding will be as [it] is, and you then will once more act as Creator. For this reason, my friends, meditation is of an extreme amount of importance. For this reason, my friends, meditation is actually the only real avenue to this understanding. For this understanding cannot be given by words. It can only be reached through knowing. And this knowing can only be reached through meditation.

Many upon your planet have been known as masters. Each of these men became aware of truth, aware of truth from the truth that was within them. [Each] perceived this awareness through the process of meditation. If an individual maintains his interest in things that are external, if he continues to use the intellect for analysis of each of his daily activities and for each of his confrontations as he progresses through his life, he will then be working in a very, very shallow way, with a very, very shallow objective and a very shallow opportunity to understand. It is necessary for him to avail himself of a truth that is not intellectual, a truth that cannot be explained in words, a truth that is only a feeling, a knowing, a truth that is. This may be done, my friends, through meditation. For this reason we seek to bring an understanding of the necessity for meditation.

All men in all places are taken to understanding the single truth that lies within them, the truth of the creation. For the truth of one thing is the truth of another. For all things are one and the same, impossible to separate. They have all been created by the same Thought. They are all made of the same substance and they are all related in the same way. Avail yourselves of this knowledge through meditation. Become aware of this. Become aware of it in such a way that it is the knowing within you that is not an intellectual knowing, but a knowing that transcends everything that you could think or do. A knowing that is. A knowing that is the love, the infinite wisdom of the Creator, the Creator of us all.

This is only available to you, my friends, through meditation. You cannot spell it out. You cannot set it down on paper. You cannot express it in words, for all of these things fall very short of this understanding. This understanding, my friends, is infinite. It is total wisdom, total love. It is within you when you learn to express it in every thought and every deed, in every move, in every breath. Regardless of what you do, regardless of what confronts you, when you are expressing this understanding you are then at one with the truth, at one as you were meant to be, meant to be as a result of the original Thought, the Thought of your Creator, the thought of our Creator.

Reach this understanding. Reach it through meditation. In reaching this understanding you will reach the only joy that there is, a joy that is so profound, so total, so far-reaching that you will not be able to express it. You will only experience it and then you will know it. This knowledge, my friends, is what you seek. It is available quite easily. All that is necessary is that you reach out. Reach out by going within, going within to all there is. For this is the direction to the infinite—infinite wisdom that is yours and your Creator's.

It has been a very great privilege speaking to you through this instrument. We have others here tonight who will speak through other instruments. I will leave this instrument at this time to allow another of my brothers to speak through one of the other instruments. I am Hatton. It has been a very great privilege to speak with you. Adonai. Adonai vasu.

(Carla channeling)

(Inaudible)

(Jim channeling)

(Inaudible)

(Tape ends.)

Thursday Meditation
October 31, 1974

(Don channeling)

I am Hatonn. I greet you, my friends, in the love and in the light of the infinite Creator. It is a great privilege to be with you, my friends, a very great privilege. The reason that I say that it is a great privilege, my friends, is that we are here for only one purpose. Our purpose is to contact those peoples of your planet who desire our contact. This is the sole reason at this time for us being here. We have come with a specific objective in mind. We have come to be of service to those upon your planet who desire knowledge, so that they may put this knowledge to use while still within the physical illusion that you now experience.

It is a very great privilege to do this, to give the service to those who desire it. It is very important, my friends, that you realize your true objective, and the means for fulfilling this objective while still within the physical illusion.

The reason for the importance is as follows: man goes through many, many experiences; some of them physical, many more of a different nature than what you presently consider physical. Within the physical illusion, he is isolated, you might say, from much of his knowledge. He is left with an intellect that is the product of his experiences within only that single illusion, and emotional biases that are the products of all his experience.

Why do you think such a condition manifests? Why do you think that you find yourself in this condition? The reason, my friends, is, first of all, you have desired this situation and secondly, having desired it, you have carried out what was necessary to bring yourself into this illusion.

Now, my friends, the reason for this excursion, you might say, from a much more delightful environment into one of severe limitation—the one in which you now find yourselves—the reason for this excursion, my friends, is for the purpose of realization.

It is difficult for many of your peoples to understand why it is necessary for such an experience to take place to reach an awareness that seemingly should be reachable any place, at any time. My friends, it is within reach any place, at any time. But it is also very difficult to test the total understanding of this realization in any experience. It is most easily tested in the experience in which you now find yourselves.

This testing, each day, this testing, each moment of time, is automatic, for it is simply your reaction to each experience that is sensed. Each of you has had reactions to experience that were reactions that you now see as foolish. If one is to reach the goal that he desires during the experience, it is necessary that he adjust his thinking so that his automatic reaction to any experience is always a reaction of love and understanding.

This was demonstrated to you by the master known to you as Jesus. He set an example of reaction to experience. If there is doubt within the minds of individuals as to how they should react to any experience, it has already been set down for you by the man known as Jesus. This man was demonstrating how to react. These reactions were not the product of his analysis or intellect. They were automatic reactions based upon a realization that he had accomplished within the same physical illusion that you now experience.

Because of the consequence of individual experiences within the present illusion, it is a much better test than a less dense illusion. The consequences within the illusion that you now enjoy are seemingly of relatively great magnitude. All of this is for the purpose of testing your ability to express love and understanding. Each of the experiences, regardless of how they seem, are simply illusory tests, operating upon you directly to produce an opportunity for you to display your understanding of love.

This is the only reason for the illusion which you now experience, my friends. If this is the only reason for this illusion, it should be obvious that once an individual is aware of this, that he spend his time in learning to react to each experience with only an expression of love and understanding.

Many of the peoples of your planet, in fact most of the peoples on your planet, have no conscious knowledge of what I have just given to you. Therefore, they go about experiencing the activity within their illusion, and reacting in a manner that is not consciously directed by their understanding.

They, nevertheless, learn from the activities and experiences of the illusion, but the process of learning is much extended over the process of the individual who is consciously aware of what he is doing. We are here at this time to aid those of the people of Earth who wish aid in understanding, consciously, what they are attempting to do.

Many of those of you who continue throughout a total experience within the physical with no conscious knowledge of the real purpose of that experience waste that entire experience and make no progress whatsoever. The progress upon planet Earth has been extremely slow for many, many of the peoples who are on the planet. This slowness of progress has been unfortunate. There have been ample communications of the objective that they desire in reality. However, due to unfortunate circumstances, a very large number of them have never become aware of their true objective while in the physical.

For this reason, they have required repeated experiences in the physical, and will require in the future repeated experiences to make the simple step from reacting to experience blindly, and, shall we say, without suitable expression of love and understanding, to a future goal which is exactly the opposite.

My friends, what we are telling you at this time is the only important thing that you need to know. We can tell you of many wondrous things, but what good is it to be told these things if they are not within your ability to experience? We are telling you simply how to achieve the ability to experience all of the wondrous things that you might wish to know.

To do this is very simple. It is simply to express love and understanding, regardless of the experience that confronts you. All that confronts you is illusion—everything. This is very clear to us. It is not always clear to you. It is not clear to you because the illusion in which you find yourselves is a very, very good illusion, a very satisfactory illusion, a very efficient illusion. It is accomplishing exactly what you wish for it to accomplish. It is accomplishing a deception. It is putting before you continual tests of your ability to express our Creator's love.

Why should you have to be continually tested, my friends? Why should you continually go through these experiences? You have chosen to do this. The reason for this, my friends, is that you wish to accelerate rapidly the progress of your spiritual understanding.

Realize in meditation the truth of what I say, and then realize in meditation the way to implement your desires, to bring them quickly into reality. Do not make the mistake of so many of those who have gained some intellectual knowledge of their true desires. Do not make the mistake of assuming that the simple intellectual knowledge of these desires is of any real benefit. It is not, my friends. The only thing that is of real benefit is if you are able to express with no reservation the love and understanding of your Creator.

This is what the entire game is about. And it is a game, my friends, especially from our point of view. You have chosen to be participants in a game, a game within an illusion. An illusion that is bounded by a narrow layer upon the surface of a small planet in an infinite amount of space.

Consciousness is evolving throughout all of the creation. In your particular place in the creation it is evolving. You are experiencing personal evolution. If you can maintain at all times an awareness of reality, and therefore an awareness of the game in which you find yourselves, you may do precisely what you have set out to do: lift yourself a very great degree in spiritual understanding.

This is what we are all attempting to do. This is our only objective. Anything else is simply a part of a game. And there are many, many games in this creation, my friends, at many levels. Each of these are played with different sets of rules, but they all have the same goal: the goal of understanding, the goal of arriving at that ability to express love that is the Creator's.

This, my friends, then is the activity of all consciousness, throughout all space. It is hard to believe that there are so many activities going on as they are. But they are infinite, each at its own level of awareness, each seeking to go farther, to become more aware, to return to the infinite knowledge of the Creator.

But each is involved in what we might term a game. We say this, my friends, not to make fun of the process, but to recognize its position within reality. We find ourselves within an illusion—a different illusion than your own. We are playing a game, my friends, a game with different rules. But yet it is a different part of the entire enterprise. It is the part that is adjacent to your part. We can call it a game, my friends, because we must contact you in this manner. We must communicate using, at all times, techniques which allow you to accept or reject our communications. For this reason, we compare our activities to a game, for we, too, are operating within certain rules.

And yet we, too, are attempting to rise, to understand more, to become more aware. We are attempting to do this at this time through the process of service. A process of service which will produce for you the evolution which you desire. You may do the same thing, at a different level. You may do the same as we. Having gained certain understanding you may pass on, within your illusion, your understanding, especially [if] you understand the rules of the game.

For many of your people, within your illusion, have attempted to pass on their understanding with no understanding of the rules of the game that they are experiencing. For this reason, much of what they have attempted to give to those around them has been misunderstood or rejected, for they have attempted to serve in a way that was with limitation with respect to understanding. All of this understanding, in an intellectual sense, my friends, is of little value, unless you augment this understanding with real knowledge through the process of meditation. This is the only way that you can totally encompass in your thinking and in your emotional biases the realities that are permanent; realities that are not a product of the game.

Man upon Earth at this time is very, very involved, for the most part, within his illusion. There is warfare, and plans for warfare. There are political ideas. There are thousands and thousands of objectives and ideas that are totally involved with the game, having no objective outside, no objective in reality. All of these ideas, all of these objectives, all of these activities, whether it be within your political systems, within your business, within your government or military structures, whether it be in any myriad of activities carried on upon your planet's surface, this makes no difference. If the individual immersed in these activities has no realization of their real value—and their real value is nothing, simply nothing—if that individual has no understanding of this, then he is not making the use that he should of his existence within this illusion.

We are afraid at this time that almost all of the peoples of your planet are so oriented. This is not to say that many of them are not of a high spiritual nature. It is simply to say that they have not made that transition that identifies what they are doing, that identifies the objective that they really seek. We are hoping to help many of the peoples of this planet make that transition while they are in the physical. This must be done at some time or another. This is a very important step in the advancement of spirit.

It has been said upon your planet that it is necessary to realize this while in the physical. This, my friends, is a very important step. The more depth within you that this realization reaches, the more benefit you will achieve from it. This, of course, may be done through the process of meditation.

Do not let the illusion that meets you with each dawning day be too much of an illusion, my friends. Recognize it for what it really is, and then recognize each day what your objective is, and you will make full use of the illusion.

It has been a very great privilege to speak with you this evening, I am Hatonn. I shall now allow my brother to speak through the other instrument. It has been a very great privilege. Adonai. Adonai vasu.

(Carla channeling)

I am Oxal. I greet you in love and light. I am glad to be using this instrument. She is not used to our contact. However, we are eager to use this instrument, and if you will be patient, we will spend a brief period working with this contact.

(Pause)

I am anxious to tell you how glad I am to be with my brothers at this time. I have been with you through the communication from my brother Hatonn. I add only one thought, and this one is an obvious one. And yet it is well to remind those who desire understanding of this thought.

My friends, to give love, to emit a vibration of understanding, is to form a consciousness which is not an illusion, but what one may call a reality, although as an ultimate form, one could not call it a reality. But one may call it a reality to express love compared to the illusion as you understand it.

And how does one express love, and how does one express understanding, and how is it possible to express these things at all times? What I wish to tell you, my friends, is that it is impossible to express these things if you are attempting to relate to the illusion. It is impossible, my friends, to react with love and understanding if you are dealing with the imperfect, foolish and sometimes ridiculous people that you will encounter in your daily life.

Of course it is impossible, my friends. The illusion is designed so that it is possible to act correctly only with knowledge. It is only possible to express love when you begin to have an awareness of the Creator.

My friends, each person may seem to be a human entity. Yet he is the Creator. Each natural object, each manufactured object, the very air around you, my friends, has a consciousness which is the Creator. You yourself, the originating agency of this love which you wish to express: you are the Creator.

If you can remember that the one known as Jesus saw each individual entity as part of the Father, then, my friends, you will be able to better express the love of the Creator.

Those who have need of you; those whom you need, are liars. There is no need, except for the Creator. To understand this is to free oneself from illusion.

I have offered these thoughts to you, for in my experience, they are helpful. As my brother has said, we have experienced the density which you enjoy. If we were to discover that we needed the gross corrections that you yourselves pursue, we would reimmerse ourselves within it.

Within our own density, we are seeking to make corrections, corrections in our understanding. And yet we may compare the two densities to two problems of which you may have intellectual knowledge. One is the problem, shall we say, of tuning in a channel. You are now attempting to discover the correct channel. This is the reason for experience. We have this correction, and yet there are finer corrections, which you would understand as the controls on a television for the clarity of the picture. The difference between these examples and the two densities, my friends, is that with changes in density, as the corrections become finer, the differences obtained become more profound.

We look forward to many, many densities beyond our own, that are far finer than our own. Yet we are content to be learning within our own, and we wish very much to aid you with yours.

I also wish to allow another member of the Confederation to speak, and so I will leave this instrument at this time. It has truly been a pleasure to use this instrument. I am known as Oxal. Adonai.

(R channeling)

I am with this instrument. It is a privilege to be with you. I greet you in the love and in the light of our infinite Creator. I will at this time condition each of you, if you desire it.

For we would very much like to use the instrument known as B to relay our thoughts to those who desire them. It will be a simple process, if she will avail herself.

(Tape ends.) ❦

Friday Meditation
November 1, 1974

(Carla channeling)

I am Hatonn. I greet you, my friends, in the love and the light of our infinite Creator. I am here, my friends, that I may aid you. And yet I am here to sting you and to stimulate you, as a gadfly. I am not here to give you comfort, in that I do not wish to put you to sleep, but to awaken you.

You, my friends of this group, are very close to your desire. You, my friends, are close to the opening. Going through this opening will unite you with your desire, and then, my friends, the progress you will make will be much accelerated.

But we must wake you. We must help you to become aware not only of the beauty but of the freedom and of the terrible responsibility of freedom.

It is so easy, my friends, to forget that you are free. Your intellectual minds insist that you accept all of the words and all of the conditions. They insist that you accept hot and cold. And then you accept right and wrong. And that you accept each and every description of your illusion. And yet, my friends, this illusion is a cunning system of limitation. The limitation is designed to produce heightened awareness, strong emotion, and the resultant understanding. And yet, if you believe too strongly [in] the illusion, you will react blindly to it, and you will not understand, and you will not find the freedom, and you will not find your desire. And this is your responsibility, my friends.

We speak of beauty to those who are beginning, for truly, all is beauty; all is joyful; all is full of love. All these things are true. But they are more than true, my friends, they are actual. And, in that they are actual, there is no beauty, there is no joy, there is only one thing, and that is the Creator.

And yet, we cannot say to you, that is the Creator and that is reality, for that is a word. We are speaking the very limitations that we wish to bring you past. Your desire is to come past these limitations, so that you may express the infinite and incandescent love and light that is within you and is the Creator.

And so we are here, in love and in light, to sting you, to stimulate you. For there is peace beyond peace, and there is understanding beyond all things. And these things must be found through the paradoxes of spiritual awareness, through the limitation of all that is a word.

As you abide in meditation, you will come ever closer to the unity between yourself and your desire. We are here to urge you towards that goal.

I will transfer this contact after a short period of conditioning. I am Hatonn.

(Don channeling)

I am Hatonn. I am now with this instrument. It is a privilege to speak through this instrument. I am aware that there are certain questions. I will attempt to answer them. It is very difficult to perceive the illusion when you are so totally immersed within it. But there are things which you may do to augment your ability to see through this illusion.

There is nothing that manifests itself. It is not a *(inaudible)*. It is only necessary that you realize this and the difficulty will be *(inaudible)*.

I am with this instrument. I shall continue.

(Pause)

I am sorry for the delay. It is a privilege to once more contact this instrument. We have stated that it is necessary to recognize the illusion. This is extremely necessary. The illusion is all about you, and yet is of no real consequence. Everything that occurs within the illusion you experience is caused by your thinking. The illusion is caused by the thinking of those that are within it. Everything that exists throughout the creation is created by thought, and the illusion that you now experience is created by thought. Everything that you are experiencing is created by thought. This is sometimes very difficult for you to understand but, nevertheless, it is true.

Everything that you experience is created by thought. Everything that you will experience is created by thought. All changes between what you experience now and what you will experience in the future—these changes are created by thought.

Therefore, my friends, there is only one thing of any importance: that is thought. And, as far as you are concerned, my friends, the only thought that you are able to control is that thought which you call your own. Therefore, it is necessary to completely and totally understand your own thinking prior to dealing with anything else. Once you have totally understood your own thinking, you are then in a position to create much more thought.

And what will you create, my friends? There is only one thing you can provide: an example. An example of thinking. If this is done by enough of the people upon your planet, your planet will achieve a state of thinking that is truly within the thought of our Creator.

I am having difficulty with this instrument.

(Carla channeling)

I am Hatonn. I am once more with this instrument. We are very privileged to be able to use each of the instruments. It may be interesting to you to know why we use different instruments at different times. The material, shall we say, of each person's mind and thoughts has a distinctive and characteristic turn or flavor. And these flavors are our tools for constructing those things which we wish to say to you through these instruments.

We know what the group desires, for we know ourselves, and we are one with ourselves and you. And so, in each communication, we attempt to fulfill the desire of the group as we find it.

To do this, we have the choice of those who are instruments within the group. Depending upon the desire of the group, various of the instruments are preferable at various times. In the case of this communication we desired to use the instrument known as Don, because his turn of mind made it more possible to get certain ideas across in a certain way.

We will attempt to conclude the message through this instrument. Due to her slightly different turn of mind, the information will come out slightly altered. It is still correct, and it will be verified by the other instrument that he was receiving the same information, but he could not get it precisely due to certain conditions.

We were simply attempting to speak in two different ways of one thing. Through this instrument, we can talk about lack of limitation. With the other instrument, with a, shall we say, more neutrally oriented background in language, we could talk more specifically.

Through this instrument we must simply say that your limitation, your illness, your lack, your need—all of these things are due to only one thing, and that is your belief that you are limited, that there are lacks, that there are limitations, that there are illnesses.

My friends, what do you believe? Unfortunately, you are very tempted to believe in limitations of all kinds. If you could believe the truth, you would have no lack, no limitation, no illness, nothing of any kind except the unity which is the truth.

Friday Meditation, November 1, 1974

My friends, you are perfect and you are fulfilled. Your only mission is understanding and service. Understanding brings its own service: therefore, your only mission need be understanding. The service follows of itself.

Do not believe in limitation, and you will become unlimited.

With this idea, I leave you. I has been my privilege to be with you, and I hope that I have been able to give you some thoughts that may aid you. I leave you in love and in light and in the presence of the infinite Father. I am Hatonn. Adonai.

Sunday Meditation
November 10, 1974

(Don channeling)

I am Hatonn. I greet you in the love and the light of our infinite Creator. We are here to serve the peoples of your planet. We are here to bring to them exactly what they desire. We are here to bring to them the only thing that is of value. This, my friends, is understanding.

Many of the peoples of this planet, my friends, are aware that there is much more to this creation and to their lives than that which they find within their present physical illusion. Many of your peoples are at this time seeking outside their illusion. To these who seek, we offer our understanding.

We do not attempt to say that we have ultimate wisdom. We only suggest that that which we have to offer may be of value. For we have found, in our experience, as we have passed through the same experiences as those of Earth, that there is a most beneficial direction in seeking to serve.

We are acting through instruments such as those here tonight to give to those who seek an understanding. We are limited at this time in methods of our communications. We are limited by the overall desire of the peoples of planet Earth. For many of those who dwell upon planet Earth at this time are not seeking what we have to offer. For this reason, we cannot come among you and hope to meet you and present that which we have to bring to you. For it would be an infringement upon the free will of those who do not desire our understanding.

We are in great numbers about your planet. We orbit your planet in our craft. We come no closer than is necessary. It is necessary only to stimulate the seeking among those of your people who truly wish to seek but are unaware, consciously, of their desire.

Our presence is meant to stimulate seeking. Through this process, we hope to contact as many of the peoples of your planet as would desire our contact. We hope in the very near future to be able to contact many more of the peoples of your planet, the peoples who would desire understanding. It is difficult to contact those peoples of your planet because of this, shall I say, mixture of types. But it is well worth our effort if we are able to contact but one.

We will continue to act as we do now, speaking through instruments such as this one, until a sufficient number of the peoples of your planet have become aware of truth. At this time, we will be able to meet directly with some of those on your surface. This, my friends, will be in the not-too-far-distant future. We are constantly striving to bring, through many channels of communication, the simple message to the peoples of Earth, the simple message that will leave them with a simple understanding of all that there is.

My friends, understanding in its purest essence is totally simple. Tonight, we shall speak through the other instruments of the simplicity of this understanding. It has been a privilege to speak through this instrument. I will at this time transfer this contact to one of the other instruments.

(Carla channeling)

I am Hatonn. I am with this instrument, and I greet you once more.

My friends, each of you within this room is truly seeking. We are aware of this, and we are most privileged to be here, and to be to be allowed to aid you in what ways we can. And the first question, my friends, is this one: what are you seeking? Is this not the first question, my friend?

Are you seeking the answer to who you are? There are many, many questions which come under the, shall we say, general heading of spiritual enlightenment. And we would like to tell you a little story, for we believe that in knowing the simple answer to this first question lies the open door to a great deal of further inspiration.

Imagine, my friends, the open skies and beautiful, puffy clouds, as they slowly gather and drift, blown by the wind across the green country. The sun shines warmly upon the country, and nature abounds in the warm sunlight. And the clouds grow heavy, and the waters gather, and they unburden themselves upon the thirsty ground. And the life-giving water enters all the plant life, and the plant life teems and grows and flourishes. And then, my friends, the clouds pass, and the sun shines forth once more, and the countryside turns and reaches for the sun, in a never ending cycle of growth and appreciation.

What questions, my friends, did the flowers, and the trees, and the shrubs, and the crops ask? Do you think they asked, my friends, why they are the color that they are? Do you think that they questioned their shape, or asked how they may be useful?

Their beauty is a blessing, and their fruit of benefit. Plants give love and service without question, for they know the one question. They know that they are reaching for the sun and for the water which gave them their life.

And you, my friends, who gave you your life, and who nourished you, but the Creator? The one Creator, my friends, Creator of us all. And in Him we all abide, some of us knowingly; some of us not. The reality is independent of our awareness of it.

What is your question, my friends? What are you seeking? I suggest to you that you are seeking the Creator. You are seeking, as you may say, the Thought that created you. This is a simple, a very simple idea; perhaps too simple for the intellect to accept. And all we suggest, my friends, is to disengage the intellect and allow your moments of meditation to speak to you regarding your true desire. Once in possession of the knowledge of your true desire, that which you desire will come to you.

My friends, so much time within the physical illusion is wasted. We say wasted, from our point of view, upon the pursuit of questions such as, "Why am I this shape? Why is my situation so and so?" These are questions which deal entirely with the illusion, my friends, which are brief, phenomenal and unimportant in the extreme. Questions which waste your time while your true desire must wait until you can give it attention.

It is written in your holy works, "Seek, and you shall find." This is a true extremely accurate statement, my friends. If you wish to open the door, and open the next door, and so on, you have only to knock.

I would at this time be privileged to transfer the contact to another instrument. I am Hatonn.

(H channeling)

I am with this instrument. My friends, as you sit here this evening, you *(inaudible)*. What we do in these messages is meant to aid you *(inaudible)*. We of the Confederation are able through our desires to see what is most beneficial *(inaudible)* through a channel such as this one. *(Inaudible)*. We stress meditation *(inaudible)*.

(R channeling)

(Inaudible)

(T channeling)

I am now with this instrument. Greetings once more in His love and His light. In reality, my friends, all is indeed very simple. In the physical illusion, things become extremely complex. We come to you in the physical illusion with the purpose of jogging your desire. *(Inaudible)*.

Once, my friends, we had what you would call a change of course. Then, my friends, we were able to give the true realization *(inaudible)*. This knowledge, my friends, now resides with you, deep within your consciousness. *(Inaudible)*.

Indeed, once you, to some degree, decide *(inaudible)*.

Indeed, many things that you encounter in your meditation *(inaudible)* indeed known to you in your physical consciousness *(inaudible)* but this the gradual pulling aside of the curtain that surrounds the physical illusion.

(Inaudible)

(Carla channeling)

I am Laitos. I greet you, my friends, in the love and light of the One Who is All. It is my special privilege and duty to give you the conditioning wave, if you desire it. For the benefit of the newer members of this group we would like to speak a few words about the conditioning wave before we begin.

That which we deliver through these channels to this meeting is sent upon a certain type of vibration. This vibration is of a certain characteristic pattern which, as you have said earlier in conversation, is much like the tuning of one of your electronic instruments.

The conditioning wave, as we call it, is the blanket vibration of a spiritual nature which carries all communications through the instruments. It is accompanied by the impulse, which when correctly received, may be translated into various movements which indicate actual contact between us of the Confederation and you upon the surface of your planet.

For those of you who wish only to experience the spiritual vibration, this conditioning wave is useful. And for those who are interested in becoming what is known as channels, the conditioning wave's functions are two-fold: first, to strengthen the spiritual vibration which will carry our thought impulses; second, to exercise the physical being which houses the instrument, so that the instrument will be quite sure that we are actually transmitting thoughts and are not a figment of your imagination.

I will therefore, at this time, offer the conditioning wave to those who desire it. If you will relax and avail yourself, we will make our presence felt. I will leave this instrument now, and greet each of you. I am Laitos.

(Pause)

(H channeling)

I am *(inaudible)*. I wish to once again greet you in the love and light of our infinite Creator. For those who request this conditioning wave, we wish to express our sincere gratitude, for we are in need in the days to come of instruments. *(Inaudible)*.

We are pleased to aid you in your service, if this is your choice. It has been my privilege to join with you tonight. *(Inaudible)*. I leave you in His love and His light. I am the one known as Laitos. Adonai vasu borragus.

(T channeling)

Greetings, my friends, in the love and the light of the One Who is All. I have but a very few words to say.

(Inaudible)

I will leave you now, in His love and His light *(inaudible)*. I am Oxal. Adonai vasu.

L/L Research

Tuesday Meditation
November 12, 1974

(Carla channeling)

[I am Hatonn.] I am in more precise contact with this instrument than with the other instrument. There is a lack of the usual relaxation with both of these instruments. I am aware of the question. I have been giving concepts to both instruments and have not yet been able to achieve a clear contact. This instrument has been having difficulty relaxing due to a state of some discomfort which varies due to variations within the illusion.

The cycle is fairly rapid, therefore, the contact is cycling in accuracy. The other instrument simply needs to relax. There is one who will attempt to condition both instruments and will attempt to transfer this contact to the other instrument, if possible, and attempt to relay the information you desire.

I greet you, and I give each of you the assurance that we wish to serve you to the best of our ability and to the best of yours. This type of information is not particularly important, yet, we will serve you as you wish to be served. [I] leave this instrument in love and light. I am Hatonn.

(Don channeling)

I am with the instrument. I am Hatonn.

(Inaudible)

(Carla channeling)

I am now with this instrument. I would like at this time to answer a question which has not been asked consciously, yet is within this instrument and may help each of those present.

That which is known upon your planet as illness is due to lack of understanding of the principle of living which is that there is only one, one place and one Being. The time is the present; the place is here; the Being is love. These things equal what is known in your intellectual framework.

It is in the misunderstanding of these truths that all lack, which shows itself to you as physical discomforts, physical needs, mental agony, and emotional need, come forth. If, my friends, you were able to live completely within the moment and to realize the love which is all around you, and to sense the immediacy of your surrounding, you would no longer be other than truly perfect within the illusion as well as outside of the illusion.

This instrument, my friends, is having some trouble receiving even these abstract thoughts, for she is maintaining a state of tension within her physical being, due to the fact she is living in the future and is awaiting the next time in which an uncomfortable feeling will come within her physical being. And yet, my friends, it is this tension that produces the future discomfort. Without the tension, perhaps, a lingering misunderstanding of a more basic type which we may call karma may yet manifest. Yet this can be made shorter and easier, and finally can be made to disappear, simply by application of a higher truth than the law of which you call karma.

There is a higher truth, my friends. Each of you may consider that your discomforts, whatever they may be, may be alleviated and finally removed by the application of the higher law of love and understanding of the eternal present and the eternal immediacy of the entire Creation.

You are one being, my friends. One perfect being. In reality, this is true. The realization of reality causes your illusion to correspond with that reality. Live in harmony, my friends, with reality.

I am aware that there was a question which was asked about what you call the New Age. This, my friends, is a large subject, or, shall I say, we may speak upon it at length. And yet, if you may understand what we were saying about the truth of love, oneness, of here and now, you may begin immediately to comprehend your New Age.

This instrument is having difficulty maintaining the quality of the content. And so, we will leave the instrument.

We are most privileged to have been able to have spoken through each of the instruments this evening. Before we leave, we would be privileged to attempt to contact one of the new instruments, if he will relax and avail himself to our contact.

I leave this instrument in the love and light of our Creator. I am Hatonn.

(Tape ends.)

L/L Research

Friday Meditation
November 15, 1974

(Carla channeling)

I am Hatonn. I greet you, my friends, in the love and in the light of the infinite Creator. It is a great privilege to be with you this evening. I and my brothers of Hatonn, though far, by your standards, are quite near by our standards to you at this time. We watch over you and it is with pleasure that we pursue our service to you. I am aware that there are questions, and so I would wish to concentrate upon answering some this evening.

My brother, Laitos, is here and as you request his conditioning he will give it to you as I and my brothers speak to you through this instrument and through others. I would ask for your kind permission to answer one question that has not been asked.

I would simply like not to let the opportunity pass to remind you, my friends, of the unity of all things. Meditate, my friends, upon the complete unity of yourself and all that you see. Do this not once, and not simply in present circumstances, but at all times and especially in difficult circumstances. For, my friends, insofar as you love and feel at one with those things which are difficult for you, to that extent will those circumstances be alleviated. This is not due to any laws within our physical illusion, but is due to the law of love. For that body which is of spirit, which is interpenetrated with the physical body, is higher than your physical body. And those changes which you make by love upon your spiritual body, will, of necessity, reflect themselves within the physical illusion.

All is one, my friends. My voice is now the voice of this instrument; my thoughts are her thoughts. Please believe, my friends, that the vibration we offer you is not a vibration of personality, but is a vibration of the Creator. We are also channels. There is only one voice. Within this vibration, we are self-consciously aware that this voice is the voice of the Creator. It is simply a matter of lifting vibrations which are not so self-aware of the Creator. That, too, is spiritual vibration, and all things will eventually come into harmony in relation to your understanding.

Even if the universe for those around you remains disharmonious and difficult, if your mind is stayed upon the unity of the Creator, your own universe will become harmonious. And this is not by your doing but by the simple love of the Creator.

Meditate upon this, my friends. It is not an easy lesson. And it will require a great deal of meditation, before the practice is as easy as the intellectual acceptance.

There are questions. I now open the meeting for questions.

T: Yes, I have a question. Hatonn, would you say something commenting on the newspaper article about the nine planets of the solar system lining up in one line?

I would be happy to speak in general of this event. We have told you many times that there is a season upon your planet which shall be highly traumatic within your physical illusion. The physical reasons for this are varied. And, my friends, your scientists will spend a great deal of time, while they can, in attempting to catalog and describe each of the conditions which will produce disaster, on this physical plane [of] your planet.

That which your scientists speak of is quite so, and will be part of the program which has been predicted by all of those holy works which you have upon the face of the Earth. It is not either permissible or possible for us to tell you precisely what events will occur, or when they will occur, due to the fact that the vibration within the mind and heart of the peoples upon your planet is determining and will determine the precise events. There is within the planet Earth a great deal of karma which must be adjusted as the cycle changes and these things will manifest. At precisely when, and how, we cannot say. Nor would we wish to, my friends. For the rain and the wind and fire will destroy only those things which are in what you call the third density of vibration.

You may value those things, because you cannot imagine what a fourth density existence will be like. We suggest to you, my friends, that you spend no time concerning yourselves with the effort of maintaining your third-density existence after the vibration change to forth density has been completed.

If, within your spirit, your graduation day has come, those things necessary for your emergence into fourth density will be done for you. All will be accomplished by helpers which you must be aware that you have.

It is extremely possible that damage will occur to those things which you identify with yourself in the third density. If we may speak plainly, you will observe the valley of the shadow of death. These very words, my friends, we have spoken to you before and yet you cling to that physical body and those physical surroundings as though your spirit were attached quite permanently.

May we suggest to you that you can find your spirit neither in your head, nor in your hands, nor in your chest, nor in your legs, nor in your feet, that nowhere can you find your spirit; nowhere can you operate to remove it, nor to aid it. Your spirit resides within a shell. The shell may be removed, but that is no matter. The spirit does not perish.

Again to the cycle change. You will be undergoing a journey which is quite unlike journeys from third density to other planes within third density. We believe that those who graduate will thoroughly enjoy this journey.

There will be a great deal to undertake. You may certainly aid those about you in the days to come, my friends, if you will but know in your heart that your spirit is not dependent upon the state of your body, and if you can realize that the valley of death is but a shadow.

If you have confidence in those days, you will shine like a beacon, that you may carry many with you toward their graduation.

Have I answered your question satisfactorily?

T: Yes, thank you.

Are there questions?

E: Yes, does the mass landing you speak of so often have anything to do with the harvest you mention?

I would like to answer this question through one of the other instruments, if he would avail himself. I am Hatonn.

(H channeling)

I am Hatonn. I shall attempt to answer any questions regarding this matter.

The landing to which you have referred is one, shall we say, of a more scientific expedition. There are many things that we of the Confederation are aware of. Though we have not passed the need of some technology, we are not totally independent upon machinery, shall we say.

The vessels which we occupy are in need of energy. The energy which they require can be obtained upon your planet. We have previously recharged the energy of our ships in this manner many times. It has been quite long since we have last done this. There was some explanation of this within the book from which you have gained your information.

This landing shall be in the very near future. We shall also be very beneficial to your peoples, for many will observe *(inaudible)*. It may awaken within many the search for knowledge, and from that search they may obtain the fourth density—the day of harvest of which you speak.

It is near, yet there are many things which must occur before that day. Be not wary, my friends. Be not anxious. The services you shall render shall indeed gain for you that day of harvest.

Between now and that day do what you feel [you] believe in. Be not lying idle, for in idleness, you are wasting. For each second that you waste, you have taken from another an opportunity to receive your services.

Are there any other questions?

P: Yes. In the Old Testament there are many references to the Lord by the old prophets. Were they actually in contact with you or any others of the Confederation?

There are, within the book to which you refer, many circumstances which occurred to those who wrote and to those they knew. Many times people were said to have had visions. A few have climbed mountains, seen the face of God.

My friends, we tell you when we refer to God as the Creator, we tell you that He is all that exists. To look upon the face of the one next to you is to look upon the face of the Creator. Those who experienced those great moments were not totally aware of this. They met with beings who, to them, radiated the beauty and the love and the knowledge of the Father, which they considered to be held by the one called God.

We have, many times, chosen ones upon your planet within its dense vibration to contact and share with them great knowledge, and they have shared it with others.

We do not wish to be considered as gods. We are but your equals. We are sorry that we have been misunderstood, but we have done the best that we can do, and we feel that the knowledge that we have shared has been helpful. It could have been much more helpful if not improperly used and interpreted by your many religions.

My friends, you shall not find peace within a religion. You do not need to support the spirit with money or goods. The religions upon your planet teach physical ideas, and when they approach the spiritual points, many of them brush them aside. There are those upon your planet which are beneficial, but many which are not.

But to answer her question. We have been referred to in the Bible in many, many portions. And we say to you, as the master Jesus attempted to tell the people of your planet, you are yourself a god. Within you lie the powers which have been demonstrated by the one known as Jesus. He himself told those around him that they were capable of doing greater things than he.

Are there any other questions?

N: I get all these negative thoughts when I am trying to meditate. Is there a word or method I can use to keep my mind clear of these unwanted thoughts?

(Tape ends.)

Year 1975

January 31, 1975 to December 28, 1975

Sunday Meditation
January 31, 1975

(Don channeling)

[I am Hatonn.] I am with you, my friends. I am here in this room. I am using this instrument to communicate with you. I realize that this form of communication is a little strange, I will say, to some of you. But, my friends, if you will truly reflect upon what you would call your environment, you will find that it is in truth beyond your understanding, so why should this communication, as I have called it, be any more strange than that which you find about you?

I will not try to prove to you, my friends, that I am, as you have said, a being from another planet. I will not try to prove to you that these words that you hear are my thoughts rather than the thoughts of this instrument. I will simply state to you what we, your friends from space, have come to give to you. This is our purpose, my friends. Not to offer you proof, but simply to possibly stimulate your thinking. For this reason we choose to communicate with you in what you might term odd ways. But I can assure you that there is good reason for this form of communication.

I and my brothers who are visiting this planet at this time are not strangers to this planet. We have been here many, many times in your past, and we will continue to visit your planet, and we will continue to work with your peoples. We are working with your peoples at this time in many ways. It is not necessary that we communicate with your people in this fashion to help them. Most of our work is done in a manner that you would call below the level of consciousness. Most of your people are not aware of our contacts. We simply present ideas. These ideas may be accepted or rejected by your people. We hope that in time we will be able to lead your people out of the darkness in which they dwell. This darkness is not necessary. Your peoples may join ours in the light of the infinite Father, as you would call that state of consciousness which is the oneness of the creation.

We are here to help you understand. And, my friends, your peoples need this understanding. In truth, my friends, this is all your peoples need for, in truth, this is all that there is. For when this understanding is acquired, all that there is is acquired. For all that there is is a state of mind.

Your thinking, my friends, is in truth all that there is, for without your thinking there is nothing. Your thinking governs all that you experience. And in this we are here to aid you with: your thinking.

For many, many generations have been engrossed, I will say, in a false world. In a world of thought, which was meaningless. Your peoples have not been aware of anything. Your peoples, as the lower forms of life, if you could call them that, upon your planet have acted from what you might term instinct. They have evolved what we might term intellectual philosophies, which are in truth meaningless, for, my friends, you have no basis for understanding that can be termed intellectual.

Your peoples have been unaware, for the most part, of that single source of understanding which would allow them to free themselves from the pain of the physical existence in which they now find themselves. We are here to attempt in various ways to aid each of your peoples to find their way back to the Father and the true creation.

This may be done by any, any of your peoples, at any time. It is simply an individual choice. Much has been given, in many, many forms, to the people of this planet. Much misunderstanding has come about. Most of what has been given to your peoples has been recorded and has become the basis for the various religions which are in effect upon your planet at this time. But, my friends, we find that almost all of this has been misinterpreted. For this reason, we seldom try to communicate concepts of truth in what you would term a verbal form or fashion, for very little is accomplished. The misunderstandings that have occurred in interpretation in the past will occur in the present.

We rely, therefore, upon a more satisfactory method of communication, one that does not depend upon the interpretation of your languages. We are able to contact your people directly, mentally. But we are only able to contact them if they avail themselves to our contacts. It is not necessary that they be aware that they are availing themselves to our contacts; it is only necessary that they quiet their conscious mind and make themselves receptive to us.

For those of you who are aware of our purpose, we suggest what you have termed meditation, for in this manner you will make yourselves receptive to that which we have to offer. We will only offer suggestions. We will only offer concepts. We will never impose our will upon your peoples. For this, my friends, would be breaking the very laws which we are attempting to explain or deliver into the consciousnesses of those who inhabit this particular planet.

We find that on this planet man has become engrossed in the intellectual creations or toys which he has devised to entertain him. Those creations may be what you term your world government or your scientific creations. They are, in truth, of no consequence, and are, of course, but a transient in the experience of their creators. You have but one thing that is not a transient. You have, my friends, only your thinking to keep for all of eternity, as you call it.

Your thinking, my friends, is all you have to develop and it is all that is really yours. The physical body in which you now find yourself is not in truth yours, and is transient. All that you create, whether it be material or whether it be intellectual, is transient.

Your people have a way of engrossing themselves with these transients that I have spoken of. They have a way of becoming addicted, shall I say, to that which in truth is of very little importance.

Your peoples today are involved in what you term your politics. your science, your business, and the affairs of your world. This has been the situation upon this planet for many centuries. Your peoples have so engrossed themselves in the study of these transient conditions that they have in truth lost that which is theirs as a gift of their Creator.

We are attempting to bring to your peoples an awareness of that which is not transient. We are attempting to bring to your peoples that which will reawaken an awareness that in truth is all that there is. For, my friends, truth is all that is lasting, an awareness, my friends, of the true creation of the infinite Father. This creation, my friends, is not a petty creation; is not a creation of no consequence; is not a creation that will be transient in the infinite scan of what you call time.

The individual can select at any time [to follow the proper] path of true development, or he may continue to involve his thinking with that which is of no real consequence. It was spoken to your peoples by your last great teacher that, "When I became a man, I put away the things of childhood." An interpretation of this, my friends, is what I have attempted to give you.

It is only possible to understand what we attempt to give you if you avail yourself to us through meditation, for the words which we are forced to use in speaking to you in your language are totally inadequate for the delivery of the concepts which we would attempt to present to you. For, my friends, the first thing that we would attempt to do is to help you become aware of the creation.

This creation, my friends, is overlooked by your peoples. This is something that is difficult for us to understand. We cannot understand how your peoples can stand upon the surface of what you call a planet, and totally overlook the creation of the infinite One. For this, my friends, is all that there is. There is nothing but this creation, this infinite creation of the infinite Father. This creation, my friends, is far more fantastic than any of the toys of your civilization.

Become aware of this first, my friends. Use your time for meditation and contemplation of the true creation; that which is you, and that which surrounds you. Become aware of this, my friends, and you will begin to understand what we are attempting to deliver unto you. Your peoples are not even aware of themselves. This awareness will grow, as you avail yourself in meditation. As this awareness grows, you will more closely attune your thinking to that which was intended by the Creator of us all. As your thinking becomes more attuned, you will begin to experience that which was intended. This has been experienced by some of your peoples. It may happen at any time and in any physical incarnation, as you speak of it, and this may have occurred to you as an individual in some earlier experience.

We are suggesting that you utilize in the fullest extent the opportunity that you have in this experience to, shall we say, revitalize this awareness. We have difficulty, my friends, in communicating these concepts. We have difficulty in using this instrument. For there are no words within your language. There are no concepts within your language for this communication.

We can only suggest to you that there is much, much beyond that which your civilization in presently experiencing. We can only suggest to you methods of achieving and experience of far greater satisfaction. We will be pleased to work individually with each of you. It is only necessary that you desire our aid.

My friends, I will suggest that you think of that which is written in your holy works: "Seek, and ye shall find. Knock, and the door shall be opened unto you." These words indicate to you, my friends, that it is first necessary that you desire more than it is possible to experience in the physical. It is necessary, my friends, that the individual seek first. This seeking, my friends, is necessary. This seeking, my friends, is the only real purpose for your existence in the physical. There is an infinite amount of time, as you call it, available. The individual may initiate his seeking at any time. Once this has been done, aid to the seeking will be supplied in what we might call a direct proportion to that seeking. In each case it will be an individual matter.

Seek ye first the kingdom of heaven, and all else shall be added. But first it is necessary to seek. This is quite necessary.

I hope, my friends, that I have been of some service to you this evening. I cannot prove to you at this time that I am who I say that I am, and if I could, in truth it would make no difference. For if I stood among you, and spoke to you, and reached out and touched you, it would make no difference. It is an individual matter, my friends, and it will always be an individual matter. For you, and only you, can affect your own thinking. For this is you, my friends. The miracles that occur about you in your daily life are routine to your thinking, but they are in truth miraculous.

Your people think they must have something different from worldly experience, if it is to be called a miracle. For this reason, and some others, we find that it is necessary to remain aloof from your peoples.

Become aware of the miracle of the creation about you which is you. When you are able to do this, then perhaps we will meet you in a more tangible fashion.

I will leave you now. I am Hatonn. I leave you, my friends, in the love and the light of the One Who is All. Adonai. Adonai vasu borragus.

Sunday Meeting
November 2, 1975

(H channeling)

I am Hatonn. Greetings, my friends, in the love and in the light of our infinite Creator. We have come to share with you what we consider to be thoughts that would be of benefit to you. We have also come as has been desired. And for this reason, we are pleased to share with you this moment of meditation.

We identify ourselves as the Confederation of Planets in Service to the Infinite Creator. Yet in truth, my friends, we are one with you, in spirit. For in spirit all things reside. And from one spirit comes the source for all experiences. And from one spirit shall all things become known. It is the destiny, shall we say, or the birthright, for each individual to evolve in awareness so that he may truly comprehend the origin of his being. And that origin, my friends, is contained within the oneness of the entire creation; the knowledge that all things form, with the whole, an entire being, infinite in experience and knowledge.

Infinite in all things is this being. Yet within you is it contained. And to know this being, it is only necessary to turn within yourself, and speak in silence to the one universal spirit known as the Creator. You truly contain this knowledge, and it is yours to gain at your own choosing. We of the Confederation believe that those present shall at their own rate achieve the awareness of which we speak. And for this reason, we share these thoughts. At this time, I shall transfer this communication to another instrument. I am Hatonn.

(Carla channeling)

I am now with this instrument. I am Hatonn. And again I greet you, and thank you for the privilege of being allowed to speak with you. It is indeed a privilege to speak with you. This, shall we say, illusion in which you dwell does not seem to be as we describe it to you, my friends, does it? It does not seem to be within you. And this is why we call it an illusion …

(Inaudible)

(Tape ends.) ♣

L/L Research

Sunday Meeting
November 23, 1975

(H channeling)

I am Hatonn. Greetings, my friends, in the love and the light of our infinite Creator. I identify myself to you by using the name Hatonn. I wish to emphasize, though, that this is only a means of identification which we have chosen to use through these communications. In reality, the name "Hatonn" would be considered the identity of what you would call the planet from which we come. Upon our planet, or shall I say, within our realm, the people, which number greatly, have united in consciousness and are desirous of one thing. And that one thing, my friends, is to know the Creator, and to be instruments of His love. And through this desire, we have come to serve the people on your planet.

So we of Hatonn, being of one mind, have heeded the cause of the peoples upon your planet, for there are many who are subconsciously pleading for assistance. We have come for this purpose, to assist in whatever way we may at this time.

We of the Confederation of Planets in the Service to the Infinite Creator consist of a large number of what you would call planets. We come from many areas of the universe, yet we are all united. We are all one, in reality. And in speaking of this oneness, we will emphasize also that you yourselves are as important to the concept of oneness as is, or shall I say, as are all of these. For, my friends, if you exclude but one member, but one unit within this vast creation, then you do not realize the concept of oneness. One, as you understand it, means a unit without any extension. But one as we understand it is a unit of infinity. My friends, as you understand infinity, there is no end or beginning. And if there are no ends, or no beginnings, to the concert of one, or infinity, what else could it be called but a unit, one unit of infinite experience, which contains all things, all knowledge, all beings within the universe.

Oneness, my friends, is indeed not limited. Oneness is all things. Within one, all things are found. Within yourself, my friends, the true identity of the concept of one has been implanted by our Creator. Within each being on your planet and throughout the creation there is the concept of one, there is its knowledge and understanding. Within you lie the answers to all problems. Within you lie the experiences of all other beings, for once you realize and are totally aware of the oneness of the entire universe then you cannot separate the experiences of your brothers from the experience of yourselves. You shall not realize self-identity as you do now. For self-identity, my friends is something which you have adopted for a short period of time while existing within the physical realm. It has been adopted by you so that you may learn. And within this physical realm, the lesson you must learn is love. And love is one, and love is all.

These words may seem contradictory, yet that is because you have taken these concepts and you have separated them within your physical illusion. My friends, realize that within the creation there are no separations. All things are indeed united and can never in any way be truly separate of each other. Your thoughts, as thoughts of all other beings, are emanated truly from one source of intelligence. And that intelligence, my friends, is the love of the Creator. And it is the Creator.

You are creators, as are all other beings. And all together, as we understand it, are the Creator. We do not know as a fact all realities or all truths, yet as close as we have been able to understand it, this is the truth: that all beings unite, all things take away the separations which we have implanted within them, unite to form the omnipotent being we call the Creator. We are but particles of His consciousness.

Yet within each particle are His abilities. We must learn to focus our consciousness on His love, which is readily available to all. And we must learn to utilize properly the abilities which have been implanted within us. For within us, my friends, is the ability to create, the infinite ability to create experience through all eternity. This should be thought of, for you should not take lightly your ability to create. For as you go through your day, you have many thoughts. Many thoughts are kind and loving. Yet within your world you are constantly bombarded by negative experiences and thoughts. Your thoughts, negative and positive, are in reality creations of experience within other realms than [this consensus] reality. Therefore, you must learn to control and utilize properly your ability to create.

I would transfer this contact at this time. I am Hatonn.

(Carla channeling)

(Inaudible)

(Tape ends.)

Sunday Meeting
November 30, 1975

(Carla channeling)

I am Hatonn. I am the one known as Hatonn. I greet you in the love and the light of the infinite Creator, the Creator of us all. It is, as always, my privilege to be with you, especially at this time, for I speak to those at a special time. We do not wish to make occasions where there are no occasions. Yet we say to you this is, within each of your experiences, a time of dedication. You may call it a rededication. Yet within this small group, my friends, there is a dedication that is not always found. Therefore, we say, "Greetings" in a special sense, from those of us who are privileged to be with you at this time.

My brothers, you have heard many of our words, and it is as though we appear to you as tailors, measuring and cutting and detailing and analyzing, and attempting to tailor for you the spiritual path, using our tools and laying it all together in a measured way. And this, of course, is because we have used these channels and we have used words. In reality, we are not tailors, and there is no measure. In reality, our message is infinite, and there is no set pattern for progress. And that which we truly have to give you lies within the silence. We find that each of you is aware of this, and yet the words are comforting, and so we are very happy to speak with you.

You must know that in many ways, you are no longer dependent upon these words, for you carry within you the ability to receive thoughts. Each of you does not need the channel any longer. Yet, what one needs for survival and what one needs to be at his peak are two different things. And that is why it is a very, very good thing that you are still meeting to hear us, as well as to meditate. There is within each of you that which desires always to let go for a moment and simply be taught, be led. This is proper. And so we welcome the opportunity to speak.

Tonight, we would like to give you a few thoughts on the nature of innocence. We want you to think of your own nature, and of what you consider to be your sins, your errors, your mistakes. You who try, sometimes very hard, to be upon the spiritual path, often are very hard upon yourselves because you have erred, made a mistake. You have manifested that which was not positive. And you say, "Why have I done this? Why did I make this error? I did not mean that! Why did I do it?" And you concentrate on the error. And this does not seem to prevent you from making an error the next time.

My friends, we have said to you many times, "We greet you in love and in light." We greet you in infinite perfection. We greet perfect beings who are totally innocent. We would like to suggest to you that instead of concentrating upon your mistakes, you ask yourself how much time you have spent this day investigating that portion of your unique person which is totally perfect. How much awareness have you had this day of the love and the light of the Creator you have within you? How aware have you been of your own innocence?

When you concentrate upon your mistakes, you dwell within the world of mistakes. And mistakes will occur again and again. If your consciousness is dwelling at a higher [resonance] within the realm where you know that you are a creation of the Father, you know that you can manifest His love. Then the opportunity for you to make a mistake and manifest that which is not love will be that much farther from you. Meditation is not upon your mistakes; is not upon the past. It is upon the eternal present, and upon your innocence. You are a child of love.

We emphasize this at this time because you are attempting to dedicate yourself in a far deeper way than you have previously attempted to do. And the key to the deeper dedication is to be able to focus yourself not upon the world of mistakes, but upon the world in which that spirit within you which is the Creator, which you may find it desirable to call the Christ spirit within you, will manifest.

My friends, it is written in your holy works that you do not know when this spirit will come. He may come in the morning. Or He may come in the evening. Or He may come at midnight. And if your lamp is lit, all will be well. And if it is not lit, you will miss Him. To dwell in the state of awareness that you are watching for the One Who is All: this is the source of the inspiration that will affect the kind of service that you wish to give, the kind of life that you wish to dedicate yourself to. You cannot analyze your own motives, your own acts or other people's motives and acts. They will tangle you all up, my friends. Only dedicate yourself, not just now, but in all the nows, to the Father. Watch and wait, for you do not know when He will come.

Within the innocence of your soul, that which is perfect will always be coming into you. So concentrate on that. It is especially difficult within your peoples' lives at this time to make this change in emphasis, for people more and more have become each other's watchdog, and this is accepted within your culture, as you may call it. And those who attempt not to concentrate upon the negative are often considered unaware, or even stupid. Yet we assure you that the will that you create by your continued innocence of heart will be a light within this world, this world of yours which is dark at this time.

My friends, it is as though the world were deep, deep asleep, and a few of you are attempting to remain awake. For you, my friends, love may yet light up the sky. For those who sleep, it may be a long night.

Other people's reality will remain real for them. Yours will also remain real for you, no matter how, shall we say, difficult the times may get for those about you. It is truly written that to those which are innocent in heart, those things which are needed will come.

I am so happy to be able to speak with you, and I will tell you it is close to my heart that each of you within this room has the ability to speak our thoughts. It is hoped that each of you will be able to help others.

At this time. I would like to leave you so that, my brother, Laitos, may speak through another channel. I leave you, my friends, in the love and light of the infinite Creator. I am known as Hatonn. I am you. Adonai.

(B channeling)

I am Laitos. I also, my friends, greet you in the love and the light of our infinite Creator. It has been some time since I have been able to use this instrument …

(The rest of the tape is inaudible.)

Sunday Meeting

December 7, 1975

(H channeling)

I am Hatonn. Greetings, my friends, in the love and the light of our infinite Creator. It is as always a pleasure and indeed a privilege to be allowed these few moments with you.

I wish to briefly acquaint myself and my brothers and our purpose with the new member. I have stated my identity as that of Hatonn. I wish to stress that my identity is the same as that of all the inhabitants of what you would consider to be our planet. We of the planet Hatonn have grown through our evolution to a point of unification of consciousness. We have gone beyond the need for extreme self-identification such as is desired by the inhabitants of your planet.

And for this purpose, we simply state ourselves as inhabitants of Hatonn. There are others within what we call our Confederation who would identify themselves by other names, and this method of identification which they use is the same which I have explained to you that we have chosen to use.

All the members of the Confederation of Planets in Service to the Infinite Creator have reached this unification of consciousness and desire. This brings us to our purpose. Our purpose is the same as our desires and our desire is to share our love and knowledge with the inhabitants of planet Earth, and with all others who would request it. We of the Confederation claim not to be beings of a supreme nature. We are not infallible in our judgment or knowledge.

Yet through our experience, we do feel that we have attained a greater understanding of the universe than those upon the planet Earth. Some upon your planet may find this statement offensive. Yet we must stress that this is truth, as we understand it. We do not wish to convey to anyone who would not choose, our thoughts. We only wish to share what we have with those who also wish to share with us. By this, we mean that we shall not force anyone to accept what we have to offer.

Our purpose is simple, as is our desire. We of the Confederation wish to serve the people upon planet Earth, and nothing else. We have no motive other than to increase your own knowledge and understanding by sharing with you our knowledge and understanding.

For in service to another, inevitably you are serving yourself. For as many philosophies upon your planet have stated, the universe and all that is in it are one being, and no more, with each being and each particle within it being exactly that: one particle within a whole, all united within consciousness and spirit. And through this unification comes about the undeniable fact that service to one is service to all, and to oneself. You, my friends, are the creator and the gods which are spoken of in the scriptures, as is everyone and everything within this universe. Accept separations within your consciousness, and they shall exist temporarily for you. But deny them, my friends, and the ones which you have been accepting for so long shall begin to fade from your awareness. And you shall begin to awaken to the true concept of oneness. And you shall begin to know the truth: that there are no separations.

We of the Confederation are beings as yourself, with no greater capabilities than what you possess. The only difference between ourselves and those within this room is that we, through our own efforts, and mostly through the use of meditation, have broadened our awareness and experience beyond that which you have done.

We dwell in a dimension, if you wish to call it that, which does not contain physical reality as you know it. In our domain, spirituality and spiritual awareness overwhelm all existence. If you are not within the harmony of the laws of creation, then you are not able to exist within our domain. Within our domain, there is not that which you consider to be negative. All that there is is love and light, love being the physical manifestation of all things.

Love is all things. The Creator is love, and He resides within you. Each time that you express your love, you have created. And each time you pass up a chance to show love, you have also passed up your chance to develop your birthright of being a creator.

My friends, what you do not understand is that you are not limited. You have been taught that there is a supreme Being, but you have been taught to accept this Being as one Who is not within you. You have been taught to accept this Being as being, in actuality, a physical being of supreme nature. This is a fallacy, in a sense, for all beings are physical beings of a supreme nature, for from the supreme Being we have come, and within Him shall we reside, and within us also shall He reside.

If you could but only once see with your eyes the creation as it truly is meant to be, as it truly is, you would see nothing, my friends, but light. You would not see entities or objects. You would only see particles of light, dashing in front of you. For this is reality is all existence. We are the particles which constitute and create the Creator. And in turn, we have been created by the Creator. Without you, without each individual, the Creator could not exist.

And without the Creator, all things could not exist. All things are interdependent, and all things are one supreme Being.

I shall transfer this contact at this time. I am Hatonn.

(Carla channeling)

I am with this instrument. I am Hatonn.

As many times as we have gone over these concepts, we find that it is not clear within any of your minds just what the relationship is between you and the Creator. Somehow, it seems to your conscious mind that to say that you are the Creator, the Creator cannot get along without you, you are Gods, etc., is somewhat laughable and even, shall we say, egocentric. And, my friends, if we were saying these things to you at the level at which these words unfortunately speak, indeed it would be terribly incorrect information. We ask that you attempt to relax your mind. Remove yourself from the tightness of your everyday thinking. And begin to see that you are very close to yourself, and very far from the nearest star, so that you seem to be much larger than the star. It is a matter of perspective. In reality, the star is a majestic, magnificent, enormous entity, compared to you. And if you are one with the star, then the star is one with you, and neither complete without the other. It is no more than the understanding which is recorded in your holy works, where it is written that sparrows, which are two for a penny, never fall without the Creator knowing that they have fallen. All things, large and small, lie within the Creator, for they lie within the creation.

We do not know what the Creator is. We do not know His nature. We do not know His actions, His purposes, His intentions. The Creator is infinite, invisible. This we know, for this He has shown to us again and again: that He created us in a vibration of pure love, and that He considers all of us as Himself. And so we tell you this, not knowing the ultimate reason, only knowing that reason enough for our infinite existence as entities within a loving creation exist and may be told to all.

We come to give you a message of love. We come to tell you that you are gods, not because you are so wonderful, but because the Creator is wonderful.

And the Creator is within you. Stand away from your personality and see if you can find that faraway sun within you, that star shining in the darkness and depths of your soul. There shines the Creator: in some cases terribly distant, yet always there, and always shining. All you need do, my friends, is look up. Within yourself, begin to seek for that star. The Creator is within you, and the Creator will work through you.

And so you may say, my friends, the Creator is you. For all practical purposes, my friends, you may cause your life to become a channel through which the Creator may live and move. In many cases, it may seem as though this human personality of yours may never get, shall we say the hang of showing the Creator's love to others. It may seem that the possibilities of the situations which you are in are very, very limited for showing love. But I say to you: that it is truly written that the place whereon you are standing is holy ground. You do not need to put yourself into a situation which may seem outwardly spiritual in order to be in a spiritual situation. For, my friends, the universe is a spiritual universe, and what you are going through is an illusion called the physical existence.

Spirituality, as it is called, may often seem to be a joke. One cannot be spiritual in a church and walk away from the church and become nonspiritual. This, may I say, my friends, makes no sense at all. For one is spirit and one carries the spirit within the temple of his body, into and out of church. Into and out of every situation. When the situation seems difficult, wait for a moment for the realization to come to you that in you is a spirit, and within that spirit is enough love to carry you through that situation so that you may show the love of the Creator.

I will close through another channel. I am Hatonn.

(B channeling)

I am Hatonn. I am now with this instrument. I would at this time like to say just a few words more. My friends, in order to take advantage of the creation which, as I have stated, is within each of you, it is not something that is always available to you, unless practiced. You will find, my friends that when used continuously through your existence, it is always available. But, my friends, you also know, due to the illusion which is now taking place, it is hard to see at times.

Continue with your meditations. And never give up hope. For, my friends, you are part of the Creator. This you will realize more each day. And it is true, my friends. In the creation there can be no sorrow.

I will leave you at this time. I am Hatonn. Adonai. ☥

Sunday Meeting
December 21, 1975

(H channeling)

I am Hatonn. Greetings, my friends, in the love and the light of the infinite Creator. It is very pleasing to be able to speak with all present this evening. We are grateful to meet so many new members. I should state at this time that I and all with whom I am working consider ourselves to be brothers. We are unified in our purpose and in our thought. And many would immediately ask of our purpose. My friends, our purpose is to love and serve the people of planet Earth and throughout the Creator's infinite universe.

We of the Confederation of Planets in Service to the Infinite Creator have come to Earth at this time to offer whatever assistance we may be able to render. And presently we are limited to this assistance in the form you are experiencing now. We are communicating through instruments such as the one speaking to mass numbers of inhabitants upon your planet. The words which we speak are offered with love and as guidance, intellectual guidance along the pathway of enlightenment.

Yet we stress, my friends, that the intellect is only a minor tool in your development. My friends, you know as well as all other people that possess an intellect that your intellectual capacities are quite limited. There are many things which you have accepted as truth that are unexplainable through your intellectual process. Uncomprehendable, yet true. My friends, truth is greater in capacity, or should I say, in size, than what the intellect is capable of perceiving. Truth is infinite, and all things within the creation are unlimited, as is your experience, and as is your knowledge. For your knowledge truly lies within the core of your being; within the oneness of the Creator; within His presence within you. My friends, your journey throughout this universe and throughout this creation is one of cycles which never end, which are constantly expanding in knowledge and experience. Upon your pathway you shall encounter many circumstances through which you may learn. And your present encounter upon the planet Earth is one of very great importance in the scheme of your progression.

My friends, man upon planet Earth presently stands upon the threshold of unlimited knowledge, unlimited love. Unlimited, my friends, infinite, never ending. It is your birthright to know these truths. Yet there is only one way to truly comprehend and to truly be enlightened. And as you may well be aware, that way is through the practice of meditation.

My friends, we have told you that the truths, the unlimited and infinite truths, lie beyond the capacities of your intellect. Therefore, in order to explore these truths, to learn and know of these truths, you must go beyond the intellect. Allow it to still itself. Allow it to rest. And let the spiritual intellect begin to avail its information to you. You may not hear words, my friends, but you shall hear truth and love. In your moments of silence, you shall hear the universe speaking through the lips of the Creator the truths of infinity and love.

I shall transfer this communication. I am Hatonn.

(N channeling)

I am Hatonn. Again I greet you in the love and light of the infinite Creator. My friends, although I stress to you the necessity for meditation seemingly constantly, I do not stress it enough. But still, my friends, we do not want to force this upon you. The decision is yours. And either way that you decide will be the path that you have chosen. We know in our experience of no other way for a somewhat speedy path, shall we say, than meditation. But the choice is yours.

We are aware of some questions in your minds, and you may have noticed some of them have already been answered. My friends, although the idea of our presence may seem rather uncommon at this time, we say to you that we have been with you for a very long time. If any of you desire our thoughts, or our presence, at the moment that you desire it, we are with you. We can only help you if you desire it. For that is our way. We leave the free will of each person in creation alone. For you see, through your own desire can be the only way we may assist you. But it is our sincere desire to be able to be with you. We consider it a very great honor to be of assistance. We are with you, my friends.

At this time I will transfer this contact to another instrument. I am Hatonn.

(Carla channeling)

I am now with this instrument. I am Hatonn, and I greet you once again in the love and the light of the infinite Creator. As we speak to you about meditation as a method of furthering your interests within this life, we wish to stop for a moment and take advantage of your experiences at this particular time. We ask that you consider your environment at this particular time, the darkness and the chill of winter. How many hours have been spent in darkness and cold? Think, my friends, of the true nature of that which is unfolding within one of your religious systems of belief. There is a story that is told that is a true story, the story is of a child born in the darkest winter. Poor, cold, hungry, the child that grew to be the master whom you know as Jesus. My friends, each of you is waiting to be born. Each of you is in the dark, in the cold. For it is within the darkness and the chill that all things come together to be born. It is the nurturing, saving darkness. And the chill is necessary. And with meditation, my friends, you nurture and comfort that soul within you as it struggles towards its spiritual birth.

There has been within your history, we are aware, much misunderstanding as to the reason for the mother of the one known as Jesus being called a virgin. You must realize that it is to indicate to all that the spirit is not of man but of the Father. Each of you is of the Father. Each of you is waiting to be born. Nurture that within yourself. No matter that the environment may seem less than perfect. It surely cannot be more imperfect than a cold, cold stable, and a stall, and animals for companions. The realities are of the Father, my friends.

We greet you always in love and in light. Love moves in the darkness, and its energy brings forth the light. Each of you is formed in perfect love. Each of you shines with perfect light, my friends.

But there are many, many colors. How many colors can you think of? Perhaps the number is infinite, for there are shades and gradations within each color that go on and on. And each one is distinguishable from the next. And yet in reality, each is a part of the white light. So are you, my friends. And all that you meet are other portions of the same light, formed in perfect love also. How hard it is to see the perfection of the Father in each person! For each person is a different shade, and some shades seem to clash with yours. But all are formed of white light. All are one with you, and you with them.

Why are you here? We may say, to find out why you are here. For the Creator Itself knows Itself, and the desire that caused you is a desire to realize selfhood. The Creator is waiting to be known as the Father. He waits within you, and can be found through meditation.

Your patience, please. We are having some difficulty with this instrument.

(Pause)

I am Hatonn. I will attempt to say one more thing through this instrument before I leave her. I am aware that there are questions. I would like to answer one of a more general type, and that is simply to say that there are within the Confederation of Planets in the Service of the infinite Creator many different types of entities. There are some, not many but some, who are actually of the same physical, as you would call it, plane of reality as you are. There are many more who are as we, in that we are able to assume the vibrations of your world and appear as, shall we say, physical objects. However, we are also able to adjust our vibrations to what you would call the astral plane of existence, so that we are moving within another continuum, and are invisible to you although very much with you. There are also many within the Confederation of Planets who are totally on this level, or on a higher level of vibration. Yet all of us are here with one hope only, and that is to be of service to you. There are many levels of vibration upon planet Earth, and in each of them there is the same confusion. We are helping on the physical, and others help within the worlds which interpenetrate the physical.

All are Earth. And were you not to be here in the physical, but by reason of what you call death have passed into one of the other planes, you would also be aware of our presence. Our presence, we genuinely hope, is of support and love. We come to tell you that there is no end to the Creator, as far as we know, and we have been somewhat further than you. We come to reach a hand out, for those before us have done it for us, and so we do it for you.

And one more thing, my friends. We do this because, at the level of understanding which we have reached, we find we cannot progress further except by service to others. For within our universe, the law which is in your universe called the Golden Rule has become completely and totally obvious. So that what we give determines, immediately and completely, what we get. We cannot receive further knowledge unless we give freely of what we have now. Therefore, it is to our advantage, and for our progress, that we are here.

I would like to transfer, one last time, to another channel. I am Hatonn.

(B channeling)

I am Hatonn. I am now with this instrument. I will say but a few words through this instrument, and that is, my friends, that all that was created by the infinite Creator is what is known to you as love.

Now, my friends, due to ties that you have evolved upon your planet, this concept is seemingly sought by those of your planet. My friends, through living out your existence surrounded in love, you may say that you protect yourself from all that you do not wish to experience. For, my friends, there is nothing stronger than love. But, my friends, it is not something to hold onto. For, my friends, you do not evolve by holding on. We ask you to meditate daily. Surround yourself in this love. To all that you come in contact with. My friends, it is an existence that we have experienced for some time. And, my friends, I can honestly state that the happiness we experience cannot even be imagined by you. This is, as we said, your birthright.

We wish to share this with you, and this is the message that we have for you this evening. It has been an extremely great honor to share in this meditation with you. I leave you in the love and the light of our infinite Creator. Adonai. ✣

Sunday Meeting
December 21, 1975

(Carla channeling)

I am Hatonn. I am now with this instrument, and for a brief time I will speak using this instrument. We speak to you once again because there are things which we wish to say to you that do not apply to all those who are in the larger group. For always, my friends, there are various peoples at various levels of understanding. And we do not speak beyond the ears of those who hear, for that only breeds confusion.

To you we speak of shepherds. For truly, you may look upon your little world as being made up of those who need care, and those who may do the caring. We speak to you of the compassion of the shepherd. Where does the compassion come from? What will inspire you to the compassion of the shepherd with his sheep?

We ask that you remember that the universe is not deadly serious, but rather is a universe of love and joy, of lightness and laughter. It is not necessary that you be so deadly serious that you insist upon absolute compassion within yourself. It is enough, my friends, if you accept a certain lighthearted desire to pretend, shall we say, to be somewhat similar to a compassionate shepherd. You are not attempting to fool the sheep into thinking you are compassionate. You are attempting to fool yourself, from a condition of illusion to a condition of reality. You know, my friends, you cannot bludgeon yourselves into this state of shepherd. Yet you must shepherd yourself, gently and coaxingly and with humor. You may act similarly to that which you would consider to be compassionate and slowly you will discover that you are not acting. But allow yourself that imperfection of ambition which is within the illusion. For you are learning, my friends.

What differentiates you from the sheep, then, who are also learning? There is a broad line that cannot be crossed by sheep, and that line is the desire to know. Sheep will be led, and if they are lost, they must be found. But the shepherds, my friends, have desire to know, in order that they may serve. This desire of yours, to know the Creator and to serve Him—this desire is all that you need to be upon the path of the shepherd. Follow it in joy and humor, for being deadly serious will cause you to stumble.

I believe that the period of preparation for the one known as H is satisfactorily completed. And so I will transfer. I am Hatonn.

(H channeling)

I am Hatonn. I am once again with this instrument. We have had some difficulty, yet we shall continue through this instrument. As all are aware, we are presently within a time, or shall we say, a season, of your year, and this season is one of great expectations of great joy and love. The season we speak of is that of what you would call Christian, the celebration of the birth of the infant Jesus. And of him we would wish to speak.

Jesus, as you call him, was a being who resided upon the planet Earth for the purpose of demonstrating a proper, shall we say, way of living, a proper way of loving. My friends, this great teacher did not die for you. He demonstrated for you that there was in all actuality no death. For no matter how much they were able to torture him and maim his body, he was able to overcome his oppressors with love. And with that same love he was able to demonstrate to all the great power contained within his love: the power over life and death, the power over nature.

My friends, you may have been taught that his death was necessitated in order to relieve us of our bondage and sins. In a concept such as this, there is also truth, for is not the realization of the power of love redemption? My friends, the answer is love. The realization of love is indeed your redemption. So in all actuality the physical death was not your redemption, for all beings have experienced this. But the awakening to the abilities and the power within the concept of love, indeed, was your salvation.

We of the Confederation of Planets state that we are the same dimensional existence as this great teacher. Yet we do not claim right to his accomplishments, for we must acknowledge that the great teacher known as Jesus was the one of the greatest teachers whom we have encountered, or whom you have encountered. And he is still present upon your planet, in the form of consciousness and residing over the spiritual vibrations which are channeled to the people of planet Earth. He is your assigned teacher, and we are his assigned helpers. This is our claim. Accept it if you will. We realize that this one point to many has been the one point of our information that was unacceptable or controversial, shall we say. But remember, my friends, the story we have told you of the love of the teacher Jesus: love, my friends, is what is important. With it, you may discern the truth. Know the love that you possess. Learn to understand this. And through the knowledge you shall find the capacity to channel the abilities contained within the love. At that time, my friends, once you have mastered the concept of love, my friends, once you understand this concept, then shall you not also be capable of achieving that which the great teacher Jesus demonstrated for us?

This is the purpose, my friends. Love was the ingredient that caused, or shall we say, made able, these accomplishments. Not the being himself in physical form, but the love within the being. That love is also within you. It is within all things. Accept this, my friends: love is all. Love is omnipotent. Love is Jesus, and love is you. And all together, all of these loves combined, all of these beings combined, are the Creator. From the Creator we have come, and we are manifestations of His thoughts of love. His love being equal for all enables all to achieve the same. Each being shall achieve these great heights of awareness. Yet each being shall achieve them when they so choose. Think of this, my friends. Do not look upon yourself as an omnipotent ruler or teacher. Look upon all, all of the beings you have known or shall ever know, as being these teachers and rulers and overseers of the creation and its inhabitants.

It has been a privilege to speak with you once again this evening. And in the spirit of the season, we thought that these concepts would be quite appropriate. And we wish to all a loving and a happy Christmas. Adonai vasu borragus. ☙

L/L Research

www.llresearch.org

Sunday Meeting
December 28, 1975

(Carla channeling)

I am Hatonn. I am privileged to speak with this gathering, and I greet you in the love and the light of our infinite Creator. I am with you, and I bring you my peace.

It is written in the words of your most recent master, the one known as Jesus: "Not as the world gives, give I unto you." And as I offer you my peace, may I say, this is so. It is not peace as the world would give, of which I speak, but a truer peace. I am a member of the Confederation of Planets in the Service of the Infinite Creator. I come across galaxies, countless, through a dimensionless gateway, and into your so-called reality, into your special place, into your universe, where you exist. My brothers and I come because you have called us. Because within this universe, the cry goes out from those who are in need, who wish to know reality.

And there are always those who listen. Cries do not go forth unheard, in this infinite universe. And we have heard you, and have come. Others have heard you, and have come. Those of your planet who are able to give, are ready to give unto you, at the finer levels of your planetary sphere. And we from other spheres are here also. For we can tell you one way, a complementary way, another way: all paths are one. There are those who can listen to us who cannot listen to others who would tell you what we will tell you. And so we come, and others come, when those upon your planet call for help. For we are all brothers; all beings upon each level in the infinite Creation are all brothers.

There are several different topics upon which I will to speak this evening. But, my friends, I believe I desire first of all to speak to you of love. It is known to us that each of you desires to seek wisdom, to seek spirituality. Yet we would say to you at this time, please allow this search for knowledge to begin and end within your own experience. You are not seeking a substitute, a different reality in place of the present reality. You are seeking to know your own reality for the first time. You are even now, at this moment, dwelling in reality. It is truly written: Heaven is all about you. You are not seeking a far-away, long-distant kingdom. For the kingdom of Heaven is with you, within you, and about you. Your experience contains the kingdom that you seek.

Let us again observe the teachings of the one known as Jesus. If you do these things to the least of these, my brethren, you do them unto me. The kingdom is all about you, and the Creator is within the face that is across from you, on the street, and in your house. Each stranger, each friend, and each enemy is the Creator. Know ye not that all men are brothers? You seek love, you seek to know the Father, and yet the Father is in each face that you see.

My brothers, look at each other, and, for the first time, truly see the very best within each other. Within the one known as Jesus was a sight which was of love. Those who were about him could be described in rather unfavorable terms. Those whom he loved could be described as harlots, tax-collectors, publicans, beggars; there were many sick and crippled. And in no case did the one known as Jesus see them as anything but the Father, the Father who was directly before him on the physical plane. He looked with love. He saw the possibilities within each of his "fallen" friends. To the sinner, he said, "This day, you will be with me in paradise." My friends, these things are familiar to you, and so I use this channel, and this mode of discussion, as a good example. There are other masters, and they have showed this Creator-within in other words. But we believe that it is through this example that you will most easily understand what we are saying to you. We look at you, and we see the light, we see the perfection, and it is our delight to be in communication with you.

It is very possible for you to become one with this vibration. And, my friends, this vibration of love, this vibration of compassion will transform your life into that of the Kingdom of Heaven. It is a matter of balancing between two opposite attitudes in your seeking. There are two dangers, and we [say] this with a sense of humor, for the dangers are not real. It is the balancing between them that causes your progress. These two dangers, my friends, are pride and humility. Woe be unto the man who begins to feel that it is his love that is setting those about him on the path of light, that [it] is his compassion that is such a light to others. Woe be unto this man, for the love of the personality is limited. It will run out, and in its wake will come much sadness.

Woe also to the person who says, "I am unworthy. In my humility I must admit I cannot be a fit channel for the love of the Creator. Do not expect me to keep trying the impossible, for I am not worthy, and I cannot do this."

In neither case, my friends, have you quite hit the balance. And if you find yourself in either the pride or the humility, balance between confidence and the knowledge of your own imperfections as a personality. You see, both of theme things are true, and neither of them matter. You are a channel through which the Creator may express Himself. The Creator is love, and His expression is love. When you see someone, to your outer eye, he may be nothing but, shall we say, a very common-looking or even unpleasant piece of stone. A large rock, awkward and peculiarly colored. Yet to the eye within, the eye of love, this rock will be the shape which the master may carve from the rock so that it becomes a beautiful statue, a statue with beautiful lines and coloration, with all the potential of that piece of rock set free in beauty of line. People are both their raw materials and the possibility of perfection. It is the Creator Who causes these possibilities to become manifest in the physical world.

You cannot do it—of course not. You can only say to the Creator, "Please, live this moment for me. Allow my eyes to shine with your light."

It is to the outer eye a very dark world. Darkness is all about you. My friends, within the darkness, there is light. If you wish to allow it to shine forth, it can never be denied. The light may not light up all of the darkness, but where you are, it will be light, if you allow it to be so. Picture your eyes as windows, and make sure the shades are up, so that the light may shine through. The shades are made of prejudice, judgment, petty feelings and negativity of all kinds. Your personality has been given to you so that you may work these things out. Again and again, you will find yourself pulling the shades down. Always it is the precise moment of now that is important. If you have been in error, simply choose at this moment to release that error, and let the shades up, and let the light shine through. What has happened in the past is completely done with.

We are having a slight amount of trouble contacting the one known as H, and we will pause at this time for a period of conditioning. I will leave this instrument. I am Hatonn.

Introduction

(H channeling)

I am Hatonn. I extend my greetings once more in the love and light of our infinite Creator. My friends, before time began, as you might say, you chose to embark upon a journey, and upon this journey you were to have a great number of experiences. These experiences may be interpreted as life experiences. Throughout countless dimensions of existence, you have and shall continue to travel. The purpose for your journey is to learn and develop your abilities as creators within this universe. You were aware of your abilities, yet for some reason you felt the need to experience those things which you may create and learn the value of your creations and also learn of the things which you would avoid. For my friends, with your thoughts you create. And if you are not aware of the effect of your creation upon the entire creation around you, then you may mistakenly create experiences which are not desirable. So as you travel, you should be aware of your abilities. Yet you should be aware of the imperfection you have chosen to accept within certain experiences. My friends, within each experience you must and shall abide by guidelines presented as laws to you through the love of your Creator.

You may ask why we are speaking of this journey, and we say that we speak of your journey and of ours, for at the present time we are aware that we are truly upon this journey, and we are aware that this journey shall at one time come to its destination, and we are aware that this destination is the point from which the journey began. It is a circle which you travel, a circle of infinity, of infinite experience, and one which, if properly used, shall not have to be repeated. For you shall journey upon many circles of experience, and each shall be a stepping-stone in the progression of your awareness of the reality of the oneness of the universe.

Yet be aware, my friends, there shall be the passage of no-time; between the beginning of your journey and the end there shall be no passing of time. For in all reality, there exist no variants such as you know as time. Is it possible to measure infinity, or to separate it in equal portions? We say this is not true. Time is but a part of your present experience. The concept of time is alien to your true identity and experience. Upon the journey which you travel there are times in which you experience feelings that you are not progressing. You become overanxious for enlightenment. You feel that you have slipped in your progression. All of these feelings, these emotions, are concepts within time. My friends, in due "time" you shall realize that each of us has already begun and completed his journey. We have gone nowhere. We have done nothing. Yet we have gone to all places, and we have done all things. Yet no time has elapsed.

Do not become concerned with your progression. My friends, your spiritual progression is as natural to your being as breathing is to your body. It may seem that some progress more swiftly than others. Yet once you have arrived, you shall truly become aware of the presence within the love and light of our infinite Creator, of all beings. Do not separate any portion of this creation. Do not place yourself above or below any being within this creation. We travel together, and together we shall realize where we have been and what we have done. Leave yourself open, remain receptive for the love of the Creator, and be not concerned with factors of time. Be aware that the desire that you have to receive the love and the knowledge of the love of the Creator is all that is needed.

Nothing else, my friends. Nothing else within this universe is worthy of desire. Desire only love, for it is all things.

I shall once again transfer this communication. I am Hatonn.

(Carla channeling)

I am again with this instrument. We are conditioning this instrument rather extensively for it is sometimes necessary to indicate to certain instruments that we are actually the source of these messages, and even the more experienced instruments sometimes need this assurance.

I would like all of you now to go with me to a field in which the odors of flowers are heavy in the air. We ask you to relax now. Stand with your feet on the springy, soft green grass. Feel the warm sun beaming down upon you, upon your shoulders, your head. Listen, my friends, to the music of creation. Feel the love and the light in its physical incarnations within the creation of your universe. We ask that you meditate. If you listen to us ever, you will hear us ask this. Within meditation, you may find the key that will open the door. No matter how many times we tell you this, it will never be enough. Meditate and listen; the love will be beating against your ears. And look; the light will be flooding your inner eyes, and touching you in many, many ways. If you will only listen and see and understand, within.

As I leave, my brother Laitos will pass among you. He will give you his energy and the vibration which we call the conditioning wave. We ask that if you desire it, you simply sit in silence and make yourselves receptive.

My brothers and sisters, I leave you in love and in everlasting light. I am the one known as Hatonn. Adonai vasu borragus.

Year 1976
January 4, 1976 to February 15, 1976

Sunday Meeting
January 4, 1976

(B channeling)

(Inaudible)

(Carla channeling)

I am Hatonn. I am now with this instrument. And again I greet you in the love and the light of the infinite Creator. Is it not so, my friends, that both illusion and reality, to the extent of our understanding, are made up of cycles, so that what you call the cycle of your world is rooted in meaning. The cycle of numbers is echoed in the natural cycle of the creation of the Father. And the ingredients of this cycle are what you call love and light. At what is known as the New Year the future is just coming to be and the past is dead. And at this time, as you would call it, you are able even within the illusion to see that this is so. You see, my friends, it does not matter how deep into the illusion you may go, the pathway always follows directly back to the Creator. Even though the days and the dates and what you call holidays are truly a creation of man, yet they lead directly back to the creation of the Father, to the very essence of life and death that makes up the cycle of this progression.

The infinite we *(inaudible)* is wrought of these cycles. Treasure therefore the lesson of this New Year. And know that, eternally and for each moment, your past shall be dead, your future shall lie aborning before you. There is, eternally, both the night that has passed and the day that is to come; the sunset and the sunrise.

And what, my friends, does this mean to you? How can this understanding lead to a richer experience for you within this illusion? My friends, the secret within the illusion is reality. The entire challenge of your life, as you know it, is to comprehend the reality which the illusion is wrapped around. As you act out your part within the illusion, you are acting out a path which leads directly to the truth. And if you understand your pathways you have arrived at an instantaneous understanding. This is not separate from your life, but at the very core. We ask that you meditate so that you may remain in contact with the reality that lies at the center of this illusion. which you call physical life.

Yet it is so easy not to pay attention. It does not seem that the cycle will end, and that death as you know it will succeed life as you know it. It does not seem that you will be called to account, not for the illusion but for that mysterious center of reality that you have been nurturing all your physical life. Yet, my friends, this is so. There will come a day when the old year of your physical life will expire, and the New Year of your life within spirit will succeed it.

And upon that day, the past shall be dead, and the future will be aborning.

It does not happen, in all cases, when it is expected. At each moment, allow your energy to penetrate to the center of your world, so that you live not only the drama of illusion but the reality at the center. And what is this reality, my friends? Love. Love within all, and all within love. "The least of these, my brethren, is the same as I," said the master known to you as Jesus. Reality for you, my friends, lies within each meeting. Even the least of those has been born in love and if you can realize this love within him, you have given him the reality within his center. Such service as this is what links you to your center; is what keeps you within reality. The consciousness of love will continue forever. Your consciousness of love will be your spiritual personality for eternity. Within this consciousness, the cycles of life and death are merely periods which seem as meaningless as the ticking noise of a clock seems in a year.

Within the consciousness of the physical illusion, life and death are weighty and serious matters, and shocking even to discuss. Within the consciousness of love, all is one and there is nothing to fear. And no one to resist. All that you see is love. We say this to some of you especially who are anointed with the ability, yet who have not used this ability on all occasions. We say this because, as your ears are opened, and your hearts unstopped, my friends, it is well that you are all *(inaudible)*.

It is a simple matter to love those you may dislike. It only needs meditation. Know, my brothers, that within the center of your being, love abides.

I would like to remove myself from this instrument for a time so that a brother may speak. I will return. I am Hatonn.

I am Laitos. I greet you in the love and light of our infinite Creator. It is my very great privilege to be with you, and I cannot express my enjoyment of this moment. I would like to attempt to exercise some instruments who have not been used to being within a larger group. Therefore, I will attempt to say only very little through each of them. However, we are very delighted that we can begin to exercise these instruments, as instruments who wish to deliver our messages are most gratefully received. I will attempt to transfer to the one known as W. If he will relax, I will say a few words through him. I am Laitos.

(W channeling)

I am Laitos.

(Carla channeling)

I am again with this instrument. We are delighted to have been in contact with the one known as W. We wish to assure him that the experience of channeling will become easier and easier as he becomes used to this service. I will attempt now to contact the one known as N. I am Laitos.

(Pause)

(Carla channeling)

I am again with this instrument. We ask the one known as N to refrain from analysis. It is not necessary that this be done as our communications will occur only if they are repeated without an attempt to analyze them. I will again attempt to contact the one known as N. I am Laitos.

(N channeling)

I am Laitos. I …

(Carla channeling)

I am Laitos. I am again with this instrument. My brothers and sisters, it is my privilege always to work with those who wish to become instruments, and we thank those older and newer instruments for their desire to serve. We can only say to you that this service will be desired by those whom you will meet in the future. And it is the will of the Creator that you are doing. We are not absolute founts of the truth, for we are as you, brothers and sisters. Yet our desires are truly of the Creator. And that which we give you is of that vibration. I am with you all, and at any time that you wish, the vibration of conditioning will be available. I say to you, my friends, meditate. I leave you in the love and the light of the One Who is All. I am Laitos.

I am Hatonn. I am again with this instrument. I would like to answer questions and I would answer the one which is within the mind of this instrument first. The one known as S requests some information from us. It is in love and light that we send our thoughts to her.

My sister, it is well known to you that planetary forces are such that it is not proper that we attempt to mold your experience within this sphere. Nevertheless, we may send to you various thoughts regarding your thought-patterns at this time. My sister, there is within you that which is to come alive. Within your mind is that which is dead. We are referring to the intellect. The intellect can be a useful tool in dealing with this illusion. Yet it is a destructive and damaging tool when used to work with emotions or spirit. That which is to come alive within you is of the spirit. There is no deadness within your spirit. There is no limit to your sense soul. There is no shape or form which you can contain your abilities within. You, my sister, *(inaudible)*. We ask that you unfetter your spirit, and let it soar, unhindered. It cannot go too far. For the distance is *(inaudible)* for the creation is one, and one thing only, and where can your spirit go except the creation? Trust your deeper soul. Trust your spirit. And do not attempt to contain it within intellectual rigidity.

We have been most happy to have accompanied you in each of your journeys, the physical ones, the mental ones, and most of all, my sister, those of the spirit. This we do for you and for all who are our brothers and sisters in desire and seeking. It is a privilege to be with you. You must know that we have attempted again and again to speak these words to you. We know that you will recognize as something already heard that which we say. Trust also your ability to understand our messages unspoken. We ask that, if you have further questions, to ask directly and only after this asking, to work through a channel. Our goal, my sister, as with all our contacts, is to be independently able to aid you.

Are there other questions?

Questioner: I want to channel and yet I didn't get a contact tonight. Why can't I be contacted like N and W?

I say that there is only one requirement for that service of channeling as you call it, and that is desire. My brother, there is a requirement which must be fulfilled before the desire may be mirrored in manifestation. This requirement is a disciplined mind. Some are of nature given a clear mind. Others engage within their intellects in what you call analytical thought to an extent that causes them to find it difficult to clear their minds. It is not necessary to perfectly clear your mind, or shall we say, to perfectly meditate, in order to receive our messages. However, it is much easier for our conditioning to affect the consciousness of one who has been able to, to a reasonable degree, clear his mind. The difficulty with your attempts to channel at this point, my brother, is that within your daily existence, your habits of mind are such that tend to attack each problem with analytical or intellectual examination. This approach does not yield immediately to the techniques of meditation. However, desire will produce that which you desire. Seek and ye shall find. Continue with your meditations and that which you seek will come.

Have you further questions?

Questioner: I hear a sound wave. Could you tell me what it is?

Sound wave? Are you referring to that which you hear during meditation?

Questioner: Yes.

There are various reasons for various people hearing certain tones. In your case, my brother, you are receiving from the interior of your physical being a vibration which is an indication of interface between physical and higher worlds. If you will examine your physical being at the time that you are aware of this sounds by closing your ears with your hands, you will find that the sound is within you. This is only one of the sounds which can occur. Others may hear others. Are there other questions?

Questioner: Are you aware of the UFO abduction in Snowflake, Arizona? Was that you?

We are very aware of it. We have a campaign, my friends. It is a campaign to alert and awaken those within the physical at this time who wish to seek the truth, and need something to start them following in the direction of the truth. For many years we have been within your skies, and various of our peoples have appeared in various ways as a kind of advertising, as you would say. The time has come when this campaign may be increased. There are within your peoples more and more a desire, more indication of other realities than the physical. We are *(inaudible)*. We would like to land and walk among your peoples, and if one day a majority of the peoples desire our presence, we will indeed do this. At this time, we are simply able to make a more, shall we say, intriguing contact than previously. We are not saying, my friends, that all of the sightings are of the Confederation. This is not so. Neither was the vessel which was sighted a totally Confederation vessel. However, it was working in cooperation with us for a specific purpose. We wish you well. And it is a great gladness to us that we are more and more able to appear not as, shall we say, gods but as fellow travelers.

Is there a further question?

M: The sighting that I had when I was a little boy—was that your ship, your representative I saw?

Yes.

M: Was there a reason that I couldn't see the man, and then I saw him later by myself?

I am having difficulty with this instrument. One moment.

(Pause)

We wanted that you be isolated when you became fully aware intellectually of our presence. We wished that the experience be of a singular nature, for it was intended that there would be an effect upon you that would cause you to remember and act upon this sighting. There was within this meeting light which was not given to the others. Many events have occurred in a following manner from this incident which was, shall we say, intended to occur. And within you is a knowledge which we were privileged to exchange with you and not others. Each person has a vibration, from eternity to eternity. At any given moment, each person vibrates in an individual manner. Therefore, as we vibrate in our individual manners, from dimension to dimension, there are some who, with their higher vibrations, may see us. We are able to appear to some, or to others, by adjusting our rate of vibration. This is, as we say, done usually for a purpose. That purpose being to alert individuals who are ready to receive this stimulus.

Does that satisfy you?

M: Yes.

Are there any more questions?

(Pause)

Within the darkness of the universe lies a tiny spark. And if you look at it steadily, it grows, and grows, and becomes a flaming sphere, and finally it totally engulfs you. And so in meditation, know the infinity behind your closed eyes. Find that spark of pure love, and then let it expand until it has totality.

(Tape ends.)

L/L Research

L/L Research is a subsidiary of Rock Creek Research & Development Laboratories, Inc.

P.O. Box 5195
Louisville, KY 40255-0195

www.llresearch.org

Rock Creek is a non-profit corporation dedicated to discovering and sharing information which may aid in the spiritual evolution of humankind.

ABOUT THE CONTENTS OF THIS TRANSCRIPT: This telepathic channeling has been taken from transcriptions of the weekly study and meditation meetings of the Rock Creek Research & Development Laboratories and L/L Research. It is offered in the hope that it may be useful to you. As the Confederation entities always make a point of saying, please use your discrimination and judgment in assessing this material. If something rings true to you, fine. If something does not resonate, please leave it behind, for neither we nor those of the Confederation would wish to be a stumbling block for any.

CAVEAT: This transcript is being published by L/L Research in a not yet final form. It has, however, been edited and any obvious errors have been corrected. When it is in a final form, this caveat will be removed.

© 2009 L/L Research

Sunday Meeting
January 11, 1976

(Carla channeling)

I am Hatonn. I greet you in the love and the light of the infinite Creator. I am with you, as always. I have little to add through this instrument on the subject of suffering. The very word in your language indicates how real the illusion is to you. And indeed, this is as it should be. If the illusion were not "real," you would not learn from it. It would not be an effective catalyst and you would not progress sufficiently under its stimulus.

That which seems to be suffering is precisely as valuable as a lesson problem is in school. You learn the lesson in order that you may pass the test. There are easy tests, and there are hard tests. If one is able to pass a harder test, one advances more quickly, perhaps to the next grade, instead of to the next semester within the same grade.

There are many of those upon your planet at this time who have elected to utilize this particular physical experience in order to obtain the greatest possible lesson, to take the greatest possible test and advance the greatest possible amount. These people have chosen their tests. These people chose to advance rapidly, within a path that is totally made of love. Within the illusion, it may seem that there is suffering. This suffering is a valuable gift. It is burning away the dross, that the gold may appear.

We have spoken earlier tonight, my sister, on the necessity of penetrating the apparent quality of the illusion, in order to perceive reality. Penetrate to the center of this illusion, which you call suffering, and know that in love a perfect being is seeking its path.

Each entity will suffer. Each entity will proceed on its path. For each entity there will be dark nights—and then, the dawn! Do not admire those who seem not to suffer, for it is truly written that the last shall be first, and the first, last. There is one whom you know who is physically, shall we say, abased; this ultimately will cause her exaltation.

Do not dwell within the illusion, my sister. The intellect cannot deal with the reality within it. Seek only to know the Creator. Do you not know, my sister, that all is love?

S: Yes.

We would like to ask you whether you have in fact received this answer from us previous to this channeling?

S: Yes.

My sister, we ask that you be more confident, for you are receiving the knowledge that we have to offer you. It is simply that you are not fond of words, and neither are we. Therefore, we do not find it possible to contact you through words. We accept and are very grateful to deal with channels in speaking with you, and you never need to hesitate to ask for a channeled message. Yet we wish you to know, in those instances when it may not be immediately possible for us to talk to you through a vocal channel, that you are receiving our messages

There are no sure things, my sister. You cannot put your faith in any outside appearance, even our voice through a channel. Depend primarily upon that which you perceive.

We have a desire to speak briefly of your own abilities at this time. You have had considerable self-doubt due to the influence of your physical environment and your emotional influences. By which we mean that the illusion produces difficulties which test one's ability to feel confidence in one's protection. Within the illusion, there is good and evil; what you call Christ, and what you call anti-Christ. Yet within the Creator, all is one. When there is seemingly, in your intelligence, a negativity or a possible negativity, we ask that you not attempt to outwardly discern, or intellectually discover, its negativity or positivity. Rather, immediately go within, until you find the Creator. Within the Creator, my sister, all is one, and there is no knowledge of separation of any sort that can possibly harm you. Nor can you harm anyone. No harm can come to you; no harm can go from you. Unity! Unity! All is love. The world around you is an illusion. All is love. Throughout all eternity, your spirit is safe and secure—for these things are without meaning within unity.

I cannot express to you my sympathy and understanding of what you are experiencing. For each soul, my sister, there is a great solitude. One soul is on one path. And no one or no thing can keep that soul company on that path. For each entity is the Creator, is primary, and must teach itself what it already knows. Sometimes, my sister, in this loneliness, we have bad dreams. We are not speaking of literal dreams; we are speaking of times when a shadow seems to be over our lives. We are not free of these upon the plane from which I speak. Yes, we have advanced, yet we do not know all. We are alone in our way, as we speak of unity, yet we have loneliness when we are not able to totally live this understanding. These moments grow fewer and fewer as you continue to seek. It is a matter of being in reality instead of the illusion. When the shadow falls across you, my sister, know it for an illusion. If you must speak aloud to remind yourself, you may

say, "All is love." And you will feel reality flow within you at that moment.

Your brothers and sisters are with you. Have you any more questions?

(Pause)

We send you our love and our light. We will leave this instrument, my sister, for now, but we are always with you. We leave you only in leaving this instrument's vocal vibrations. Adonai. ☙

Sunday Meeting
January 11, 1976

(H channeling)

I am Hatonn. Greetings, my friends, in the love and in the light of our infinite Creator. It is our purpose this evening to speak with you through this instrument, for we wish to share with you our thoughts. Our thoughts are many, yet all are expressed in one concept, and that concept is of love. It is, we feel, our knowledge that your existence and the existence of all things have emanated from the concept of love. Whatever your impression of what we call the Creator, we see no other way to envision the action of our existence, other than through the love which was given that created us.

We claim to be members of a confederation of planets yet we feel that there can be no justification of this claim, for, my friends, a confederation means a drawing together of units to form a body, and in truth, my friends, there are no units. There is only the existence of one thing, and this one thing that exists cannot be separated.

This is very difficult for the human intellect to comprehend. We describe ourselves as a confederation of planets because it is the closest thing which your language barrier would permit us to use to describe our situation. My friends, in our experience we have found that the use of the intellect, though it is necessary for your existence upon the plane which you have chosen, it is of little use in the comprehension of infinite truth. My friends, in order to know and understand the meaning of what we say, we once again must stress the need for meditation. For within your period of silences you are open to the creative thought within your own being that is in truth the Creator's love, and the Creator Himself. All truth is known to you, only you have forgotten how to tap the memory.

My friends, in your moment of silence, day after day, you shall suddenly, at one time, realize that the effort was well worth it. Yet when we say suddenly, in our terms, you cannot expect great revelations of truth within days or months, but one day you will realize that you have become more aware and are beginning to understand.

All of the people upon your planet are searching for the answer to their existence. All of the people upon your planet are anxious to know the truth. The truth is pure and simple: you are the truth, and within you it lies.

I shall transfer this contact. I am Hatonn.

(Carla channeling)

I am now with this instrument, and again I greet you. When we say, my friends, that the truth lies within you, we say that which is most easily misunderstood by your peoples. And indeed, when the master known as Jesus said, "Thou shalt love thy neighbor as thyself," this truth also is most often misunderstood by your peoples. It has most often been understood to mean that we must love each other's good points and bad points, as you call them, within this physical illusion. That we must love each other's failures as well as successes. That the truth lies within the illusion.

We do not wish to indicate that the truth which lies within you has a thing to do with your outer covering, shall we say, of deeds and actions. Nor did the master known as Jesus mean to indicate that you must love the outer wrappings of others. What we are suggesting, and what the master was suggesting, is that you penetrate the illusion, penetrate the wrapping of deeds and misdeeds, and discover within that illusion the reality of the Creator, the reality of love. Within you lies the truth. Within you lies love. Within each fellow man lies the same truth.

My brothers, to love another, as we mean it, is to love that within them which is one with that which is within you. To love yourself is not to love the outer wrapping of personality, but to honor and hallow that divinity that you are, which is at your very center. It is not possible to love your neighbor or yourself from a human level. You may have felt that you had failed if you had not loved completely, yet it is the law of the physical Illusion that a "love" will be bound by the law of good and evil. Therefore, there will be successes and failures. Love will not abide within the physical illusion. It cannot. Laws are to be followed, and the law of good and evil, of action and reaction, is unbreakable within the physical illusion.

There is a higher law, my friends, the law of love. Not the human love; that will fail. But the love which you will find at the center of your created being. My friends, you cannot try to love. Only let go of your feelings, and release them completely into the care of the love that created you. It is not expected that, at the human level, you will be able to love as the Creator desires. It is only as those who open to the center of their being that the love within flows through in the physical being, and out into the physical illusion. You may release this from within you just as a person may, on a very dark night, raise all the window shades in his house, so that the light within may pour out onto the world around him. The light within you, my friends, shines brightly. Whether you know it or not, whether you feel it or not, you have such power within you, my friends. You have such beauty of soul, such love, that it is indescribable. Be it known unto you, however, that love abides within each of you. And the power of this love is total.

Have you been operating on this power, or have you been attempting to live out an illusion using the illusion's terms? Why do you think, my friends, that you are here? Have you not come to the conclusion that you are here to find something out that is obviously shown to be the reality about you? In there any question in your minds but that the routine of your daily life does not express that which you know to be the truth? My friends, let your seeking cease its restlessness. Turn within. In opening yourself to your own center of truth, you open yourself to the infinity of that which it is your birthright to know. That which you need will come to you, if you begin to seek it in a correct manner. The correct manner, my friends, is to know that the truth is within, and then to turn within and ask that that which you need to know be shown to you. Perhaps, my friends, you will find truths directly in meditations. Perhaps the truths will occur in your daily life in unexpected ways. Whatever you need, if you are seeking it from the Creator, the Creator will provide. Seek and ye shall find. This is the truth that we state over and over to you. Seek the truth. Seek in meditation.

I would like to leave this instrument so that my brother Laitos might speak. I am Hatonn.

(H channeling)

I am Hatonn. My friends, I wish only to add that it is our purpose to give our thoughts and our services to those who would request them. If it be against your will, we shall be aware of your will, and we shall acknowledge your right to express and receive your desire. Ask and you shall receive. This is a law which we may not violate. In the love and the light of our infinite Creator, I shall leave you. I am Hatonn. Adonai vasu borragus.

(Carla asks if there were any questions, because she still feels a presence. S has been grieving because of her mother's extreme difficulties and asks about the possible reason for her mother suffering so greatly.)

(H channeling)

I am Hatonn. I have chosen to speak through this instrument due to lack of familiarity. One moment, please, while I condition the instrument.

My friends, to all present we must say that within your present existences you experience a varied number of emotions. For those whom you are closest to, the emotions are as if there are no separations between the two. You speak of suffering and it be not yours, yet are you not indeed suffering? Your suffering, my friend, is not of a physical nature. It is one of spirit, the spirit of your being within you. Caring not of your emotions, it is expressing love for the one whom you love. The circumstance is unavoidable. Yet the lesson is one which is very valid. You must learn, my friends, the reality of unity. What appears to you upon this plane to be the suffering of a loved one is only a projection of your existence and your love. Though it appears to be suffering, it is only an infinite expression of love within this infinite creation, which to the intellect is incomprehensible. My friends, the more you suffer, the more you allow your emotions to believe it is suffering. The longer you deny the lesson—you do not suffer. Your spirit is expressing love.

Is this adequate?

S: Yes.

Be there any other questions?

Questioner: Is it possible to just ride out the waves of living, not worrying or hassling about everyday problems? Can we count on the Creator to that extent? Should we?

My friends, we have taught you that your existence is one of your own projection of consciousness, guided by laws of the Creator. In order to abide by His law, it is only necessary to lend your existence through meditation to the Creator. Your so-called hassles may or may not disappear, and certainly your ability to care shall increase. But if it is your belief that you are guided by the consciousness of the Creator, and if you make yourself available for guidance, your experiences are those which are of benefit to you. What you need to learn, the Creator can foresee. Abide by His guidance; accept His will. And then you shall become aware that there is no real need for apprehension, for you are on a path of enlightenment and truth, and in order to achieve your goal, you must undergo a process of learning which is sometimes, within the physical plane, very difficult.

Are there any other questions?

Questioner: I would like to know what comment you could make about the advantages or disadvantages of chanting prior to meditation. Also any comments about another group to which I belong.

It is very difficult through these type of contacts to relay through the instrument specific names such as your organization. But we would speak on this. There are advantages to anything that you do which you truly feel is aiding your spiritual progression. Many people use many methods of rendering themselves open to the Creator. The form of chanting uses, or shall we say incorporates, sound waves which in turn create within your physical body vibrations which enhance your progression into meditation. Also, it is a very good substitute for what is known as a mantram. Yet we must stress that there is no one most beneficial means of achieving states of meditation. For each and every individual, there is a different manner of achieving this state.

Upon organizations, we must say their purposes are of a positive nature; their recognition of themselves as being organizations deny the truth of unity they teach. This may sound harsh, but it is the truth.

Are there any more questions?

(Pause)

It has been my privilege to answer questions. Once again I leave you in the love and light of our infinite Creator. I am Hatonn. ☥

Sunday Meeting
January 18, 1976

(Carla channeling)

I am Hatonn. I greet you, my friends, in the love and in the light of our infinite Creator. His presence is within all of you. You are listening to the one known as Hatonn, but in reality, you are listening to love. You are listening to the Creator. For all that you hear is the voice of the Creator.

My friends, I have been speaking with you through concept within silence. We were having no difficulty with this channel, yet we desired that you have some silence to reach a level where we could communicate with you in the silence. And we are privileged to have accomplished this.

My friends, to answer a question which has been on the minds of some of you, and to further your own understanding of meditation itself, we want to quickly discuss with you what happens during your channeling, as you call it. You see, not all channeling is the same. You have observed with the channels within your particular group a type of concept channeling which is given by a type of electromagnetic vibration which actually can be felt above the head of the channel. It has a physical manifestation within the consciousness of the channel's physical vehicle, in that as each individual experiences this particular electromagnetic condition known as the conditioning, this will call forth some reaction within the vehicle. Within some, there will be the feeling of heat; within some, the opposite feeling, of cold. There are many completely different reactions to this conditioning wave, these differences being due, my friends, to the stage of your individual spiritual centers within your several vehicles. You know of these centers as chakras. In someone whose chakras are to some extent open, there will be quite a different experience from the one whose chakras are not for the most part opened. And each is at a different stage in his development. This is why every reaction differs.

Now, we have never used with this channel, although we have with other channels within the group, a stronger and more physical type of beam. We do not like to use this beam, because it causes discomfort within the instrument. We can actually use the instrument's voice-box, speaking with our voices, shall we say, in that we exercise the muscles of the speaker. We do not like to do this. It is not necessary that we do this, within this group, for this group is concerned with philosophical and spiritual concepts, and this is most desirably done through the vocabulary and concepts which we can give to each individual. Now, these are the channeling ways.

There is another vibration, which is far more desirable, and not at all the same as the channeling wave. You see, my friends, the channeling wave, although it is conceptual, will be expressed in vocabulary. It is an electromagnetic wave, it is within the physical illusion, and it is attempting to coincide the vibration of the channel with the vibration of our thought. It is, shall we say, a cut-and-dried, limited and intellectual wave. We are not putting it down, as you would call it. It is very useful and is totally given in love, and with a spiritual desire to aid you.

But, my friends, the basic vibration of the Creator, perfect love, is a vibration which is given not only through us, but through your aides and guides, whom you would call angels, through your own inner self, through teachers upon your own spiritual planes, as you would call them—everywhere, everywhere, my friends, within the creation. This original Vibration of love is reality. In meditation you are seeking not an electromagnetic wave from us; you are seeking perfect love. What we can give you in this channeling wave is a means of service to others. Also, it is, as we are well aware, a comfort to some of you to know that we are present. For, indeed, our presence is a supporting one in that we love each of you, and wish only to comfort you and help you through your experience.

Seek beyond these words. Meditate to perfection. What this channel gives to you in words is only a poor physical food for your physical mind. Spiritual food, my brothers, lies in silence, in contemplation, in what you would call prayer: in listening to the original Thought of creation, the original Vibration that, out of nothingness, created all that there is. Listen now to the silence again. And listen beyond words. I will return to this instrument after a little while.

(A pause of several minutes.)

I am with you, my brothers. I am Hatonn. It is a joy to me to see that my words have meaning to you. Your vibrations are known to us. The vibrations of all your peoples are known to us. Your thoughts and your desires are known to us. Your free will is completely preserved, yet you are known to us. It is this knowledge that allows us to be with each of you as you desire us. We feel the desire that quickens within you to know love. There have been many who have dedicated their lives to a love of one kind or another, and for this love a man may sacrifice years and years in a position which he may hate, in order that he may take care of those that he loves. A woman may sacrifice many, many desires in order to nurture her mate and her children. Love seems always to offer sacrifice. Have you pierced the veil of this truth of love, my friends? It is written that the master known as Jesus said, "In order to love Him, we must pick up a cross."

My brothers, this is truth: love is sacrifice. There is a further and transforming truth that can only be learned once the leap has been made into love, once the sacrifice has been freely given, not grudgingly, but freely. That which you give is given to yourself. Truer words never were, my friends. As you love, so you will be loved. What you are, what your reality is, is totally a result of your thought. To sacrifice to another is your only way of giving. That which does not cost you anything is not a true gift. To give, it must be infinite; it must be all. It may not be physically of any moment or importance. Yet within yourself, to be a gift it must be at some cost to yourself, and freely given. Then, my friends, you have considered your brother as the master and yourself as the servant. And you are interested in serving your brother. And then, you have found the secret of love. For all of the creation was designed to be of service to each other part of the creation. That which you give enriches you beyond measure—and that which you hold back will strangle you. How often people think that they are poor, when in fact they simply have not given enough away. How often have you been lonely, my friends, when you could reach out and aid another's loneliness? Do you not know that to sacrifice is to love—and to love others is only to love yourself?

This is not an easy lesson. We know that. Go back into the silence when you have difficulties, and you will have difficulties. As often as you can, regularly, find love within you. And then, give it away. For you are truly rich, my brothers.

I would like to speak through another instrument, and so I will leave this instrument. I am Hatonn.

(N channeling)

I am Hatonn. I greet you again, my friends, in the light and love of our infinite Creator. Perfect love is within your reach. It is not a dream upon which you focus at certain times, and then cast away as something far in the future, or something unattainable. It is real. It completely engulfs you at all times. We understand, my friends, the difficulty that you have realizing this, but we know that it is with you, nevertheless. If you are truly seeking on the spiritual path, if you desire the higher thoughts and vibrations, then expect, my friends, to attain these things. You must believe that it can happen before it will happen.

Through each day, as each of you go about your affairs, there seems to be many things to be taken care of, earthly things. But, my friends, the spiritual cares of you need to be taken care of from within. The Creator—the creation—is within you at this very moment. It can be manifested, if you desire it: perfect love.

At this time I would like to contact a newer instrument. May I suggest to relax and we will give our best to help you. I am Hatonn.

(Pause)

I am Hatonn. I am again with this instrument. There seems to be difficulty making contact with the newer instrument. At this time I will transfer to the one known as Carla, to speak through a more experienced channel to aid in contacting the newer channels. I leave you now through this instrument. I am Hatonn.

(Carla channeling)

I am now with this instrument. I am Hatonn. I can relieve the worst of the anxiety of the one known as W by impressing him with a vocal version of his contact. We have been attempting to contact the one known as W. We will again attempt to do so. My brother, we were attempting to contact you without the use of your name, for you have been able to hear our contact fairly clearly, and we were hoping to build up your confidence. It is the next step of the newer channel, after he has been able to consciously perceive our contact, to have the confidence to go ahead with that perception in the absence of the name. For, as you can well imagine, it would be difficult for us to say the name if the person were the only channel present. Therefore, we try to get the new channel over the need for the use of his name as soon as possible, so that if he desires to be of service in a group in which he is the only channel he will have the confidence to go ahead with his contact. We are sorry that we, shall we say, rushed you a bit.

Now, we ask that you relax. We will not say much through you, but would like to give you a brief message. I will now transfer to the one known as W.

(W channeling)

I am Hatonn. I am with this channel. Once again, I greet you in the love and the light of the infinite Creator. During our days, much of our time is spent in needless worry over things that really do not matter. And the things in our lives that really do matter, such as meditation and seeking the truth, are always left for another day or put off until tomorrow, when in truth these are the most important things in your whole life. This is the reason you were put here on this planet, to search and seek and try to find a way back to the infinite Creator.

At this time, I would like to try to transfer to a newer channel. I am Hatonn.

(Pause)

I am Hatonn. I am back with this channel now. At this time I would like to leave this channel and transfer back to the one known as Carla. I am Hatonn.

(Carla channeling)

I am with this instrument. I am Hatonn. It is with pleasure that I return to this instrument. We are most privileged to have a newer channel making such good progress with us. We will leave this instrument, and yield to one of our brothers. We will return. I am Hatonn.

I am Oxal. I have good contact with this instrument. I am Oxal. I greet you in the love and the light of our infinite Creator. I am Oxal. I am Oxal.

I am Oxal. Very good. Very good. Good contact. I am Oxal. Now, I am extremely pleased to speak with you. I wish to primarily contact the one known as N. We have found through our vibration check that it will be a stronger contact with the one known as N with this particular type of vibrational equipment. Therefore, we have decided to contact the one known as N. This contact is a slightly different type and is more nearly in the physical plane, which is why it can be of a stronger nature. We transfer now to the one known as N. We ask that she relax and allow her thoughts to become clear. We will not say very much through her, but we wish to say a few sentences in order that she may have the experience of giving a message to a slightly larger group. We wish to say to our sister that it is not difficult because the energy of the group will aid you once you begin. The larger the group, the greater the energy. Therefore, it is easier to be sure of your contact. We will now transfer to the one known as N. I am Oxal.

(Pause)

I am Oxal. I am very pleased to have made this contact. We request that this instrument relax.

(N channeling)

I am Oxal. I am with this instrument. As we were saying, we request that N relax and attempt not to analyze the thoughts which we are sending her through her brain. We realize that it is very difficult to distinguish our thoughts from the ones that you already have, for there is no real physical difference except your feeling of our vibration and conditioning. Many people who are attempting channeling for the first time expect a great sensation physically and we do not attempt to do this, for as we explained earlier, with this type of group it is not necessary. So we say to the one known as N, through practice and experience you will gain more control, so you may relax your body and not try to analyze the thoughts which we are sending you. I will attempt once more to say a few more words through the one known as N. I am Oxal.

(Pause)

I am Oxal. I wish to speak further concerning the vibration which conditions the channel. We are happy to use this as an instrument of conditioning. There are many forms of conditioning, depending upon the instrument whom we wish to channel through. There are various stages at which the channel may be used. At times, it may be easier to channel through one or another certain instrument. I will leave this instrument now. I am Oxal.

(Carla channeling)

I am again with this instrument. I am most pleased that we have been able to make contact with the one known as N. You may have wondered why I used this instrument at the beginning to repeat myself so many times. I was attempting to give an example to the one known as N that it is important not to analyze what is given.

(Tape ends.)

Sunday Meeting
January 25, 1976

(Carla channeling)

I am Hatonn. I greet you, my friends, in the love and the light of the infinite Creator. I am He who is among you. I am He who is within you. I AM. My brothers, dwell now within the I AM that you are. For I AM, not only now but always. Before this world was created and when it is long since passed again into infinite space, I AM. The creation began with consciousness, the consciousness of one vibration, each and every particle totally unified, totally homogeneous, of only one identity, that identity being love. We use the word "love" to you because of the bias which it contains within your language. The word "consciousness," my friends, is a slightly more accurate word, yet this consciousness is the consciousness which creates. Therefore, we must use the word love. For the force of love as you understand it in your density is the indwelling of the creative force within your sphere of experience. So the creation began in an infinite and constant state of love, vibrating infinitely and in unity. And this creation sent forth the power of love to differentiate into entities that could dwell in self-knowledge, in unity, yet in knowledge of unity

This, my brothers, is described in your Garden of Eden, and in all worlds and universes there are descriptions which, within each culture, describe the state of self-awareness of unity. This was the beginning of the cycles.

And there arose within these entities in your Garden, shall we say, a knowledge to be self aware, not only of unity, but of separation. And in doing so, in choosing this path, the dimensions were born. For these entities had chosen a path which, in separation, cannot express the unity of all with all. The vibrations of knowledge of separation must travel downward through many, many frequencies, and as consciousness traveled downward, it formed a great and infinite array of potential experiences on many, many levels, one of which you are now at this time experiencing,

You are experiencing separation. That is the meaning of your physical being. With your senses, you can only feel that which is within yourself, only that which comes to your own ears and eyes and hands. You can only taste that which is given to your own experience. This incarnation, my brothers, is an incarnation of loneliness and pain, for separation is such.

Why have you come here, my friends? Why now do you vibrate in sympathy with loneliness and separation? Why now must you accept pain? May we say, my brothers, so all entities will choose to do while they are learning to seek the healing from that pain.

We seek to give you, shall we say, some distance on your problems. Not that they are not important, we do not say that. Nor do we say that they are a more nothing, to be ignored—for you were not invested with a physical form in order to ignore what is happening to you in the physical. Yet know that these things are occurring to you in such a way that you will not be tested beyond your ability, for you have yourself chosen these lessons. You have yourself chosen this pain. And you hope very dearly, in your higher self, to learn from this pain the lessons that you have come here to learn. It is a hard thing to ask yourself to trust in your own judgment when you do not have the ability to face your higher self in the flesh, so to speak. You cannot say to your higher self, "Look, I think this is more than I can take. I don't think I can handle this. Why don't we go back and do this over?" You don't have that satisfaction, my friends. You must trust that the self that placed you in the situation you are now in knew and understood your capabilities and, though ambitious of learning as much as possible, did not plan things so as to test you beyond your limit. The more lessons you learn, my friends, in this incarnation, the more progress that you will make. It is not to rejoice at pain, but to understand that within pain there is the peace, when you are convinced within yourself that you have tried as much as possible to learn the lesson that is buried within the experience.

We have said to you many times, you must go within and seek the Father. If you are seeking the Father the Father will provide that which is necessary to you. And today we emphasize also that which is secondarily true: in your fellow men, seek to do service. Your energy may go most effectively for that one seeking within the physical. In the inner worlds, seek to know the Father, and in the outer world, seek to do service to the Father Who is all around you. The Creator will aid all who trust in Him, no matter how they are acting, just as the pain which you are now experiencing will fall, as is written in your holy works, on the just and the unjust alike.

Yet, in your own experience, it would be much more helpful for you to use energy in helping to the best of your ability those about you, whether or not they are seeking to help you, whether or not service seems to be offered unto you. It is written in your Holy works: one must love one's Creator and one's fellow man as oneself. We say to you again, it is not necessary to love one's fellow man, or to love oneself on the level of the human, as you call it. Yet you see the Creator, and love the Creator, in him and in you, for that is the same. Then you are loving yourself and yourself in him and the Creator in each of you.

There is a cliché that is within this channel's mind, that every cloud has a silver lining. And we would add to that that sometimes a fruit may seem to be inedible, for the skin may be tough and pitted. Yet when you peel it, the fruit within is still succulent and tasty and delicious. Experiences are like this, even the most inconvenient. Be of good cheer, my friends, and remember to attempt not only to seek the Creator in meditation, but to seek the Creator within your fellow man. With the armor of your inner guidance, and your light before you on the path, there is nothing that can harm you.

We have wanted to give you these words of comfort, for each of you is undergoing at this time some difficulty, not the same, yet as we have said, all difficulties within the physical have one thing in common, that is, the emotional or physical or mental pain. Be of good cheer. There is no pain within the garden—and the garden is within you.

I would leave you at this time, my friends. I leave you in the love and the light of our infinite Creator. I am Hatonn. Adonai.

(B channeling)

I am Hatonn. I am now with this instrument. My friends, you have often heard [us] speak about love, and my friends, you must understand, speaking of the infinite Creator, what one word best describes all facets of what you know of life? Now, my friends, you are well aware of the great power of this word. My friends, if you were only familiar with this one love, or my friends, familiar with this one word, and this word only, my friends, your progress would be so swift!

Surround yourselves in this. For, my friends, it is truly a suit of armor that nothing in all the universe may penetrate. For, my friends, when you surround yourself in love, you are indeed surrounding yourself in the Creator. The Creator is love and, my friends, nothing can penetrate this. As we all travel on our many ways, it is very true that this group sitting here today has been and has asked to be together. For, my friends, you all have a very important mission to perform. Now as we speak of this trouble that surrounds us all, one reason, my friends, that it is very necessary for you to be together—by the positive grounding that this group provides, my friends, you receive enough stimulation, stimulations, my friends, that you all very much need. And as you have advanced, my friends, we also advance. And as you have asked for our presence, we are with you at all times. There are many times, my friends, that situations will seek you out. But, my friends, the positive always draws negative; by the overcoming of these negatives, you are indeed that much stronger. For, my friends, we are all together in love. If this could only be seen, my friends.

I would at this time like to try this experiment: think to yourselves, my friends, love and fellowship and brotherhood, to all those in this room. As you think this word love, you will see or feel that it is escaping from every cell of your body. Now, my friends, never deny the help of your brother. If you would attempt, my friends, to sit for one moment in silence, and pass this love to all those in this room. We are now in the room with you, my friends, and we too will experience this. And what we will feel is true love. Allow this energy to escape and flow into your being. I will pause for one moment. I am Hatonn.

(Pause)

I am again with this instrument. I am Hatonn. My friends, you have experienced this energy. Now ask yourselves, what thought could penetrate this force field of love? For, my friends, it overpowers all. When you have these small troubles, my friends, as I said earlier, seek your Creator within you, and your brother's help. For, my friends, you will all ground each other. Love is beautiful. Love is all we know. No negativity can overcome this energy, and no problem cannot be worked out.

I will attempt at this time to transfer this contact. I am Hatonn.

(H channeling)

I am Hatonn. I am now with this instrument. My friends, as we speak to you, we realize that due to your existence within the physical illusion your understanding of the concepts which we present to you is, shall we say, very shallow. Yet what is important is that you—those who are present—have truly begun to understand. Understanding is far beyond that which is intellectual. True understanding of the concept of love and all things contained within it is, shall we say, a sense, as you would call it, within your core. Within the creative consciousness of your existence, understanding awaits you. And though you are not truly aware of its presence, it constantly is flowing from within the core of your existence into your physical reality. My friends, all things which you experience within this illusion are presented and have been chosen by you as lessons. We suggest that you become more patient within this experience for, my friends, the reason that you become, shall we say, tangled up within your emotions is that you become apprehensive of the passing of time and the weight of the circumstances you experience upon that passage of time. You feel as though there is no tomorrow in which you may enjoy yourself. You ask yourself why you should experience this misery any longer. My friends, realize that without misery there can be no joy. Without the passage of time within your illusion, there can be no lessons. These things which you experience are truly difficult, yet they are the seeds upon which you grow. Some may choose to ignore these facts. Yet none may ignore them forever. Eventually, all shall come face-to-face with reality. And your progression is something which you cannot avoid. Ponder these thoughts, and in your daily routines, be thankful, although it may be difficult, for the experiences which are somewhat trying, yet bountiful in knowledge and love.

Also you should remember that the greater the lesson which you are learning, in most cases, the greater the difficulty which shall be experienced in the process of learning. Yet realize that you have the capacity to withstand whatever difficulties may arise. You are infinite, in your ability to learn, understand and persevere. I now leave you, in the love and the light. I am Hatonn. Adonai

(Carla channeling)

I am Oxal. I wish only to say a very little bit, for the light is very strong, and it is my desire to let you know that I am with you also in the light. May peace flow from you like a fountain, and from that peace may the waters of joy transform all within your world into that transcendent state when your eyes are opened, and you see and understand. I leave you in the physical, yet always bathed in the love and the light, never in the physical, but of the highest. You are transcendent beings, and though you may have pain, yet always within you there is the water of peace and the fountain of joy, for it is not a river that begins within the physical illusion, but from the highest estate. "Not as the world gives, give I unto you," said your great master. Peace—my peace, the Creator's peace—I leave with you now. Adonai, in the love and the light. I am Oxal. Adonai. ☙

Sunday Meeting
February 1, 1976

(Carla channeling)

I am Hatonn. I greet you, my brothers and my sisters, in love and peace, in the infinite light of all that there is. I especially greet those of you who are new to our group. It is a great privilege to be able to speak with each of you, and a very great pleasure to speak for the first time to those whom we now meet.

We are here, my friends, only to be of service to each of you. All of those upon the surface of your planet who desire at this time to listen to thoughts that will be of service to their spiritual development are those very people whom we wish to serve, and we are here for that reason and for that reason only, to share with you our knowledge, such as it is, to reach a hand back down one rung of the ladder, just as those one rung above us have reached their hand down to us.

For so, my brothers, it is. The infinite, universal creation has infinite densities, infinite progressions. And in each progression there is a brotherhood of those upon the same path, those striving towards the same understanding. And as one reaches one higher rung, one of the privileges of learning is responsibility for those below. For we can no longer ascend higher unless we are endeavoring to the utmost to bring those just below us with us. You see, my brothers and sisters, it is the nature of all things within the creation to be of service to the other portions of the creation. Upon your planet, the creation of the Father manifests this service over and over again, in cycles which complement each other, so that your natural growths give forth oxygen that your animals and yourselves breathe, while you give off that which is helpful to the plants. The air itself is a perfect blend so that you might flourish. The rain falls in such a way that that which you need for your survival grows in plenty upon the surface of your planet. All dwells in harmony, in an attempt to be of service to that which is around it.

To take another example, my friends, it is written within your holy works that the various portions of your own physical body are not separate from each other but are mutually helpful to each other, for the benefit of the whole. My friends, this is true not simply of your body as an entity, but of all that there is in the universe as an entity. The universe is one thing, one complete whole, and all that is in it functions in mutual service to all the other parts. This functioning is in harmony with the perfect love that created the universe. This unity is love and this love is all that there is.

I would like this evening to speak on several things and I will skip around to a certain extent, my friends, because there are several topics that it is, shall we say, necessary to hit upon at this time. First, I would like to speak with you about light. There are those within your group who have already noticed that I was attempting to speak with you as a group earlier. This is quite so. The group at the time was extremely willing to hear my message. However, because the channel felt that it would not be the proper thing to do, we were not able to get through, for as you well know we will not force ourselves upon you, but only come when it is your desire.

We had a desire at that time to talk to you about light. We will now so do. Light, my brothers—imagine yourselves armed, completely covered with an armor of light. The light is so bright and so white, you are so radiant, that no one can look directly at you. You shine like the sun. It is not possible for any harm to penetrate that armor of light, nor is it possible for any harm to leave your mind, your heart, or your hand through this aura of light. You are protected from within and from without.

There are many, many times, my friends, when in your fear you attempt to use your armies, those little armies of soldiers which you call words, and you send your words and your mean actions and your petty emotions out like little soldiers to combat those little enemies, those people about you who seem to be sending their soldiers against you, saying and doing things that make you unhappy. You feel that you are vulnerable to them and so you fight back, shall we say, with your little army of words. And you become disturbed and excited. You are not yourself, in the sense that you are no longer a light-being, but a small, dark animal fighting for its position. You have lost the grandeur and the majesty of that within you which is pure light and pure love and you are reacting as a weak person.

My friends, you need no armies, you need no intellect. You need no fights, for you are completely protected by light.

(A pause, during which the wind roars against the windows of the house.)

You are aware, my friends, of that which is a great disturbance in your outer environment, and we use this to tell you these storms within your emotions may seem just as difficult, just as dark, and just as terrifying. If you feel anger, if you feel discomfort or, my friends, those of you who were with the group in this afternoon meeting, those of you who felt the slightest need to, shall we say, defend yourselves against someone who did not seem to understand—you were not seeing this person, my friends, as a light being, to whom you should give love only. You were seeing him as someone to be convinced, his army against your army, words against words. Love and light, my brothers, my sisters, need no words, but only a simple radiation, a radiation from within of the love and the protection from all that may be without of your armor of light. Never, ever, sell yourselves short. Never let yourselves become in need of that army, if you can possibly remember who you are and what protection you do have. You may play, instead of from weakness, from a position of great strength. The love lies within you, the light shines through you, and there will be nothing which love cannot conquer.

I would like to transfer and continue through another instrument. I am Hatonn.

(H channeling)

I am Hatonn. I am now with this instrument and shall continue. My friends, the light of which we speak is not light as you may perceive it within your intellect. The light of which we speak, to best describe it, is the physical manifestation of the love of your Creator. All that appears to you within your physical environment appears due to the love which is expressed by our Creator. All things which are visible to your eyes are comprised of units of light. Various are the colors which you may perceive. Yet you have learned that through a prism a white light may enter and it is dispersed as many different colors. Therefore, all colors, all physical manifestation, has been derived from the pure and infinite glowing white light, which is the physical representative of the love of our Creator.

And you may ask yourself What or Who is our Creator? This, my friends, we cannot answer. We can only say to you that to the best of our knowledge, our Creator is all things. He resides within and without all other beings. Within His light we reside. Within His creation we reside. Many things we could say that would express our concept of the Creator, yet we have found through our experience that in order to understand the concept of the Creator, there is but one way. In order to attain this understanding you must go within yourself, beyond the physical limits of your intellect and into the core of your being and communicate, communicate with your Creator. This communication shall not take place in the form of conversation. All that you need to hear is silence. All that you need to see is light. And all that you need to understand is yourself. For within you are the answers to the questions that you may ask.

My friends, you have been told many times, through many sources, that the Creator resides in all areas. This means that He is within you. No closer could you ask to be. If it is your desire to truly know and understand the universe and your Creator, then it is only necessary for you to go within yourself and seek that which you desire. Seek and you shall find. This may sound familiar, and it has always been, and shall always remain to be, true. You are the citadel of your existence. You are the center of the universe.

Do not underrate your abilities or your importance to the overall functioning of the creation. For, my friends, if you were not necessary you would not exist. For, as we understand it, within this creation of love all things are interdependent upon each other, for in all reality there is but one thing, though you do not recognize it through your physical senses. There is but one unity, one presence, throughout the entire creation and that is the Creator.

You have been told that you have been created in His image and likeness and we say unto you that if you believe this to be true, then you cannot deny what we are speaking. You are the Creator. We all together are the Creator. Further than this we cannot say for this is our understanding and we do not proclaim to possess infinite knowledge of all matters. We can only state what we have learned through our own experiences and allow you to accept or reject as you will. But in order that you understand what we say, it is necessary that you practice the art of meditation, not as you are witnessing it now, but alone. Though these sessions are quite helpful, the true answers lie in the silence of your personal meditation. For understanding is infinite, my friends, and the intellect is limited. Therefore, you must go beyond the reaches of what you term your intellect.

It is our desire to assist those upon your planet who desire to transcend physical experience. And in order to do so it is definitely required by your very nature that you, to some extent, utilize your intellect. Therefore, we have provided, upon request, these sessions. We of the Confederation of Planets in Service to the Infinite Creator are well aware of your present experience, for we have ourselves experienced quite similar existences and we of the Confederation, during those existences, chose to follow in the love and the light of our infinite Creator through the process of meditation. Light, my friends, is love and love is all.

I shall once again transfer this communication. I am Hatonn.

(Carla channeling)

I am Hatonn. I wish each of you now to become more carefully aware of the entities beside you, who dwell now within this room in a unified group, all seeking the light. Become aware, my friends, of each infinitely precious spirit, of the great treasure patiently, through eons of time, from experience to experience, each of these entities has built and built upon experience to come to the place where the entity is now, the place on the ladder, the place in the progression, on the path, however you wish to put it. Each of you, my brothers, is on the same path. You may think sometimes that you are alone, but within this room you are all one. Allow the light within you to spread out until it touches those about you and rest in that light and in the one perfect love.

And now I leave you. I will return later. I am Hatonn.

(Carla channeling)

I am Oxal. I greet you in the love and the light of the infinite Creator. I speak through this instrument due to my difficulty in contacting the one known as R. It has been a long time since I have been able to use the one known as R. It would indeed be a great privilege to be able to give a short message through this instrument. I will attempt again to contact the one known as R. I am Hatonn.

(Pause)

(Carla channeling)

I am Oxal. I am again with this instrument. We are having difficulty with the one known as R, and so we will attempt to contact the one known an N. I am Oxal.

(H channeling)

I am Oxal. We are experiencing some difficulty in achieving contact with instruments who are not, shall we say, familiar with the personal vibration of our contact. There is some variance between the energies experienced from the different brothers within the Confederation and it is very difficult, many times, to differentiate between these contacts. As for the instrument known as R, I would wish to add that though it has been a great length of time, your knowledge is far too advanced for you to allow your apprehensions to overcome your desire. And once again I shall attempt to communicate through the instrument. I am Oxal.

(Carla channeling)

I am Oxal. We are having some difficulty this evening, and so I will briefly conclude through this instrument and then depart. We wish to say to the one known as R and to the one known as N to be not discouraged, for though it may take a bit of time to become totally confident, either for the first time or again, yet the ability is still there and the service that you have done and will do, my sisters, is wonderful to behold.

We wanted to say to you a few words about harmony, a few words about progression. My friends, that which you hear at this time within your density outside your dwelling place is an instance of disharmony. There are two definitions of normalcy within the air. One is warmer and one is colder and within this duality there is inevitable conflict. And the result of this conflict can be heard by your ears at this time. And the destruction which is wrought shall at times be very great, simply because there is a duality between heat and cold and the result is a terrible confrontation in which that duality is resolved and harmony again reigns.

Within that density which you now enjoy there is a natural and inevitable swing. That swing is towards progression, progression not only of your spirit but of all that there is: physical, intellectual, emotional, heavenly, ethereal—any density, any type, anything that you can name in existence has an inevitable progression from lower to higher. And it takes place at an inexorable pace, step by step, time by time. Each of you and the planet upon which you now reside will progress, from this time and place into the next, from this cycle into the next. It was designed that within the schoolroom which you now enjoy you would learn your lessons and you would progress in harmony with your planet. My friends, this has not happened, and there are many, many of your peoples who are in disharmony with the planet itself as it progresses inevitably into the next cycle. The vibration of all that exists within the physical plane upon your planet is slowly being transformed by its very crystalline structure into a vibration which is not what it was. The space into which your entire solar system now passes is of a vibratory nature which is not what it was and it has been planned that your thoughts, your spirits, and your progressions would be in harmony so that they are not what they were also. Unfortunately, many, many of your peoples are exactly what they were. They have chosen not to progress at all. They are thinking of self, they are thinking of power over others and their grade, if you wish to put it that way, is under fifty percent, by which we mean that they are thinking of themselves without regard to others more than fifty percent of the time. This is written in a holy book of your planets and it is, unfortunately, so.

The cycle into which you are passing will inevitably come into conflict with this kind of thinking and the storm will rage about those upon this planet who are not able to achieve harmony with the new vibration, which is a vibration of love of a higher nature. It is a vibration in which there is much less deceit, in which it is much clearer to you that your brother is also yourself. You see, my brothers, you are all one and to do service to your brother is only to serve yourself. In this density it has not been very clear that this is so and in the next density it will be much clearer.

We are aware that you do not wish to be swept away, shall we say, in the ruins of this confrontation. And we ask you, please, to think of these words if you find yourself in a position where you have closed the outside world away and are thinking only of yourself. Remember, my friends, your self is, in total essence, in total harmony with all that there is. To close yourself off from it is to come into inevitable and destructive confrontation with reality. Please get off of that 50 percent fence that you are now on. Pull yourself onto the side of harmony. Even if your actions are not perfect, if you simply desire to be better, your vibrations will have been pulled off that fence and you will begin to come into harmony with that reality you face more and more each day.

I will leave you, my friends. I wished to share this with you and it is indeed a great privilege to share this with you. I leave you in joy, for it is truly a joy to share with you the love and the light of the Father. I am Oxal. Adonai.

(H channeling)

I am Hatonn. As I said earlier, I have returned. It has been my privilege to allow my brother Oxal to speak with you. Though I have little left to say, I would wish to extend to all present my presence. And while I complete this communication, my brother Laitos shall dwell among you within this room. We ask that you relax and listen and know of our presence. If you are open and receptive to us, then you indeed shall be aware of our presence. We of the Confederation of Planets in Service to the Infinite Creator come from what you consider to be many places. We have come across vast portions of the universe. We have transcended what you consider to be time and we can experience instantaneous travel from one point to another. Through the use of what you may call your God-given abilities, you also can achieve these things. And I say unto you, be patient.

(Pause while someone entered the meeting.)

I shall continue. I expressed to you the need for patience. For, my friends, those upon your planet experience great annoyance and distress over the passage of time. Many things you attempt to do and to solve rely upon the passage of time within your present concepts …

(Tape ends.) ♣

L/L Research

L/L Research is a subsidiary of Rock Creek Research & Development Laboratories, Inc.

P.O. Box 5195
Louisville, KY 40255-0195

www.llresearch.org

Rock Creek is a non-profit corporation dedicated to discovering and sharing information which may aid in the spiritual evolution of humankind.

ABOUT THE CONTENTS OF THIS TRANSCRIPT: This telepathic channeling has been taken from transcriptions of the weekly study and meditation meetings of the Rock Creek Research & Development Laboratories and L/L Research. It is offered in the hope that it may be useful to you. As the Confederation entities always make a point of saying, please use your discrimination and judgment in assessing this material. If something rings true to you, fine. If something does not resonate, please leave it behind, for neither we nor those of the Confederation would wish to be a stumbling block for any.

CAVEAT: This transcript is being published by L/L Research in a not yet final form. It has, however, been edited and any obvious errors have been corrected. When it is in a final form, this caveat will be removed.

© 2009 L/L Research

Sunday Meeting
February 1, 1976

(Carla channeling)

Greetings in the love and the light of the infinite Creator. Before I speak with you I wish that you feel the warmth and vibration of the energy that is with you at this time. We are sending you our vibration which enhances the natural vibration of this group in such a way that it may more easily coincide with that which may be called spiritual vibration. Pause and feel this energy

(Pause)

Before we begin to answer your questions, we would like to respond to a mentally asked question. It is something that this instrument does not particularly like to do, but we feel it is good for both the instrument and the questioner to occasionally experience this form of channeling.

We say to you, my brothers, you are upon a round ball, not totally round, my brother, but round enough. Consider yourself standing on the surface of the ball. One side of this ball is in light, and the other is in darkness. And it may seem to you very real that you are in darkness now, and that you have been in light earlier today, and that tomorrow the light will come again, and after that, another period of darkness. For you are upon the surface of a ball, and what is real to you is what is real for that ball. And sometimes there is light, and sometimes there is darkness.

Problems, difficulties, pain, lack, limitation; these things are just like the ball that you are standing on. Only you hold these balls. Consider them as evanescent bubbles. When you turn them in your hand, they rotate half in light and half in darkness, and as you see the dark side of the trouble, you experience the lack and the limitation, and the trouble seems very real to you, but lo, the trouble turns in your hand, and the solution is come upon you, and it also seems real to you. And the bubble bursts, and is no more, and in your hand is another bubble, and it is turning its dark side to you. And as you hold it in your hand, it turns, and it turns, quickly or slowly, and eventually the light side shows. Day dawns upon that particular trouble, and your solution is come upon you.

We ask that you consider, my brother, that the man standing upon the ball is not just the man upon the ball. For there is that within him which is kin to all that there is. He is not a prisoner of light and darkness, for within him is the sun. Within him, even within the intellect of this man, in imagination, there is the ability of this man to go to the point of view of the sun, and from the standpoint of the sun there is no night, and the turning of a ball in infinite space has no meaning, for there is eternal, infinite, unbelievably wasteful light. There is no darkness, from the standpoint of the sun.

Your difficulty at this point is a problem of thinking of yourself as a person standing upon a ball, and holding a ball, both balls being subject to light and darkness. Consider your difficulty from the standpoint of the eternal light and oneness of the sun, and the bubble will burst.

There is a point to the standpoint of the man upon the ball. You are a plant within the cosmic garden, and that which is necessary for your growth is given unto you. Your growth is not in the body but in the spirit, and that which is, shall we say, fertilizer is the infinite array of emotional reactions that you have to these same problems. Through the reactions of your emotions, and through choosing what reactions you will encourage within your own consciousness, you are turning and developing your own cosmic growth. Let that cosmic sun shine upon you and your problems.

I will now open the meeting to questions. Who would like to ask a question?

Questioner: How can I meditate better?

My sister, it is my great pleasure to be able to speak with you. We are very pleased for the opportunity. For each person, as this instrument has said, there is a uniquely personal way to get past the difficulties of the conscious mind and settle into a more meditative or contemplative state. In your case, my sister, it is recommended that, for a period of five minutes or so, you take one of the works which personally has spiritual meaning for you, whether it be that which you know as the Holy Bible, or whether it be any other work which has meaning for you personally. Your mental discipline is such that you are accustomed to making good use in a physical sense of your time. Therefore, the main difficulty with your taking time for a meditation period is that it is a waste of time within the intellectual framework.

The greatest bridge from the intellect to the spiritual is inspiration. Therefore, reading words of inspiration will at some point give you the inspiration and desire to pause and contemplate that which you have read. At this point, your own intellect will find it permissible to do so, for you will be learning. And truly this, although it is not meditation proper, is an extremely useful method of learning. It is a gateway into the spiritual. If you cannot go further than the contemplation of an inspirational thought, then this will be fine. At some point, as you do this daily, however, you will find that you have stopped thinking about that inspirational thought, and you have not yet thought of anything else. Perhaps that inspiration has led you to another inspiration, and then to another, and then you have a pause. My sister, if that pause lasts five seconds, within that five seconds you have made contact with the silence within, and within that silence is that which we have called the sun. Within that silence is the Creator. Five seconds with the Creator, my sister, is ample. Seek and ye shall find. This has been said over and over.

Do not be disheartened if meditations remain short for some time. It is not how long your meditations last, but how earnestly you are seeking. If you knock at that door, it shall be opened. It will not be tomorrow that you are able to spend minutes, and then a quarter of an hour, in deep meditation, yet through the door of contemplation you will become comfortable with the meditation. You see, my sister, there are people who are, shall we say, less energetic, and therefore they do not require their time to be productive. Once you begin to see in your own consciousness the joy and the productive changes which are occurring as a result of your meditation, short as it is, you will no longer consider it as a waste of time. At that point, your being will relax and allow the silence its rightful place.

The physical vehicle in all of those among your peoples has been trained to be very active, and even among those who are the least energetic you will find resistance to meditation, for the body itself is not comfortable doing nothing. This is unfortunate but true. It is much better to be totally inactive, and then to move with true purpose, than to be partially active at all tines and have no purpose of a lasting quality. Therefore, we wish you a very productive outcome to your seeking. We assure you that this will be so.

Does that answer your question?

Questioner: *(Inaudible).*

Are there other questions?

Questioner: I would like to know if I could have some way of knowing, physically or absolutely, that I am channeling, really channeling, when I think I am channeling from the Confederation. I need to be absolutely sure that I'm not channeling myself, because I would hate to give anybody wrong advice or say something that's not right.

This is a difficult question to answer, my brother. There is no channel that does not dwell within doubts many times. Moreover, due to the type of beam that we are using with you, although it is electromagnetic in a physical sense, it is not the type of wave in which total control is ours and you have no free will. We have experimented with this beam and we do not like it, even when the instrument is fully willing to give over to us. It is uncomfortable to the instrument, and it is not necessary in order to give to you philosophy.

We prefer using a type of communication which deals within your free will. We see your vocabulary as spread out within your awareness, and we pick out of your awareness the closest concepts to what we are trying to say. This is why different channels give different messages to a certain extent.

Now, it is partially their subconscious, and it is partially us. Do you understand this? Do you see what I mean, my brother?

Questioner: Well …

This does not answer your question, but it tells you the basic answer, which is that you will never know for sure whether it is us until such time as channels are not actually necessary. Now, we must back up a bit.

Channels are necessary because we cannot and will not go against the free will of those upon your planet. Some of those upon the planet are seeking the truth. To those people we come to give our message. Many, many of those peoples upon your planet are not seeking the truth at this time. This is their prerogative. We do not wish to upset their applecart. We do not wish to make them know that our reality is superior to theirs, they are inexorably headed for our reality, and they will be forced into learning our lessons. We do not wish to do this to anyone. We wish only to talk to those who wish to listen. We cannot appear among you at this point for this reason. So we use telepathic channels which no one can prove are actually speaking. This unprovability is essential to the vibration upon this planet at this time. We must not be proven to be here at this time, until the majority of those upon your planet want what we have come to bear witness to.

This channel has become convinced that she is channeling something of a higher reality. This channel is not totally convinced that we are UFO entities. This is fine with us. We do not care who you think we are. The reason that this channel is convinced that she is channeling is that in many instances that which she has channeled has been confirmed by events or by people as being, shall we say, on the nose, and the instrument knows that she did not previously have any awareness as to what was channeled. Therefore, she knows that there was an information source that was coming through her.

We suggest to you what we have suggested often, that it matters not where the information comes from, it matters only whether the information is valid, whether it is helpful. As a matter of fact, we are from another planet. We are in craft about your planet. We are people, and we speak to people: we are here in love and peace. This is our nature, and this to our message. Proof is not with us. Proof is not of our vibration. Love is what we have come to offer, and love is proven only in love.

We ask you, my brother, simply to have confidence. When you feel a desire to help, to give service in this way, pray, as you would call it. Speak to the light within you in a way which communicates to your own vibration. Either say to yourself, "I wish only to do work for the Creator"; say to yourself, "Let me be an instrument of Thy peace"; say to yourself whatever is your true desire in the Father to do this work. In that way, there is no possibility of your channeling that which is not of the Father. It is when one is not careful of one's vibrations that one begins to channel those entities which are quite astral, which, while sometimes very high vibration, are also sometimes not. If you wish a spiritual communication, set your vibrations to that. Then, speak what comes to your mind. The essence of channeling is not to worry about what you are saying, but to go ahead, catch those balls, and throw them on, catch those words and speak them. You have arranged your vibration, you have set yourself to do the work of the Father: then, do it. You need not question intellectually something that is not intellectually happening to you.

This may sound very difficult at this time. What will make it easier for you is experience in this service. As you begin to have a backlog of experiences in which everything came out all right, in which that which was given to you was well-received, you will begin to realize that once you prepare yourself as the instrument, then that which is given through the instrument is not of your concern.

Does this answer your question?

Questioner: Yes.

Is there another question?

Questioner: When we meditate, do we get rid of karma?

No, my sister. Do you wish an explanation?

Questioner: Yes, please.

There is a law within the density which you now know as the physical. This law is visible within the physical illusion as cause and effect. There is no action without a reaction. Nothing that happens has not been caused. That which you do is reflected in experience. This is karma.

This is a law. The law does not become abrogated. There is a higher law, and this is the Law of Love. If you invoke this law, this law will dissolve the karma. Yet you invoke this through action. In meditation, you align yourself with all that there is. You have brought into your consciousness the Creator. Yet karma is that which is in the physical, and to dissolve karma, there must be action of a final kind which resolves the reaction. This action partakes of love, but love-in-action.

It is as though you would say that there was a fire, raging out of control. And you stood by it, and you said "What is this destructive thing? And how do I manage to overcome it?" And as you meditated, it came to you that you would overcome fire with water.

And there you sit in meditation, with a pail of water in your hand. But, my sister, you have not put the water on the fire. Go from the meditation with the understanding, and put out that fire. Do it consciously, and know that the law of love is overcoming the law of karma.

Is this clear, my sister?

Questioner: Yes.

As we sit here, my brothers and sisters, we are like islands in a stream. This phrase has been used by one of your writers, and we take it from this channel's mind, for it in very apt at this time. You seem like islands in the stream. You are separate, and the waters are rushing past you, and you are each in a different place, attempting to understand the nature of that which is around you. Yet you are fixed, still, and as the waters rush past you, you see only that which touches you.

My friends, you are the water. One drop of water, that is one with all of the water that reaches from one corner of the world to the other, that indeed touches all that there is, that knows all that all the other drops of water know. Release yourself from that island, in meditation, and become one with the water. Water does not seem strong, yet it is water—gentle, flowing, unified water—that dissolves the rock.

Are there any other questions?

Questioner: Should we believe in reincarnation?

My sister this is, to the best of our knowledge, what happens. If it is uncomfortable to you, it is perfectly all right not to believe in it. However, reincarnation of the entity within a certain experience, then removed from that experience and re-evaluating it, then deciding what needs to be learned and going back in to the density of experience, coming back out and evaluating again—this, to the best of our knowledge, is the nature of each of you.

You are infinite, eternal beings. Your transit within this particular physical vehicle is very brief. Your transit within the Creator is infinite. We do not know where the trail ends. We are not at the end of it. We see far ahead, just as you do. We see a little further ahead than you. We certainly do not know the end. We do not know the whole. Although we ourselves are still reincarnating, it is on a density where we are more in control of our experience and our stays within each vehicle are quite a bit longer as you would measure time. We do not say that the eternal essence of all that there is is reincarnation. We only say that, at this point in our evolution, this is the nature of the residing spirit. It has a residence, and a higher residence that percolates, shall we say, into the lower residence and takes up for the learning, for the experiencing, the lower residence.

Does this clarify the matter?

Questioner: Yes.

Is there another question?

Questioner: Yes. I am having trouble channeling. How can I practice? Usually I mediate alone.

The best route for you to follow, probably, my brother, is that, instead of trying a full-scale message—we do not suggest this when you are without at least three in the group—you attempt a much more informal and brief type of channeling. This is actually the best type to do alone, at least until you have developed the ability to make contact with us in a solid way. It is for your own protection, so that you will not get astrals. We discussed this earlier, and suggested that before initiating contact, the instrument pray. We suggest this to you. If prayer is not your chosen word for what we are suggesting, we give you the option of considering yourself a radio, and tuning yourself consciously to the very highest frequency, so that you take in only the purest of light frequencies.

If you wish to test your abilities to channel, take your problems of the day, your questions, and your unmentioned but simply felt mood, and say, "What have you to say about this?" You will receive an impression. This impression will be a very short answer. Listen to it, and evaluate it. Do not take it as read or disbelieve it, but in an open-minded and careful way, evaluate your answers. See what you think about the source, about the level of response. In this way it will not be very long before you begin to build up some confidence in your contact. Answers given in this way are quite short, but to the point.

Within conversations with others, it is entirely possible to ask for words, so that you might, shall we say, plant a seed while not formally channeling. It is not necessary to sit in a dark room with your eyes closed in order to get our words. Our thoughts are simply the thoughts which are within you but which are amplified by the spiritual vibration so that you may hear them. Therefore, it is only necessary to make a momentary contact with the desire to be of service. Then, that which you need to say will be forthcoming. Again, it is not necessary that this be sustained. Very often, those people who have come to you with a question will not need very much but only the seed that they may take with them and let grow on their own. These things may be done without ever becoming what is known as a vocal channel. They are done because of desire to be of service. This type of channeling is just as important as the more formal type of vocal channeling, and in the case of the seed-planting, is very helpful in cases where the person asking the questions is only beginning to seek. This person would not come to a meeting, and would be uncomfortable if he did come. We could not talk to him through a channel. We would not be able to get through, for his free will would then be violated. Yet the seed can be planted, if he asks a question that has a spiritual answer. This also is a service, my brother, and can be practiced in any situation.

Now, we wish to add: if you can find two or three who wish to channel, it is possible to be more formal, but we do not suggest that it would be best to attempt this on your own.

Does this answer your question?

Questioner: Yes. Thank you.

You are welcome. But it is we who thank you, I assure you, for the privilege of serving you. Are there any other questions?

Questioner: Yes. I wonder if you could comment on an experience I had about eight years ago when I was followed very closely by a UFO on my way to and from a destination.

We will attempt to answer this question. There are times, my sister, when the light which is within is manifested outward in an unusual manner. The entity which you saw was not a Confederation entity but a spiritual entity of your planet which was activated by your rising vibration within this density. You are a person who has made some progress in understanding within this experience, and as awakenings occur within the real self, the eyes are opened to higher densities. Within the higher densities there dwell what you know as angels. These angels are not boring harp-players who flap around with wings. They are beautiful, ethereal light-beings. In physical manifestation, they are of physical beauty, and in etherean manifestation they are very bright. You had a sight of an angel who was of your sector. It was with this harbinger that a new era within your spiritual development began. We have appeared also to you, but this particular sighting was not ours.

Does this answer your question?

Questioner: Yes, and thank you.

It is a great pleasure to be with this group. I would leave you now. Yet I do not leave you. I never leave, but as you desire our help, we are here. We have the ability to hear ten thousand at once, and understand each. We hear and we are heard.

(Tape ends.) ❧

Sunday Meeting
February 15, 1976

(H channeling)

I am Hatonn. Greetings, my friends, in the love and the light of the infinite Creator. It is indeed my privilege to share this moment with you. And while speaking with you this evening, I and my brothers shall pass among you, and if you are open, you shall sense our presence.

We of the Confederation of Planets in the Service of the Infinite Creator have come to your planet to assist you in whatever manner that we may. Yet presently, the manner which you are witnessing now is our most effective means of assistance. We wish to share with you some of our ideas. Throughout many experiences each individual forms for his or herself opinions judging from the experiences. As you pass on throughout your journeys, you shall form many of these opinions. These opinions may better be expressed as concepts. Your experiences shall be infinite in number, and your concepts shall also be infinite. Yet all of the experiences and all of the concepts which you have formed can be described as being within the concept of love.

Love, my friends, is not what man perceives within his intellect. Love is not the emotion that is felt for another. Love is not attachment to any given thing. Love is totally detached, yet infinitely united within truth, within the light of the Creator. All things are united due to the existence of love. In experiencing the concept of love, there are many things which must be learned before you can truly comprehend the infinity of the concept. Love is all that exists. Love is all things which you experience and which you can see. Love at many times may appear to be what you might call negative in its effect upon you or others, yet, my friends, you must indeed, in order to learn, be exposed and have experience on what you would call both sides of the coin. You must be aware of the negativity which exists within your present experience as only an assistant to your learning process. You are assisted by those acts which you consider to be negative in that they allow you to weigh within yourself the value of that which you consider to be negative and that which you consider to be positive.

My friends, in order to learn, you must have full knowledge before a full concept can be realized. Therefore, do not allow yourself to think that any action or experience pertaining to yourself is not one of love. No matter what its appearance may be upon the physical plane, you must realize that upon the spiritual planes it is assisting your growth, your understanding, and your knowledge. By your experiences you shall learn that which is necessary to evolve into what you would call a higher dimension of existence.

My friends, you are here at this time primarily to learn and understand the concept of love. Your daily experiences are your lessons, and your daily reactions to those experiences shall bear upon your final, shall we say, judgment of your experience. With the proper outlook, these experiences can always be found within the realms of the concept of love. This is difficult to understand at times—and even more difficult for us to relate to you—that you must be aware of the omnipresence of love.

I shall transfer this communication. I am Hatonn.

(Carla channeling)

I am now with this instrument. I greet you again, in the love and the light. My friends, that which surrounds you in your daily lives is a seeming mixture of the good and the bad, the plus and the negative. This appearance is not only your reality in the outer world, but it is a symbol for that which is on the inner planes the spiritual truth for all of those who are in your density and upon your physical plane. You see, my friends, you all seem to suffer, separate from each other. And in that you are separate from each other, you are broken and unhealthy and in pain. You do not know oneness with each other. You cannot understand each other. And, not understanding each other, you experience what seems to be negativity, and what seems to be pain, my friends. And this is for a reason.

You experience that which you perceive to be a state of unhealthiness. It is, on the outer plane, the precise symbol for that on the inner planes which is also unhealthy and ununified. The healing—and the only healing which you can achieve—is the healing of love. To be made whole again within is to be made aware of your unity with all that there is on the outer planes. As you act on the outer planes, so will your consciousness behave on the inner.

How can you call this healing into what seems to be a divided planet? Because we use this channel and because we speak to this group, we use examples which are found within one of your holy works, known as the *Bible*. We ask you to remember the story of the man who was a prophet. And from a far country a leper came, and he said to the prophet, "Heal me!" And the prophet said, "Do you think that I am a God, that I could heal you? Nay, only go wash in the river of Jordan seven times." And the leper, who was a rich man, went away, saying, "Indeed, I thought that such a prophet would at least call upon his God for me, pray over me, but he didn't." And he was unhappy. And his servant said to him, "Master, he asked you to do something that was very easy. Would you not have obeyed him if he asked you to do something difficult?" The leper said, "Why, yes I would have, for I wish to be healed." The servant said, "Then, Master, go wash in the Jordan seven times, for it is very simple, and you want to be healed." And the leper did so and he became whole.

My friends, this experience you are now going through is much like that story, in that you are at this point in some manner or other sick, lonesome, unhappy, in some pain or some sadness of physical existence, whether it be in the mind, in the emotions, in the body. And you desire to be healed. You desire to be a whole person. We are not prophets. We do not wish to behave as prophets. Yet we say to you: your prophet is love. Your higher self has arranged the basic elements and ingredients of your life experience, so that your life itself may tell you where the Jordan is, that you may wash and be whole. You need not search for a difficult way to find love. Love is close to you now, at this very moment.

When you have your next painful experience, ask your own experience, your own life, your own situation, "Where can I be healed? Where is love in this situation?" If you are quiet and if you meditate, truth will come to you. The water will become evident. And that portion of your consciousness will be made whole by your understanding of love. Know ye, my friends, that we are all one. In pain or in pleasure, healing is in knowing that the Creator lies in every breath of air that you breathe, in every plant that gives you pleasure, in every bite of food that gives you health, in all of the friends and all of the enemies—you are looking at the Creator. All is one.

Never mind that within this physical body you cannot hear and see the Creator. That is a mere experience. The truth applies before this experience, after this experience, and if you wish it, during this experience. It is before you in such evidence, my friends, that unity with each other is the goal. Know ye not the pleasure of an overreaching type that comes when two minds meet as one? When an understanding between two people has reached a perfect balance? Have you not felt, within the realm of your physical relationships, those moments of unity that are not, as you would say, of the body, but of a higher type? In experiences such as this, directly within your physical illusion, you are seeing unity, and you feel its divinity. Yet you can only become unified with a very few people on this plane. What we ask you to do in meditation is to begin to bring the healing love within your consciousness, so that you feel that love with everyone, and in all situations.

You see, my friends, you must have the consciousness of love before you enter the situation. Then, you will receive from that situation love. Without the consciousness of love, you receive what you send out, be that whatever it may. It is written many times in your holy works, "As ye sow, so shall ye reap." So, love to the very best of your ability, and you will reap it a hundredfold. Many of you have wondered at times: "How can I be of service? I do not have a great deal of money. I do not have very special talents. I do not know what to do to be of service." We say to you, "Meditate and find love. And then open yourself to your own self."

Within your life experience there is guidance. The guidance will show you who and how to serve. Love is infinite. You cannot put a dollar value on the heart, and it takes no special talent to be a channel for love. If you can begin to make your life function in this new way, if you can begin to know the Creator personally and let Him love through you, then that which comes to you will become more and more a reflection of that love. It may take a certain amount of time, but if you begin now, we assure you that it will be very, very soon that you will feel the universe about you warming to you, becoming a friendly place, becoming your home.

I would like to speak through one more channel. I am Hatonn.

(B channeling)

I am Hatonn. I am now with this instrument. As you have been told before, my friends, we are, shall we say, all upon our paths to learn one great lesson, which is of a very high estate. As you know, you were conceived in love, and there *is* only love. Through the many years of experience, as you call them on this planet, many things have, shall we say, taken place that are difficult. But as you look around you now you see, from every angle, this concept coming back. And, my friends, I say that the greatest lesson that you are to learn upon this planet is that of love.

We realize that it is not an easy thing. But, my friends, as we speak to you in love, we can truthfully say that it is the greatest thing. Now, my friends, you cannot learn merely by wanting to, but it is the first step. As you apply yourselves to this word "love," you will find that your progress will grow to be many times accelerated. And after a period of time, you will come to see in all that is within your grasp, love. For, my friends, I repeat again, love is all. When you have captured this love, you have all.

As you know, my friends, I and my brothers are with you always and are willing to help in any service that we can. It has been an extremely great honor to share in your meditation. I will leave this instrument, in the love and light of our infinite Creator. I am Hatonn.

(Carla channeling)

I am Hatonn. I am with this instrument, greeting you in the love and the light of the infinite Creator. I would like to ask if there are questions at this time.

Questioner: Yes. Was that a UFO I saw two weeks ago tonight on the way home from this meeting?

We do not wish to communicate with you on this matter at this time. It is important for you to evaluate and determine that which you see, until you are at a certain place where you are not easy to dissuade by any information, from our source or any other. We do not wish to interfere in any way with your progress. At a point where you are satisfied within your mind as to the spiritual content of this experience, we will be glad to communicate further. However, we feel that to speak at this time would be to interfere with your free will. It is for this very reason that we do not prove ourselves to you, or to the general public, shall we say. We are regretful if this is unsatisfactory to you, but precious to us above all else is the preservation of your free will, so that you may choose your path and your destiny.

Is there another question?

Questioner: I saw a light in the sky recently. Did it have anything to do with a change in my consciousness?

No, not as you understand it.

Questioner: *(Inaudible).*

Is there another question? If not, we would like to take this opportunity to answer a question that is within the mind of one of you, and may be of some interest to the others. It is never easy to know how to be of service to those about you. And yet, it is all-important to be of service. For there are many, many who are waking from their sleep, and now know that there is something that they need to receive. And they are seeking. We say to you: be very, very careful to listen with utmost clarity to what people ask of you, and answer according to their needs. We ask that you familiarize yourself, not only with the paths that are pleasant and amenable to you, but also with those paths which may not satisfy you, but which seem to be leading towards the one goal, which is the understanding of love. There are many such paths, and each one has been made by those for whom it is the very best path. Rather than attempting to coerce anybody to follow the "best" path, encourage each person to follow any path. If no path suits this person, encourage the person in new and creative ways, remembering only the goal: that the person begin to seek outside the physical confines for that "more" which is there.

If a person has come to you, he knows that there is more. In whatever you do to be of service, enlarge that understanding. Never discourage it, whatever way the person may be seeking. This takes compassion, and a very gentle spirit. There is nothing more harmful than the person who is sure that there is only one path. We say this to you because it is something that is not easy to see, and yet in the days to come, those about you, when they sense that you know something, will be asking what that is. Do not be a stumbling block to anyone. Know that the Creator is on all paths towards spirit. Only attempt to discourage that seeking which separates man from his creation. This is all that needs to be discouraged. Any loving and unifying direction will end in the Creator.

We will leave you at this time, not leaving you truly, but only the vocal mechanism of this channel. We are always with those who seek and request our aid, for we feel the vibration of your desire. I leave you in the love and the light of our infinite Creator. I am known as Hatonn. Adonai vasu borragus. ☙

www.ingramcontent.com/pod-product-compliance
Lightning Source LLC
Chambersburg PA
CBHW080419230426

43662CB00015B/2153